MESSAGE OF THE FATHERS OF THE CHURCH
General Editor: Thomas Halton

Volume 7

MESSAGE OF THE FATHERS OF THE CHURCH

THE EUCHARIST

by
Daniel J. Sheerin

Michael Glazier
Wilmington, Delaware

ABOUT THE AUTHOR

DANIEL J. SHEERIN received his doctorate from the University of North Carolina at Chapel Hill. He has taught at the University of Delaware, University of North Carolina at Chapel Hill and the Catholic University of America. He is presently on the faculty of the University of Notre Dame. He has done wide research on the writings of the Greek and Latin Fathers.

First published in 1986 by Michael Glazier, Inc.
1935 West Fourth Street, Wilmington, Delaware 19805

Distributed outside U.S., Canada, Australia, and Philippines by Geoffrey Chapman, a division of Cassel Ltd., 1 Vincent Square, London SWIP 2PN.

Library of Congress Catalog Card Number: 85-45562
International Standard Book Number:
  Message of the Fathers of the Church series:
    (0-89453-312-6, Paper; 0-89453-340-1, Cloth)
  EUCHARIST
    (0-89453-319-3, Paper)
    (0-89453-347-9, Cloth)

Cover design: Lillian Brulc

Typography by Richard Reinsmith

Printed in the United States

Contents

Editor's Introduction

The *Message of the Fathers of the Church* is a companion series to The *Old Testament Message* and The *New Testament Message*. It was conceived and planned in the belief that Scripture and Tradition worked hand in hand in the formation of the thought, life and worship of the primitive Church. Such a series, it was felt, would be a most effective way of opening up what has become virtually a closed book to present-day readers, and might serve to stimulate a revival in interest in Patristic studies in step with the recent, gratifying resurgence in Scriptural studies.

The term "Fathers" is usually reserved for Christian writers marked by orthodoxy of doctrine, holiness of life, ecclesiastical approval and antiquity. "Antiquity" is generally understood to include writers down to Gregory the Great (+604) or Isidore of Seville (+636) in the West, and John Damascene (+749) in the East. In the present series, however, greater elasticity has been encouraged, and quotations from writers not noted for orthodoxy will sometimes be included in order to illustrate the evolution of the Message on particular doctrinal matters. Likewise, writers later than the mid-eighth century will sometimes be used to illustrate the continuity of tradition on matters like sacramental theology or liturgical practice.

An earnest attempt was made to select collaborators on a broad inter-disciplinary and inter-confessional basis, the chief consideration being to match scholars who could handle the Fathers in their original languages with subjects in which they had already demonstrated a special interest and competence. About the only editorial directive given to the selected contributors was that the Fathers, for the most part, should be allowed to speak for themselves and that they should speak in readable, reliable modern English. Volumes on individual themes were considered more suitable than volumes devoted to individual Fathers, each theme, hopefully, contributing an important segment to the total mosaic of the Early Church, one, holy, catholic and apostolic. Each volume has an introductory essay outlining the historical and theological development of the theme, with the body of the work mainly occupied with liberal citations from the Fathers in modern English translation and a minimum of linking commentary. Short lists of Suggested Further Readings are included; but dense, scholarly footnotes were actively discouraged on the pragmatic grounds that such scholarly shorthand has other outlets and tends to lose all but the most relentlessly esoteric reader in a semi-popular series.

At the outset of his *Against Heresies* Irenaeus of Lyons warns his readers "not to expect from me any display of rhetoric, which I have never learned, or any excellence of composition, which I have never practised, or any beauty or persuasiveness of style, to which I make no pretensions." Similarly, modest disclaimers can be found in many of the Greek and Latin Fathers and all too often, unfortunately, they have been taken at their word by an uninterested world. In fact, however, they were often highly educated products of the best rhetorical schools of their day in the Roman Empire, and what they have to say is often as much a lesson in literary and cultural, as well as in spiritual, edification.

St. Augustine, in *The City of God* (19.7), has interesting reflections on the need for a common language in an expanding world community; without a common language a man is more at home with his dog than with a foreigner as far as intercommunication goes, even in the Roman Empire, which imposes on the nations it conquers the yoke of both law and language with a resultant abundance of interpreters. It is hoped that in the present world of continuing language barriers the contributors to this series will prove opportune interpreters of the perennial Christian message.

Abbreviations

ACO	*Acta Conciliorum Oecumenicorum*
ACW	*Ancient Christian Writers*
AH	*Analecta Hymnica Medii Aevi*
ANF	*Ante-Nicene Fathers*
ARI	E. Yarnold, *The Awe-Inspiring Rites of Initiation: Baptismal Homilies of the Fourth Century,* Slough, England, 1972.
Bouley	A. Bouley, *From Freedom to Formula: The Evolution of the Eucharistic Prayer from Oral Improvisation to Written Texts,* Washington, D.C., 1981.
Bouyer	L. Bouyer, *Eucharist: Theology and Spirituality of the Eucharistic Prayer, tr* C.U. Quinn, Notre Dame, 1968.
CCSL	*Corpus Christianorum, Series Latina*
CCSG	*Corpus Christianorum, Series Graeca*
CSCO	*Corpus Scriptorum Christianorum Orientalium*
CSEL	*Corpus Scriptorum Ecclesiasticorum Latinorum*
EEC	Willy Rordorf *et al., The Eucharist of the Early Christians, tr* M.J. O'Connell, New York, 1978.
FC	*The Fathers of the Church*
GCS	*Die griechischen christlichen Schriftsteller*
HBS	*Henry Bradshaw Society Publications*

LNPF	*A Select Library of Nicene and Post-Nicene Fathers of the Christian Church*
PE	A. Hänggi, I. Pahl, *edd, Prex Eucharistica: Textus e variis liturgiis antiquioribus selecti,* Fribourg, 1968.
PEER	R.C.D. Jasper, C.J. Cuming, *Prayers of the Eucharist: Early and Reformed, 2nd ed, New York, 1980.*
PG	*Patrologia Graeca*
PL	*Patrologia Latina*
SC	*Sources chrétiennes*
SL	C. Jones, G. Wainwright, E. Yarnold, *edd, The Study of the Liturgy,* New York, 1978.
TU	*Texte und Untersuchungen*

Note: Abbreviations of the titles of the books of the Bible are those used in the English language version of *The Jerusalem Bible.*

General Introduction

> O Christ our God, you are surpassingly glorified,
> for you have established our Fathers as luminaries on earth,
> and through them you have guided us to the true faith,
> O much-merciful One, glory to you!
> — Troparion for the Sunday of the Fathers
> of the First Six Ecumenical Councils.

This volume is an endeavor, in keeping with the purpose of the series in which it appears, to place before the modern reader the message of the fathers of the church concerning the eucharist in the words of the fathers themselves. Thus, what is offered here is a collection of readings of sufficient length to place eucharistic teachings in their contexts. This effort has led to the exclusion of certain occasional remarks of the fathers about the eucharist familiar from *enchiridia* and the footnotes of learned works. Obviously, not all patristic texts relevant to the eucharist could be included here. I hope that the process of selection has not misrepresented or disfigured the fathers' message.

The selections in Sections I-III, IVA, and V have been assembled in part according to literary genre, in part according to occasion and purpose of composition. This scheme is abandoned in Section IVB-D for a more topical arrangement. The presentation of the individual selections is more or less uniform. Indications are given of the serial

15

number of the selection in the volume according to the Table of Contents (e.g. IVB1), of the author, of his dates, of the work being excerpted, and of the location of the excerpt within the work. After the abbreviation *ed* the source of the text is given, after *tr* the source of the translation adapted for presentation here. The abbreviation *lit* introduces an item of secondary literature. The basis for the choice of these, and of the items listed under the heading "Suggestions for further reading" at the conclusion of the introductions to some of the sections, has been that these are apposite, compendious materials, readily accessible to English-speakers. Biographical sketches of the individual authors are provided in the introductory note to the first selection from an author in the volume. The numbers assigned to the selections in the Table of Contents are also used for cross reference within this volume, thus (IVA7) refers the reader to IVA7, Augustine of Hippo, *On the Merits and Remission of Sins* 1.34, the seventh selection in subsection A of Section IV.

Citations of scriptural quotations and allusions are provided in parentheses. Scriptural passages are translated as they appear in the Fathers' texts. The Psalms are numbered according to the Septuagint.

Introductory material for the five sections of the volume and for the individual selections is of an historical and literary-historical kind, in order to place the passages into context, and, when appropriate, to indicate how the message of the fathers has come down to us. No essay has been made to synthesize partistic teachings into a patristic theology of the eucharist. Essays at synthesis are possible, and, indeed, necessary, though few have appeared in English in recent years. The fathers themselves rarely approached the eucharist in a wholly comprehensive, synthetic way. Texts in this collection which might be called treatises on the eucharist have definite limitations. Cyprian addresses a particular disciplinary problem in his Letter 63 (IVA4). Gregory of Nyssa's model catechesis on the eucharist (IIA2) is, to a degree, idiosyncratic, and has specific goals. The same may be said of Cyril of Alexandria's detailed presentation of

the eucharist (IIIB10) which was given within the parentheses of an exegetical homily. The selection from John of
Damascus' *Accurate Exposition of the Orthodox Faith*
(IID2) is brilliant and comprehensive, but it does not by any
means exhaust the patristic teachings which it attempts to
synthesize. By and large, patristic teaching about the eucharist was fitted to an occasion, presented under a variety of
circumstances, to a variety of audiences, to meet a variety of
needs. The arrangement of the selections in this volume is
intended to indicate and underscore this fact.

A word about language. I have tried to provide accurate
translations in modern English. I must confess occasional
failures in this, partly due to my ignorance, and partly due to
the fact that the sayings of the fathers cannot always be
translated into modern English because of the immiscibility
of some of their thought and expressions with contemporary iodiom. Technical terms (they are not many) have been
shifted into English transliterations, or, occasionally, English equivalents. No attempt has been made to articulate
patristic understandings of the eucharist with those of later
centuries. Thus, the reader of this volume will find neither
the "—ations" (transubstantiation, impanation, transsigni-
fication, transelementation, transfinalization, transenta-
tion, etc.) nor the "presences" (real, *aktual-*, effective, etc.).
This is not to depreciate later and contemporary efforts to
interpret and commend the eucharist to successive generations. But we are concerned here with the message of the
fathers, the touchstone of all that follows, and it is best
presented in its own terms, in its own context.

Clarification of a few patristic expressions may be
appropriate. One is "to approach." This means simply to
come forward and receive the eucharist. Another which has
in the past caused difficulty may be simply dealt with. It is
the use of the language of symbol to speak about the eucharist. We encounter the expressions "in the type (*typos*) of the
bread His body is given to you, and in the type of the wine
His blood" and "the antitype (*antitypos*) of the body and
blood of Christ" in Cyril of Jerusalem (IIA3); the expression
"the antitypes of the holy body and blood of your Christ" in

the Liturgy of St. Basil (VA3); and "antitype," along with "symbols" (*symbols*) in Theodoret (IVA9). We find the Latin equivalent of both (*typos* and *antitypos* seem to be used indifferently in a eucharistic context) in the term "figure" (*figura*) in Tertullian, (IVA3), Ambrose (IIA4), and Gaudentius of Brescia (IIA5). These terms have a long and, perhaps, complex pedigree (some work has been done on their history; much more is required). It is safe to say that, whatever the specific resonances of these terms which proceed from exegetical and liturgical contexts in individual authors, their basic meaning is, to use an anachronism, "sacramental sign." The contexts in which they occur guarantee the orthodoxy of the significance of these expressions.

A negative reaction against such usage is registered by John of Damascus (IID2), though the rejection of this sort of language had set in earlier. In fragments of their commentaries on Matthew, we find Theodore of Heraclea (*d* 355) rejecting the term *typos*, and Theodore of Mopsuestia (*d* 428) rejecting *symbolon* (TU 61.93,133). Theodore also rejects the language of symbol in his mystagogical catechesis (see ARI 215). For a rejection of *antitypos* see Anastasius of Sinai's *Hodegos* 23 (CCSG 8.307). The basis for these rejections seems to have been a gradual shift in the understanding of type and antitype towards the modern understanding of a symbol as something wholly other than what it represents.

In such a lexical situation, confusion and suspicion could easily arise, as in the story of the simple old monk in the *Apophthegmata Patrum* (PG 65.156-160). The old man insisted that the eucharistic bread was not the body of Christ, but its antitype, nor could he be dissuaded from this until, at a eucharistic liturgy, he beheld a vision of an angel carving up a boy on the altar (this part of the story is alluded to in IIB2), and, when he received communion, he saw a lump of flesh in his hand. This grotesque story points up the risk of extremes, both of sacramentalism and realism.

The eucharist was for the fathers a mystery, rather like a splendid, many-faceted gem which they held up, before themselves and their people, to the light of the Spirit. Confusion and error arise, of course, when one facet is concentrated on to the exclusion of the others.

Suggestions for further reading

See the synthetic effort of R. J. Halliburton, "The Patristic Theology of the Eucharist" (with bibliography), in SL 201-208, and the judicious remarks of J. Pelikan, *The Christian Tradition: A History of the Development of Doctrine* I (Chicago, 1971) 167-170, 236-238. On symbolic language about the eucharist see ARI 93-94, 135, 136-137, and Darwell Stone, *A History of the Doctrine of the Holy Eucharist* (London, 1909) I 29-33, 61-70; the curious should follow up with the work of K. J. Woolcombe in *La Vie spirituelle*, Suppl. 4 (1951) 84-100 and V. Saxer in EEC 145ff (NB note 27).

By way of conclusion, I wish to thank Professors Michael Slusser and Robert Taft for their advice and encouragement, and, especially, Professor Thomas Patrick Halton, the General Editor of *The Message of the Fathers of the Church*, for sharing with me his learning and zeal for the fathers. Finally, I wish to dedicate this volume to my wife, Jeannette, and with her to the Archimandrite Joseph Francavilla and the people of Holy Transfiguration Melkite Greek-Catholic Church, with a prayer for all of us

> Tu qui cuncta scis et uales,
> qui nos pascis hic mortales,
> tu nos ibi commensales,
> coheredes et sodales
> fac sanctorum ciuium.

I. "Mercy, Peace, a Sacrifice of Praise!": The Testimony of the Apologists.

Introduction

Section I is divided into two parts. The first gives a modest sampling of the repeated charges of cannibalism, incest, misanthropy, and impiety brought against the early Christians in a variety of historical and literary settings. The second part contains a number of defenses and explanations of the Christian faith, all focused on the eucharist, "the sacrifice of Christians."

The work of the apologists, as commonly understood, was to defend and explain Christianity against the accusations of its enemies. It will be seen, however, upon reflection, that the apologists are Janus-like, facing outward, towards the adversaries of the faith, but also facing inward, strengthening the belief of the members of the church against doubts arising from their encounters with non-Christian and heterodox communities, and arming them for their own witness to the faith.

The communities against whose criticism the works of the apologists were directed were three: first, the polymorphous pagan community, intellectual and vulgar, with its various philosophies, state cults, and more personal mystery religions; second, the vital Jewish community, with its ancient traditions which were held in common by the Christians,

21

and its compelling contemporary appeal, both in the Holy Land and in the Diaspora; third, the heterodox communities, of various origins and of varying degrees of proximity to catholic Christian thought and observance.

Responses to these three groups' criticisms and teachings which involved the eucharist are presented in different sections of this volume. Responses to the pagans are given in this section. Responses to heterodox groups are collected in Section IVA. Responses to Judaism—or, more precisely, responses to problems, real or imagined, which arose in the Christian community as a result of claims or counterclaims made by Jewish communities and judaizing Christians in the matters of covenant, sacrifice, and fidelity to tradition— are not collected in one section, but are to be found scattered through the volume. (Note: The list of Old Testament types and prophecies in the Appendix to the Introduction to Section III provides a good index to these passages.)

IA. Athenagoras of Athens (see IB4) in his concise opening statement enumerates the most common pagan accusations against the Christians: "They allege three charges against us: atheism, Thyestean banquets, Oedipal couplings" (*The Plea* 3.1). Charges of atheism (absolute atheism, or, more often, a codeword for non-conformity to the state cults), of cannibalism (and attendant human sacrifice), and of incest are reported everywhere in Christian apologetic literature. Our concern here is, of course, with the charge of human sacrifice and cannibalism.

Suspicions of human sacrifice, cannibalism, omophagy (the eating of raw flesh), and various blood-rituals readily occurred to the popular mind in antiquity in connection with foreign and/or secret religions and black magic. That some such allegation would have been made against the Christians was, perhaps, only to be expected given the currency of such suspicions (*cf* the bizarre charge of ritual cannibalism against the Jews reported by Josephus, *Against Apion* 2.8). Another contributing factor was the attitude towards the Christians, presumably not an uncommon one, indicated by Tacitus when he wrote of the Christians who suffered in connection with the fire at Rome in 64: "a great multitude of them were convicted, not so much on the charge of arson as on account of their hatred for the human race" (*Annals* 15.44).

The ubiquity of the charge of cannibalism against the Christians presents an interesting analogue to the perennial blood-libel against the Jews, but the analogy breaks down. To bring a charge of ritual murder and blood-ritual against people whose Law creates an abhorrence of anything resembling such practices (see, e.g., IIIA2, IIIA3, IIIB2) is plainly a case of invincible prejudice. The charge of ritual cannibalism brought against the unoffending Christians, on the other hand, may have been born of prejudice, but a community which could produce a sacred text like "Unless you eat the flesh of the Son of Man and drink his blood...," a community whose communal life was centered around eucharist and agape, could not, perhaps, afford to ignore such a charge.

IB. It is worth focusing on the charge of cannibalism and the responses to it because it evoked from the early Christians explanations of the eucharist directed to an unbelieving world. The explanations could be, as in the case of Justin's (IB2), far more revealing and detailed than were available later, when the discipline of non-disclosure of details of the eucharistic liturgy to the unbaptized was in force (see Introduction to IIA). Secondly, the charge of cannibalism and the responses to it are worthy of attention because the Sacrament of the Body and Blood of Christ is not without its horrific aspects, a horror described in the account of the reaction of the people to Christ's eucharistic discourse in John 6. This potential revulsion is alleged in various texts (see IIA5, IIIA3, IIIA5, IIIB3, IIIB6, IIIB8, IIIB10) to explain, in part, why the eucharist is a *sacrament*.

In addition to the more sensational charge of cannibalism, the general charge of atheism or impiety (nonparticipation in the state cult) touched upon the eucharist, for the Christians abstained from the common sacrifices of the civic community, offering their own peculiar sacrifice and excluding others from participation in it. This inevitably led to charges that the Christians were undermining the state by declining to participate in the propitiatory sacrifices required by the polytheistic state cult. One defense, among others, brought against this charge by Christians was the explanation of what was involved in the true understanding of God and the sacrifice due to Him (IB4, IB6, and IVA2).

Yet another line of criticism against Christianity was taken from its novelty, its having appeared so late on the scene as compared to Judaic and classical-pagan religion and culture. Such criticisms were countered by extravagant claims for the priority of Christianity in the church of the Old Testament (see IIA4, IVA4), and the characterization of all that was valid in Judaism and wholesome in classical antiquity as derivative, one way or another, from Christianity. In the case of the sacraments, the sensitive area was their similarity to certain ceremonials of the mystery cults, a connection enhanced, eventually, by the appropriation of some of the language of the mystery cults to Christian initiation (see Introduction to IIA). Defense of the eucharist against such a line of criticism appears in Justin (IB2) in connection with the Mithraic mysteries, and as a part of a vigorous offense against paganism in Firmicus Maternus (IB5) in connection with the cult of Attis. In each case, the similarity of Christian to pagan mysteries is attributed to demonic instigation of the pagans to imitate (anticipate?) the Christian rites.

Suggestions for further reading

A. Henrichs, "Pagan Ritual and the Alleged Crimes of the Early Christians," in *Kyriakon: Festschrift J. Quasten*, Munster, 1970, 18-35.

D. H. Tripp, "The Mysteries," in SL 54-55.

E. Yarnold, "Mystery Religions," in ARI 55-62.

R. L. Wilken, *The Christians as the Romans Saw Them*, New Haven, 1984.

A "The dripping blood our only drink, the bloody flesh our only food": The Charge against the Christians.

IA1. The Churches of Vienne and Lyons, *The Acta of the Martyrs of Lyons* 14-15.

ed H. Musurillo, *The Acts of the Christian Martyrs* (Oxford, 1972) 64-66.

Eusebius of Caesarea has preserved in the fifth book of his *Ecclesiastical History* an encyclical letter of the churches of Vienne and Lyons in Gaul to the churches of Asia and Phrygia. This letter describes the sufferings of Christians during the persecution of 177 under the emperors Marcus Aurelius and Lucius Verus. The letter is considered to be authentic, though it may have received some re-working in the third century.

Here we see the common slanders against the Christians, cannibalism among them, combining with judicial abuse and popular prejudice in an atmosphere of out-and-out persecution. The developments described here contradict Athenagoras of Athens, who, in his *Plea for Christians* addressed to Marcus Aurelius around this time (see IB4), said, among other things in Chapter 35 in refutation of the charge of cannibalism: "Moreover, we have slaves, some of us many, some of us few, and it is impossible that such behavior could escape their notice, but no one of them has ever contrived such lies against us."

14. In addition, some pagan household slaves of our people were arrested, since the prefect had given a general order that all of us be investigated. By the plotting of Satan, these slaves, frightened by the torments which they saw the saints suffering, charged us falsely, at the prompting of the soldiers, with Thyestean banquets, Oedipal unions, and such things as we may neither speak nor think about, let alone believe that any such things have anywhere been done among human beings. 15. When the report of these things was spread abroad, everyone became savage towards us, with the result that even those who may have been moderate before, because of friendship, became indignant, and raged against us. Indeed fulfilled was the statement of the Lord that "A time will come when anyone who kills you will think that he is offering worship to God" (Jn 16.2).

IA2. Tertullian (*c* 160-*c* 225), *Apologeticum* 7.14-8.1-5,7.
ed CCSL 1.100-101.

Tertullian was born at Carthage into a pagan family, and received an excellent traditional education in literature, philosophy, and law. He was converted to Christianity *c* 190, but fell into the Montanist heresy *c* 212. Tertullian was a prolific, profound, and energetic writer, and produced works in defense of Christianity against pagans and heretics alike, as well as treatments of Christian faith and practice. We encounter him in this volume, here, as an apologist, and later (IVA3), as a defender of the faith.

Tertullian's *Apologeticum*, completed in 197, is a well-reasoned plea for toleration of Christians addressed to Roman provinical governors. The short selections given here deal with the enormity of the popular slanders against the Christians, and with their improbability. In 8.7, Tertullian reduces the whole business to absurdity with a characteristically sarcastic realization of the popular view of Christian initiation and worship.

7.14 Quite aptly, then, it is Rumor alone who has knowledge, so far, of the crimes of Christians. It is she whom you bring forward to inform against us. But the charges which she once spread around, and has strengthened by the passage of time into popular belief, she has not yet been able to prove. So I can call Nature herself as witness against those who assume that such things are worthy of belief.

8.1 Look! We are setting up a reward for the commission of these atrocities: They promise the reward of eternal life! Assume, for the time being, that you believe this, for I want to ask you, in this connection, if, supposing you believe this, you would place so great a value on everlasting life that you would attain to it with a conscience like this. 2. Come on, sink the sword into a baby, hostile to none, guilty of nothing, a son to all. Or, if that is someone else's job, you just stand in attendance as a human being dies before he has lived. Await the newly-departing soul. Catch the fresh blood. Soak your bread in it. Eat! Enjoy! And while you are reclining at the banquet, check out the seating arrangements. Make careful note of where your mother and sister are, so that when the dogs bring on the darkness, you will make no mistake. For you will be guilty of sacrilege unless you commit incest.

4. Thus initiated and "sealed," you will live forever. I want you to answer whether eternity is worth so much to you. But if it is not, then you must not believe such things about us. Even if you believed all this, I say you would not be willing to act in this way, and, even if you were willing, you would be incapable of it. Why, then, are others able, if you are not?

Why are you incapable, if others can? 5. I suppose we are of a different species, dog-headed, or like the big-foot, with a different arrangement of teeth, or a different musculature, one avid for incestuous lust! If you believe these things about a human being, then you too are capable of them. You yourself are a human, just as the Christian is. If you cannot do these things, then you should not believe the reports of them. For you are a human, and the Christian is just what you are.

7. I imagine it is customary for those who wish to be initiated first to obtain an interview with the "Father" of the rites, and to make a list of the necessary preparations. He gives the list: "You need [1] a baby, still tender, who has no fear of death, and will smile under your knife; [2] bread, to use to soak up the juicy blood; [3] lampstands, lamps, and some dogs, and meat scraps to get them to knock over the lights; [4] most important, you will need to come with your mother and sister."

IA3. Minucius Felix (*fl* 200-230), *Octavius* 8.4, 9.5-6.

ed M. Pellegrino (Torino, 1963) 10-11, 12-13.

> All we know of Minucius Felix has been derived from his *Octavius*. He was possibly of North African origin, and probably resident and active as a lawyer in Rome in the first third of the third century. The *Octavius* is an apology cast into the form of a dialogue, modeled on Cicero's *De natura deorum*. It takes its name from Octavius, the Christian interlocutor. Our selections are from the invective against the Christians by the pagan Caecilius Natalis. 8.4 alleges the irreligious character of Christianity, and 9.5-6 prefer the charges of infanticide, cannibalism, and promiscuity. Note the probable reference in 9.6 to Marcus Cornelius Fronto (*c* 100-*c* 166), from Cirta in Numidia. He was the leading orator of his

day, and tutor to the emperors Marcus Aurelius and Lucius Verus. Fronto's speeches are lost; this is the only reference we have to an anti-Christian speech of his.

8.4 They [the Christians] establish the rank and file of their profane conspiracy from men gathered from the dregs of the uneducated and from gullible women who are easily taken in, due to the weakness of their sex. They are joined together by nocturnal assemblies, by fasts at appointed times, and by inhuman meals, not by any rite, but by sacrilege, a nation which lurks and fears the light, silent in public, prone to chatter in dark recesses. They despise the temples as tombs; they spit on the gods, they ridicule our rites; they are pitiful, yet, if one dare to say it, they pity our priests; they treat elective office and the purple with disdain, though they themselves are half-naked.

9.5-6 Now the story of how they initiate recruits is as revolting as it is well-known. They coat a baby with batter, to fool the unwary, and they place it before the one to be initiated. The baby is then slaughtered with hidden and secret wounds by the recruit who has been urged on to strike blows which are apparently quite harmless because of the covering of batter. It is unspeakable: they slurp up the baby's blood, and eagerly hand around his limbs. By this victim are they leagued together; by the shared knowledge of this crime they pledge themselves to silence. These rites are more foul than all sacrileges combined.

The nature of their "banquet" is well-known. Everyone talks about it, and the speech of our man from Cirta bears witness to it. They meet for the meal on an appointed day, with all their children, sisters, mothers, people of each age and sex. There, after a huge meal, when the party has really got going, and the fire of drunkenness and incestuous lust has waxed hot, a dog, which has been tied to the lampstand, is provoked to rush and leap forward by the tossing of a scrap of food beyond the length of the rope by which it is tied. Thus, when the light, a potential witness, has been overturned and extinguished, they throw themselves haphazardly into couplings of unspeakable lust in the wanton darkness, and, if they do not all commit it in fact, nonetheless, they are all guilty as accessories to incest, since whatever is capable of happening in individual cases is what the entire group really wants.

B *"The Sacrifice of Christians":*
Explanation and Polemic

IB1. Pliny the Younger (*c* 61-113), *Letter* 10.96.6-8.
ed. R. A. B. Mynors (Oxford, 1963) 338-339; *lit* A. N.
Sherwin-White, *The Letters of Pliny* (Oxford, 1966)
702-708; D. H. Tripp in SL 51-52; R. L. Wilken, 1-30.

Gaius Plinus Caecilius Secundus served as pro-
praetorian legate, with consular authority, for the
emperor Trajan in the province of Bithynia-and-Pontus
beginning in the year 109 or 110, until his death in 113.
Pliny undertook no program of persecution of the Christians in particular, but took cognizance of them in
response to prosecutions by private citizens. Pliny seems
to have been as unclear about the precise legal position of
Christians as are modern historians.

This extract is from Pliny's report to Trajan of his
investigation and disposition of the Christian question. It
contains an account' of the first explanation offered by
Christians to the civil government of their rites and practices. Pliny's first information was received from apostate
Christians, but it seems to have been confirmed by the
testimony of faithful Christian women who, being slaves,
were interrogated under torture. Liturgical scholars have
disputed the precise nature of the observances mentioned

by Pliny's witnesses. The insistence of these people, perhaps volunteered, perhaps in response to Pliny's interro-
gation, that the food consumed in their assemblies was
"of an ordinary and harmless kind" seems to be aimed at
allaying the fears of the mainstream pagan community
about Christians engaging in omophagy or cannibalism.

6. Others, whose names I obtained from an informer,
declared that they were Christians, and then denied it. They
said that they had been, but had given it up, some three years
ago, some more, some even twenty years ago. All of them did
reverence to your image and the statues of the gods, and
cursed the name of Christ. 7. They insisted that this was the
extent of their crime, or error: it was their practice to meet,
on an appointed day, before sunrise, to sing together among
themselves a hymn to Christ, as to a god, and to bind
themselves by an oath, not for any criminal activity, but not
to commit theft, or robbery, or adultery, not to perjure
themselves, not to refuse to return property left with them
when called upon to do so. Upon the completion of these
activities, their practice was to separate, and to assemble
again to take food, but of an ordinary and harmless kind.
They said they abandoned this practice after the promulga-
tion of my edict whereby, following your instructions, I had
forbidden the existence of societies. 8. So I considered it all
the more necessary to investigate the truth of the matter by
interrogating, under torture, two female servants who were
called deaconesses. I discovered nothing but perverse
superstition.

IB2. Justin Martyr (*c* 100-*c* 165), *First Apology* 65-67.

ed G. Rauschen (Bonn, 1911) 104-110; *lit* T. G. Jalland,
"Justin Martyr and the President of the Eucharist,"
Studia Patristica 5 (TU 80) 83-85, M. Jourjon in EEC
71-85, Bouley 109-117.

Justin was born into a gentile family of Nablus in Samaria at the end of the first or beginning of the second century. After considerable study of pagan culture and philosophy, he was converted to Christianity sometime shortly before the period 132-135. After his conversion, he taught in Ephesus, and then, around 150, he carried his teaching to Rome, where he died a martyr *c* 165.

It was in Rome that Justin wrote his *First Apology*, addressed to the Emperor Marcus Aurelius, his son Verissimus, and his adopted son Lucius, sometime in the period 152-155. The *Apology* is a defense and explanation of Christianity. It alludes directly to the standard slanders against the Christians only in passing, in Ch 26, as it discusses the heterodox, who, for all their false teachings, are still called Christians by pagan society: "Now whether they [*sc* the followers of Simon Magus, Menander, and Marcion] engage in these mythological practices, the overturning of the lamp, the haphazard couplings, and the devouring of human flesh, we do not know; but we know quite well that they are neither persecuted nor slaughtered by you, at least, not on account of their teachings."

Justin's real and effective defense of Christians against these charges was to explain, simply and candidly, what the worship of the Christians really was. He describes both a postbaptismal eucharist and the Sunday eucharistic liturgy. This is our first description of the eucharistic thought and practice of the church in Rome. For later developments see VA2 and VA4. The occasional vague elements in Justin's account are explained by Jalland, in the article cited above, in terms of varieties of practice and church polity existing in Rome in Justin's time.

65. But we, after thus washing the one who has believed and joined us, bring him to the place where are assembled those called the brothers, to offer prayers in common for ourselves, for the newly-illumined person, and for all other persons wherever they may be, in order that, since we have

found the truth, we may be found worthy also through good works to be reckoned good and devout and observers of what has been commanded, and thus attain to eternal salvation. At the conclusion of the prayers we greet one another with a kiss (1 Pt 5.14). Then bread and a cup containing wine and water are presented to the one presiding over the brothers. He takes them and offers praise and glory to the Father of All, through the name of the Son and of the Holy Spirit, and he makes a lengthy thanksgiving to God because He has counted us worthy of such favors. At the end of these prayers and thanksgiving, all express their assent by saying *Amen*. This Hebrew word, *Amen*, means "So be it." And when he who presides has given thanks, and all the people have acclaimed their assent, those whom we call deacons summon each one present to partake of the bread and wine and water over which the thanksgiving was said, and they carry it also to those who are absent.

66. We call this food the "Eucharist." No one is allowed to partake of it except him who believes that our teachings are true and has been cleansed in the bath for the forgiveness of his sins and for his regeneration, and who lives as Christ commanded. Not as common bread or as common drink do we receive these, but just as through the word of God, Jesus Christ, our Saviour, became incarnate and took on flesh and blood for our salvation, so, we have been taught, the food over which thanks has been given by the prayer of His word, and which nourishes our flesh and blood by assimilation, is both the flesh and blood of that incarnate Jesus. The apostles, in their memoirs which are called gospels, have handed down that they were commanded to this: Jesus took bread, and, after giving thanks, said "Do this in remembrance of me; this is my body." In like manner, He also took the cup, gave thanks, and said "This is my blood." And to them alone did He communicate this. The evil demons, in imitation of this, have ordered the same thing to be performed in the Mithraic mysteries. For, as you know or may easily learn, bread and a cup of water, along with some incantations, are used in their mystic initiation rites.

67. Henceforward, we constantly remind one another of

these things. We who have possessions come to the aid of the poor, and we are always together. For all the favors we enjoy we bless the creator of All, through His Son, Jesus Christ, and through the Holy Spirit. On the day which is called the day of the Sun we have a common assembly of all who live in the cities or in the country, and the memoirs of the apostles or the writings of the prophets are read, as much as there is time for. Then, when the reader has finished, the one presiding provides, in a discourse, admonition and exhortation to imitate these excellent things. Then we all stand up together and say prayers, and, as we said before, after we finish the prayer, bread and wine are presented. He who presides likewise offers up prayers and thanksgiving, to the best of his ability, and the people express their assent by saying *Amen*, and there is the distribution and participation by each one in those things over which thanksgiving has been said, and these are sent, through the deacons, to those not present. The wealthy, if they wish, contribute whatever they desire, and the collection is placed in the custody of the president, and he helps the orphans and widows, those who are needy because of sickness or any other reason, and the captives and the strangers in our midst; in short, he takes care of all those in need. The day of the Sun, indeed, is the day on which we all hold our common assembly, because it is the first day. On it God, transforming darkness and matter, created the world; and our Saviour Jesus Christ arose from the dead on the same day. For they crucified Him on the day before that of Saturn, and on the day after that of Saturn, the day of the Sun, He appeared to His apostles and disciples and taught them the things which we have passed on to you also for your consideration.

IB3. Justin Martyr, *Dialogue with Trypho* 41.

ed G. Archambault (Paris, 1909) 182-186; *lit* J. Nilson, "To Whom is Justin's *Dialogue with Trypho* ?" *Theological Studies* 38 (1977) 538-546.

Justin wrote his *Dialogue with Trypho* around 160. It is an extrapolational, almost fictional account of a dispute which occurred in Ephesus between Justin and Trypho the Jew. According to Nilson, the work is aimed primarily at the non-Christian, gentile population in Rome, who could not distinguish between Judaism and Christianity. This brief section touching upon the eucharist occurs in the course of Justin's discussion of how the Mosaic Law contains figures of things having to do with Christ.

The offering of fine flour, gentlemen, I said, which was prescribed to be offered for those cleansed of leprosy (Lv 14.10) was a type of the bread of the eucharist which our Lord Jesus Christ commanded us to offer in memory of the Passion He endured for the sake of those whose souls are cleansed of all evil, in order that we might, at the same time, thank God for creating the world and all it contains for man's sake, for freeing us from the evil in which we were born, and for destroying utterly the principalities and powers through Him who became passible in accordance with His will.

Wherefore, concerning the sacrifices you used to offer, God says through Malachy, one of the twelve: "My will is not in you, says the Lord, nor will I accept your sacrifices from your hands. For from the rising of the sun to its setting my name is glorified among the gentiles, and in every place incense and pure sacrifice are offered to my name. For my name is great among the gentiles, says the Lord, but you have defiled it" (Ml 1.10-12). In this passage God already speaks of the sacrifices which we, the gentiles, offer Him in every place, namely, the bread of the eucharist and the cup, likewise, of the eucharist. He foretells that we glorify His name, while you defile it.

Furthermore, the command of circumcision, obliging you without exception to circumcise your sons on the eighth day, was a type of the true circumcision by which we are circumcised from error and wickedness through our Lord Jesus Christ who arose from the dead on the first day of the week. For the first day of the week, while it remains the first of all days, yet is called the eighth according to the number of days of the cycle, and still it remains the first.

IB4. Althenagoras of Athens (*fl c* 176), *The Plea* 13.2-4.

ed W. R. Schoedel (Oxford, 1972) 26-28; *lit* L. W. Barnard, *Athenagoras: A Study in Second-Century Christian Apologetic* (Paris, 1972) 153-162.

> We know of Athenagoras only from his works, *On the Resurrection of the Dead*, and the work from which this excerpt is taken, *The Plea for Christians of Athenagoras the Athenian, Philosopher and Christian*, which he addressed to the emperor Marcus Aurelius and his son Commodus on the occasion, according to recent opinion (T.D. Barnes), of their visit to Athens in September 176. Our excerpt is from the portion of *The Plea* which deals with the charge of religious non-conformity and atheism on the part of Christians, for it is in this section, not in the refutation of the charge of cannibalism in Chapter 35, that Athenagoras makes oblique, but unmistakeable reference to the eucharist, "an unbloody sacrifice, a spiritual worship."

Because the majority of those who accuse us of atheism have no conception at all of divinity, not even in a dream, and they are untrained and unconversant with scientific and theological thought, they measure out piety by the conventional practice of offering sacrifices, and thus they accuse us of not holding to the same gods as the cities. Concerning both charges, O sovereigns, please consider the following. First, as to our not offering sacrifices: 2. The Fashioner and Father of the universe has no need of blood, nor of the savor of fat, nor of the fragrance of flowers and incense. He is Himself the consummate fragrance, in need of nothing and self-sufficient. Instead, the best sacrifice to Him is that we know who it was who stretched out the heavens, gathered

them into a sphere, and fixed the earth as a center, who
brought together water into the seas, and divided light from
darkness, who adorned the sky with stars, and made the
earth to cause every seed to spring up, who made animals
and fashioned men. 3. So, then, since we believe the Creator
to be God, who contains and rules all things with the knowledge and craft whereby He creates them, and we raise up
pious hands to Him, what need has he of a hecatomb?

4. And men avert the immortal gods with sacrifices
and propitiatory prayers, with libation and savory
fat, as they pray when one transgresses and sins.
(*Iliad* 9.499-501)

But what to me are whole-burnt-offerings of which God has
no need? Indeed, to offer sacrifices is necessary, but to offer
an unbloody sacrifice, a spiritual worship (Rm 12.1)!

IB5. Julius Firmicus Maternus (*fl c* 346), *On the Error of the Pagan Religions* 18.

ed A. Pastorino (Firenze, 1956) 183-197; *cf* ACW 37.
80-84, 194-197.

We have only bits and pieces of information about
Julius Firmicus Maternus. A native of Sicily, he entered
the legal profession; in the period 334-337, he wrote the
Mathesis, the most extensive extant Latin treatise on
astrology. He was converted to Christianity, and *c* 346 he
addressed to the emperors Constantius and Constans the
treatise *On the Error of the Pagan Religions*, an invective
against the remaining pagan cults and a plea for their
extirpation.

Chapter 18 is the first of a series of denunciations of the
pagan mystery cults, which, by diabolic inspiration,
designedly approximate features of Christian worship.
Here Firmicus denounces the baneful mimic-communion
of the initiates of Attis, and proclaims the authentic food
and communion of the Christians. His description of the
eucharist contains many scriptural proof texts, most of
them drawn from Cyprian's (see IVA4) collection of
testimonia, The *Ad Quirinum*.

18,1. Now I would like to discuss the signs and tokens
whereby the crowd of pitiable people identify themselves in
these superstitious observances. For they have special signs,
special passwords, which the Devil's instruction has handed
down to them in the assemblies of these sacrilegious men.

In some temple, to gain admission to the inner sanctum,
someone, a candidate for damnation, says: "I have eaten
from the timbrel, I have drunk from the cymbal, I have
gained knowledge of the mysteries of religion," which is said
in Greek as follows [he quotes in Greek]: "I have eaten from
the timbrel, I have drunk from the cymbal, I have become an
initiate of Attis."

2. O man so wretched, to acknowledge thus the outrage
you have committed! You have drunk the baneful, venom-
ous poison, and you lap up the deadly cup, driven by
sacrilegious fury. Death is always the result of this food,
death and punishment. That which you boast you have
drunk wounds the soul to death, and throws the seat of the
soul into confusion by a defiled protraction of evils.

There is another food which bestows salvation and life,
another food which both commits and restores man to God
Most-high, another food which relieves the sick, recalls the
wandering, raises up the fallen, which grants the boon of
eternal immortality to mortal men. Seek the bread of Christ,
seek the cup of Christ, that humanity may disdain earthly
frailty, and be fattened on the food of immortality.

3. But what is this food, what the cup, which Wisdom
proclaims with a loud voice in the books of Solomon? For
He says: "Come, eat of my bread, and drink the wine which I
have mixed" (Pr 9.5). Melchisedech, too, the King of Salem
and priest of God Most-high, proffered to the returning
Abraham the grace of a blessing with bread and wine (Gn
14.18-19). Also, when Isaac had blessed Jacob, and Esau
was begging and demanding the same thing, his father
answered him; "I have made him your master, and I have
made all his brothers his slaves; in wheat and wine I have
established him (Gn 27.37)." Then Esau wept over his mis-
fortune with a pitiable lament, because he had lost the grace
of wheat and wine, that is, of future happiness.

4. Moreover, that this divine bread is bestowed by God on

those devoted to Him, the Holy Spirit says through Isaiah: "Thus says the Lord: Behold, those who serve me shall eat, but you will go hungry. Behold, those who serve me will rejoice, but you will be put to shame. The Lord will kill you" (Is 65.13-15). Not only is this bread denied by God Most-high to the sacrilegious and impious, but a punishment is promised as well, and the doom of bitter death is decreed, that divine chastisement may eventually be inflicted on the hungry mouths. 5. The worshipful oracle of the thirty-third psalm is in harmony with this, for David says through the Holy Spirit: "Taste and see that the Lord is sweet" (Ps 33.9). Sweet is the heavenly nourishment, sweet the food of God, nor does it allow the woeful torment of lamentable hunger, and it drives out the toxin of former poison from the hearts of men. And the ensuing words of the oracle declare that this is so, for it says: "Fear the Lord, O His saints, for there is no hunger for those who fear Him. The wealthy have grown poor and gone hungry, but those who seek the Lord will not want for any good thing" (Ps 33.10).

6. O you who strut in the temple in the robe of office, who shine with purple, whose head is loaded with a crown of gold or laurel, disgraceful want pursues your error, and the burdensome load of poverty hangs over your neck. That poor man whom you despise has abundant riches. Abraham prepares a place for him in his bosom (Lk 16.22ff). Then you will beg of him, through the interposed gulf of flames, a tiny droplet of trickling water, to ease the wounds of your conscience. But even though he wishes to do so, Lazarus will be able neither to give nor to obtain for you any relief of your pain. The merits of each are repaid in kind. Life is awarded to him, because of misfortunes in this world; but to you, because of advantages in this world, the penalty of everlasting torment is assigned.

7. Moreover, that the identity of this bread might be learned without ambiguity, that men might not be duped and their hopes disappointed by distorted interpretations and contradictory expositions, the Lord Himself established the matter with His holy and worshipful mouth. For He said in the Gospel according to John: "I am the bread of

life. He who comes to me will not hunger, he who believes in me will never thirst" (Jn 6.35). Likewise, in the ensuing words, He establishes the same point in a similar way, for He says: "If anyone thirst, let him come and drink. He who believes in me. . . " (Jn 7.37-38). And again, to communicate the true character of His grandeur to those who believe, He says: "Unless you eat the flesh of the Son of Man, and drink His blood, you will not have life in you" (Jn 6.54).

8. Therefore, have nothing to do with the bread of the timbrel, O you would-be gods, who are only mortal men! Seek the grace of the food of salvation, drink the cup of immortality. By His banquet Christ recalls you to the light, and restores life to comatose bodies and limbs gangrenous from noxious poison. Restore ruined human nature by heavenly food, that whatever is dead in you may be reborn by divine kindness. You have learned, now, what your best interests require. Choose which you want. From your food death is born; from this food immortal life is given.

IB6. Augustine of Hippo (354-430), *The City of God* 10.4-6,20; 17.20.

ed CCSL 47.276-279; 588-599; *tr* M. Dods (Edinburgh, 1872), revised.

Augustine, the greatest of the fathers of the church, has left us an ample account of his earlier life and conversion to Christianity in his magnificent *Confessions*. After his baptism in 387, he made his way back to North Africa. He was ordained to the priesthood in Hippo in 391, and was made coadjutor bishop and successor to bishop Valerius there in 395. He presided over the see of Hippo until his death in 430, and has "given the world the most extensive and humane theology it has yet seen."

In this volume, we meet Augustine as catechist, exegete, and pastor, but our first encounter with him is in his role of apologist. Pagan literary and philosophical culture had continued to enjoy great prestige, in spite of the virtual christianization of the mediterranean world. Criticisms of Christianity by influential pagans, and their allegations of a Christian subversion of the Roman state and religion obtained a wider audience following the sack of Rome by the Goths in 410. Naive Christian optimism and pride in the universal Christian empire had suffered a blow. These and many other factors led to Augustine's composition of his monumental work of defense and explanation, *The City of God*.

In Book Ten of *The City of God*, along with other matters, Augustine deals with the nature of authentic sacrifice and worship. He sets out his arguments in Chapters 4-6, excerpted here, concluding at the end of Chapter 6 with the description of the perfect sacrifice, the sacrifice of Christians. He draws a connection between the body of Christ, which we are, and the sacrifice of the altar, a theme developed in his catecheses on the eucharist (IIA6). Augustine provides a reprise and clarification of his theme in Chapter 20, where he focuses on the priesthood of Christ.

4. Sacrifice is due to the True God alone.

But to say nothing for the present of other things which have to do with religion's service by which God is worshipped, certainly no man would dare to say that sacrifice is due to any except God. Many parts, indeed, of divine worship are abused in showing honor to men, whether through an excessive humility or pernicious flattery. Yet, while this is done, those persons who are thus worshipped and venerated, or, in an extreme case, even adored, are considered to be humans. But who ever thought of sacrificing except to one whom he knew, supposed, or pretended to be a god? Moreover, how ancient a part of God's worship sacrifice is, is shown adequately by those two brothers, Cain and Abel, of whom God rejected the elder's sacrifice, but looked favorably on the younger's (Gn 4.4 *ff*).

5. Concerning the sacrifices which God does not need, but wished to be observed for the signifying of those things which He requires.

And who is so foolish as to suppose that things offered to God in sacrifice are needed by Him for some purposes of His own? Though divine scripture deals with this in many places, so as not to be tedious, let it be enough to quote this brief passage from a psalm: "I have said to the Lord, You are my God, for you do not need my goods" (Ps 16.2). We must believe, then, that God has no need, not only of cattle, or any other corruptible and earthly thing, but even of man's righteousness, and that all right worship of God profits not God, but man. For no man would say he did a benefit to a fountain by drinking, or to the light by seeing. And the fact that the ancient fathers offered animal sacrifices, which the people of God now reads of, but does not practice, means nothing else than that those sacrifices signified the things which we do for the purpose of drawing near to God and inducing our neighbor to do the same.

A visible sacrifice, therefore, is the sacrament, that is, the sacred sign of an invisible sacrifice. Hence that penitent in the Prophet, or it may be the Prophet himself, entreating God to be merciful to his sins, says: "If you desired sacrifice, I would have offered it. You delight not in whole-burnt-offerings. The sacrifice to God is a contrite spirit; a heart contrite and humbled God will not spurn" (Ps 50.18-19). Observe how, in the very words in which he said that God does not desire sacrifice, he shows that God does desire sacrifice. He does not desire, therefore, the sacrifice of a slaughtered beast, but He does desire the sacrifice of a contrite heart. Thus, that sacrifice which he says God does not desire signifies the sacrifice which, he goes on to say, God does desire.

God does not desire sacrifices in the sense in which foolish people think He desires them, that is, for the sake of His own pleasure. For if He had not wished that the sacrifices He requires—one of which is a heart contrite and humbled by penitent sorrow—should be symbolized by those sacrifices which He was thought to desire as if pleasing to Him, He would never have commanded their offering in the Old Law. And so they were destined to be altered when the opportune and appointed time arrived, in order that men might not suppose that the sacrifices themselves, rather than the things symbolized by them, were pleasing to God or, indeed, acceptable in us. Hence, in another passage from another psalm, He says: "If I were hungry, I would not tell you; for the world is mine and its fullness. Will I eat the flesh of bulls, or drink the blood of goats?" (Ps 49.12-13), as if He should say: "Supposing such things were necessary for me, I would never ask you for what I have in my own power." Then he goes on to indicate what these signify: "Offer to God the sacrifice of praise, and pay your vows to the Most High. And call upon me in the day of trouble; I will deliver you, and you will glorify me" (Ps 49.14-15). So in another prophet: "Wherewith shall I approach the Lord, and reach my high God? Shall I reach Him with burnt-offerings, with yearling calves? Will the Lord be pleased with thousands of rams, or with ten thousands of fat goats? Shall I give my first-born for my offense, the fruit of my body for the sin of my soul? Has He shown you, O man, what is good? And what does the Lord require of you, but to do justly, and to love mercy, and to be prepared to walk with the Lord, your God" (Mi 6.6-8)? In the words of this Prophet, these two things are distinguished and set forth clearly: that God does not require these sacrifices for their own sake, and that He does require the sacrifices which they symbolize. In the epistle entitled *To the Hebrews* it is said: "To do good and to be sharers forget not, for with such sacrifices God is pleased" (Heb 13.16). And so, when it is written, "I desire mercy rather than sacrifice," nothing else is meant than that one sacrifice is preferred to another; for that which in common speech is called sacrifice is the symbol of the true sacrifice. Now mercy is the true sacrifice, and therefore it is said, as I have just quoted, "with such sacrifices God is pleased." All the various divine ordinances, therefore, which we read concerning the sacrifices in the service of the tabernacle or the temple, we are to refer to the love of God and of our neighbor, for "On these two commandments," as it is written, "depend all the law and the prophets" (Mt 22.40).

6. *The true and perfect sacrifice.*

Accordingly, a true sacrifice is every work which is done that we may be united to God in a holy fellowship, and which is referred to that final Good in which alone we can be truly blessed. And, therefore, even the mercy whereby we aid men, if it is not done for God's sake, is not a sacrifice. For, though made or offered by man, yet sacrifice is a "divine thing," to such a degree that the ancient Latins called it by this very term. Thus man himself, consecrated in the name of God, and vowed to God, is a sacrifice insofar as he dies to the world that he may live to God. For this is a part of that mercy which each man shows to himself, and so it is written: "Have mercy on your soul by pleasing God" (Si 30.24). Our body, also, is a sacrifice when we chasten it by temperance, if we do so as we ought, for God's sake, that we may not present our members as instruments of iniquity to sin, but as instruments of righteousness to God (Rm 6.13). Exhorting to this sacrifice, the Apostle says: "I beg you, therefore, brothers, by the mercy of God, to present your bodies as a living sacrifice, holy, acceptable to God, your spiritual service" (Rm 12.1). If, then, the body, which the soul uses as an inferior servant, or as an instrument, is a sacrifice, when its good and proper use is referred to God, how much more does the soul itself become a sacrifice, when it refers itself to God, that, inflamed by the fire of His love, it may lose the shape of worldly desire, and be remolded, subjected to Him as to unchanging beauty, and become pleasing to Him, because it has received of His beauty? And this, indeed, the Apostle adds by way of a conclusion, saying: "And be not conformed to this world, but be trans-

formed in the newness of your mind, that you may prove
what is the will of God, what is good, what acceptable, what
perfect" (Rm 12.2).

Since, therefore, true sacrifices are works of mercy to
ourselves or our neighbors, done with reference to God; and
since works of mercy have no other object than that we be
freed from distress, and that, thereby, we become happy;
and since there is no happiness apart from that good of
which it is said, "It is good for me to cling to God" (Ps
73.28), it comes about, accordingly, that the entire
redeemed City, that is to say, the congregation and society
of saints, is offered to God as a manifold sacrifice through
the Great Priest, who also offered Himself to God in His
Passion on our behalf, that we might be the body of so great
a Head, according to the form of a servant (Ph 2.7). For it
was this form He offered, in this He was offered, because it is
according to this that He is Mediator, in this He is the priest,
in this the sacrifice.

Accordingly, when the Apostle had exhorted us to present our bodies as a living sacrifice, holy, acceptable to God,
our spiritual service, and not to be conformed to this world,
but to be transformed in the newness of our mind, that we
might prove what is the will of God, what good, what
acceptable and perfect, because we ourselves are the entire
sacrifice, he says: "For I say, through the grace of God
which is given to me, to every man that is among you, not to
think of himself more highly than he ought to think, but to
think soberly, according as God has dealt to every man the
measure of faith. For as we have many members in one
body, and all members do not have the same function, so
we, though many, are one body in Christ, and every one
members one of another, having gifts which differ according
to the grace that is given to us" (Rm 12.3-6). This is the
sacrifice of Christians: "We, though many, are one body in
Christ" (1 Co 10.17), and this is the sacrifice which the
church continually celebrates in the sacrament of the altar,
known to the faithful, in which she teaches that she herself is
offered in the offering she makes.

20. Concerning the highest and true sacrifice which the Mediator of God and Man Himself became.

Whence that true Mediator—in that "taking the form of a servant" (Ph 2.7) He was made the "Meditor of God and man, the man, Jesus Christ" (1 Tm 2.5)—although "in the form of God" (Ph 2.6) He might receive sacrifice along with the Father with whom He is also one God, yet in the form of a servant He preferred to be the sacrifice rather than to receive it, lest, even under this circumstance, anyone might suppose that sacrifice was to be offered to any creature. Wherefore, He is both priest, making the offering Himself, and also Himself the offering. He wished that the sacrament of this reality should be the daily sacrifice of the church, which, since it is the body of Him, the Head, it learns to offer itself through Him. The manifold and varied former sacrifices of the saints were the signs of this true sacrifice, since this one sacrifice was prefigured by many, as one entity may be named by many words that it may be commended without tediousness. All false sacrifices have given way to this supreme and true sacrifice.

> In the second half of *The City of God*, Augustine traces the progress of the heavenly and earthly cities through time. Book Seventeen is devoted to the times of the prophets. Chapter 20 deals with David and Solomon, and, in particular, with the prophecies of Christ contained in the books of Solomon. Our excerpt is concerned with Proverbs 9.1-5, and its prophecy of the eucharist.

17.20. Likewise, in the same book [*sc* Proverbs], there is that passage which we already touched upon earlier, when we were discussing the barren woman who bore seven sons [17.4]. It is usually interpreted as having been uttered concerning Christ and the church, as soon as it came into existence, by those who know that Christ is the Wisdom of God (1 Co 1.24):

Wisdom has built herself a house and has set down
seven columns. She has slain her victims, mixed her
wine in a bowl and prepared her table. She has sent
her servants, inviting with a lofty proclamation to
her bowl, saying: "Who is foolish? Let him turn to
me." And to those lacking good sense she has said:
"Come, eat of my bread and drink the wine which I
have mixed for you." (Pr 9.1-5)

Here, surely, we recognize that the Wisdom of God, that
is, the Word coeternal with the Father, has built in the
Virgin's womb a house for Himself, a human body, and has
joined it to the church, as limbs to the Head; He has offered
as victims the martyrs; and has prepared His table with
bread and wine, where also is revealed the priesthood
according to the order of Melchisedech (Ps 109.4; Heb 5.6);
He has summoned the foolish and those lacking good sense,
because, as the Apostle says, He "chose the weak things of
the world to confound the strong" (1 Co 1.27). He says what
follows to these weak ones: "Abandon folly, that you may
live; and seek prudence, that you may have life" (Pr 9.6). To
become a partaker of that table is to begin to have life. For
also in another book, which is called *Ecclesiastes*, where it
says: "There is no good for man, save that he eat and drink"
(Qo 8.15), what makes better sense of what it says than to
understand that it has to do with the partaking of this table,
which the Priest, the very Mediator of the New Covenant
(Heb 9.15; 12.24) according to the order of Melchisedech
provides in His body and blood? For that sacrifice has taken
the place of all those sacrifices of the Old Covenant, which
were offered as a shadow of the sacrifice to come, in connection with which, moreover, we recognize the voice of the
same Mediator speaking through the Prophet in the Thirty-
ninth Psalm: "You had no desire for sacrifice and oblation,
but you have framed a body for me" (Ps 39.7), because His
body is offered in place of all those sacrifices, and distributed to those who partake. In addition, that this Ecclesiastes
is not thinking of the feasts of fleshly pleasure in this remark
about eating and drinking, which he often repeats and urges

strongly, is made clear where he says: "It is better to enter a house of mourning than a house of drinking" (Qo 7.3), and a little later, "The heart of the wise is in the house of mourning, and the heart of the foolish in the house of feasting" (7.5).

II. "O Taste and See": Eucharistic Instructions.

Introduction

This section is devoted to specifically eucharistic instruction provided within the Christian community. We proceed from A, the catechesis on the eucharist provided for the newly baptized, to B, the mystagogy which replaced it as adult baptism (and catechetical instruction) became uncommon, and from the renewal of eucharistic catechesis in C, festal sermons for Great and Holy Thursday to D, examples of the treatment of the eucharist as a part of encyclopedic works on the liturgy and on the faith.

IIA Eucharistic catechesis from the period before the Peace of the Church (313) is not well documented. The basic structure of the catechumenate, with its program of probation and instruction, is thought to have emerged by the beginning of the third century. And although there are indications of the energy and care expended on the instruction of catechumens, no formal eucharistic catechesis survives from before the fourth century. Our first selection, from Clement (IIA1), a leader of Alexandria's celebrated Catechetical School, provides and obscure and idiosyncratic example of what it may have been like.

The reasons for the dearth of eucharistic catechesis from the earlier period relative to the abundance of specimens from the fourth and fifth centuries are matters for speculation. The so-called *disciplina arcani* (see below) cannot be invoked as an explanation, for it seems to have been in force already in the time of Origen and Tertullian. More likely causes may be the increasingly formalized, more economic program of instruction required by the flood of converts which followed the toleration and establishment of the church, and by a change in literary conventions which promoted the copying and recopying of catecheses on the sacraments. In any case, we find ourselves in the later fourth and fifth centuries in the classic period of the catechumenate and of eucharistic catechesis.

An understanding of these texts, and of many others in this volume, will be enhanced if we digress briefly to explain the *disciplina arcani* and the place of eucharistic cathechesis in Christian initiation. *Disciplina arcani* (discipline of secrecy) is a modern term for the practice which proscribed the disclosure of the details of the sacraments, the mysteries of the Christian faith, to the unbaptized. The discipline was typically extended to include the Creed (see IIA7.2), the Lord's Prayer (see IIA6.2), and the details of the rites of baptism, chrismation, and the eucharist (hence the dismissal of non-Christians and catechumens alike upon the conclusion of the Liturgy of the Word; see IIB1, IIB2, IVB6, IVB7, IVD2).

The gradual, and then accelerating process of instruction in these mysteries typically began with admission to candidacy for baptism, which usually took place at the beginning of Lent. In the course of a program of teaching about the faith which extended throughout the Lenten season, the candidates (*competentes*, applicants [for baptism]; *electi*, the chosen; *photizomenoi*, the illumined) were taught the Creed and the Lord's Prayer (see IVC4). But instruction in the three sacraments of initiation—baptism, chrismation, and eucharist—was deferred, almost everywhere, until after the sacraments had been received at Pascha; such instruction was usually given in Bright Week.

In language borrowed from the pagan mystery-cults, the baptized were called initiates, and the sacramental catechesis they received was sometimes called a *mystagogia*, an introduction to—and an instruction in—the *mysteria*, "the mysteries," a term applied to baptism, chrismation, and, most particularly and frequently, to the eucharist. Hence the instructions on the sacraments have come to be called, following the title given them in the transmission of the Jerusalem catecheses (IVA3), mystagogical catecheses.

The texts collected in the present volume contain abundant allusions to the distinction between the uninitiated and the initiated, i.e. between the unbaptized and the baptized, and to the special factual and experiential knowledge of the eucharist which was reserved for the initiates (also called "the Faithful") alone (see IB6, IIA2, IIA4, IIIB4, IIIB7, IVA5, IVC4, IVD2). References to the force of the *disciplina arcani* occur as well (see IIA2, IIA5, IIIA2, IVA9, IVB7, VB1). An examination of some of the texts will show, however, that in the case of the eucharist at least, secrecy about the mysteries had more to do with the details of the eucharistic liturgy than with the fact of the sacrament of the body and blood of Christ (see the profusion of teaching in the exegetical and festal sermons, delivered, in most cases, to baptized and unbaptized alike). One is inclined to ask "Why the secrecy?", given the amount of information about the sacrament available to the regular or even occasional non-Christian or not-yet-baptized catechumen churchgoer, and the amount of detailed information to be gleaned from the collection of bits and pieces from the indiscrete talk of the faithful, whose degrees of earnestness must have varied widely as their number increased. The desire to prevent parodies of the mysteries and the desire to enhance their awesomeness (see Introduction to IV) must have played a part. Another factor was surely a calculated exploitation of curiosity.

A difficult challenge to the pastor of souls was posed by the people who, though admitted at some stage of their lives to the catechumenate, postponed entering candidacy for baptism for various reasons, none of them commendable.

The following extract from a sermon of St. Augustine delivered probably at the beginning of Lent, on the eucharistic discourse of John 6, shows that master of psychological manipulation shamelessly exploiting the curiosity of this class of people, called "hearers" in the church of Hippo:

As we heard when the Holy Gospel was being read, the Lord Jesus Christ has urged us, with the promise of eternal life, to eat His body and to drink His blood. Of those who have heard these words, some are doing this already, but some do not yet do it. Those who have been baptized and are the "faithful," you know what He meant. But those among you who are still catechumens, and are called "hearers," they were able to be hearers when the reading was given, but they could not be comprehenders as well, could they? And so, our remarks are addressed to both groups.

Let those who already eat the Lord's flesh and drink His blood consider what it is they are eating and drinking, lest, as the Apostle says, they eat and drink condemnation for themselves (1 Co 11.29). But let those who do not yet eat and drink make haste, now that they have been invited to such a feast.

In these days the government is providing food. Christ provides food everyday. His table is the real community table. Why is it, O "hearers," that you see the table, but do not approach the feast?

And maybe, when the Gospel was being read, you were saying to yourselves: "I wonder what He means by 'My flesh is truly food, and my blood is truly drink (Jn 6.56).' How is the Lord's flesh eaten, how is the Lord's blood drunk? I wonder what He means."

Who has shut you out so that you do not know this? It is veiled, but if you want, it will be revealed. Make your profession, and you have answered your question! The faithful already know what the Lord meant; but you are called a catechumen. You are called a "hearer," but you are deaf! The ears of your body are open, for you hear the words which were said; but the ears of your soul are closed, for you do not understand what was said. I am arguing; I am not explaining.

Look! Pascha is at hand. Sign up for baptism. If the festival does not motivate you, let simple curiosity prompt you, that you may know the meaning of "He who eats my flesh and drinks my blood abides in me, and I in him" (Jn 6.57). So you may know, along with me, what this means, knock, and it will be opened to you (Mt 7.7). And as I say to you "Knock, and it will be opened to you," I also am knocking. Open to me! As I sound in your ears I am knocking on your heart. (Sermon 132; PL 38.734-735)

This opening of the heart could only be achieved by enrolling for baptism, and receiving the sacraments of initiation. Curiosity would be satisfied by a personal experience of the mysteries, and only then, by receiving an explanation of their details. Most of the principal monuments of mystagogical catechesis on the eucharist have been collected in IIA. They offer us a hint of the fascination and joy of the newly baptized, and show us the subtlety and delight of the fathers in their work of illumination. (Note: A notable omission from IIA is the mystagogical catecheses of Theodore of Mopsuestia (*d* 428), which are extant only in Syriac translation. These are omitted because of their prolixity and their ready availability in a recent translation (in ARI 211-263), and because the tendency towards allegorization of details of the eucharistic liturgy which they display finds a more compendious, and, in the case of IIB1, more influential manifestation in the mystagogies which took the place of the mystagogical catechesis.)

IIB Opportunities for detailed, formal instruction about the eucharist became more restricted as infant baptism became the universal practice, and as the administration of the sacraments of Christian initiation were made available throughout the year. The gap created by the disappearance of eucharistic catechesis was filled by the composition of explanations of the liturgy, by the inclusion of eucharistic teaching in encyclopedic treatments of the faith, and, beyond the chronological scope of this series, by the elaboration of treatises on the eucharist, as controversy or clerical formation required.

The liturgical commentaries apply to the elucidation of liturgical places, objects, persons, actions, and prayers the techniques developed for the allegorical exegesis of scripture, a transference of method already partially evident in eucharistic catechesis. Of the two early examples of mystagogy included in this section, Germanus of Constantinople (IIB1) expounds the eucharistic liturgy with some system and restraint; the letter attributed to Germanus of Paris (IIB2) does so diffusely and extravagantly. However one may feel about such an approach, it is important to bear in mind that the allegorical exposition of the liturgy dominated Christian piety for more than a thousand years.

IIC An annual opportunity for instruction concerning the eucharist was provided by Great and Holy Thursday, the locus within the yearly celebration of the paschal mystery for the commemoration of the institution of the eucharist. The eucharist is never the unique focus of festal homilies for Holy Thursday, as may be seen in our examples; sometimes the eucharist is dealt with only in passing, primary emphasis being placed on the betrayal of Christ by Judas. Instruction on the eucharist, and the rekindling of the people's fervor for the sacrament was by no means limited to Great Thursday, and could be provided in the course of preaching (see IVB2, IVC6), and as an excursus in the course of scriptural exposition (see e.g. IIIA, IVB4, IVB5, IVC2, IVD1, IVD2), in occasional sermons designed to correct abuses (see IVD 3-4), and, above all, through the prayers and chants of the eucharistic liturgy (see VAB).

IID Violence, ignorance, and secular and ecclesiastical politics brought on the conclusion of the age of the fathers. In the eleventh hour, Providence supplied masters of synthesis who could pass on the message of the fathers in a compendious form, ready of access, portable, and relatively cheap to reproduce. The concluding selections in this section are from two such syntheses, Isidore of Seville's pioneering liturgical encyclopedia, and John of Damascus' manual of the Christian faith which contains the finest synthesis of patristic thinking on the eucharist ever to appear.

Suggestions for further reading

E. Yarnold, ARI 3-62; SL 95-109.

F. van der Meer, *Augustine the Bishop*, tr B. Battershaw, G.R. Lamb, London, 1961, 353-382.

K. Hein, *Eucharist and Excommunication...*, Bern, 1976, Chapter 3, Excursus, "Judas Iscariot at the Last Supper," 38-50.

R. Taft, "The Liturgy of the Great Church: An Initial Synthesis of Structure and Interpretation on the Eve of Iconoclasm," *Dumbarton Oaks Papers* 34-35 (1980-81) 45-75.

A Catechesis

IIA1 Clement of Alexandria (*c* 150-*c* 215), *Paedagogus* 1.42-43; 2.19.3-20.1.

ed SC 70.186-190; 108.46-48; *tr* FC 23.40-41, 111-112, revised; *lit* A. Méhat in EEC 99-131.

Clement, a child of pagan parents, found the truth he had been seeking in the teachings of Pantaenus, the head of the Christian catechetical school in Alexandria. He succeeded Pantaenus around 200, only to be driven by persecution into exile, never to return. He wrote the *Protrepticus* (*Exhortation*) to call pagans to Christianity, and the *Paedagogus* (*The Tutor*) for the instruction of those converted to the faith. The purpose of the *Paedagogus* suggests that some extracts from it which bear on the eucharist may aptly be included here, although it is not a catechesis of the classic type.

The articulation of Clement's views of the eucharist with the rest of his unusual theology is a matter of interpretation (see, e.g., that of Méhat, cited above). These passages are, for a variety of reasons, obscure in part, but they speak clearly enough of the role of the eucharist in the life of the Christian and the life of the church, and of the nourishment and transformation which proceed from it.

42.1 O mystical wonder! There is one Father of the universe, and one Logos of the universe, and one Holy Spirit, everywhere the same. There is only one virgin-mother, and it is my delight to call her the church. This mother alone does not have milk, because she alone did not become a wife. She is at once virgin and mother, undefiled as a virgin, loving as a mother, and she summons her children and nurses them with a holy milk, with the Logos who is suited to infants. 2. She has no milk, because the milk was the Child, this lovely Child, her very own, the body of Christ, and she has fed with the Logos the new people which the Lord Himself wrapped in the swaddling clothes of His precious blood.

3. O the holy birth, the holy swaddling clothes! The Logos is everything to the infant: Father, and Mother, and Teacher, and Nourisher! "Eat my flesh," He says, "and drink my blood." The Lord supplies these as the foods most appropriate for us. He proffers His flesh and pours out His blood, and nothing is lacking to the children for their growth. 43.1 O paradoxical mystery! He commands us to put off the old, fleshly corruption, and the old nourishment as well, to partake of another, new way of life, that of Christ, to receive Him, if possible, and store Him up in ourselves, to put the Saviour in our hearts, in order to destroy the passions of the flesh.

2. Or you would rather not understand it in this way, perhaps something less out-of-the-ordinary? Then listen: The flesh is an allegory for us of the Holy Spirit, for indeed the flesh was created by Him; the blood suggests to us the Logos, for indeed as abundant blood has the Logos been poured out upon our life. The union of both is the Lord, the food of infants, the Lord, Pneuma and Logos. 3. The food, that is, the Lord Jesus, that is, the Logos of God, is Pneuma incarnate, hallowed, heavenly flesh. The food is the milk of the Father by whom alone we infants are nursed. And He, "the Beloved" (Mk 1.11), and our Nourisher, the Logos, poured out His blood for our sakes, thus saving humanity. Through Him we have come to trust in God, and have taken refuge at the Father's "breast causing forgetfulness of care"

(*Iliad* 22.83), the Logos, and He alone, as is fitting, furnishes us infants with the milk of love; and truly blessed are they alone who suck at this breast.

2.19.3.   Subsequently, the holy vine produced the prophetic cluster. This was a sign to those who had received elementary instructions drawing them from their wandering to rest (Nb 13.24-27), the Great Cluster, the Logos who was crushed for our sakes, since the Logos willed that the blood of the grape (Gn 49.11) be mixed with water, as His blood also is mingled with salvation. But the blood of the Lord is twofold: there is His fleshly blood by which we have been redeemed from corruption, and there is His pneumatic blood by which we have been chrismated. And this is what it is to drink the blood of Jesus, to partake of the Lord's incorruptibility. But the strength of the Logos is Pneuma, as blood is of the flesh. 20.1 Thus, wine is mixed with water, and Pneuma mixed with man in an analogous way. And the one, the mixture of wine and water, nourishes unto faith, and the other, Pneuma, leads to incorruptibility. And, again, the blending of both, of drink and of Logos, is called eucharist, a gift laudable and lovely. Those who partake of it in faith are sanctified in both body and soul, that divine mixture, man, which the Father's will blends mystically with Pneuma and Logos. And quite truly was Pneuma akin to the soul which it supported, and flesh akin to the Logos, the flesh for whose sake "the Logos became flesh" (Jn 1.14).

IIA2 Gregory of Nyssa (*c* 335-394), *The Great Catechetical Oration* 37.

ed J.H. Strawley (Cambridge, 1903); tr J.H. Strawley (London, 1917), revised.

Gregory was the younger brother of Basil the Great. After an excellent religious education at the direction of Basil, as well as training and practice in the profession of oratory, he turned to the monastic life. He was summoned thence to the pastoral care of the see of Nyssa, a

suffragan see of his brother's. In addition to many speculative works in dogmatic and ascetical theology, Gregory
has left us the thorough and practical, but sublime *Great
Catechetical Oration*, written *c* 385. Prepared for the
guidance of catechists, it is not an actual catechetical
speech, but, rather, a model presentation of the faith—at
once didactic and apologetic. The exposition of the sacraments is given in Chapters 33-36 (baptism), and in Chapter 37 (the eucharist), the chapter given here. His logical
presentation of the eucharist, which draws on philosophy,
physiology, common sense, and sublime theology, is typical of his work.

37. But since human nature is twofold, a composite of
soul and body, those who are being saved must grasp Him
who leads the way towards life by means of both. Now the
soul, being blended with Him by faith, received from it the
beginnings of its salvation. For the union with Life involves
a sharing of life. But the body comes into an association and
blending with its Saviour in a different way.

Those who have through treachery received poison neu-
tralize its destructive force by means of another drug. But
the antidote, like the poison, must enter the vital organs of
the person, in order that the effect of the remedy may, by
passing through them, be distributed through the entire
body. So, when we had tasted of that which brought destruction to our nature, of necessity we needed in turn something to restore what was destroyed, in order that such an
antidote passing into us might, by its own counteracting
influence, repel the harm already brought into the body by
the poison.

What is this, then? It is nothing else but that body which
was shown to be mightier than death and which inaugurated
our life. For just as a little leaven, as the Apostle says (1 Co
5.6), makes the whole lump like itself, so the body which was
made immortal by God, by passing entire into our body
alters and changes it to itself. For just as when a deadly drug
is mingled with a healthy body, the whole of what it is

mingled with becomes as worthless as the drug, so also that immortal body, passing into him who receives it, changes the entire body to its own nature.

But it is not possible for anything to enter the body, unless it is mingled with the vital organs by way of food and drink. Therefore the body must receive the life-giving power in the way that its nature permits. But since only that body which is the receptacle of divinity has received this grace, and since it has been shown that it is not otherwise possible for our body to become immortal, unless it participates in immortality through association with that which is incorruptible, it is fitting to consider how it became possible for that one body, though continually distributed to countless believers throughout the whole world, to become in its entirety the possession of each, through the portion received, and yet to remain whole in itself.

In order, then, that our faith, with a view to logical consistency, may experience no ambiguity concerning the question proposed, it is fitting that our argument should turn aside for a moment to discuss the physiology of the body. For who is not aware that the very nature of our body does not possess life by an essential character of its own, but maintains itself and continues in existence through the influx of a force from without, by a ceaseless motion drawing to itself that which it lacks and casting off that which is superfluous?

A leather bottle full of some liquid, if the contents escape at the bottom, will not preserve its own shape around the volume unless some other liquid in turn enters from above to fill up the void. Thus he who sees the rounded circumference of this vessel knows that it does not belong to what he sees, but that it is the liquid flowing into it and contained in it which gives its shape to that which contains the volume. So also the constitution of our body has nothing that we can recognize of its own to maintain itself by, but continues in existence by means of the force which is introduced into it.

Now this force is nourishment and is so called. It is not the same for all bodies that are nourished, but each body has some appropriate nourishment assigned to it by Him who directs its nature. For some living creatures are nourished by digging up roots, others find their food in herbs, others again feed on flesh, while man finds his chief sustenance in bread. In order to retain and preserve moisture he has to drink, not water only, but water often sweetened with wine, in order to assist the heat within us. He who sees these elements, then, sees, in effect, the bulk of our body. For, by passing into me, those elements become body and blood, seeing that the nourishment, by the power of assimilation, is changed in each case into the form of the body.

After thus investigating these points, we must bring back our thoughts to the problem before us. The question which we were asking was how that one body of Christ gives life to all mankind, that is, to as many as have faith, being distributed to all and yet suffering no diminution in itself. Perhaps, then, we are not far from the probable explanation.

It is admitted that the subsistence of the body comes from nourishment, and that this nourishment is food and drink, and that in food bread is included, and in drink water sweetened with wine. It is admitted, further, that the Word of God, who, as we explained at the beginning, is both God and Word, mingled with our human nature, and when He entered our body, He did not devise some other constitution for our nature, but provided for the continuance of His own body by the customary and appropriate means, maintaining its subsistence by food and drink, the food being bread. As, then, in our case, in accordance with what we have already repeatedly said, he who sees bread sees, in a way, the human body, for the former by passing into the latter becomes what it is, so too in His case, the body which was the receptacle of divinity, receiving the nourishment of bread, was, in some sense, identical with it, seeing that the nourishment, as we have said, was changed into the nature of the body. For that which is characteristic of all men was acknowledged in that flesh also, that that body also was maintained by bread, while through the indwelling of God the Word, it was translated to the divine dignity. With good reason, then, do we believe that now also the bread which is sanctified by the word of God is changed into the body of God the Word.

For that body, too, was potentially bread, and it was sanctified by the indwelling of the Word who dwelt in the flesh (*cf* Jn 1.14). The manner, then, whereby the bread which was changed in that body was changed to divine power is the same which now brings about the like result. For in that case the grace of the Word sanctified the body which derived its subsistence from bread and, in a sense, was itself bread; whereas in this case, likewise, the bread, as the Apostle says, is sanctified by the word of God and prayer (1 Tm 4.5). Not by the process of being eaten does it go on to become the body of the Word, but it is changed immediately into the body through the word, even as the Word has said: "This is my body."

But all flesh is nourished also by moisture, for without being combined with this the earthly part of us cannot continue in life. As we maintain the solid part of the body by solid and firm food, in a similar way we make an addition to the moist element from the nature which is akin to it. And this, on entering our bodies, is changed into blood by the faculty of assimilation, especially if through wine it receives the power of being changed into heat. Since, then, that flesh which was the receptacle of divinity received this element also in order to maintain itself, and the God who manifested Himself mingled Himself with our perishable nature in order that by communion with his divinity humanity might at the same time be divinized, for this reason He plants Himself, by the economy of His grace, in all believers by means of the flesh which derives its subsistence from both wine and bread, mingling Himself with the bodies of believers, in order that, by union with that which is immortal, man also might partake of incorruption. And this He bestows by power of the eucharistic prayer [*eulogia*], transforming the nature of the visible elements into that immortal thing.

IIA3 Cyril of Jerusalem (*c* 313-387), *Mystagogical Catecheses* 4-5.

ed SC 126.134-174; *tr* FC 64. 181-186, 191-203, revised; *lit* ARI 65-67; E. Yarnold, "The Authorship of the Mystagogical Catecheses Attributed to Cyril of Jerusalem," *Heythrop Journal* 19 (1978) 143-161; *Clavis Patrum Graecorum*, ed. M. Geerard, 2.297.

The fourth-century church of Jerusalem has left us a remarkable set of catecheses. This set includes: an introductory *Procatechesis*; a series of eigthteen Lenten catecheses; and a set of five paschal catecheses for the newly baptized. The *Procatechesis* and the Lenten catecheses are securely ascribed to Cyril of Jerusalem. They are thought to have been delivered *c* 348-349, perhaps while he was still a presbyter. The authorship of the mystagogical catecheses has been disputed. One school of thought urges an attribution to Cyril's successor, John II, the opinion favored in the *Clavis patrum graecorum*. Yarnold, however, in the article cited above, has made a strong case for the possibility of Cyril's authorship, and, in consequence, it seems best to keep to the traditional ascription. The disputed authorship in no way diminishes the importance of these sermons. They would have been delivered in Jerusalem, to the newly baptized, during Bright Week, in the Church of the Anastasis.

Mystagogical Catecheses 1 and 2 deal with baptism; the third deals with chrismation; and 4 and 5 with the eucharist. No. 4 provides doctrinal exposition of the sacrament, theological and typological. No. 5 expounds the eucharistic liturgy; it contains precious information about the liturgy, and—most interesting and touching—precise directions about how to receive communion (para 20-22).

MYSTAGOGICAL CATECHESIS 4

And the reading is from the Letter to the Corinthians: "For I

received from the Lord what I also passed on to you..."
and the rest (1 Co 11.23 *ff*).

This teaching of the blessed Paul is itself enough to give
you full assurance about the divine mysteries by admission
to which you have become one body and blood with Christ.
For Paul just now proclaimed "that on the night on which
He was betrayed, Our Lord Jesus Christ took bread and,
after giving thanks, broke it and gave it to His disciples
saying: 'Take, eat; this is my body.' And taking the cup, He
gave thanks and said; 'Take, drink; this is my blood'" (1 Co
11.23-25+Mt 26.26). When the Master Himself has declared
and said of the bread, "This is my body," who will still dare
to doubt? When He is Himself our warranty, saying, "This is
my blood," who will ever waver and say it is not His blood?
2. Once at Cana of Galilee He changed water into wine by
His own sovereign will. Is it not worthy of belief, then, that
He changed wine into blood? If as a guest at a physical
marriage He performed this amazing miracle, shall He not
far more readily be confessed to have bestowed on "the
friends of the Bridegroom" (Mt 9.15) the benefit of His own
body and blood?
3. With perfect confidence, then, let us partake as of the
body and blood of Christ. For in the type of bread His body
is given to you, and in the type of wine His blood, that by
partaking of the body and blood of Christ you may become
one body and one blood with Him. Thus, when His body
and blood are imparted to our bodies, we become Christ-
bearers, thus, as the blessed Peter said, "partakers of the
divine nature" (2 P 1.4).
4. Once, speaking to the Jews, Christ said, "Unless you eat
my flesh, and drink my blood, you do not have life in you
(Jn 6.53')." Not understanding His words spiritually, they
were scandalized and drew back, thinking that He was
proposing the eating of human flesh (Jn 6.61,67).
5. The Old Covenant also had the loaves of proposition (Lv
24.5-9), but they, as belonging to the Old Covenant, have
come to an end. The New Covenant has its heavenly bread
(Ps 77.24) and cup of salvation (Ps 115.4), which sanctify

soul and body. For as bread corresponds to the body, so also the word is fitting for the soul.

6. Do not then think of the elements as mere bread and wine. They are, according to the Lord's declaration, body and blood. Though the perception suggests the contrary, let faith be your stay. Instead of judging the matter by taste, let faith give you an unwavering confidence that you have been privileged to receive the body and blood of Christ.

7. The blessed David suggests to you their power when he says: "You have prepared a table before me, against those who oppress me" (Ps 22.5). What he means is this: Before your coming, the devils prepared a table for mankind, a table defiled and polluted [*sc* pagan altars], filled with diabolic power; but after your coming, Lord, you have prepared a table before me. When man says to God, "You have prepared a table before me," what else does he mean but the mystical and spiritual table which God has prepared for us against, that is, opposite to and opposed to the demons? And very aptly, for that table gave communion with demons, but this gives communion with God.

"You have anointed my head with oil." He has anointed your head with oil upon your forehead, through the seal of God which you have, that you may be made "the impression of the seal: the Sanctification of God" (Ex 28.36).

"Your cup, also, which inebriates me, how excellent it is!" You see mentioned here the cup which Jesus took in His hands and of which, after giving thanks, He said: "This is my blood, shed for many for the forgiveness of sins" (Mt 26.28).

8. For this reason, in Ecclesiastes (9.7-8), Solomon also alluding to this grace in a riddle, says: "Come hither, eat your bread with joy," that is, the spiritual bread. "Come hither," he calls, a saving, beatific summons, "and drink your wine with a merry heart," that is, the spiritual wine. "And let oil be poured out upon your head," you see how he hints also at the mystical chrism. And "at all times let your garments be white, because the Lord approves of your deeds." For before you came to the grace, your deeds were "vanity of vanities" (Qo 1.2).

Now that you have put off your old garments and have

put on those which are spiritually white, you must go clad in white always. I do not, of course, mean literally that your clothes must always be white, but that you must be clad in those truly white and shining spiritual garments, so that you may say with the blessed Isaiah: "Let my soul rejoice in the Lord, for He has dressed me in the garment of salvation, and with the robe of gladness has He clothed me" (Is 61.10).

9. You have learned and become quite convinced that the perceptible bread is not bread, though it is bread to the taste, but the body of Christ, and that the perceptible wine is not wine, though taste will have it so, but the blood of Christ; and that it was of this that David sang of old: "Bread strengthens the heart of man, to make his face shine with oil" (Ps 103.15). Strengthen your heart, partaking of this bread as spiritual, and make cheerful the face of you soul. God grant that, your soul's face unveiled, with a clear conscience you may, "reflecting as in a mirror the glory of the Lord," go "from glory to glory" (2 Co 3.18) in Christ Jesus our Lord, whose is the glory unto the ages of ages. Amen.

MYSTAGOGICAL CATECHESIS 5

And the reading is from the Catholic Epistle of Peter: "Laying aside, then, all malice, deceit, and slander..." and the rest (1 P 2.1 *ff*).

1. By the kindness of God you have, in our former meetings, received sufficient instruction about baptism, chrismation, and the partaking of the body and blood of Christ. We must now pass on to the rest, intending today to crown the work of your spiritual edification.

2. You saw, then, the deacon who offers the water for the washing of hands to the celebrant and to the presbyters who encircle the altar of God. Not that he offered this water on account of any bodily uncleanness, of course not, for we did not enter the church unwashed; rather, the ablution is a symbol of our obligation to be clean from all sins and transgressions. The hands symbolize action. So by washing

them we signify plainly the purity and blamelessness of our conduct. Did you not hear the blessed David explaining the mystery of this ceremony when he says: "I will wash my hands among the innocent, and will circle your altar, O Lord" (Ps 25.6)? The hand-washing, then, signifies freedom from the liability of sin.

3. Next the deacon cries: "Welcome one another," and "Let us kiss one another." You must not suppose that this kiss is the kiss ordinarily exchanged in the streets by ordinary friends. This kiss is different, for it effects a commingling of souls, and pledges complete forgiveness. The kiss, then, is a sign of a true union of hearts, and of the banishing of any grudge. On account of this Christ said: "If, when you are offering your gift upon the altar, and there you remember that your brother has anything against you, leave your gift on the altar. Go first to be reconciled with your brother, and then come back and offer your gift" (Mt 5.23-24). The kiss, then, is a reconciliation and is, therefore, holy, as the blessed Paul declared somewhere, saying "Greet one another with a holy kiss" (Rm 16.16; 1 Co 16.20), and Peter "Greet one another with a kiss of charity" (1 P 5.14).

4. Then the priest cries: "Lift up your hearts!" For truly is it necessary at that most awesome hour to have one's heart on high towards God, and not below, occupied with earth and the things of earth. In effect, then, the priest commands everyone at that very hour to banish worldly thoughts and workaday cares, and to have their hearts in heaven towards the God who loves mankind.

Then, assenting to this by your confession, you answer: "We have lifted them up to the Lord." Let no one present be so disposed that while his lips say "We have lifted them up to the Lord," in his mind his attention is engaged with worldly thoughts. At all times we should be mindful of God, but at least, if this is not possible due to human frailty, we must strive for it at that hour.

5. Then the priest says: "Let us give thanks to the Lord." Indeed, we ought to give thanks to the Lord for calling us, when we were unworthy, to so great a grace, for reconciling

us when we were enemies (Rm 5.10-11), and for granting us the spirit of adoption (Rm 8.15).

Then you say: "It is fitting and right." In giving thanks we do, indeed, a fitting and right act; but He did, not a right act, but one which went beyond justice, by His kindness counting us worthy of such marvelous blessings.

6. After that we call to mind the heavens, the earth and the sea, the sun and moon, the stars, the whole rational and irrational creation, both visible and invisible, Angels and Archangels, Virtues, Dominions, Principalities, Powers, Thrones, and the many-faced Cherubim, saying, in effect, the Davidic text, "O magnify the Lord with me" (Ps 33.4). We call to mind also the Seraphim whom Isaiah, in the Holy Spirit, saw encircling the throne of God, "with two wings veiling their faces, and with two their feet, while flying with two, and saying: 'Holy, Holy, Holy, Lord of Hosts'" (Is 6.2-3). We recite this doxology which comes to us from the Seraphim that we may be sharers of the hymnody of the heavenly hosts.

7. Next, after sanctifying ourselves by these spiritual songs, we implore the merciful God to send forth His Holy Spirit upon the offerings, that He may make the bread the body of Christ, and the wine the blood of Christ. For whatever the Holy Spirit has touched is hallowed and changed.

8. Next, when the spiritual sacrifice, the bloodless worship has been completed, over this sacrifice of propitiation we beseech God for the common peace of the churches, for the good estate of the world, for the emperors, for the army and the allies, for those in sickness, for the distressed; for all, in a word, who need help, we all pray and offer this sacrifice.

9. Next we call to mind also those who have fallen asleep: first of all, patriarchs, prophets, apostles, and martyrs, that God, through their intercessory prayers, may accept our supplication. Next we pray also for the holy fathers and bishops who have fallen asleep, and generally for all who have fallen asleep before us, believing that this will be of the greatest benefit to the souls of those on whose behalf our supplication is offered in the presence of the holy, most dread sacrifice.

10. And I wish to convince you by an illustration. For I know that many say: "What does it avail a soul departed this world, whether with or without sins, to be remembered at the oblation?" Well, suppose a king banished persons who had offended him, and then their relatives wove a garland and presented it to him on behalf of those undergoing punishment, would he not mitigate their punishment? In the same way, when we offer our supplications to Him for those who have fallen asleep, even though they are sinners, we do not weave a garland, but offer Christ slain for our sins, propitiating the merciful God both on their and our own behalf.

11. Next, after this, you say that prayer which the Saviour gave to His own disciples, with a clear conscience designating God as our Father and saying: "Our Father who art in heaven." Oh, the greatness of God's love for men! To those who had revolted from Him and had been reduced to the most dire straits He has granted so great a pardon and sharing in grace that they may even call Him "Father, Our Father who art in heaven." They also are a "heaven" who "bear the likeness of the heavenly One" (1 Co 15.49), since God is "dwelling in them and abiding in them" (2 Co 6.16).

12. "Hallowed be thy name." God's name is by nature holy, whether we call it so or not. But because it is sometimes profaned among sinners according to the words "Through you my name is continually blasphemed among the gentiles" (Is 52.5), we pray that the name of God may be hallowed in us; not that from not being holy it becomes holy, but because it becomes holy in us when we are made holy and our actions are worthy of our sanctification.

13. "Thy kingdom come." It is the mark of a pure soul to say with confidence "Thy kingdom come," for it is the man who has listened to Paul saying "Therefore do not let sin reign in your mortal body" (Rm 6.12), and has purified himself in action, thought, and word, who will say to God "Thy kingdom come."

14. "Thy will be done on earth as it is in heaven." God's heavenly, blessed angels do the will of God, as David said in the Psalm: "Bless the Lord, all you His angels, mighty in strength, who do His word" (Ps 102.20). In effect, then, this

is what you mean by this petition: As among the angels your will is done, so on earth let it be done by me, O Master.

15. "Give us this day our superessential bread." Ordinary bread is not superessential, but this holy bread is superessential in the sense of its being ordained for the essence of the soul. This bread does not pass into the stomach and so is discharged into the privy (Mt 15.17). Rather, it is absorbed into your whole system to the benefit of both soul and body. "This day" means "daily," as in Paul's "while yet it is called today" (Heb 3.13).

16. "And forgive us our trespasses, as we forgive those who trespass against us." Our sins are many, for we err both in word and in thought, and do many deeds which deserve condemnation. Indeed, "If we say that we have no sin, we lie," as John says (1 Jn 1.8). So we make a bargain with God, begging Him to pardon our sins according as we forgive our neighbors. Bearing in mind, then, how much we receive in return for so little, let us not delay or put off forgiving one another. The offenses committed against us are small, paltry, and easily settled; but the offenses which we have committed against God are great, too great for any mercy save His. Beware, then, lest, on account of slight and trifling transgressions against you, you debar yourself from God's forgiveness of your most grievous sins.

17. "And lead us not into temptation," O Lord. Is it this what the Lord teaches us to pray for, not to be tempted at all? How, then, is it said in another place, "A man untempted is a man unproved" (Si 34.9-10; Rm 5.3-4), and again, "Consider it all joy, my brothers, when you fall into various temptations" (Ja 1.2)? But entering into temptation could mean being overwhelmed by temptation, for temptation is like a raging torrent which is difficult to cross. Some people in time of temptation manage to cross without being overwhelmed by the raging waters, their prowess as swimmers saving them from being swept away by the tide. But if others who are not of the same sort enter, they are engulfed, like Judas, for example, who entered into the temptation of avarice and did not swim across, but was overwhelmed and drowned, physically and spiritually. Peter entered into the temptation of the denial, but, though he entered, he was not

drowned, but swam nobly across and was delivered from the temptation.

Listen, again, in another passage, to a company of triumphant saints giving thanks for their deliverance from temptation: "For you, O God, have proved us; you have tried us by fire, as silver is tried. You have brought us into a net, you have laid afflictions on our back, you let men ride over our heads. We have passed through fire and water, and you led us out into respite" (Ps 65.10-12). You see them speaking boldly because they passed through and were not trapped. And "you brought us out," it says, "into respite." Their being brought into respite refers to their rescue from temptation.

18. "But deliver us from the Evil One." If "lead us not into temptation" referred to not being tempted at all, He would not have said: "But deliver us from the Evil One." The Evil One from whom we pray to be rescued is our adversary, the Devil.

Then, after completing the prayer, you say "Amen," which means "So be it," thus setting a seal upon the petitions of the prayer taught by God.

19. Next the priest says: "Holy things for the Holy." Holy are the offerings after they have received the visitation of the Holy Spirit, and you are holy after you have been privileged to receive the Holy Spirit. So holy things and holy persons correspond. Next you say: "One is holy, one is Lord, Jesus Christ." For truly One is holy—holy by nature; we also are holy, not, indeed, by nature, but by participation, ascesis, and prayer.

20. After this you hear the chanter inviting you with a divine melody to the partaking of the holy mysteries, in the words "Taste and see that the Lord is good" (Ps 33.9). Entrust not the judgement to your bodily palate, but to unwavering faith. For in tasting we are bidden to taste not bread and wine, but the antitype of the body and blood of Christ.

21. Coming up to receive, then, do not have your wrists extended or your fingers spread, but making your left hand a throne for the right, for it is about to receive a King, and cupping your palm, receive the body of Christ, and answer

"Amen." Carefully hallow your eyes by the touch of the sacred body, and then partake, taking care to lose no part of it. Tell me, if someone gave you gold-dust, would you not take the greatest care to hold it fast, so as not to lose any of it and endure its loss? How much more carefully, then, will you guard against losing so much as a crumb of that which is more precious than gold or precious stones?

22. After partaking of the body of Christ, approach also the cup of His blood. Do not stretch out your hands, but, bowing low in a posture of worship and reverence as you say "Amen," sanctify yourself by partaking of the blood of Christ. While it is still moist upon your lips, touch it with your fingers, and so sanctify your eyes, your forehead, and other senses. Then wait for the prayer, and give thanks to God who has counted you worthy of such high mysteries.

23. Preserve these traditions unstained, keep yourselves free from sin. Never cut yourselves off from communion, never through the pollution of sin deprive yourselves of these sacred, spiritual mysteries. "And may the God of peace sanctify you completely, and may your whole spirit, soul, and body be preserved for the coming of our Lord Jesus Christ" (1 Th 5.23), to whom be glory unto the ages of ages. Amen.

IIA4 Ambrose of Milan (*c* 339-397), *On the Sacraments* Book IV. 1-29, Book V. 1-17.

ed CSEL 73.46-65; *tr* FC 44. 297-314, revised.

> Ambrose was born of an aristocratic Christian family. He was trained in rhetoric, and pursued a career in law and in the civil service. In his office as governor of the region around Milan he intervened to maintain order in the catholic-arian tension which followed the death of Auxentius, the arian bishop of Milan. Ambrose, though still a catechumen, was chosen bishop by acclamation; after receiving the sacraments of Christian initiation, he was consecrated bishop of Milan on 7 December 374 (or 1 December 373, opinion varies).

The mystagogical catechesis of Ambrose comes to us in two forms. One is the treatise *De mysteriis* (*On the Mysteries*), written *c* 390. It is a polished treatise in the form of an oration—perhaps composed in that form, perhaps a reworking of earlier catechetical sermons. The second is the *De sacramentis* (*On the Sacraments*), a collection of mystagogical sermons, now arranged in six books: 1-3 on baptism and chrismation; 4-5 on the eucharist (5.18-30 explains the Lord's Prayer). Ambrose's authorship of *On the Sacraments* has been questioned and denied in the past, but it is now solidly established. Less polished, but far more detailed than *On the Mysteries*, the discourses of *On the Sacraments* are thought to be stenographic versions of Ambrose's preaching. The sermons of *On the Sacraments* are dated to the period 380-390, and they, or something like them, would have been heard by a famous neophyte, Augustine, the African rhetorician, after his baptism at Pascha in 387.

On the Sacraments, Book IV

1. In the Old Covenant the priests were accustomed to enter the first tabernacle frequently; the highpriest entered the second tabernacle once a year. Recalling this plainly to the Hebrews, the Apostle Paul explains the order of the Old Covenant (Heb 9.1-7). For there was the manna in the second tabernacle; there was also the rod of Aaron, that had withered, and later blossomed again, and the altar of incense. 2. To what does this point? That you may understand what the second tabernacle is, the one into which the priest brought you, the one into which the highpriest was accustomed to enter once a year, that is, the baptistry, where the rod of Aaron blossomed. It was dry before, but afterwards it blossomed. You too were dry, and you began to flower by the watering of the font. You had become dry by sins, you had become dry by errors and transgressions, but now you have begun to bear fruit, "planted by the courses of

water" (Ps 1.3). 3. But perhaps you may say: "What had this to do with the people, if the rod of the priest became dry and blossomed again?" What is the people itself if not priestly? To them was said "But you are a chosen race, a royal priesthood, a holy nation," as the Apostle Peter says (1 P 2.9). Each one is anointed into priesthood, each is anointed into the Kingdom, but it is a spiritual kingdom and a spiritual priesthood. 4. In the second tabernacle there is also the altar of incense. It is the altar of incense because it emits a good odor. Thus, you also now are the good odor of Christ (2 Co 2.15), now there is no stain of transgression in you, nor odor of grave error.

5. Next is your coming to the altar. You began to approach, the angels watched. They saw you approaching, and they perceived the human condition which before was foul with the dark squalor of sins all of a sudden gleaming brightly, and so they said "Who is this that comes up from the desert whitened" (Sg 8.5)? So even the angels are amazed. Do you want to know how they marvel? Hear the Apostle Peter saying that those things have been conferred on us which even the angels long to see (1 P 1.12). Listen again; "Eye has not seen," it says, "nor ear heard what God has prepared for those who love Him" (1 Co 2.9). 6. Next consider what you have received. The holy Prophet David saw this grace in a figure and longed for it. Do you want to now how he longed for it? Listen, again, as he says "You will sprinkle me with hyssop, and I shall be cleansed. You will wash me, and I shall become whiter than snow" (Ps 50.9). Why? Because snow, although it is white, quickly becomes darkened from some dirt, and is ruined. That grace which you have received, if you keep what you have received, will be everlasting and constant.

7. You came, then, with longing. Inasmuch as you had seen so vast a grace, you came to the altar longing to receive the sacrament. Your soul says "And I will go unto the altar of God, to God who gives joy to my youth" (Ps 42.4). You put off the old age of sins, you took up the youth of grace. The heavenly sacraments have bestowed this on you. Again,

then, hear David as he says "Your youth will be renewed like
the eagle's" (Ps 102.5). You have begun to be a good eagle,
you seek heaven, you disdain earthly things. Good eagles
are about the altar, for "Where the body is, there too the
eagles" (Mt 24.28). The altar is in the form of the body, and
the body of Christ is on the altar. You are eagles, renewed by
the washing away of transgression.

8. You came to the altar, you observed the sacraments
placed upon the altar. And, to be sure, you marveled at the
object itself, but the object is common and familiar. 9.
Perhaps someone may say: "God bestowed on the Jews such
a great favor, He rained manna upon them from heaven.
What more has He given to His faithful, what more has he
granted to those whom He has promised more?"

10. Hear what I say: the mysteries of the Christians are
earlier than those of the Jews, and the sacraments of the
Christians are more godly than those of the Jews. How?
Listen. When did the Jews [*Judaei*] come into existence?
From Juda, of course, the great-grandson of Abraham, or,
if you wish to understand it so, from the Law, that is, when
they received the Law of God [*jus dei*]. Therefore, from the
great-grandson of Abraham they were called Jews in the
time of the holy Moses. At that time God rained manna
from heaven on the Jews as they murmured. But for you a
figure of these sacraments went before, when Abraham was
alive, when he gathered 318 servants born i⁻ his house, and
went forth, and pursued his enemies, and delivered his
nephew from captivity. Then he came as a victor. Melchisedech the priest went to meet him, and offered bread and
wine (Gn 14.14-18). Who had the bread and wine? Abraham
did not have it. But who did have it? Melchisedech. He,
then, is the author of the sacraments. Who is Melchisedech?
Who is described as "the king of righteousness, the king of
peace (Heb 7.2)?" Who, then, is the king of righteousness
other than the Righteousness of God? Who is the peace of
God, the wisdom of God (1 Co 1.30)? He who was able to
say "My peace I give to you, my peace I leave to you" (Jn
14.27). 11. So first understand that these sacraments which

you receive are earlier than whatever sacraments the Jews say they have, and that the Christian people began before the people of the Jews began, but we in predestination, they in name.

12. Melchisedech, then, offered bread and wine. Who is Melchisedech? "Without father," it says, and "without mother, without genealogy, having neither beginning of days, nor end of life" (Heb 7.3). This is what the Epistle to the Hebrews has, "without father," it says, and "without mother." There you have one "likened to the Son of God" (Heb 7.3). The Son of God was born by heavenly generation "without mother," because He was born of God the Father alone. And, again, He was born "without Father," when He was born of the Virgin. For He was not begotten of the seed of man, but was born of the Holy Spirit and the Virgin Mary, brought forth from a virginal womb. Melchisedech was also a priest, in all respects "likened to the Son of God," for Christ too is a priest to whom is said "you are a priest forever according to the order of Melchisedech" (Ps 109.4 + Heb 7.17). 13. Therefore, who is the author of the sacraments but the Lord Jesus? These sacraments came down from heaven, for all counsel is from heaven.

But it was a truly great and divine miracle, that from heaven God rained manna upon the people, and the people did not labor and did eat (Ws 16.20). 14. You are perhaps saying "My bread is the ordinary kind." But that bread is bread before the words of the sacraments. When consecration has been added, from being bread it becomes the flesh of Christ. So let us argue how it is possible that what is bread is the body of Christ.

The consecration, then, in whose words is it, in whose speech? The Lord Jesus'. For all the rest that are said earlier are said by the priest: praise is given, and prayer is offered to God, supplication is made for the people, for rulers, and the rest. When it comes to confecting the venerable sacrament, then the priest uses not his own words, but he uses the words of Christ. Thus, the word of Christ confects this sacrament. 15. What is the word of Christ? Surely that by which all things were made. The Lord commanded, the heaven was made. The Lord commanded, the earth was made. The Lord commanded, the seas were made. The Lord commanded, every creature came to be. You see then how effective is the word of Christ. If, then, there is so great a power in the word of the Lord Jesus that things which were not began to exist, then how much more effective, that those things which were exist, and are changed into something else! The heaven was not, the sea was not, the earth was not, but hear David as he says "He spoke and they were made, He commanded and they were created" (Ps 148.5). 16. Therefore, to answer you, it was not the body of Christ before the consecration; but after the consecration, I tell you, it is then the body of Christ. He spoke and it was made, He commanded and it was created. You existed, but you were an old creation. After you were consecrated, you began to be a new creation. Each, he says, "is a new creation in Christ" (2 Co 5.17).

17. Hear, then, how Christ's word has regularly changed every creature, and changes, when He pleases, the laws of nature. You ask how? Listen. And, first of all, let us take an example from His begetting. It is usual that a human being is not begotten except of man and woman, and by conjugal association. But because the Lord pleased, because He chose this sacrament, it was of the Holy Spirit and the Virgin that Christ was born, that is, the "Mediator of God and men, the man Jesus Christ" (1 Tm 2.5). You see, then, that a man was born, born of a virgin, contrary to the laws and pattern of nature.

18. Take another example. The people of the Jews were hard pressed by the Egyptians, they were shut off by the sea. By divine command Moses touched the water with a rod and the water parted, not, of course, according to the custom of its nature, but according to the grace of heavenly command (Ex 14. 21-22). Take another example. The people were thirsty, they came to a spring, the spring was bitter. Moses cast wood into the spring, and the spring, which was bitter, was made sweet, that is, it changed the usual disposition of its nature, it received the sweetness of grace (Ex

15.23-25). Take also a fourth example. The iron head of an axe fell into the water. As iron, according to its nature, it sank. Eliseus threw in the wood. Immediately the iron head was raised and floated on the water, quite contrary to the behavior of iron, for it is heavier material than the element of water (2 S 6.5-7).

19. From all this, then, do you understand how great is the efficacy of heavenly utterance? If heavenly utterance operated in an earthly spring, if it operated in other things, does it not operate in the heavenly sacraments? Therefore you have learned that from bread the body of Christ is made. And what of the wine and water? It is put into the cup, but becomes blood by heavenly consecration.

20. But perhaps you say "I do not see the appearance of blood." But, it has the likeness. For just as you took on the likeness of death (Rm 6.4), so too, you drink the likeness of the precious blood, that there may be no horror of blood, and yet the price of redemption may be effective. You have learned, then, that what you receive is the body of Christ.

21. Do you wish to know how it is consecrated with heavenly words? Hear what the words are. The priest says: "Bring it about for us that this offering may be approved, spiritual, acceptable, which is the figure of the body and blood of Our Lord Jesus Christ. On the day before He suffered, He took bread in His holy hands, looked up to heaven, to you, holy Father, almighty, eternal God; He gave thanks, blessed, broke it, and gave it to His apostles and disciples, saying: 'Take and eat of this, all of you, for this is my body which will be broken for many.'" Pay attention! 22. "Likewise, after they had eaten, on the day before He suffered, He also took the cup, looked up to heaven, to you, holy Father, almighty, eternal God; He gave thanks, blessed, and gave it to His apostles and disciples, saying: 'Take and drink of this, all of you, for this is my blood.'" Notice, all these words up to "Take" are the Evangelist's, whether in the case of the body or the blood. From then on the words are Christ's, "Take and drink of this, all of you, for this is my blood." Observe these features one by one.

"On the day before He suffered, He took bread in His holy hands." Before it is consecrated, it is bread; but when Christ's words have been added, it is the body of Christ. Then hear Him as He says: "Take and eat of this, all of you, for this is my body." And before the words of Christ, the cup is full of wine and water; when the words of Christ have been added, then is made the blood which redeems the people. So behold in how many ways the word of Christ is able to change all things. Moreover, the Lord Jesus Himself has borne witness for us, that we receive His body and blood. Should we doubt at all about His trustworthiness and testimony?

24. Now return with me to my point. It is a great matter, and one worthy of reverence, that manna rained upon the Jews from heaven. But understand. What is greater, manna from heaven or the body of Christ? The body of Christ, of course, for He is the Creator of heaven. In addition, he who ate the manna died; but he who has eaten this body, it will become for him the forgiveness of sins and he "shall not die forever" (Jn 6.49-50; 11.26). 25. Not idly, then, do you say "Amen," confessing already in spirit that you receive the body of Christ. Therefore, when you approach, the priest says to you "The body of Christ," and you say "Amen," that is, "True." What the tongue confesses let the heart hold fast, with the knowledge, moreover, that this is a sacrament whose figure has gone before.

26. Next, realize how great a sacrament it is. See what He says: "As often as you shall do this, so often will you make a remembrance of me, until I come again." 27. And the priest says: "Therefore, mindful of His most glorious Passion and Resurrection from the dead and Ascension into heaven, we offer to you this immaculate victim, a spiritual victim, an unbloody victim, this holy bread and the chalice of eternal life. And we ask and pray that you receive this offering upon your altar on high through the hands of your angels, just as you deigned to receive the gifts of you servant, Abel the Just, and the sacrifice of our patriarch, Abraham, and what the highpriest Melchisedech offered to you." 28. So, as often as

you receive, what does the Apostle say to you? As often as we receive, we proclaim the death of the Lord (1 Co 11.26). If His death, then we proclaim the forgiveness of sins. If, as often as blood is shed, it is shed for the forgiveness of sins (Heb 9.22), I ought always to receive Him, that He may always forgive my sins. I, who sin always, should have a medicine always.

29. Today, for the time being, we have explained matters as much as we were able. But tomorrow, Saturday, and Sunday we will speak about the order of prayer as best we can. May our Lord God preserve for you the grace which He has given, and may He deign to illumine more fully the eyes which He has opened up for you, through His Onlybegotten Son, our King and Saviour, our Lord God, through whom He and, with whom He has praise, honor, glory, magnificence, power, together with the Holy Spirit, from the ages, and now, and always, and unto all ages of ages. Amen.

On the Sacraments, Book V

1. Yesterday our discourse and exposition was brought up to the sacraments of the holy altar. And we learned that the figure of these sacraments had gone before, in the time of Abraham, when the holy Melchisedech, "having neither beginning of days nor end" (Heb 7.3), offered sacrifice. Hear, O man, what the Apostle Paul says to the Hebrews. Where are they who say that the Son of God is of time? As for Melchisedech, it is said that he has neither beginning of days nor end. If Melchisedech does not have beginning of days, could Christ? The figure is not greater than the truth. You see, then, that He Himself is "the first and the last" (Rv 1.17), first, because He is the Creator of all, last, not because He determines the end, but because He completes all things.

2. We have said, then, that the cup and bread are placed on the altar. What is put into the cup? Wine. And what else? Water. But you say to me: "How is it, then, that Melchisedech offered wine and bread? What does the admixture of water mean?" Hear the explanation. 3. First of all, the figure

which went before in the time of Moses, what does it mean? When the people of the Jews were thirsty and murmured because he could not find water, God ordered Moses to touch the rock with his rod. He touched the rock, and the rock poured out a great amount of water (Ex 17, Nb 20), just as the Apostle says, "And they drank from the rock which followed, and the rock was Christ" (1 Co 10.4). It was not an unmoving rock that followed the people. You too must drink, that Christ may follow you. See the mystery: Moses, that is, the prophet, with his rod, that is, with the word of God. The priest, with the word of God, touches the rock, and water flows, and the people of God drink. Then the priest touches the cup, water abounds in the cup, it leaps unto eternal life (Jn 4.14), and the people of God, who have attained to the grace of God, drink.

4. Have you learned this then? Consider another point. At the time of the Lord's Passion, since the Great Sabbath was at hand, because our Lord Jesus Christ, or, rather, the thieves were still alive, men were sent to strike them. When they arrived, they found our Lord Jesus Christ dead. Then one of the soldiers touched His side with a lance, and from His side there flowed water and blood (Jn 19.31-34). Why water? Why blood? Water to cleanse, blood to redeem. Why from His side? Because from where sin comes, from there also comes grace (Gn 2.21-22); sin through a woman, grace through our Lord Jesus Christ.

5. You have come to the altar. The Lord Jesus calls you —or your soul, or the church—and He says "Let him kiss me with the kiss of his mouth" (Sg 1.1). Do you wish to apply it to Christ? There is nothing more welcome. Do you wish to apply it to your soul? There is nothing more pleasant. 6. "Let him kiss me." He sees that you are clean of every sin, because transgressions have been washed away. On that account He judges you worthy of the heavenly sacraments, and therefore invites you to the heavenly banquet, "Let him kiss me with the kiss of his mouth."

7. Yet on account of what follows, your soul—or the human condition, or the church—sees that it is cleansed of

all sins, that it is worthy to be able to approach the altar of Christ—for what is the altar of Christ but an image of the body of Christ?—it sees the wondrous sacraments, and says "Let Him kiss me with the kiss of His mouth," that is, "Let Christ impress a kiss on me." Why? "For your breasts are better than wine" (Sg 1.1), that is, the experience of you, your sacraments are better than wine, than that wine which, although it has sweetness, has joy, agreeableness, yet has in it worldly joy; but in you is spiritual delight. So, even then, Solomon portrayed the marriage either of Christ and the church, or of the spirit and the flesh, or of the Spirit and the soul. 9. And he added: "Your name is oil poured out. Therefore the maidens have loved you" (Sg 1.2). Who are these maidens, but the souls of individuals who have put aside the old age of the body, renewed through the Holy Spirit? 10. "Draw us, let us run after the fragrance of your ointments" (Sg 1.3). See what he is saying: You cannot follow Christ, unless He Himself draws you. Indeed, that you may realize this, He says: "When I am lifted up, I will draw all things to myself" (Jn 12.32). 11. "The king has brought me into his chamber" (Sg 1.3)—the Greek has "into his storeroom" or "into his pantry"—where there are good liquors, good odors, sweet honey, diverse fruits, various delicacies, so that your meal may be flavored by many delicacies.

12. So you have come to the altar, you have received the body of Christ. Hear again what sacraments you have obtained, hear holy David as he speaks. Indeed, he foresaw these mysteries in spirit, and rejoiced, and said that nothing was lacking to him (Ps 22.1). Why? Because he who shall receive the body of Christ shall never hunger (Jn 6.35). 13. How often have you heard Psalm 22 and have not understood it! See how applicable it is to the heavenly sacraments: "The Lord feeds me, and nothing will be lacking to me. He has set me in a place of pasture. He has brought me upon the water of refreshment. He has converted my soul. He has led me on the paths of righteousness for His name's sake. For though I walk in the midst of the shadow of death, I will fear

no evils, for you are with me. Your rod and you staff, they have comforted me" (Ps 22.1-4). The rod is dominion, the staff suffering, that is, the eternal divinity of Christ, but also His bodily suffering. The former has created, the latter has redeemed. "You have prepared a table before me against those who afflict me. You have anointed my head with oil, and your intoxicating cup, how glorious it is" (Ps 22.5)!

14. And so you have come to the altar, you have received the grace of Christ, you have obtained the heavenly sacraments. The church rejoices in the redemption of many, and is glad with spiritual exultation that a household dressed in white attends her. You have this in the Canticle of Canticles. Rejoicing, she invites Christ, having prepared a banquet which seems worthy of heavenly feasting. And so she says: "Let my brother descend into His garden and take the fruit of His fruitbearing trees" (Sg 4.16). What are these fruit-bearing trees? You were made dry wood in Adam, but now, through the grace of Christ, you sprout as fruitbearing trees.

15. Gladly did the Lord Jesus accept, and with heavenly kindness He replied to His church. He says: "I have come down into my garden, I have gathered the vintage of my myrrh with my perfumes, I have eaten my bread with honey, I have drunk my wine with my milk. Eat," He says, "my brothers, and be intoxicated" (Sg 5.1). 16. "I have gathered the vintage of my myrrh with my perfumes." What is this vintage? Know the vineyard, and you will recognize the vintage. It says: "You have transplanted a vineyard out of Egypt" (Ps 79.9), that is, the people of God. You are the vineyard, you are the vintage. Planted like a vineyard, you have borne fruit as in a vintage. "I have gathered the vintage of myrrh with my perfumes," that is, to make the fragrance which you have received. 17. "I have eaten my bread with my honey." You see that in this bread there is no bitterness, but there is every sweetness. "I have drunk my wine with my milk." You see that the gladness which is not alloyed by the filth of sin is of this sort, as often as you drink, you receive the forgiveness of sins and you are intoxicated in spirit. Therefore, the Apostle says: "Be not drunk with wine, but be filled with the Spirit" (Ep 5.18). For he who is drunk with

wine sways and totters, he who is drunk with the Spirit is rooted in Christ. And so, glorious is the drunkeness which effects sobriety of mind. This is my short and hurried explanation of the sacraments.

IIA5 Gaudentius of Brescia (*fl* 406), *Tractate Two on Exodus.*

ed CSEL 68.24-32; *tr* S.L. Boehrer, *Gaudentius of Brescia, Sermons and Letters* (diss., Washington, D.C., 1965), revised.

Gaudentius became bishop of Brescia sometime between 384 and 397. He was a prominent figure in the Italian episcopate of his time, and took a leading part in the delegation sent by Pope Innocent I in 406 to seek the restoration of John Chrysostom to the see of Constantinople.

The majority of Gaudentius' works survive due to the interest of his townsman Benevolus, sometime *Magister memoriae* to the emperor Valentinian II and a strong anti-arian. Unable to attend the paschal services due to illness, Benevolus, through still a catechumen, had requested that Gaudentius send him copies of his paschal discourses. Gaudentius complied, sending, along with other material, copies of ten sermons which he had delivered in the Pascha-Bright Week period: eight on Exodus, and two on the Marriage Feast at Cana. Of these sermons, *Tractates* 1-4 seem to be mystagogical catecheses. They are, however, strange examples of this type, for they lack any direct reference to the rites of baptism, chrismation, and eucharist; Gaudentius may have removed such references in the process of editing his sermons for the catechumen Benevolus.

Tractate Two, the eucharistic discourse, was given to newly baptized on the Easter Vigil, after they had left the baptistry.

*To the neophytes after they returned from the font,
concerning the explanation of the mysteries, which
is not suitable for the catechumens to hear, though
the same matters, written in the gospels, seem to be
accessible to all.*

Upon the resurrection of Christ from the dead, punishment has been inflicted on the Egyptians through the sacrament of baptism. While hell looked on in alarm, the enemies of God, that is, the adversaries of His people, were destroyed by the return of the Lord for the Resurrection of His own body. For the prophetic Spirit cries out: "Let God arise and His enemies be scattered; may those who hate Him flee from His face; let them vanish as smoke vanishes; as wax melts before fire, so let sinners perish before God; and let the just keep feast" (Ps 67.2-4). Our devoted Father has sent redemption to His people, (Ps 110.9), mindful of His holy covenant which He granted to our fathers, to Abraham and to his seed forever (Lk 1.55). For God, who had the power to do so, has raised up sons for Abraham from these once hard stones (Mt 3.9), the gentiles.

"Now let all those who are redeemed by the Lord, whom He has redeemed from the hand of their enemies, and gathered together from afar, from the rising and the setting of the sun, from the north and from the sea, declare that He is good, that His mercy is forever" (Ps 106.2-3,1). For "in the exodus of" that "Israel from Egypt, the house of Jacob from a foreign people, Judah" alone "was made His sanctuary" (Ps 113.1-2), but now, "Blessed are all who fear the Lord, who walk in His ways (Ps 127.1), Blessed are those whose iniquities are forgiven and whosw sins are covered (Ps 31.1), For there is no distinction of Jew and Greek, for the Lord is the same, generous to all who call upon Him" (Rm 10.12), because, as it is written: "Anyone who will call on the name of the Lord will be saved" (Rm 10.13).

Therefore, let as many of us who, by calling on the Lord, receive salvation upon the destruction of the Egyptians learn to eat the Passover, but not as the foolish Jews who still follow the shadow after the coming of the Truth, killing and eating a lamb in each of their households on the fourteenth day of the first month. From the time when the true Lamb of God came, the Lord Jesus, whose shadow that lamb was, who takes away the sin of the world (Jn 1.29), and said: "Unless you eat my flesh and drink my blood you shall not have life in you" (Jn 6.54), from that time on the Jews in vain practice carnally that which, unless they do it spiritually with us, they are not able to have life in them. "For the law is spiritual" (Rm 7.14), as the Apostle says, and "Christ, our Passover, has been sacrificed" (1 Co 5.7).

It is required that, beginning tomorrow, with God's help, we begin to explain what spiritual forces were prefigured in the very history of the Exodus where the celebration of the Passover is recounted: the meaning of the tenth day, of the fourteenth, the meaning of the sacrifice of an unblemished male lamb of one year at evening time, of the blood to be smeared on the posts, of the gathering of neighbors, of the sandals and the staffs, of the yeast and of the unleavened bread. For today, only those things are to be selected from the reading which cannot be presented when the catechumens are present, but which must be explained to the neophytes.

Not one, but many lambs were killed in the shadow of that passover of the Law. One was killed for each household, because a single lamb could not suffice for everybody, for that was a figure and not the reality of the Lord's Passion. A figure, indeed, is not the truth, but an imitation of the truth. For man also has been made to the image of God, but he is not for that fact God, even though it is in the sense that he is called God's image that he may be termed "god" as well. For by nature there is one God, but by appointment many (Ps 81.6).

Therefore, in this truth wherein we live, One has died for all, and in the mystery of the bread and wine in every church this same One as sacrificed restores, as believed vivifies, and as consecrated sanctifies the consecrators. This is the flesh of the Lamb, this His blood. For the Bread who came down from heaven says: "The bread which I will give you is my flesh for the life of the world"(Jn 6.51-52). Rightly, also, is His blood manifested in the appearance of wine, for when He Himself says in the gospel "I am the true vine"(Jn 15.1), He makes it quite clear that all wine offered in the figure of His Passion is His blood. Thus the most blessed patriarch Jacob had prophesied about Christ, saying: "He will wash His robe in wine, and His garment in the blood of the grape" (Gn 49.11). Indeed, He was to wash the robe of our body, His garment, in His own blood.

Nature's Creator and Lord, then, who produces bread from the earth, because He is able and because He has promised, again makes His own body from the bread. And He who has made wine from water has also made His blood from wine.

We must observe in the same reading how this Lamb ought to be eaten. It says: "You shall not eat anything of it raw, nor boiled in water, but roasted with the feet and the entrails"(Ex 12.9). There are two spiritual meanings in these words, but if you would follow up one, you will know both. Every part of the divine scripture, both of the Old and of the New Testament, contains the Son of God, either promising that He will come into human nature, or declaring that He has already come. So it is that the blessed Philip, himself found by Christ, finds Nathaniel, and says to him: "We have found the one of whom Moses and the prophets have written in the Law, Jesus, the son of Joseph, from Nazareth"(Jn 1.45).

What more are we to say, my dear ones? In Him is contained the entire Law, both old and new, and, one might say, He is the life of the Law. For He spoke through Moses when He says to Him: "I will open your mouth, and I will teach you what you must say" (Ex 4.12). He spoke also through the prophets when He says: "I who spoke" in the prophets, "behold I am here" (Is 52.6). And He spoke also through the apostles, when Paul says: "Do you seek a proof of Christ who speaks in me" (2 Co 13.3)? Therefore, this flesh of the immaculate Lamb, that is, the meat of His doctrine, should not be consumed raw, without interpretation, nor should it be boiled in water, that is be dissolved and cooked down by the discussions of those who flow downwards like water, understanding nothing of what is above. Rather, it says that it is to be "roasted by fire," that is, made firm and seared by the divine Spirit, for fire tends upwards. For this reason the Lord said to the Jews: "You are from below, I am from above" (Jn 8.23).

Since we have said that the members of the Lamb of God are His scriptures, let us, then, see what is the "head, with the feet and entrails." That is, let us see that, according to the testimony of the four evangelists, by the head you understand divinity, that you take the feet for His Incarnation which took place towards the end of the age—for the feet are the extreme parts of the body—, and that in the entrails you observe hidden mysteries.

"And you will not leave," it says, "anything of it in the morning; and you shall not break a bone from it; what is left of it in the morning you shall burn with fire" (Ex 12.10). This means that if any mysteries which we are not unable to comprehend remain to be revealed in the morning of the resurrection to come—for "Now I know in part," says the Apostle, "but then I shall know even as I am known" (1 Co 13.12)—, they are to be burned with fire, that is, given over to the divine Spirit so that those things whose meanings we do not now grasp may be consumed by the spirit of a burning faith.

But as to the saying "You shall not break a bone from it," this commands that everything in the scripture which is very stout and strong should not be broken or smashed, but should remain solid. Those who do not keep this precept deservedly hear "Woe" from Him whose bones they break. "Woe to you," He says, "scribes and pharisees, hypocrites, because you tithe mint and anise and cummin, and have abandoned the weightier matters of the Law, judgement and mercy and faith" (Mt 23.23). These are the bones of the Lamb. In another place He says to them: "You make void the word of God that you might maintain your own traditions" (Mt 15.6).

But in Exodus God adds to the foregoing prescriptions

the following: "And in this manner shall you eat it," that is, the lamb, "your loins shall be girt, and you shall have shoes on your feet, and staffs in your hands, and you shall eat in haste. For it is the Passover of the Lord" (Ex 12.11).

The explanation of the shoes and staffs is lengthy and will be presented at another time. I have frequently spoken to you in detail about the girding of the loins, so I will only touch briefly on it now. It is written in Jeremiah: "And gird your lions, and you will say to the people," and the rest (Jr 1.17). It is said to the holy Job: "Gird up your lions like a man. I will question you, and you answer me. Where were you when I laid the foundations of the earth," and the rest (Jb 38.3-4). The apostles also hear: "Let your loins be girt" (Lk 12.35). Just why this was commanded so earnestly is understood in the case of John the Baptist, who was girded with animal skin around his loins. The meaning of the loins is shown by the Apostle in the Epistle to the Hebrews. He tells us: "Levi," that is, the priestly tribe, "was still in the loins of his father when Melchisedech came to him" (Heb 7.10). Came to whom? Of course, he came to the holy Abraham! Therefore, the girdle of animal skin around the loins signifies the mortification of vices, for animal skin is capable of use only if the animal is dead. It is, thus, necessary for us, according to the precept of God, first to mortify the concupiscence of the flesh, and so receive the body of Christ who was sacrificed for us in the Egypt of the world. "Therefore, let a man prove himself," as the Apostle says, "and so let him eat of that bread and drink of the cup" (1 Co 11.28).

When He says that it is to be eaten in haste, He commands that we consume the sacrament of the Lord's body and blood not with a sluggish heart and torpid mouth, but with all eagerness of spirit, as men truly hungering and thirsting for righteousness. For the Lord Jesus says: "Blessed are those who hunger and thirst for righteousness, for they shall be filled" (Mt 5.6).

Now this celebrated reading concludes its words most fittingly with: "For it is the Passover of the Lord." "O the depth of the riches of the wisdom and of the knowledge of God" (Rm 11.33)! "It is the Passover of the Lord," it says, that is, the passage of the Lord, so that you will not consider earthly what has been made heavenly by Him who has passed into it, and has made it His body and blood. For what we explained earlier in a general way about the eating of the flesh of the lamb is specifically to be observed in tasting these same mysteries of the Lord's Passion, lest you think, as did the Jew, that this is raw flesh, and raw blood and reject it saying: "How is this man able to give us his flesh to eat" (Jn 6.53)? Nor should you, thinking it common and earthly, cook this sacrament in the pot of a carnal heart which is by nature subject to the humors of the body. Rather, you must believe that what has been declared to you has been accomplished through the fire of the divine Spirit, that what you receive is the body of that heavenly Bread and the blood of that sacred Vine. For when He gave the consecrated bread and wine to His disciples, He said: "This is my body, this is my blood" (Mt 26.26,28). Let us believe, I pray you, the One whom we have believed. Truth does not know deceit. Therefore, when He was speaking about the eating of His body and the drinking of His blood to the crowds who wondered and murmured "This is a hard saying, who can hear it?" (Jn 6.61), He added, in order that through heavenly fire He might wipe away those thoughts which I have said should be avoided: "It is the Spirit which gives life; the flesh is of no benefit. The words which I have spoken to you are spirit and life" (Jn 6.64).

And for that reason we are commanded to eat the head of His divinity with the feet of His Incarnation, together with the inner mysteries, so that we may believe alike all things just as they have been handed down, not breaking that strongest bone of all, "This is my body, this is my blood."

If there is yet remaining in anyone's understanding something he has not grasped from this exposition, let it be burnt up in the ardor of faith, for "Our God is a consuming fire" (Heb 12.29), cleansing, teaching, and illuminating our hearts unto the understanding of things divine, that we may learn the cause and the meaning of the heavenly sacrifice instituted by Christ, as we give thanks unceasingly for His indescribable gift.

For this, indeed, is the legacy of His New Covenant, which He left to us as a pledge of His presence on the night on which He was handed over to be crucified. This is that provision for our journey by which we are fed and nourished on the road of this life until, on leaving this world, we come to Him. Wherefore the same Lord did say: "Unless you eat my flesh and drink my blood you will not have life in you" (Jn 6.54).

He has willed that His gifts remain with us. He has willed that souls redeemed by His precious blood be ever sanctified through the image of His Passion. For that reason He charges His faithful disciples whom He established as the first priests of His church that they perform unceasingly these mysteries of eternal life. It is necessary that they be celebrated by every priest in every single church in the entire world until Christ comes again from heaven, that the priests themselves, and all the faithful people as well, having daily before their eyes and bearing in their hands the model of the Passion of Christ, receiving it also by mouth and in heart, may possess an indelible remembrance of our redemption, and acquire a sweet medicine of everlasting protection against the poisons of the devil. Thus does the Holy Spirit urge us: "Taste and see that the Lord is sweet" (Ps 33.9).

There is a twofold reason why He has established that this sacrament of His body and blood be offered in the appearance of bread and wine. First, that the immaculate Lamb of God might give to a cleansed people a clean offering to be celebrated without burning, without blood, without stench, and one that would be easily and readily available for offering to all. Secondly, because it is necessary that bread be made from many grains of wheat reduced to flour, and that it be compounded with water and completed by means of fire, it is reasonable that the figure of the body of Christ be accepted in it. We know that He has been made one body from the multitude of the entire human race, completed through the fire of the Holy Spirit. For He was born of the

Holy Spirit, and because it thus suited Him to fulfill all justice (Mt 3.15), He enters the waters of baptism so that He might consecrate them. Then filled by the Holy Spirit who had descended on Him in the form of a dove, He returns from the Jordan, as the evangelist bears witness: "Now Jesus, full of the Holy Spirit, returned from the Jordan"(Lk 4.1). Similarly also, the wine of His blood, gathered from the many grapes of the vine planted by Him, is pressed out in the winepress of the Cross, and of its own power it begins to ferment in the capacious vessels of those who receive it with faithful heart.

You who go forth from the power of Egypt and Pharaoh, the Devil, receive with us this sacrifice of the saving Passover with all the longing of a devout heart, that our innermost parts may be sanctified by our Lord Jesus Christ, whom we believe to be present in His sacraments. His inestimable power endures forever.

IIA6 Augustine of Hippo (354-430), *Three Eucharistic Catecheses* (*Sermons* 272, 227, Wolfenbüttel 7).

lit See SC 116.352-365 for a schematic summary of Augustine's paschal preaching, and F. van der Meer, *Augustine the Bishop*, 353-382, for a detailed account of Christian initiation during Augustine's episcopacy in Hippo.

In these selections we encounter Augustine as pastor, explaining the eucharist to his *infantes*, the newly baptized of his flock. The three sermons are, to a degree, repetitive, but that should not dissuade us from including all three. For we see in them community of theme (exegesis of 1 Co 10.17, homely analogies to the production of bread and wine, explanation of parts of the eucharistic liturgy) and variety as well. Each discourse was addressed to a different group of *infantes* over the period 405X410-

413X417. The sermons call to mind the words of Augustine's friend and biographer, Possidius, that "those received the greater benefit from him [Augustine], who were able to see and hear him in person, speaking in the church." The jingling exclamation in Sermon 272, "Unity! Verity! Piety! Charity!," is as good a summary as any of Augustine's eucharistic preaching.

IIA6.1 *Sermon* 272 (dated 405-411).
ed PL 38.1246-1248.

What you behold now on the altar of God you saw there last night as well. But you have not yet heard what it is, what is means, and of how great a reality it is the sacrament. What you see, then, is bread and a cup. This is what your eyes report to you. But your faith has need to be taught that the bread is the body of Christ, the cup the blood of Christ. Perhaps this rather brief statement might be sufficient for belief, but belief requires instruction, for the Prophet says: "Unless you believe, you will not understand" (Is 7.9). So now you can say to me: "You have taught us to believe. Explain, so we may understand."

For the following thought may arise in anyone's mind. "We know whence our Lord Jesus Christ took flesh, from the Virgin Mary. As an infant He was nursed. He was brought up. He grew. He attained manhood. He suffered persecution from the Jews. He was hanged on the wood, He was killed on the wood, He was taken down from the wood. He was buried. He rose on the third day. When He willed, He ascended into heaven; to there He lifted up His body. Thence will he come to judge the living and dead. Now He is there, enthroned at the right hand of the Father. How is the bread His body? And the cup, or what is in the cup, how is that His blood?"

These things, my brothers, are called sacraments for the reason that in them one thing is seen, but another is understood. That which is seen has physical appearance, that which is understood has spiritual fruit. If, then, you wish to understand the body of Christ, listen to the Apostle as he says to the faithful "You are the body of Christ, and His members" (1 Co 12.27). If, therefore, you are the body of Christ and His members, your mystery has been placed on the Lord's table, you receive your mystery. You reply "Amen" to that which you are, and by replying you consent. For you hear "The Body of Christ," and you reply "Amen." Be a member of the body of Christ so that your "Amen" may be true.

But why in bread? I provide nothing of my own at this point, rather let us listen together to the Apostle who said, when he was speaking about this sacrament, "We, though many, are one bread, one body" (1 Co 10.17). Understand and rejoice. Unity! Verity! Piety! Charity! "One bread." What is this one bread? "Many...one body." Remember that bread is not made from one grain, but from many. When you were exorcized you were, after a fashion, milled. When you were baptized you were moistened. When you received the fire of the Holy Spirit you were baked. Be what you see, and receive what you are.

That is what the Apostle said about the bread, and he has already indicated quite well what we are to understand of the cup, even though he did not say it. For just as in the preparation of the bread which you see, many grains were moistened into a unity, as if there were taking place what holy scripture says about the faithful, "They had one mind, one heart towards God" (Act 4.32), so also in the case of the wine. Brothers, recall whence wine comes. Many grapes hang in the cluster, but the liquid of the grapes is mixed in unity. So also did Christ the Lord portray us. He willed that we belong to Him. He consecrated the mystery of our peace and unity upon His table. He who receives the mystery of unity and does not hold fast to the bond of peace, receives not a mystery for himself, but testimony against himself.

Turned towards the Lord God, the Almighty Father, with a pure heart, let us render great and true thanks to Him, as much as our incapacity can. With all our soul, let us beg His singular gentleness that He may deign to hear our prayers with favor, that He may also drive the enemy from our actions and thoughts by His power, that He may increase our faith, guide our minds, grant us a spiritual way of thinking, and bring us to His blessedness, through Jesus Christ His Son. Amen.

IIA6.2 *Sermon* 227 (dated 412-413, 416-417).

ed SC 116.234-242; *tr* P.T. Weller, *The Easter Sermons of St. Augustine* (diss., Washington, D.C., 1955), revised.

A Sermon of Blessed Augustine the Bishop Concerning the Sacraments, Delivered on the Holy Day of Pascha

I am mindful of my promise. I promised you who have just been baptized a discourse in which I would explain the sacrament of the Lord's table, which you are witnessing even now, and of which you were made partakers last night. You ought to know what you have received, what you are about to receive, what you should receive daily.

The bread which you see on the altar, sanctified by God's word, is the body of Christ. The cup, or, rather, its contents, sanctified by God's word, is the blood of Christ. Through these Christ our Lord wished to bequeath His body and His blood which He shed for us for the forgiveness of sins (Mt 26.28). If you received worthily, you are what you received. For the Apostle says: "We, though many, are one bread, one body" (1 Co 10.17). Thus did he explain the sacrament of the Lord's table, "We, though many, are one bread, one body." By means of this bread he impresses on you how you must love unity. For was this bread made from one grain? Were there not many grains of wheat? Yet before they became bread, they were separate. They were joined together through water, and that after some grinding, for unless wheat is milled and moistened with water, it never reaches that form which is called bread. So you too, in a certain sense, were first milled by the humiliation of fasting and by the sacred rite of exorcism. Next came baptism and water. You were moistened, as it were, to come to the form of bread. But there is yet no bread without fire. What, then, does fire signify? The chrismation of oil. For what feeds our fire is the sacrament of the Holy Spirit. Notice this in the Acts of the Apostles when it is read, for just now that book begins to be read—"Today begins the book called the Acts of the Apostles." Whoever wishes to make progress has the wherewithal. When you are come together to church, stop your idle gossip. Be attentive to the scriptures. We are your books. Listen, then, and see that the Holy Spirit is to come on Pentecost, and thus will He come: He manifests Himself in fiery tongues, for He breathes into us the charity whereby we blaze towards God and disdain the world, and our straw is burnt away, and the heart is purified like gold. The Holy Spirit comes, then, as fire after water, and you are made the bread which is the body of Christ. And for that reason, unity is signified in a particular way.

You recall the mysteries in their proper sequence. First, after the prayer, you are admonished to lift up your hearts. This is fitting for the members of Christ. For if you have become members of Christ, then where is your Head? Members have a head, and unless the head has gone before, the members would not follow. Where has our Head gone? What did you recite in the creed? "On the third day He arose from the dead. He ascended into heaven, and sits at the right hand of the Father." Our Head, then, is in heaven. So, at the words "Lift up your hearts," you respond "We have lifted them up to the Lord." And, lest you attribute your having your hearts to the Lord on high to your own strength, your own merits, your own efforts, since it is God's gift to have one's heart lifted up, for this reason the bishop or the priest who is offering the sacrifice, immediately after the people have replied "We have lifted our hearts up to the Lord,"

continues "Let us give thanks to the Lord our God," that we
have our hearts lifted up. Let us give thanks, for, were it not
for His gift, we would have our hearts on earth. And you
bear witness, saying "It is fitting and right" that we give
thanks to Him who has caused us to raise up our hearts to
our Head.

Next, after the sanctification of God's sacrifice, for He
willed that we ourselves should be His sacrifice, as was
shown when first was presented the idea that we too are
God's sacrifice, that is, it is a sign of the reality which we are
—after the sanctification of the divine sacrifice has been
effected, we say the Lord's Prayer, the prayer which you
were taught and have recited. After that is said "Peace be
with you," and the Christians kiss one another with a holy
kiss (Rm 16.16). This is a sign of peace. Let what the lips
express outwardly be so also in the conscience, that is, as
your lips draw near to your brother's, so let your heart not
withdraw from his.

Great mysteries are these, very great indeed! Would you
like to know what importance is assigned to them? The
Apostle says: "Whosoever eats the body of Christ or drinks
of the cup of the Lord unworthily shall be guilty of the body
and blood of the Lord" (1 Co 11.27). What is it to receive
unworthily? To receive in contempt, to receive in mockery.
Let it not seem common to you because you can see it. What
you see is transitory, but the invisible reality signified does
not pass away, but abides. Behold, it is received, eaten, and
consumed. Is the body of Christ consumed? Is the church of
Christ consumed? Are the members of Christ consumed?
Not at all! Here, on earth, His members are purified, there
they are crowned. Thus what is signified will endure eternally, even though what signifies it seems to pass away.

Receive, then, in such a way that you may take thought
for yourselves, that you may have unity in your hearts, that
you may fix your hearts always on high. May your hope be
not on earth, but in heaven. May your faith in God be strong
and acceptable to Him. For what now you do not see here,

and yet believe (Jn 20.29), you will see there, where you shall rejoice without end.

IIA6.3 *Sermon Wolfenbüttel* 7 (dated 410-412).

ed G. Morin, *Miscellanea Agostiniana* 1 (Rome, 1930) 462-464; *tr* Weller, revised.

A Discourse Concerning the Lord's Day of Holy Pascha.

O you who have been reborn into new life, and for that reason are called infants! You, especially, listen while I explain, as I promised, what is the meaning of what you see before you here. Listen also, O faithful, who have grown accustomed to see this. Recollection is good, lest forgetfulness steal us away.

What you see on the Lord's table you are accustomed to see on your own tables, as far as outward appearances go. It has the same appearance, but not the same efficacy. You too are the same people you were before, for you do not present new faces to us. Nevertheless, you are new, your old selves in physical appearance, but new by the grace of holiness. So also is this something new. Until now, as you see, it is bread and wine. But once the consecration is added, this bread will be the body of Christ and this wine will be the blood of Christ. The name of Christ, the grace of Christ brings it about that even though it looks as it looked before, yet its efficacy is not what is was before. Had you eaten thereof before the consecration, it would have filled your stomach; but now, when it is eaten, it builds up the soul.

As at your baptism, or, rather, before your baptism, on Saturday, we spoke to you about the sacrament of the font in which you were to be immersed. And we told you—I trust you have not forgotten—that baptism had, or, rather, has this power, that it is a burial with Christ, as the Apostle says:

"For we are buried together with Christ by baptism unto death, that as He is risen from the dead, so we also may walk in newness of life" (Rm 6.4). So also our task is now to commend and explain, not out of our own imagination, nor by our own presumption, nor from human arguments, but on the authority of the Apostle, what it is that you have received and are about to receive.

Hear, then, briefly, what the Apostle, or, better, what Christ says by the mouth of the Apostle concerning the sacrament of the Lord's table: "We, though many, are one bread, one body" (1 Co 10.17). That is all there is to it, as I have quickly summed it up. Yet do not count the words, but rather, weigh their meaning. For if you count them they are few, but if you ponder them, their import is great. "One bread," he said. No matter how many loaves were placed before him then, there was only one bread. No matter how many loaves are placed upon the altars of Christ throughout the world today, it is but one bread. What is meant by "one bread"? He explained it concisely, "We, though many, are one body." This bread is the body of Christ, to which the Apostle refers when he addresses the church: "Now you are the body of Christ and His members" (1 Co 12.27). What you receive, you yourselves are by the grace by which you have been redeemed. You show agreement when you respond "Amen." What you see here is the sacrament of unity.

The Apostle has shown us briefly what this bread is. Now consider the matter carefully and see how it comes about. How is bread made? Wheat is threshed, milled, moistened, and baked. By moistening, the wheat is purified, and by baking, it is made firm. What was your threshing? You were made in this way: your threshing was in fasting, in the Lenten observances, in vigils, in exorcisms. You were milled when you were exorcized. But moistening cannot be done without water. Thus you were baptized. Baking is troublesome, but beneficial. What, then, is the baking? The fire of temptations from which no life is free. And how is this beneficial? "The furnace tries the potter's vessel, and the trial of affliction just men" (Si 27.6). As one loaf results from combining the individual grains and mixing them together with water, so also the one body of Christ results from the concord of charity. And as the body of Christ is to the grains of wheat, so also is the blood to the grapes. For wine pours forth from the pressing, and what was individually in many grapes flows together into one liquid, and becomes wine. Hence both in the bread and in the cup the sacrament of unity is present.

At the table of the Lord you hear the words "The Lord be with you." We usually say these words when we greet you from the apse, and also whenever we begin prayers, because our well-being requires that the Lord be always with us, since without Him we are nothing. Recall, too, the words which sounded in your ears, the ones you say at the altar of God. For we question you, as it were, and admonish you, saying "Lift up your hearts." Do not let them sink. The heart rots on earth, lift it towards heaven. But lift the heart to where? What do you answer? To where? "We have lifted them up to the Lord." Now to keep one's heart lifted up is sometimes a good thing and sometimes a bad thing. How can it be bad? It is bad for those of whom it was said: "You cast them down when they were lifted up" (Ps 72.18). To lift up the heart, if not to the Lord, is not righteousness but arrogance. Therefore, when we say "Lift up your hearts," you answer, since to lift up the heart could be mere arrogance, "We have lifted them up to the Lord." And thus it becomes a worthy deed, and not a mark of pride. But because it is a worthy act to lift up the heart to God, is that, then, a matter of our own doing? Could we accomplish this by our own power? Have we lifted up the earth which we are into heaven? Not at all! It is His doing, it is His condescension. He stretched forth His hand, He proffered His grace, He made upward that which was downward. Thus, when I said "Lift up your hearts," and you made the reply "We have lifted them up to the Lord," so you may not attribute to yourselves the lifting of your hearts, I added "Let us give thanks to the Lord our God."

These are concise mysteries, but vast ones. Our utterances are short, but full of meaning. For you say these things quickly, without the aid of a book, without reading, without the use of many words. Remember well what you are, and in whom you must persevere, so that you may be able to attain to the promises of God.

IIA7 *Two Pseudo-Augustinian Eucharistic Catecheses* (5th-6th Centuries).

> The authenticity of these two sermons, though affirmed by many, has been called into question or denied with sufficient regularity and cogency that it seems best to present them separately as pseudo-Augustinian works. It has been suggested that Sermon Denis 3 is the product of a Gallic or Spanish author of the fifth or sixth century, and that Sermon Denis 6 dates from the same period. In my opinion, Denis 3 is definitely not the work of Augustine; Denis 6 may be Augustine's, but a demonstration of this would be welcome.

IIA7.1 Ps-Augustine, *Sermon Denis* 3.
ed Morin, MA 1.18-20; *tr* Weller, revised.

Concerning the Sacraments, on the Day of Pascha.

The duty of preaching, and the sollicitude with which I have given birth to you that Christ might be formed in you (Ga 4.19) compel me to instruct you infants who are now reborn by water and the Spirit (Jn 3.5), who see this food and drink resting here on the altar of the Lord in a light that is new, and receive it with a devotion newly acquired. We must tell you the meaning of so great and godly a sacrament, such an excellent and noble remedy, such a clean and ready sacrifice, which is offered now, not in one city on earth, Jerusalem, nor in the tabernacle built by Moses, nor in the

Temple built under Solomon, all of which were merely shadows of things to come (Col 2.17), but "from the rising of the sun even to its setting" (Ml 1.11), as foretold by the prophets, and is offered as a victim of praise to God, according to the grace of the New Covenant. No longer is a bloody victim selected from the herds of cattle, no longer is a sheep or a goat brought to the divine altars, but the sacrifice of our times is the body and blood of the Priest Himself. This was, indeed, foretold of Him long ago in the Psalms: "You are a priest forever according to the order of Melchisedech" (Ps 109.4). In the Book of Genesis (14.18-19) we read and believe that Melchisedech, the priest of the High God, brought forward bread and wine at the time he pronounced a blessing on our father Abraham.

Christ our Lord, who offered for us in His Passion what he received from us at His birth, was made the chief of priests forever, and gave us the sacrificial rite which you are witnessing, that of His body and blood. When His body was pierced by the lance, it let forth water and blood by which He forgave our sins. Mindful of this grace, working out your salvation (Ph 2.12), for "it is God who works in you" (Ph 2.13), approach with fear and trembling the partaking of this altar. Acknowledge in this bread that which hung on the Cross, in this cup that which flowed from His side. Even the ancient sacrifices of God's people prefigured in many different ways this one sacrifice which was to come. For Christ Himself is a sheep, in the innocence of His guileless soul, and a goat, because of the similitude of the body of sin (Rm 6.6). And whatever else was foretold in many different ways in the sacrifices of the Old Testament, all of it pertains to this one sacrifice revealed in the New Testament.

Take, then, and eat the body of Christ, for in the body of Christ you are already made the members of Christ. Take and drink the blood of Christ. So that there may be no division among you, eat that which binds you together. So you may not appear to yourselves to be of little worth, drink your ransom. Just as this, when you eat and drink it, becomes part of you, so also you are changed into the body of Christ when you live in obedience and devotion.

At the time when His Passion was near at hand, while keeping the passover with His disciples, He took bread, blessed it, and said: "This is my body which shall be delivered up for you" (1 Co 11.24). In like manner he blessed the cup, and gave it to them, saying: "This is my blood of the New Covenant which shall be shed for many for the forgiveness of sins" (Mt 26.28). You have read this or have heard it in the gospel, but you did not know that this eucharist is the Son. Now, however, with your hearts cleansed (Hb 10.22), with conscience clear and bodies washed in clean water (Ex 36.25), "Draw near to Him and be illumined, and your faces shall not blush" (Ps 33.6). For if you receive this worthily, since it pertains to the New Covenant whereby you hope for an eternal inheritance, and if you observe the new commandment, that you love one another (Jn 13.34), you have life in you. You eat that flesh of which Life Himself declared "The bread which I will give is my flesh for the life of the world" (Jn 6.52), and "Unless a man eat my flesh, and drink my blood, he shall not have life in him" (Jn 6.54).

Because you have life in Him, you will be one flesh with Him. For this sacrament does not bestow the body of Christ to separate you from it. The Apostle recalls that this was foretold in holy scripture: " 'And they shall be two in one flesh' (Gn 2.24). This is a great mystery," he says, "but I say it applies to Christ and the church" (Ep 5.31-32). And in another place he says of this eucharist: "For we, though many, are one bread, one body" (1 Co 10.17). You, then, are beginning to receive what you have also begun to be, provided that you do not receive it unworthily, lest you eat and drink condemnation on yourselves. For the Apostle says this: "Whosoever shall eat this bread or drink the cup of the Lord unworthily shall be guilty of the body and of the blood of the Lord. Rather, let a man prove himself, and so let him eat of that bread and drink of the cup. For he who eats and drinks unworthily, eats and drinks judgement on himself" (1 Co 11.27-29).

But you receive worthily when you are on your guard against the leaven of false doctrine, so that you may be the unleavened bread of sincerity and truth (1 Co 5.8), and if you keep that leaven of charity which the woman hid in three measures of meal, till the whole was leavened (Mt 13.33). For this woman is the Wisdom of God, who became mortal flesh through the Virgin. He spreads His gospel throughout the world until the world be leavened, the same world which He restored after the Flood from the three sons of Noah, as if in three measures of meal. This is that whole, called *holon* in Greek, wherein preserving the bond of peace, you will be "according to the whole" which is called *catholon*, whence the name "catholic" is derived.

IIA7.2 Pseudo-Augustine, *Sermon Denis* 6.
ed Morin, MA 1.29-32; *tr* Weller, revised.

A Discourse on the Sacraments of the Faithful, on the Lord's Day of Holy Pascha.

What you see here on the Lord's table, beloved, is bread and wine. But once the word is pronounced over them, this bread and this wine become the body and blood of the Word. For that very Lord, who "In the beginning was the Word, and the Word was with God, and the Word was God" (Jn 1.1), because of His mercy through which He did not disdain what He created in His own image, "the Word became flesh, and dwelt among us" (Jn 1.14), as you know. The same Word assumed human nature, that is, the soul and body of man, and became man, remaining God. Because of this, and because He also suffered for us, He left us, in this sacrament, His body and blood which He has also caused us to be. For we too have been made His body, and through His mercy we are the very thing which we receive.

Recall that this creature [wheat] was formerly in the field, how the earth bore it, how the rain nurtured it and brought it to the mature ear, and how afterwards the industry of man carried it to the threshing-floor, threshed it, winnowed it, stored it, brought it out, milled it, added water, baked it, and at length turned it into bread. Also recall yourselves. You did not exist, and you were created. You were brought to the threshing-floor of the Lord and threshed by the labors of oxen, that is to say of the heralds of the gospel (1 Co 9.9 ff). When you were put off as catechumens, you were being stored in the granary. You handed in your names, and you began to be milled by the fasts and the exorcisms. Afterwards you came to the water and you were moistened and made a unity. With the onset of the heat of the Holy Spirit you were baked, and you became the Lord's bread.

Behold what you have received. For as you see that what has been made is a unity, so you also must be one by loving one another, by holding to one faith, one hope, and undivided charity. Heretics, when they receive this sacrament, receive testimony against themselves, for they seek division, whereas this bread signifies unity. So also the wine existed in many grapes, but is now a unity, one in the savor of the cup, but after the crushing of the winepress. You also have come, in Christ's name, as it were to the cup of the Lord, after your fasts and labors, after your humility and grinding contrition, and there you are on the altar, there you are in the cup. You are there along with us. We are this together, we drink together, because we share life together.

You are about to hear what you already heard last night. But today you are going to receive an explanation of the words you heard and the responses you made. Perhaps you remained silent when the responses were made, but you learned yesterday the responses you are to make today.

Following the greeting with which you are familiar, "The Lord be with you," you heard "Lift up your hearts." The entire life of true Christians is "Lift up your heart," not the life of those who are Christian in name only, but of Christians in reality and truth the entire life is a lifting up of the heart. To lift up the heart, what does this mean? Hope in God, not in yourselves, for you are below and God is above. If you hope in yourselves, your heart is below, it is not above. So, when you hear the priest say "Lift up your hearts," you reply "We have lifted them up to the Lord." See to it, then, that you reply the truth, because your reply is entered in the divine records. As you speak, so let it be, and let not the conscience deny what your tongue declares. And since it is by God's gift, not by your own resources that you lift up your heart, the priest continues, after you have declared that your hearts are lifted up to the Lord, and says "Let us give thanks to the Lord our God." Why should we give thanks? Because we have our hearts lifted up, and yet, had He not raised them, we would still be wallowing on the earth.

Next come those things which are done in the sacred prayers which you are about to hear, so that by the presence of the word the body and blood of Christ may come to be. For take away the word, and there is simply bread and wine, but add the word, and it is something else. What is that something else? The body of Christ and the blood of Christ. Take away the word, and it is only bread and wine. Add the word, and it will become a sacrament. To this you say "Amen." To say "Amen" is to agree. "Amen" is translated in Latin as "True."

Then the Lord's Prayer is said, the prayer you received and recited back. Why is this prayer said before the body and blood of Christ are received? Because it may have occurred, through human frailty, that our mind conceived an improper thought, or that your tongue let slip an unseemly word, or that our eyes gazed upon an unbecoming object, or that our ears listened eagerly to something unsuitable. Now if anything of this sort was committed through worldly temptation and human frailty, it is wiped away then by the Lord's Prayer, that is, when we say "Forgive us our trespasses." And in this way we can approach the sacrament in the assurance that we do not eat and drink to our condemnation (1 Co 11.19).

This is followed by the words "Peace be with you." What a great sacrament, the kiss of peace! Kiss with genuine love. Do not be a Judas. Judas the betrayer kissed Christ with his mouth, but plotted in his heart. If it happens that a person is hostile to you, and you cannot win him over, then you must bear with him. You must not repay him evil for evil in your heart. If he hates you, you must love him nonetheless, and you can kiss without anxiety.

You have heard only a few words, but they are important. Do not consider them of little worth because they are few, but let them be dear because of their weight. For the present, you ought not to be burdened with more, so that you may retain what has been explained.

IIA8 Eusebius "Gallicanus" (seventh century?), *Sermon* 17 (*On Pascha* 6).
ed CCSL 101.195-208.

Eusebius "Gallicanus" is the name given to the compiler and his large collection of sermons falsely attributed in the manuscripts to Eusebius, bishop of Emesa in Syria (*d c* 359). Some have argued that the sermons are the work of Faustus, sometime abbot of Lerins, and bishop of Riez in Provence from *c* 459. Others have maintained that the collection is a later compilation from Faustus' works. A third school holds that the collection is a compilation by an unknown Gallic redactor, who drew on the works of a number of authors from the third to the sixth centuries. This third opinion has been adopted and developed by F. Glorie, the editor of the collection in the CCSL; he maintains that the collection was put together by a compiler of, perhaps, the seventh century, who drew on materials assembled earlier by Caesarius of Arles (*d* 542).

This sermon, apparently a eucharistic catechesis (see beginning of sect. 3, *etc*), would have been something of an anachronism in the seventh century; it was intended for delivery on Holy Thursday. Glorie indicates that the sermon draws on a number of authors, including Ambrose and Augustine; it is especially indebted, in para 6-7, to Cyprian's Letter 63 (IVA4). However awkward this *omnium gatherum* of a sermon may be, it exercised wide influence (see Glorie's list, in CCSL 101.193, of later authors who borrowed from it).

The magnitude of heavenly favors surpasses the limitations of the human mind. For that reason, Divine Providence has ordained that devout faith should conceive of what our reason, overcome by the vastness of the realities, cannot grasp, and that sturdy belief should nourish understanding.

Since, then, God observed from on high (Ps 13.2) the nature of our indebtedness through the first transgression, whereby through Adam we were held liable to birth and death (*cf* Heb 2.15), he fashioned the work of redemption according to the character of our captivity, that is, He would offer a death not owed for a death that was owed, for we had no basis for life, as He had no reason for death. He took up matter from our mortality, so that life, supplied from his immortality, might be able to die for those who were dead.

And so, because He was going to take away from our eyes (Ac 1.9) the body which He had assumed, and place it among the stars, it was opportune that He should, upon this day, consecrate for us the sacrament of His body and blood, that what was offered once as a ransom might be always venerated through a mystery; that, because the redemption for the salvation of men labored daily and indefatigably, the offering of that redemption should also be constant, that its victim should live everlastingly in memory and be present always in grace.

2. Truly a unique and complete victim, one to be valued not according to appearance, but to faith, to be appraised not by outward vision, but by inner love. Therefore rightly does heavenly authority offer assurance that "My flesh is truly food and my blood is truly drink" (Jn 6.56). And so, let every doubt of disbelief depart, since He who is the author of the gift is also Himself the guarantor of its truth.

For the invisible Priest changes visible creatures into the substance of His body and blood by His word with unseen power, saying "Take and eat; this is my body," and, with a repeated blessing, "Take and drink; this is my blood."

At the Lord's command the heights of heaven, the depths of the sea, the expanses of the land came suddenly into existence from nothing. With a like power, the power of the word reveals itself in the spiritual sacraments, and an effect upon reality obeys.

3. O you who are now reborn in Christ, ask what great and praiseworthy benefits are worked by the power of divine blessing. Ask yourself how it should not seem startling and impossible to you that things earthly and mortal are changed into the substance of Christ.

Beforehand you were in exile, an alien to life, wandering far from mercy, from the way of salvation, inwardly dead. Suddenly you were initiated by the laws of Christ, you were made new by the salvific mysteries, you passed over into the body of the church not by seeing, but by believing (Jn 20.29); and from being a son of perdition (Jn 17.12; 2 Th 2.3), you came to be an adoptive son of God through a secret purification. Your visible stature remained the same, but you became greater than yourself without increase in size. Though you were yourself the same person, yet you were much altered by the advance of faith. Nothing was added to your exterior person, yet your inner being was wholly changed. Thus a man became a son of Christ, and Christ was formed in the mind of a man.

As, then, without physical sensation your former vileness was put off, and you were clothed of a sudden with a new dignity, and just as you believe, not with your eyes, but with your mind that God has healed your wounds, cleansed your corruption, washed away your stain; so too, when you approach the venerable altar to be filled with its food, view the sacred body and blood of your God with faith, marvel at it with praise, touch it with the mind, take it up with the hand of the heart, and, most of all, consume it with an inward reception.

4. But if the manna of the Law, of which we read that "He rained manna on them that they might eat" (Ps 77.24), tasted to each as his desire wished (Ws 16.21), then one thing was eaten, and something else perceived—the flavor was

formed imperceptibly in the palate of each one. If, therefore, that manna of the Law, fallen down from heaven, surpassed in its manifold flavors the expectation of its natural appearance, and, since the dispensation of the Bestower endowed His creature with a multiplex variety, it provided a taste not to be guessed from its appearance, according to the desire of the one eating, then a new dignity came about in that food, and it refreshed each with various unexpected flavors, the honeyed gift of the rain, the manifold benefit of the dry rain.

And so, what hunger accomplished then, let faith accomplish now. Though food has taste in the body, God causes an effect in the heart through faith, as we read: "Man approaches, his heart high, and God will be exalted" (Ps 63.7-8). Therefore let blessing now work in the mind what savor accomplished in the mouth. Let the very power of Him who consecrates it strengthen you to confess and receive the sacrifice of His true body. Let what then was hidden, prefigured in the manna, be now revealed to you in grace. Its being prefigured by the appearance of the manna is plainly shown by the Prophet when he says: "He gave the bread of heaven to them; humankind ate the bread of angels" (Ps 77.24-25). And what is the "Bread of Angels" but Christ, who fills them with the food of His love and the light of His glory?

Of this bread the prophet says: "You will gather a double amount on the sixth day; you will not gather on the sabbath" (Ex 16.5, 26). Inasmuch as it is granted from the first, that is, the Lord's Day, in the Law, and is denied on the sabbath alone, already at that time it is shown that Christ is to be received by the church for which His Resurrection consecrated the Lord's Day, and it is foretold that He is to be denied by the synagogue to which the cult of the sabbath belongs, since that day, the seventh, is punished by the deprivation of the heavenly bread.

The ancient account tells of this bread that "Neither did he who had gathered more possess more, nor did he who brought together less obtain less" (Ex 16.18), because the holy reception of the eucharist is not a matter of quantity, but of power; because the body, as the priest imparts it, is as much in a small particle as in the entire loaf; because, when the church of the faithful receives, it is surely entire to each, just as it is fully present to all. From this understanding was derived the statement of the Apostle that "He who has much will not abound, and he who has little will not be diminished" (2 Co 8.15). If, perhaps, we should serve bread for the hungry to eat, an entire loaf would not go to each one, but each would receive bread in bits and morsels according to his portion. But when this bread is received, each individual has no less than the whole group: one person receives the entirety, two persons the entirety, many persons the entirety, with no diminution of it, for the blessing of this sacrament can be shared, but cannot be exhausted by the sharing.

5. We find the form of this sacrament presented even in the texts of the Jews. For we read about Melchisedech in Genesis: "And Melchisedech, the King of Salem, brought bread and wine, and blessed Abraham, for he was a priest of the most-high God" (Gn 14.18-19). In the blessing of circumcision—to—come by uncircumcision, that is, by a gentile, the glory of the church is proclaimed, and the people acquired from the gentiles is placed before the unfaithful synagogue. This Melchisedech, then, whose genealogy, or origin, was unknown (Heb 7.3) at that time, by his offering of bread and wine prefigured the sacrifice of Christ about whom the Prophet declares: "You are a priest forever according to the order of Melchisedech" (Ps 109.4; Heb 5.6).

Moses also spoke about this mystery, signifying wine and blood in one expression. He showed forth the Lord's Passion far in advance in the blessing of the Patriarch, speaking thus: "He will wash his garment in wine, and his cloak in the blood of the grape" (Gn 49.11). Observe how plainly manifest it is that the creature of wine is to be called the blood of Christ.

Learn whatever you might still be asking about this twofold appearance from the testimony of the Lord Himself: "Unless you eat the flesh of the Son of Man, and drink His blood, you will not have life in you" (Jn 6.54). The evidence is quite clear and most effective against the blasphemies of Pelagius who presumes, with lunatic impiety, to declare: "Baptism is to be given to children not because of life, but because of the Kingdom of Heaven." For by these words of God in which the Evangelist declares "You will not have life in you," it is plainly to be undersood that every soul which has not the gift of baptism is lacking not only glory, but life as well.

6. That this wine of the Lord's blood is to be mixed with water the Lord shows, not only through tradition, but also by the very nature of His Passion. From the stroke of the lance there flowed from His side blood and water (Jn 19.34), just as the Prophet foretold much earlier, saying "He struck the rock and water flowed out" (Ps 77.20), and the Apostle, "They drank from the rock which followed them, and the rock was Christ" (1 Co 10.4). You see that the mercy of Christ follows him who drinks of the grace of Christ.

But also in Solomon we read a prediction about God Himself. "Wisdom," he says, "has built herself a house" (Pr 9.1), that is, He has taken a human body in which dwelt the fullness of divinity (Col 2.9); "and she has laid down seven columns" (Pr 9.1), because the blessing of the Holy Spirit, the blessing of a seven-fold grace filled Him (Is 11.2-3); "She has slain her victims, she has mixed her wine into a bowl, and prepared her table" (Pr 9.2); and, in a subsequent verse, "Come and eat of my bread, and drink the wine which I have mixed for you" (Pr 9.5). We read, therefore, that wine was mixed with water. Now let us seek the reason why the Lord wished them to be mixed.

When, in the marriage feast of the Jews, wine, that is, faith, was running out among them—"the wine," it says, "was running out" (Jn 2.3), because the vineyard was denying its fruit, concerning which is said "I expected it to produce grapes, but it produced thorns" (Is 5.4), wherefore also it placed a crown of thorns upon the head of the Redeemer—when the Lord changed water into wine at the time of the marriage, that is, when the Bridegroom was to be joined to His church by paschal joy He changed water into wine, He plainly prefigured the multitudes of the gentiles which would come because of the grace of His blood. For that the peoples are signified by water is apparent from the sacred text, as we read: "These waters which you see are the peoples and nations and languages" (Rv 17.15). We observe that in the waters the figure of the gentiles is disclosed, but that in the wine the blood of the Lord's Passion is shown forth. And thus, when water is mixed with wine in the mysteries, the faithful people is incorporated into Christ and is joined and united to Him by a certain connection of perfect love, so that it may say, along with the Apostle, "Who will separate us from the love of Christ? Tribulation, or constraint, or persecution?" and the rest (Rm 8.35), for God is mixed with man by a received sanctification when faith is poured forth in his heart with the disposition of righteousness, devotion, and mercy.

7. Also, in this very thing which we know is made from countless grains of wheat the unity of the peoples is clearly indicated. For just as the wheat which is prepared by the customary care of the thresher is brought to a white appearance by the work of millstones, and brought together through water and fire into the substance of a single loaf, so too the various peoples and different nations, coming together into a single faith, make of themselves the single body of Christ. And the Christian people, like countless thousands of grains of wheat, is separated from the sacrilegious nations by a faith which threshes and winnows. When it is separated and gathered into a unity, as it were by the removal of the tares of the unfaithful, and processed by the instruction of the two testaments, as if by the twin labor of two millstones, it gleams and is changed into the dignity of its first origin with its innate brightness, and through the water of baptism and the fire of the Holy Spirit it is made the body of the Eternal Bread.

Moreover, just as the grains cannot be separated from the unity of the finished loaf, and just as water, mixed into the wine, can no longer return into its own substance, so too all the faithful and wise who know that they have been redeemed by Christ's blood and Passion must be joined like inseparable members to their Head by the safeguarding of faith and the most ardent piety, in such a way that they can be separated from Him not by will, not by coercion, not by any blandishment of worldly hope, nor yet, finally, be rent from Him even by death itself.

8. And let no one doubt that basic created things can, by the will of power and the presence of majesty, be changed into the Lord's body, when he observes that human nature itself, by the instrumentality of heavenly mercy, has been made the body of Christ. But just as each one who comes to the faith is still in the bond of the ancient debt before the words of baptism, but as soon as they are said he is cleansed of all trace of sin, so, when the creatures are placed on the holy altars to be blessed by heavenly words, before they are consecrated by the invocation of the highest Name, there is there the substance of bread and wine; but after the words of Christ, it is the body and blood of Christ.

But what wonder is it if He who was able to create by a word is also able to alter what He has created by a word? Rather, it seems less extraordinary if That which is known to have created out of nothing should be able to change what has already been created into something better. Inquire what could be difficult for Him for whom it was easy to bring into existence things visible and invisible (Col 1.16) by the command of His will; for whom it was easy to fashion man from the material of mud (Gn 2.7) and to clothe him with the image of His divinity (Gn 1.26); for whom it was easy to call him back up from the lower world (1 S 2.6); to restore him from destruction (Si 50.4), to restore him from the dust (1 S 2.8), to raise him from earth into heaven, to make him an angel from a man, to render a human body comformable to the body of His glory (Ph 3.21), and to raise up His artifact to the sharing of His Kingdom, so that He who had taken on the body of our frailty should assume us into the body of His immortality. For which glorious resurrection may He deign to ready you by devout works, who reigns into the ages of ages. Amen.

B Mystagogy

IIB1 Germanus I, Patriarch of Constantinople (*d c* 733), *Historia Ecclesiastica* 23-55.

ed N. Borgia, *Il Commentario liturgico di S. Germano* (2nd ed, Grottaferrata, 1912), with revisions by D. Sheerin, *Historia Ecclesiastica: The Contemplation of the Divine Liturgy by* ... *Germanus I* (Fairfax, VA, 1984) 27-29; *Lit* P. Meyendorf, *St. Germanus of Constantinople on the Divine Liturgy*, Crestwood N.Y., 1984.

Germanus was Patriarch of Constantinople from 715 to 730. He is best known as an opponent of iconoclasm, but his most lasting and far-reaching influence comes from his elucidation of the eucharistic liturgy—the most popular liturgical commentary in the East until the work of Nicholas Cabasilas in the fourteenth century. The earlier parts of the commentary deal with the church, its structures, vestments, liturgical objects, *etc.* I have omitted these from this selection; a translation of the entire treatise may be found in my work cited above. Sections 23-55 deal with the eucharistic liturgy, specifically, with the Divine Liturgy of St. Basil (VA3). A hypothetical alignment of the commentary with the Liturgy of Basil may be found in the introduction (iv-viii) to my translation of the entire work. Texts from the Litrugy are given here in captial letters.

The Divine Liturgy

The antiphons of the Liturgy are the prophets' predictions which foretold the coming of the Son of God; they shout "Our God has appeared on earth and has dwelt among men (Ba 3.38)" and "He has put on beauty" (Ps 92.1), that is, they reveal His Incarnation which we proclaim again, having embraced knowledge of it through those who have become servants, eyewitnesses, and attendants of the Word (Lk 1.2).

The entrance of the Gospel signifies the advent and the entry of the Son of God into the world, according as the Apostle says: "When He," that is God the Father, "brings His firstborn into the world He says: 'And let all His angels adore Him'" (Heb 1.6). Then the bishop shows by his vestment Christ's garment of the flesh, red and bloody, which He, immaterial and divine, did wear, dyed purple from the undefiled blood of the Virgin Theotokos; and, as the Good Shepherd (Jn 10.11), He took upon his shoulders the sheep which had gone astray (Lk 15.5). Wrapped in swaddling clothes, He is placed, no longer in the manger of irrational beasts, but upon the spiritual table of reason-endowed men, He whom the armies of angels praised in song, saying: "Glory to God in the highest, and peace on earth, good will among men" (Lk 2.14), and, "Let all the earth adore Him" (Ps 65.4). And as we, in our turn, hear: COME, LET US ADORE AND FALL DOWN PROSTRATE (Ps 94.6) ... SAVE US, O SON OF GOD, we proclaim the coming revealed to us by the grace of Jesus Christ.

The Trisagion Hymn is as follows: there the angels said "Glory to God in the highest," but here we, as the Magi their gifts, offer to Christ faith, hope, and love, as gold, incense, and myrrh, while in faith we cry out the song of songs: HOLY GOD the Father; HOLY MIGHTY ONE the Son and Word, for, having chained the Devil who was mighty against us, through the Cross He rendered impotent the one who had the power of death (Heb 2.14), and allowed our life to tread upon him (Lk 10.19); HOLY IMMORTAL ONE the Holy Spirit, the Giver of Life, through whom all creation is enlivened and cries out HAVE MERCY ON US!

The bishop's ascent to the *synthronos* and his blessing of the people is the Son of God when He had accomplished the Economy. He raised His hands and blessed His holy disciples (Lk 24.50) and said to them: "My peace I leave to you" (Jn 14.27), manifesting that He gave this same peace and blessing to the world through His apostles.

His sitting down is when the Son of God carried the flesh which He wore "up above every Principality and Power and Dominion" (Ep 1.21) of the powers on high, and offered it to God the Father. God the Father received it as a sacrifice and acceptable offering on behalf of mankind. And He said to Him: "Sit at my right hand" (Ps 109.1, Heb 1.13), and "He sat at the right of the throne of majesty on high" (Heb 1.3).

The *prokeimenon* again discloses the prophets' revelation and foretelling of the coming of Christ, like soldiers running ahead and shouting: "You who sit upon the cherubim, appear and come to save us" (Ps 79.2-3).

Alleluia in the Hebrew language is AL—"He comes, he has appeared"—, EL-"God"—and OUIA-"praise, hymn the living God."

The censer shows the humanity of Christ, the fire His divinity; the fragrant smoke discloses the fragrance of the Holy Spirit going before; for the censer [*thymiater*] is interpreted "most fragrant joy."

The Gospel is the presence of God, whereby He has been seen by us, no longer speaking to us through clouds and riddles as once to Moses, through voices and lightnings and trumpets, in sound and darkness and fire upon the mountain (Heb 12.18 ff), or to the prophets through dreams, but plainly, as true man, He has appeared and has been seen by us (Ps 17.27), the gentle and tranquil King (Za 9.9; Mt 21.5) who beforehand came down soundlessly on fleece (Ps 71.6), "and we have beheld his glory, glory as of the Onlybegotten of the Father, full of grace and truth" (Jn 1.14). Through Him God the Father has spoken to us face to face and not through riddles (Nb 12.8). Concerning Him the Father bears witness from heaven and says: "This is my beloved Son" (Mt 3.17), WISDOM, Word, and POWER (1 Co 1.24), the One announced to us in the prophets but manifested in the gospels that "as many as receive Him ... and believe in His name" may receive "the capability of becoming Sons of God" (Jn 1.12). "We have heard, and have seen with our eyes" (1 Jn 1.1) that He is the Wisdom and the Word of God. We all cry out: GLORY TO YOU, O LORD. Next the Holy Spirit cries out, who overshadowed in a bright cloud, now through man It cries: "BE ATTENTIVE, 'Hear Him'" (Mt 17.5)!

There are four gospels because there are four universal winds, according to the quadriform living creatures upon which the God of all sits. From them it is manifest that the God who rests upon the cherubim (Ps 79.2) and sustains all things (Ws 1.7) has been revealed and has given to us the gospel, quadriform, but united in one spirit. They are, moreover, four-faced (Ez 1.6, Rv 4.7 ff), and their four faces portray the activity of the Son of God. For the first is like a lion, designating His efficacy, sovereignty, and royalty; the second is like a calf, manifesting His ritual, priestly order; the third has the face of a man, plainly delineating His coming as a man; the fourth is like a flying eagle, making plain the gift alighting through the Holy Spirit. And the gospels are like in shape to those [*sc* the quadriform living creatures] in whose midst (Rv 4.6) Christ rests. The gospel according to John relates His sovereign, active, and glorious generation (*cf* Is 53.8) from the Father. That according to Luke, given its hieratic character, begins from the priest Zachariah offering incense in the temple. Matthew relates His generation according to man: "The book of the generation ..." (Mt 1.1); it, then, is the man-shaped gospel. But Mark takes his beginning from the prophetic spirit coming upon men from on high, saying: "The beginning of the

Gospel of Jesus Christ. As it was written in the prophets: 'Behold I send my angel ...'" (Mk 1.1), showing the winged likeness of the gospel.

The bishop's blessing the people teaches that the future coming of Christ will be in the six-thousand-five-hundredth year, through the number of fingers showing 6,500.

The *iliton* signifies the linen in which Christ's body was wrapped when He came down from the Cross and was placed in the tomb (Mk 15.46).

The catechumens depart as being uninitiated in Divine Baptism and the Mysteries of Christ. Concerning them the Lord says: "And I have other sheep, and I must bring them and they will hear my voice" (Jn 10.16).

The *proskomide* [immediate preparation] which is made in the treasury manifests the "Place of the Skull" (see Mt 27.33 *etc*) where Christ was crucified, in which, tradition has it, rested the skull of our firstfather Adam, showing that the tomb was near where He was crucified (Jn 19.41-42). This "Place of the Skull" was prefigured in Abraham when upon one of those hills, at the Lord's command, he built an altar of stones, heaped up wood, and placed his son there, but offered in his place a ram as a whole-burnt-offering (Gn 22.2 ff). Thus also was God the Father, the One without beginning and Ancient of Days (Dn 7.9), pleased that His Son without beginning should, "in the last times" (1 P 1.20), become incarnate of the undefiled Virgin, the Theotokos, from his [Abraham's] loins (Heb 7.5) according to the promise of the oath which He established in respect to him. He suffered as a man in His flesh, but remained impassible in His divinity. Indeed Christ carried His Cross as He went to His crucifixion, and in place of a ram was sacrificed His immaculate body, as a lamb slaughtered by a lance in His side, made a highpriest (Heb 6.20), offering Himself and offered to take away the sins of many (Heb 9.28). He died as a man, but rose as God through the glory which He had with God His Father before the creation of the world (Jn 17.5).

The Cherubic Hymn manifests through the procession of the deacons and the contemplation of the seraphic likenesses of the *rhipidia* the entry of all the holy and just, entering with Him who is the Holy of Holies, with the cherubic powers entering together and going before, as the angelic soldiery run invisibly before the great King, Christ, praising and escorting Him as He advances to the Mystical Sacrifice, borne by material hands. The holy Spirit enters ahead with them to the bloodless and spiritual sacrifice, intellectually contemplated in fire and incense and vapor of fragrant smoke. The fire shows divinity, the fragrant smoke shows the presence of the One who has come invisibly and has perfumed us through the mystical and sacrificial and bloodless worship and whole-burnt-offering. Moreover, the spiritual powers and the choirs of angels, after seeing the Economy accomplished through the Cross and death of Christ and His victory against death and His descent into Hades and His third-day Resurrection, cry out with us ALLELUIA.

This is also in imitation of the burial of Christ wherein Joseph, after taking His body down from the Cross, wrapped it in clean linen after he had anointed it with spices and ointments, and carried it, with Nicodemus, and buried it in the new tomb cut from rock. The symbol of the Holy Tomb is the altar and the repository, for on it is placed the immaculate and all-holy Body.

The *diskos* stands for the hands of Joseph and Nicodemus who buried Christ. The *diskos* upon which Christ is carried is also interpreted as the circle of heaven and it shows to us, in a small compass, Christ, the spiritual Sun, contained and beheld in the bread. The covering of the *diskos* stands for the cloth which was upon the head and face of Christ and covered Him in the tomb.

The veil, that is the *aer*, stands for the stone with which Joseph closed the tomb, which the guard of Pilate also sealed.

Behold, Christ was crucified, Life was buried, the tomb was secured, the stone sealed. The priest approaches. He comes along with the angelic powers, no more as standing upon earth, but in the supercelestial sanctuary. Before the altar of the throne of God he stands and contemplates the great and inexplicable and inscrutable mystery of God. He confesses the grace, he proclaims the Resurrection, he seals the faith of the Holy Trinity. He approaches, the angel clad in white, at the stone of the tomb, rolling it away with his hand, indicating by his posture, crying out with his voice, in trembling, proclaiming through the deacon the third-day Resurrection, raising the veil and saying: LET US STAND WELL, the first day: LET US STAND IN AWE, the second day; TO OFFER THE HOLY OBLATION IN PEACE, the third day. The people declare the grace of the Resurrection of Christ: A MERCY, A PEACE, A SACRIFICE OF PRAISE.

The priest teaches the people the trinitarian knowledge of God through grace: MAY THE GRACE OF THE HOLY AND CONSUBSTANTIAL TRINITY BE WITH YOU ALL. The people confess and pray with him and say: AND WITH YOUR SPIRIT. Then the priest, as he raises all to the heavenly Jerusalem on high in which "our feet were standing" before the Fall, "in your courts, Jerusalem" (Ps 121.2), to His holy mountain, cries out: BEHOLD, LET US HAVE OUR HEARTS ON HIGH. All make solemn affirmation saying: WE HAVE LIFTED THEM UP TO THE LORD. The priest: LET US GIVE THANKS UNTO THE LORD. The people give assent, saying: IT IS FITTING AND RIGHT, sending up hymns of thanksgiving to the Holy Trinity, to hold the eye of the soul upwards, seeking the habitation of the Jerusalem on high.

Then the priest advances "with confidence to the throne of the grace" (Heb 4.16) of God, "with a truthful heart and in fullness of faith" (Heb 10.22) making declaration to God and speaking with Him, no more through a cloud as once did Moses in the Tabernacle of the Witness, but "contemplating the glory of the Lord with face unveiled" (2 Co 3.18). He is an initiate in the divine knowledge and faith of the Holy Trinity and he addresses God one to one, declaring in a mystery mysteries hidden before the ages and from generations, but now revealed (Col. 1.26) to us through the Epiphany of the Son of God. These [mysteries] "the Onlybegotten Son of God who is in the bosom of the Father has declared" (Jn 1.18) to us. For as God spoke to Moses invisibly, and Moses to God, so too the priest stands between the two cherubim at the Throne of Mercy (Nb 7.89; Heb 9.5), bows down because of the unendurable and not-to-be-beheld glory and brilliance of divinity, and sees in his mind the supercelestial worship and is initiated into it. He beholds the splendor of the life-giving Trinity—God the Father, without beginning and unbegotten, the Son and Word, also without beginning, consubstantial and begotten, the Holy Spirit, coeternal, of the same nature and proceeding—: The Holy Trinity, according to the unconfused distinction of hypostases, that is to say of persons, according to the undivided unity of nature and inseparable divinity, kingdom, and glory. In his mind he beholds, and he proclaims the thrice-holy doxology of the seraphic powers and the quadriform living creatures, of the cherubim overshadowing and the seraphim crying aloud, with whom he cries out: SINGING, PROCLAIMING, SHOUTING THE HYMN OF VICTORY AND SAYING. Then the people, in the place of the cherubic powers and quadriform living creatures cry: HOLY, HOLY, HOLY LORD OF SABAOTH, that is, the thrice-holy and one God of Hosts, HOSANNA IN THE HIGHEST; BLESSED IS HE WHO COMES IN THE NAME OF THE LORD. *Hosanna* is "Save us now, O you who, like light, come in the name of the Lord."

The *rhipidia* and the deacons manifest the six-winged seraphim and the likeness of the many-eyed cherubim, for thus do even earthly things imitate the spiritual, heavenly, and transcendent order. The quadriform living creatures cry out, replying antiphonally to one another (Is 6.2 ff). The first, in the likeness of a lion, cries HOLY; the second, in the likeness of a calf, cries HOLY; the third, in the likeness of a man, cries HOLY; the fourth, in the likeness of an eagle, cries LORD OF SABAOTH, in three acclamations of HOLY which come together into one lordship, power, and divinity, just as the prophet Isaiah did behold when he saw the Lord upon a lofty, raised throne and the seraphic powers standing around, and from their voice the building was filled with smoke. "One of the seraphim was sent and took a coal with its hand, which it took in a pair of tongs from the altar" (Is 6.6); this signifies the priest at the holy altar holding with the tongs of his hand the Spiritual Coal which sanctifies and cleanses those who receive and share Him. For Christ entered into the holy places, heavenly, not made-by-hand, and was manifested in glory before the face of God (Heb 9.24), become for us a great highpriest (Heb 6.20) who has entered into heaven (Heb 4.14), and we have Him as an advocate before the Father and as a propitiation for our sins (1 Jn 2.1-2). He fitted to us His own holy body (Heb 10.5) as a ransom for all of us, just as He said: "Father, make holy in your name those whom you have given to me, that they too may be holy" (Jn 17.17, 11, 19), and "I will that they may be where I am, and may see my glory, for you have loved them just as you loved me before the foundation of the world"(Jn 17.22-24).

Then again the priest declares to God the Father the mysteries of the Incarnation of Christ, His ineffable and glorious birth from the Holy Virgin and Theotokos, His way of life and dwelling in the world, His crucifixion, His death, and the liberation by Him of the souls in bondage, His holy third-day Resurrection from the dead, His Ascension into the heavens, His Enthronement at the right of God the Father, His glorious Second Coming again in the future for us. And he celebrates the mystery of the "womb before the morningstar," God unbegotten, that is God the Father, and the Son born before the ages, just as He says: "Out of the womb before the morningstar have I begotten you"(Ps 109.3). The priest calls upon Him to accomplish again the mystery of His Son, and cause the bread and wine to become, that is, to be changed into the body and blood of Christ God Himself, and then will be fulfilled ". . . this day have I begotten you" (Ps 2.7).

Whence also the Holy Spirit, by the good pleasure of the Father and the will of the Son invisibly present, shows forth divine power and bears witness to the hand of the priest and seals and accomplishes the change of the proffered holy gifts into the body and blood of Jesus Christ our Lord who said:

"For them I make myself Holy" (Jn 17.19), so that "He who eats my flesh and drinks my blood abides in me and I in him" (Jn 6.56).

Having become thence eye-witnesses of the Divine Mysteries and partakers of immortal life and "sharers of the divine nature" (2 P 1.4), let us glorify the great, incomprehensible and unsearchable mystery of the Economy of Christ God. Wherefore rendering glory, let us cry out WE PRAISE YOU, God the Father, WE BLESS YOU, God the Son, WE GIVE THANKS TO YOU, to the Holy Spirit, O LORD OUR GOD, the Trinity in unity, consubstantial and undivided, possessed, beyond our reasoning, both of distinction of persons and of unity of one nature and divinity.

The fact that the priest celebrates the Divine Mystery while bowing shows that he speaks invisibly with God alone. Thence too he sees the divine glory and rejoices because of the brilliance of the glory of the face of God, and he draws back for fear and modesty, just as Moses, when he saw God in the likeness of fire upon the mountain, trembled and drew back and hid his face, for he feared even to gaze upon the glory of His face (Ex 3.6).

Memorial of those fallen asleep is made to the "God of spirits and of all flesh" (Nb 16.22), for He has dominion over both the dead and the living and rules "those in heaven, upon the earth, and under the earth" (Ph 2.10), that, in the presence of Christ the King, as the Holy Spirit summons all the living and the departed to an abode and place of rest against the coming of our God, Lord, and Saviour Jesus Christ, they may be gathered together and "go before His face" (Ps 94.2), for the bonds of all the souls in Hades were loosed through the death and Resurrection of Christ. For "He has been raised from the dead," the firstfruit and the "firstborn of those who have fallen asleep" (1 Co 15.20; Rv 1.5), and has prepared for all, as it were a path, the Resurrection from the dead, strengthening unto immortal and blessed life those who have fallen asleep in the hope of His Resurrection. Moreover, the souls of Christians are called together with prophets, apostles, martyrs, and hierarchs to assemble and "recline with Abraham, Isaac, and Jacob" (Mt

8.11) at the Mystical Table of the Kingdom of Christ.

Having come thence into the unity of faith and communion of the Spirit through the Economy of Him who died
for us and is seated at the right of the Father (1 Th 5.10; Rm
8.34), we are no more upon the earth, but we have taken our
places at the royal throne of God in heaven where Christ is,
just as He says: "O holy Father, make holy in your name
those whom you have given to me, that where I am, they too
may be with me" (Jn 17.25, 16, 11, 24, 23). We, therefore,
who have received adoption as sons (Ga 4.5) and have
become co-heirs with Christ (Rm 8.17) through His grace
and not through works (Ep 8.17), we have the Spirit of the
Son of God (Ga 4.6). Contemplating His power and grace,
the priest cries aloud and says: Abba (Ga 4.6), HEAVENLY
FATHER, MAKE US WORTHY WITH CONFIDENCE
AND WITHOUT BLAME TO DARE TO CALL UPON
YOU [AS FATHER] AND TO SAY:

The people cry: OUR FATHER, WHO ART IN
HEAVEN, HALLOWED BE THY NAME. The name is
that of the son of God, the name invoked upon us (Ja 2.7),
"Christ," whence we too are Christians and His name is
invoked upon us. THY KINGDOM COME. The kingdom
of God is the Holy Spirit, as He says: "The Kingdom of God
is within you" (Lk 17.21). Kingly rule pertains to the Holy
Spirit, with the Father and the Son, for He sanctifies and
illumines the spiritual, angelic hosts and "every man that
comes into the world" (Jn 1.9), and who believes in the name
of the Son of God. THY WILL BE DONE. ON EARTH AS
IT IS IN HEAVEN. The will of God the Father is the
Economy of the Son. GIVE US THIS DAY OUR DAILY
BREAD. Our daily bread is Christ who is, was, and shall be,
who is unconsumed, endures always, and "gives life to the
world" (Jn 6.33). We accepted Him through Baptism and
seek to receive Him always. AND FORGIVE US OUR
TRESPASSES and failings.

Then the priest cries out to all and says: "I am a man
afflicted like you, nor do I know the sins of each of you.
Look, consider, behold God; and God is holy and rests
among the saints" (Is 57.15). The people confess and say:

"ONE IS HOLY, ONE IS LORD and God, the sinless one, our Lord JESUS CHRIST with God the Father and the Holy Spirit."

And Moses indeed sprinkled the blood of goats and calves, saying to the people: "This is the blood of the covenant" of God (Heb 9.19-21, Ex 24.8); but Christ God gave His own body and poured forth His own blood and mixed the chalice of the new covenant, saying: "This is my body and my blood, broken and shed for the forgiveness of sins."

And so, for the rest, with such love, we eat the bread and drink the chalice as the body and blood of God, confessing the death and Resurrection of the Lord Jesus Christ. To Him be glory unto the ages. Amen!

IIB2 Pseudo-Germanus of Paris (seventh century), [*Exposition of the Ancient Gallican Liturgy*], Letter 1.

ed E. C. Ratcliff, *Expositio antiquae liturgiae gallicanae (HBS 98*, London, *1971) 3-17; lit* translation of anaphora of Gallican liturgy in PEER 105-108.

> In contrast to the preceding work, this liturgical commentary enjoyed very limited popularity, and survives in only one manuscript. The MS attributes the two letters of which this treatise consists to Germanus, bishop of Paris. Scholarship is divided over whether this is an authentic work of St. Germanus of Paris (*d* 576) or of an anonymous seventh-century author.
>
> Letter 1, the portion of the treatise excerpted here, deals with the eucharistic liturgy; Letter 2 explains miscellaneous liturgical observances and objects. A reconstruction of a gallican eucharistic liturgy for Christmas may be found in K. Gamber, *Ordo antiquus gallicanus (Textus patristici et liturgici* 3, Regensburg, 1965) 24-43.

We take up the principal features of the traditions of the fathers: how the solemn ritual of the Church is conducted, with what dispositions the ecclesiastical order is adorned. Germanus, the Bishop of Paris, has written about the Mass.

The Mass, the first and greatest of the sacramental gifts, is sung in remembrance of the death of the Lord, because the death of the Lord has become the life of the world, that by its being offered it may be beneficial to the salvation of the living and the repose of the dead.

Concerning the *Pre-reading* [i.e. Entrance Psalmody].

The pre-reading antiphon is sung in the likeness of those patriarchs who thundered forth, with mystic words, the coming of Christ before the Flood, like Enoch, "the seventh from Adam" (Jd 14), who was translated by God (Si 44.16). He prophesied, saying: "Behold the Lord will come with His countless saints to do judgement," and the rest (Jd 14). The apostle Jude, the brother of James, reports this testimony in his Epistle. For, just as when the patriarchs were prophesying, the hand of the Lord came upon the Ark to give the remains of the earth to the uncondemned, so also as the clergy sing, the priest comes out from the sacristy in the likeness of Christ, as if from heaven to the Ark of the Lord which is the Church, that by admonition and intercession he might foster good works among the people and eliminate evil works.

Concerning the *Silence.*

The deacon proclaims "Silence" for two reasons: that the people keeping quiet may better hear the word of God, and that our hearts may keep silent from every base thought, that the word of God may be better received.

The priest addresses the people the people saying: "May the Lord be with you always," so that while he blesses the people, he may be blessed by all, saying: "And with your spirit," so that he may be more worthy to bless the people to the degree that, by God's favor, he receives a blessing from the mouth of the entire people.

Concerning the *Aius* [*Trisagion*].

The *Aius* [i.e. *hagios*] before the Prophecy is sung in the Greek language because the preaching of the New Covenant went forth in the world through the Greek language, with the exception of the Apostle Matthew who was the first to produce a gospel of Christ, in Judea, in Hebrew letters. So, guarding the honor of the language which first received the gospel of Christ in its bosom and taught it with its letters, the Church sings the *Aius* as the first canticle, intoned by the bishop, speaking Latin with Greek. And that the joining of the Old and New Covenants may be manifested, "Amen" is said in Hebrew, like the notice which Pilate placed on the Cross, by God's inspiration, in a trinity of languages, thereby confessing, though in ignorance, "Jesus of Nazareth, King of the Jews," that is, Holy One and King.

The three boys, who as if with one voice, next sing "Kyrie eleison" three times are in the likeness of the threefold languages of Scripture: Hebrew, Greek, and Latin, or of the three ages of the world: Before the Law, Under the Law, and Under Grace.

Concerning the *Prophecy.*

The Canticle of the priest Zachariah (Lk 1.68-79) is sung in honor of St. John the Baptist, because the beginning of salvation is the sacrament of baptism which John received for his ministry by the gift of God. And because, upon the waning of the shadow of the Old Covenant and the dawning of the new brightness of the gospel, John, in the middle, as the last of the prophets and first of the evangelists, gleamed as a radiant lamp (Jn 5.35) before the face of the True Light (Jn 1.9), for that reason the Church sings antiphonally the prophecy which his father sang when he was born.

Concerning the *Prophet* and the *Apostle.*

The reading of the prophets keeps its own pattern, that is, of the Old Covenant, rebuking evil and announcing things to come, so that we may understand that it is the same God who thundered through prophecy as He who also taught through the Apostle and gleamed in the splendor of the gospel.

Concerning the *Apostle*.

For what the prophet cries out is to come, the Apostle teaches as accomplished fact. The Acts of the Apostles and the Apocalypse of John are read because of the newness of paschal joy, keeping to the order of the seasons, just as the reading of the Old Testament in the fifty-day period [before Pascha] and the deeds of the holy confessors and martyrs on their feasts, that the people may understand how much Christ loved His servant, granting the testimony of miraculous power to him whom the devout people seek as their patron.

Concerning the *Hymn*.

The *Hymn of the Three Young Men* (Dn 3.51-90) [...] which is sung after the readings is a figure of the saints of old who, sitting in darkness (Lk 1.79), were awaiting the coming of the Lord. For just as, when they were silent, an angel came, as a fourth, brought in a cloud of dew, and quelled the flames of fire (Dn 3.49-50), so also as these were awaiting Christ, the Son of God Himself, the Angel of Great Counsel (Is 9.6) came and smashed the powers of Hell, set them free, and brought in the joy of the Resurrection, as the gospel-writer teaches. Accordingly, the Church keeps an order whereby a prayer does not come between the *Benedicite* [the Hymn of the Three Young Men] and the Gospel, excepting only the responsory which is sung by the children, like the Innocents who are read in the gospel to have perished as sharers in Christ's birth (Mt 2.16 ff), or like those children who cried out in the Temple, as the Lord was going to His Passion, "Hosanna to the Son of David" (Mt 21.15), as the Psalmist sings: "Out of the mouths of infants and nurslings you have perfected praise" (Ps 8.3; Mt 21:16).

Concerning the *Aius* [*Trisagion*] before the Gospel.

Then, against the arrival of the holy Gospel, the clergy again sing the *Aius* in clear song, in the likeness of the angels before the face of Christ crying out to the gates of Hell: "Lift up your gates, O you princes, and be lifted up, eternal gates, and the Lord of Hosts, the King of Glory will come in" (Ps 23.7-10).

Concerning the *Gospel.*

The procession of the holy Gospel, therefore, goes forth like the power of Christ triumphing over death, with the aforementioned singing and the seven candelabra of lights (Rv 1.13) which are the seven gifts of the Holy Spirit, or the six lights of the Law (Ex 25.32) fixed according to the mystery of the Cross, ascending to the height of the *ambo,* like Christ to the throne of the Father's Kingdom, to thunder forth from it the gifts of life (Ep 4.8), as the clergy cry out "Glory to you, O Lord!" in the likeness of the angels who, when the Lord was born, appearing to the shepherds sang "Glory to God in the Highest."

Concerning the *Sanctus* after the Gospel.

The clergy sing the *Sanctus* which is sung at the return of the holy gospel in the likeness of the saints who, when the Lord Jesus Christ returned from Hell, sang a canticle of praise as they followed the Lord, or in the likeness of the twenty-four elders whom John describes in the Apocalypse, who cast down their crowns and sang a sweet song before the Lamb (Rv 4.10-11).

Concerning the Homilies.

The homilies of the holy fathers which are read are appointed for preaching alone, that whatever the Prophet, Apostle, and Gospel have commanded, this the teacher and pastor should proclaim to the people in plainer language, so tempering it with skill that neither rusticity should offend the learned, nor decent eloquence should become obscure to the countrymen.

Concerning the Prayer.

The singing of a prayer on behalf of the people by the deacons takes its origin from the books of Moses, so that after the preaching has been heard by the people the deacons should pray for the people, and the priests, prostrate before the Lord, should intercede for the sins of the people, as the Lord said to Aaron: "You and your sons and the whole tribe of Levi will bear the sins of my people" (*cf* Ex 28.38; Lv 10.17; Nm 18.1, 23), not of course, by suffering the punishment, but by removing them by prayers.

Concerning the *Catechumen*.

The deacon shouts for the catechumen[s] to go out according to an ancient rite of the church, the purpose of which was that the Jews and heretics, and pagans undergoing instruction, who came to baptism as adults and were being tested before baptism, might remain in the church and hear the counsel of the Old and New Testaments, and that afterwards the deacons should pray for them and the priest should say the Collect after the Prayer, but that afterwards they should go outside because they were not worthy to remain in the church while the oblation was being brought in, that prostrate on the earth outside, in front of the door, they should listen to the wondrous works of God. This concern belongs to the deacon and to the door-keeper, that the former should admonish them to depart, and the latter should take care that no unworthy person tarry in the church, as the Lord says: "Do not give what is holy to dogs, and do not cast your pearls before swine" (Mt 7.6). For what on earth is more holy than the consecration of the body and blood of Christ, and what is more unclean than dogs and swine? They are comparable, by analogy, to him who has not been cleansed by baptism and not fortified by the sign of the Cross.

We are bidden to keep silence spiritually, and to attend to the door, that is, that keeping silence from the tumult of words and vices, we should place the sign of the Cross before our faces, so that concupiscence may not come in through the eyes or anger through the ears, that base speech may not proceed from the lips, and that the heart's sole concern may be to receive Christ into itself.

Concerning the *Sonus*.

The *Sonus* which is sung during the offertory procession took its origin from this: the Lord commanded Moses to make silver trumpets which the Levites were to sound when a victim was being offered, and this would be a sign whereby the people would know at what hour the offering was brought in, and all, bowed, would worship the Lord until there would come the column of fire or cloud which would bless the sacrifice (Nb 10.2-10, 14.14; Ex 12.27; Si 50.18-20). But now, when the body of Christ proceeds to the altar, not with faultless trumpets, but with spiritual voices the Church sings in sweet melody the glorious works of Christ.

The body of the Lord is carried in towers for the reason that the tomb of the Lord was cut in the rock in the likeness of a tower, and inside was the bier on which the Lord's body rested, whence the King of Glory rose in triumph. The blood of Christ is offered in a cup because in such a vessel the mystery of the eucharist was consecrated on the day before the Lord suffered, as He says: THIS IS THE CUP OF MY BLOOD, THE MYSTERY OF FAITH, WHICH WILL BE SHED FOR MANY FOR THE FORGIVENESS OF SINS.

The bread is changed into the body, the wine into the blood, as the Lord says of His body, "For my flesh is truly food," and of the blood, "My blood is truly drink" (Jn 6.55). For of the bread He said, "This is my body," and of the wine, "This is my blood." Water is mixed with the wine, either because it is fitting that the people be united with the Lord, or because from the side of Christ on the Cross there flowed blood and water (Jn 19.34), that by the one we might be cleansed from the stain of sin, and by the other we might be prepared for the Kingdom of Heaven.

The paten on which the offering is sacrificed is so called because the mystery of the eucharist is offered in remembrance of the Passion [*pati*, to suffer] of the Lord.

The linen veil is a figure of His garment which, because it was woven in one piece, was not divided by the soldiers, that is the tunic of Christ (Jn 19.23 ff).

The corporal upon which the oblation is placed is pure linen because the body of the Lord was wrapped, with spices, in pure linen in the tomb.

The covering of the sacraments is ornate because the Resurrection of Christ excels all ornaments, or in the likeness of the vault of heaven, which now conceals the Lord from us. The silk is adorned with gold and gems because the Lord commanded Moses to make veils in the Tabernacle from gold and violet and purple and scarlet twice-dyed and fine linen (Ex 26.31), because all those mysteries went ahead as symbols of Christ.

The *Praises*, that is the "Alleluia," John, in the Apocalypse (Rv 19.1, 3, 4, 6), heard those in heaven singing after the Resurrection of Christ. And so, at that hour at which the body of Christ is covered by a veil, as Christ is by heaven, the church is wont to sing the angelic song. The fact that the Alleluia has a first, second, and third part [i.e. is sung thrice] designates the three ages: Before the Law, Under the Law, and Under Grace.

The names of the departed are read at the hour when the veil is removed because the Resurrection of the Dead will take place when, at the Coming of Christ, heaven will be rolled up like a scroll (Is 34.4).

They offer the Peace of Christ to one another to the end that through a shared kiss they may have in themselves a disposition of charity, and that he who is darkened by some discord may quickly return to grace and seek forgiveness from his neighbor and lest, by giving the Peace falsely, he come to share the lot of the Betrayer. The reception of the eucharist and the imparting of the blessing are more beneficial to the degree that Christ perceives our hearts to be in peace, because He told His disciples, when he was ascending into heaven: "Peace I leave to you, my peace I give to you (Jn 14.27). A new commandment I give you, that you love one another" (Jn 13.34), and "By this shall all know that you are my disciples, if you love one another" (Jn 13.35).

The priest gives an admonition to have "Hearts on high" so that no earthly thought may remain in our hearts at the hour of the sacred offering; and Christ may be better received in the mind to the degree that thought undivided strives to attend to Him.

The Fraction and Commixture of the Body of the Lord was declared of old by such great mysteries to the holy fathers that when the priest was breaking up the oblation, as it were an angel of God appeared to cut up the body of a shining boy with a knife and collect his blood by catching it in a cup, so that they might more truly believe the word of the Lord saying that His flesh is food and His blood is drink (Jn 6.55). By this fraction the priest means to increase [*sc* the number of morsels of the consecrated bread], at the same time he should add [*sc* unconsecrated wine to the consecrated], because then heavenly things are mingled with things earthly, and the heavens are opened to the prayer of the priest. As the priest makes the fraction, the suppliant clergy sing an antiphon because when Christ endured the pain of death all elements of the quaking earth bore witness (Mt 27.51).

The Lord's Prayer is placed there to the end that all our prayers may be concluded with the Lord's Prayer.

The Lord commanded the priests to pour down a blessing on the people through Moses, saying: "Say to Aaron and to his sons: Thus shall you bless the people: May the Lord bless you and keep you," and the rest which follows (Nb 6.22-26). Aaron then held the place of the bishop, and his sons the place of the priests. The Lord commanded them both to bless the people; but to maintain the dignity of the bishop, the holy canons have established that a bishop should give a longer blessing, the priest bestow a shorter one, saying: "Peace, faith, charity and communion in the Body and Blood of our Lord Jesus Christ be always with you." For although it is permitted to bestow that blessing which God dictated to Moses, and no one can oppose the priest because "Heaven and Earth will pass away, but my words will not pass away (Mt 24.35) [...] This Blessing, then, is given before communion so that the Mystery of Blessing may enter into a blessed vessel.

But now, with the words of the gospel, Christ shows how sweet Holy Communion is for soul and body, saying: "If you abide in me, my words will abide in you; whatsoever you ask of the Father in my name will be done to you" (Jn 15.7).

The *Trecanum* [Ps 33? Greater Doxology?] which is sung is the seal of the Catholic faith, proceeding from belief in the Trinity. For just as its first part is turned to the second, the second to the third, and, again, the third to the second, and the second again is turned to the first, so, in the mystery of the Trinity, the Father is embraced in the Son, the Son in the Holy Spirit, the Holy Spirit in the Son, the Son again in the Father.

But now, let my letter make an end. In it is shown the solemn ritual briefly described, so that in the second letter [information] about the general office may, by God's gift, be revealed to your ears.

Who lives.....

C Sermons for Great and Holy Thursday

IIC1 Ephraem the Syrian (*ca* 306-373), *Memra for the Fifth Day of Great Week* (Holy Thursday).
ed CSCO 412.27-33; *tr* this translation of E. Beck's German version in CSCO 413.51-61 was compared to the original Syriac by Edward Mathews of the Institute for Christian Oriental Research, The Catholic University of America; Mr. Mathews' suggestions for greater precision in the translation were, with gratitude, incorporated into this version.

Ephraem the Syrian, the Harp of the Holy Spirit and the glory of Syriac Christianity, was born and educated in Nisibis in Mesopotamia. He was ordained decon and began his ecclesiastical career there; but, upon the loss of Nisibis to the Persians in 363, he moved to Edessa in Syria, the center of Syriac Christianity. Ephraem has left us a set of eight sermons for Great (Holy) Week, in the form called *memra*, a sermon in verse. This sermon is the fourth in the set; it was to be chanted on Great Thursday evening, in commemoration of the Mystical Supper.

By the Holy Mar Ephraem,
Station of the Night of the Fifth of Passion Week

After Simon had been persuaded, and had proffered his feet to Jesus, and He had washed him, the Lord put His clothes back on, and reclined at the meal which was in progress. When they were all reclining at table together, Jesus arose and spoke to them: "I want you to know now why I have done this (*cf* Jn 13.12). If I do not explain them, who will understand my mysteries? If I do not give examples, who will know my will? Thus it is necessary for me to accomplish all things which the prophets have said about me. It is proper that I become the teacher and instructor for you.

O Simon, I have appointed you as my disciple, for the foundation of holy church. Earlier I called you Cephas (Jn. 1.42), because you will support my entire edifice. You are the assayer of those who will build up a church for me on the earth. If they build anything ugly, you the foundation, must reproach them. You are the source of the spring of my teaching. You are the head of my disciples. Through you I shall give drink to all nations, with the sweetness of the life which I bestow. I have chosen you to be as the firstborn in my instruction. That you may become the heir of my treasures, I have given you the keys to my kingdom (Mt 16.18). Behold, you rule over all my treasures.

Now also know and comprehend the explanation of the mysteries which you have seen, that I have made myself a servant and have served you honorably. Behold, I have humbled myself and you have seen it. I have washed your feet. I have bowed down and dried them with a towel, in the manner of a servant. You call me Teacher and Lord as indeed I am (Jn 13.13), +...+ nor am I deceptive, with a borrowed name without reality, but in fact and truth. You are my disciples, and I have chosen you before the creation and all its inhabitants existed (Jn 15.16; 17.5), and the heavenly Father bears witness that I am your God, and your Teacher. I want you to keep my commandments and to imitate me by your deeds. For if I have washed your feet, if I placed you at table and served you, how much more should you wash one another's feet and serve? I have given this example to you for a remembrance of me, to show you that the servant is not greater than his master, and the apostle not greater than He who has sent him. If you know all this, you are blessed indeed. I am not speaking of all of you, for I know those whom I have chosen; but that the scripture may be fulfilled: 'Behold, he who betrays me is at the table.' I tell you now, before it happens, so that when my word has come to pass, you may know and believe that I am" (Jn 13.14-19).

And thus was that which was written in the prophets fulfilled by Jesus, in that He took the form of a servant (Ph 2.7), and began to serve His disciples. And He so lowered Himself that He washed and dried their feet. And thus he convinced them that they should learn and teach humility.

There remained yet another act which would abolish that Passover and would become the Passover of the gentiles, a source of life until the end. Our Lord Jesus took bread (Mt 26.26) in His hands, plain bread at the beginning, and blessed it, made the sign of the Cross over it and sanctified it in the name of the Father and in the name of the Spirit, and He broke and distributed it in morsels to His disciples in His kindness. He called the bread His living body, and He filled it with Himself and with His Spirit. He stretched forth His hand and gave them the bread which His right hand had sanctified: "Take, eat, all of you (Mt 26.26) of this bread which my word has sanctified. Do not regard as bread what I have given you now +...+ eat it, and do not +disdain+ its crumbs. For this bread +which I have sanctified+ is my body. Its least crumb sanctifies thousands of thousands, and it is capable of giving life to all who eat it. Take, eat in faith, doubting not at all that this is my body. And he who eats it in faith eats in it fire and the Spirit (Mt 3.11). If anyone doubts and eats it, it is plain bread to him. He who believes and eats the bread sanctified in my name, if he is pure, it will keep him pure, if he is a sinner, he will be forgiven. He, however, who despises it, or spurns it, or insults it, he may be sure that he is insulting the Son who has called the bread His body, and truly made it so. Receive of it, eat of it, all of you, and eat in it the Holy Spirit, for it is truly my body, and he who eats it will live forever (Jn 6.51). This is the heavenly bread which has come down from on high onto the earth (Jn 6.50). This is the bread which the Israelites ate in the wilderness and did not esteem. The manna which they gathered, which came down to them, was a figure of this spiritual bread which you have now received. Take and eat of it, all of you. In this bread you are eating my body. It is the true source of forgiveness.

I am the bread of life (Jn 6.35), I am that coal which, when applied, sanctified Isaiah and his lips (Is 6.7). I am it; applied now to you, I have sanctified you through the bread. Those tongs which the Prophet saw, which took the coal from the altar (Is 6.6), depicted me in a great mystery. The prophecy went before the reality. Isaiah gazed upon me, just as you see me now. For behold, I have stretched forth my right hand, and have given the living bread to your mouths. The tongs are my right hand. I take the place of the seraphim. And that coal is my body. You are all Isaiah. And that altar is this table. That temple is this room. The Lord of that temple is I. Behold, the prophecy has been fulfilled. Isaiah received my Spirit then, he received of it and spoke about me."

After the disciples had eaten the new and holy bread, understood it, and believed that the body of Christ was their food, Jesus continued to explain and declare the entire mystery. He took the cup of wine, and mixed it and blessed it, made the sign of the Cross over it, and sanctified it, and said, giving thanks over it, that it is His blood which was to be shed. He stretched His right hand towards Simon, and gave the cup to him first, so that he could taste the blessing from it. He gave it next to the beloved one who was nearest Him (Jn 13.23). All approached and drank from the cup, that is, only eleven of them. For when Jesus had given his bread indiscriminately to the eleven, Judas also approached to receive, just as his comrades who had approached and received. But Jesus dipped the bread (Jn 13.26) in water, and thus gave it to Judas. He washed the blessing from it, and thereby marked off the offender. From this the apostles recognized that it was he who would betray him. Jesus had dipped the bread, and thus gave it to him, so that its blessing might be removed from the bread. Thus Judas did not eat the blessed bread, nor did he drink from the cup of life. He grew angry that his bread had been dipped, for he knew that he was, then, not worthy of life. And the rage about this removed him from drinking from the cup of the blood of Jesus. He went out to the crucifiers, and no longer saw the hallowed cup. Satan rushed to drive the Iscariot away from his comrades, so that he would not be a sharer with them of the living and life-giving sacrament.

The disciples had received from the right hand of Jesus the cup of salvation; they approached and all drank from it +...+ one after the other. He gave them to drink, and He explained to them that the cup which they drank +was His blood +...+ "Take, drink of it, all of you (Mt 26.27), for it is the New Covenant in my blood (Lk 22.20; 1 Co 11.25). As you have seen me doing, so also should you do for a remembrance of me (1 Co 11.25). As often as you gather in my name in the church in every point of the compass, do what I have done for a remembrance of me. Eat my body, and drink also my blood +...+ My Father gave the rainbow in the clouds that the floodwaters might be done away with by the visible rainbow (Gn 9.12ff). I, the Son of the Living Father, have come down from heaven in this sixth millennium to give the New Covenant to my church, so that through the remembrance of my body and blood and destruction and annihilation I declared upon the bold ones who sin against me, as did the men of old, might be abolished."

Our Lord taught yet another teaching of life to His disciples on that evening on which He distributed His body and mixed His blood for drink. For it was the evening which fulfilled the perfect and true Passover. It was the last of evenings, the final seal of the teachings of Christ. It was the evening which grew dark and went over from darkness into light, and to the fourteenth, on which there was no moon, the day of the new sun +...+ God had commanded the synagogue to celebrate, year after year, the feast of the unleavened bread. And on the evening of this Passover the Son gave His church the command to +celebrate+ the remembrance of the Lamb +...+ who before He was slain for us, distributed His body and blood. Thus on the evening on which the unleavened bread of the Jews was celebrated, Jesus, in the Upper Room, established the church as the heir of his blood.

O most triumphant evening, on which the mysteries were explained, the ancient covenant brought to a close, the church of the gentiles enriched! Blessed be that evening and that time, when the supper was consecrated! Blessed also be that table, which became an altar for the apostles! In this supper the Lord brought to completion the spiritual food, and mixed here the heavenly drink as Isaiah had foretold, and here He took the form of a servant (Ph 2.7) and fulfilled the word of the Son of Amos (Is 1.1; 42; 49; 52-53). In this supper He taught, teaching all about humility, because of the dissension which arose at the table among the disciples. Who surpassed the others in greatness (Lk 22.24), they thought about at that meal. He who knows the secrets of the heart at once explored their thoughts as well, and addressed them persuasively, not reproaching, with love, not with censure: "If you do not know it, know that the kings of the gentiles are their masters, and those who have rule over them are called 'benefactors,' but you should not be like the other nations. Rather, he who is greater among you should be like the least of you, and he who is called the head should be like one who serves. For who is greater, the one who reclines, or the one who serves? Behold, it is plain that the one who reclines at table is greater than the one who serves. You know that I, who am your Lord and Master, am greater. Behold, I have chosen you for my disciples. Receive and learn my commandments. And to you, who have persevered in my trials, I give the promise, just as my Father has promised me. I will give you the kingdom, and at my table I will make you glad, and the heavenly powers will wonder. You may not eat and drink with me unless you are my disciples. I shall place you as judges upon twelve thrones, and I shall gather before you the twelve tribes of Jacob. You, in my place, will judge your brothers and you will pass sentence on them" (Lk 22.25-30). Thus spoke Jesus, and they offered a hymn of praise, and went forth from the upper room to the Mount of Olives (Mt 26.30; Mk 14.26), that all which had been written might be fulfilled.

The end, and glory to God forever. Amen.

IIC2 John Chrysostom (*c* 349-407), *Sermon on the Betrayal by Judas* 5-end.
ed PG 49.380-382.

John Chrysostom, the Golden-mouthed, was a native of Antioch. He received a first-rate secular training in philosophy, and, under the pagan Libanius, the premier rhetor of his day, in rhetoric. John remained a catechumen until he came to the notice of the archbishop, Meletius, who saw to his Christian education and baptized him (*c* 368). After continued training in scripture and theology, John gave himself over to the eremetical life for some six years, until his health failed, and he returned to Antioch. There he was ordained deacon (381), and priest (386). From 386-397 he followed his particular vocation of preaching, with a success which will be apparent in the pages of this volume. On 26 February 398, John was consecrated archbishop of Constantinople against his will. His zeal, and his vehement attacks on insincerity, vice, and abuses of power cost him the favor he had initially enjoyed among the highly-placed, and won him an ever-widening circle of enemies among ecclesiastics. These trends reached a culmination in his illegal deposition at the hands of his clerical enemies at the Synod of the Oak in 403. John was exiled by the emperor, but recalled immediately. Continuing tension and violence led to another exile in 404. John Chrysostom died in exile on 14 September 407.

The grace which gleams from your mouth,
like a torch, has illumined the earth,
has laid up treasures ungrudgingly for the world,
and has manifested to us the loftiness of humility.
As you instruct us with your words,
Father John Chrysostom,
intercede with the Word, Christ our God,
for the salvation of our souls.
                    — Troparion of St. John Chrysostom.

John Chrysostom has left us a set of postbaptismal
catecheses (available in ACW 31), but none of them deals
specifically with the eucharist. Therefore, we have
included in this section an excerpt from a sermon
preached by Chrysostom on Great and Holy Thursday,
probably in Antioch. The earlier portions of this sermon
deal with the narrative of the betrayal of Christ by Judas,
and with the superiority of the Christian over the Jewish
Pascha. In our excerpt, Chrysostom speaks of Christ's
institution of the eucharist, of His perpetuation of it
through the church, and of the dispositions required for
our participation in the eucharist. Borrowings from this
sermon are apparent in the selections from John of
Damascus (IID2) and Anastasius of Antioch (VB4).

There was, then, of old a Pascha of the Jews, but now it
has been abolished, and the spiritual Pascha has come, the
one which Christ handed down at that time. For, when they
were eating and drinking, scripture says, He took bread,
broke it, and said "This is my body, broken for you for the
forgiveness of sins." Those who have been initiated know
the words. And again, the cup, saying "This is my blood,
shed for many for the forgiveness of sins." And Judas was
there when Christ said these words. This is the body, O
Judas, which you sold for thirty pieces of silver! This is the
blood concerning which, for a trifle, you made a shameless
deal with the senseless Pharisees. O the love of Christ for
mankind! O the madness, the insanity of Judas! For he sold

Christ for thirty *denarii*; but Christ, even after that, did not refuse to give, for the forgiveness of sins, that very blood which had been sold, to its seller, if he desired it. For Judas was there, indeed, and partook of the holy table. Just as He washed Judas' feet along with those of the other disciples, so too was he a sharer of the holy table, so that he would have no pretext for defense if he persevered in his wickedness. All that was His Christ showed and offered, but Judas persisted in his evil plan.

6. But it is time, finally, to approach this awesome table. Let us all, accordingly, approach with fitting seriousness and sobriety. And let there be no Judas now, let there be no one wicked, no one harboring venom, no one bearing one thing on his lips and another in his mind. Christ is here, and He who spread that table spreads this one as well. For it is not man who causes the offerings to become the body and blood of Christ, but Christ Himself, who was crucified for us. The priest stands following His model and uttering the words, but the power and the grace are God's. "This is my body," he says. These words transform the offerings. And just as the words "Increase and be multiplied, and fill the earth" (Gn 1.28), though uttered only once, became for all time what, in fact, enables our nature to produce children, so too these words, though spoken once, from then until the present time and until His Coming, at each table in the churches accomplish the perfect sacrifice.

Let no one, then, be a deceiver, no one full of evil, no one holding venom in his mind, lest his partaking lead to condemnation (1 Co 11.29). After Judas took what was offered, the devil hastened into him (Jn 13.27), not because the devil despised the Lord's body, but because he despised Judas for his shamelessness. Thus you may learn concerning those who partake unworthily of the divine mysteries, that them especially the devil invades and enters at once, as he did to Judas of old. Honors, indeed, are of benefit to those who are worthy, but those who enjoy them without deserving they propel into greater retribution.

I say these things not to frighten but to protect you. So, let no one be Judas, let no one entering here harbor the venom of wickedness. For the sacrifice is spiritual food, and, just as corporeal food, when it enters a stomach which has evil humors, further increases the illness, not because of its own nature, but because of the weakness of the stomach, so too is it the case with the spiritual mysteries. For they too, when they enter a soul full of evil, corrupt it all the more and destroy it, not because of their own nature, but because of the frailty of the soul receiving.

Accordingly, let no one have wicked thoughts within, but let us cleanse our minds, and as we are approaching a clean sacrifice (Ml 1.11), let us make our souls holy. And this can be accomplished in a single day. How? In what way? If you have anything against your enemy, get rid of your wrath, heal the wound, let go of your hostility, that you may receive healing from the table, for you are approaching the awesome and holy sacrifice. Show reverence for the goal of the sacrificial offering. The slain offering is Christ. And for whom was He slain, for what purpose? That He might make peace between heaven and earth (Col 1.20), to make you a friend of the angels, to reconcile you to the God of all, to make you, an enemy and adversary, a friend. He gave His life for those who hated Him. Will you continue in enmity with your fellow servant? And how will you be able to approach the table of peace? He did not refuse even to die for you, and do you refuse to let go of your wrath towards your fellow servant? What kind of forgiveness does such behaviour deserve? "He is abusive, and terribly rapacious," you say. But what is this? Your loss has altogether to do with money. He has not yet wounded you as Judas did Christ. But nevertheless, He has given His blood which was shed for the salvation of those who shed it. What can you say that equals this? If you do not forgive your enemy, you injure not him, but yourself. For you may have harmed him frequently in the present life, but you have rendered yourself unable to plead for pardon in the day to come. For God hates nothing so much as a man who harbors grudges, as a heart swollen, a soul seething with resentment. Hear, at least, what He says. "When you offer your gift upon the altar, and, standing there before the altar, you remember that your brother has something against you, leave your gift upon the altar, and go and be reconciled with your brother, and then offer your gift" (Mt 5.23-24).

What are you saying? "Shall I forgive him?" Christ is saying "Yes!" This sacrifice was instituted for the sake of peace with your brother. Accordingly, if the sacrifice was instituted for the sake of peace with your brother, but you do not establish peace, you partake of the sacrifice in vain, the work has become of no profit to you. Do first, then, that for the sake of which the sacrifice is offered, and then you will properly enjoy its benefits. The Son of God came down for this purpose, to reconcile our human nature to the Lord. But He did not come down for that purpose alone, but also for the purpose of making us, if we do likewise, sharers of His title. For He says: "Blessed are the peacemakers, for they shall be called sons of God" (Mt 5.9). You, according to human capacity, must do what the Onlybegotten Son of God has done, be an agent of peace, for yourself and for others. For this reason, at the very time of sacrifice He recalls to us no other commandment than that of reconciliation with one's brother, showing that it is the greatest of all.

I had wished to prolong this discourse, but what has been said is sufficient for those who pay attention, if they remember it. Let us always be mindful, dearly beloved, of these words, and also of the holy kisses and of the awe-inspiring embrace which we give one another. For this joins our minds, and causes us all to become one body, for, in fact, we all share one body. Let us blend ourselves into one body, not mingling bodies with one another, but joining our souls to one another with the bond of love. For thus will we be able with confidence to enjoy the table set before us. For we may have countless good works, but if we still harbor grudges, all is pointless and vain, and we will be unable to derive any profit unto salvation. Conscious, then, of these matters, let us abandon all anger, and, cleansing our consciences, let us, with gentleness and all forbearance, approach the table of Christ. With Him, to the Father and the Holy Spirit is all glory, honor, and power, now and ever, and unto the ages of ages. Amen.

IIC3 Theophilus of Alexandria (*d* 412), *Sermon on the Mystical Supper.*

ed PG 77.1016-1029, with improvements to the text provided by M. Richard in *Revue d' histoire ecclésiastique* 33 (1937) 46-56.

Theophilus presided over the see of Alexandria from 385 until his death in 412, when he was succeeded by his nephew Cyril. He has suffered from an evil reputation for his violent suppresssion of pagan cult centers, his about-face attack on Origenism, and his sleazy and successful plot against John Chrysostom (which culminated in Chrysostom's deposition from the see of Constantinople by the Synod of the Oak in 403). Theophilus is not without his admirers as well, both in ancient times and in the present. Recent study has moved towards a view of him as having been no better and no worse than many great bishops of his time.

Theophilus' *Sermon on the Mystical Supper* presents him to us in a microcosm, for it combines some of the most lyrical and exalted preaching on the eucharist which Christian antiquity has left to us with the violent attack on the Origenist monks with which he concludes the work. Marcel Richard, in the admirable study cited above, has restored this sermon, long attributed to Cyril, to Theophilus; he has also made sense of its text, and has established as the date of its delivery Great Thursday (29 March) in the year 400. The sermon is a splendid example of Greek festal oratory.

What is more delightful, what sweeter to those who love God, who truly long for life, than to enjoy God unceasingly and to find repose in His divine remembrances. For if those who fill themselves with food and drink, and foster their own precarious luxuries keep their bit of flesh quite thriving and bold, in how many ways will those who have concern for their souls, and are fed upon the water of refreshment

(Ps 22.2), that is, of the divine preaching, shine forth, clad and adorned, according to the Prophet, in apparel of cloth of gold (Ps 44.10)? For "they shall grow wings like eagles; they shall run, but not grow weary; they shall march, and not hunger" (Is 40.31).

Since, then, from the spiritual race-course we have arrived at the goal of the life-giving mysteries, and gifts beyond understanding are offered to us from the Lord as the provisions of immortality, come then, as many of you as seek the delight of things ineffable, who are sharers of a heavenly calling (Heb 3.1), who have, with all eagerness, put on an unfailing faith as a wedding garment, together let us hasten to the Mystical Supper. Today Christ feasts us, today Christ serves us, Christ, the Lover-of-Mankind, refreshes us. Awesome is what has been said, awesome too is what is accomplished. The Fatted Calf (Lk 15.23ff) is sacrificed; the Lamb of God who takes away the sins of the world (Jn 1.29) is slain. The Father rejoices, the Son is willingly offered in sacrifice, not today by those who war against God, but by Himself, to show that His salvific Passion was willingly endured.

Do you want me to declare to you the greatest proof of what has been said? Pay no attention to my brevity and poverty of speech, but rather to the nobility of those who proclaimed these things beforehand, and to their credibility in these matters. For it is not some low-lifes or riff-raff and common types collected from the crossroads by bright young politicos who proclaimed these things, but Solomon, great among kings, was sent ahead as the herald of the King of All. He who was the lord over lofty thrones spoke forth the mysteries of the Most High. He, bedecked with purple and with a diadem upon his head, pronounced the edicts of Him who establishes and removes kings (Dn 2.21). Do you see how great is the nobility of the herald? Observe the power of the things foretold to you through him. "Wisdom," he says, "has built herself a house, she has set down seven columns. She has slain her victims, she has mixed her wine in a bowl and has prepared her table. She has sent out her servants, inviting to her bowl with a lofty proclamation, saying: 'He who is foolish, let him turn to me.' And to those lacking wits she said: 'Come, eat my bread, and drink the wine I have mixed for you. Abandon folly, and you shall live,' and 'Seek prudence that you may thrive,' and 'Order your understanding with knowledge'" (Pr 9.1-6).

Beloved, these words are tokens of the things now being celebrated, which are the delights of the banquet here. The munificent One is here; the divine gifts are set forth; the mystical table is made ready; the life-giving bowl is mixed; the King of Glory summons, the Son of God welcomes, God incarnate, the Word, invites. The Hypostatic Wisdom of the Father has built for Himself a temple not made by hands (Heb 9.11), He distributes his body like bread and bestows His life-giving blood like wine. O awesome mystery! O inexpressible economy! O incomprehensible condescension! O unsearchable kindness! The Creator offers Himself to the creature for his enjoyment! Life itself bestows Himself on mortals for their food and drink!

"Come, eat my bread," He urges, "and drink the wine I have mixed for you. I have prepared myself to be food, I have mixed myself as drink, for those who desire me. Willingly I became flesh (Jn 1.14), though I am life. By free choice I shared in blood and flesh (Heb 2.14), though I am the Word and Hypostatic Image (Heb 1.3) of my Father, in order to save you. Taste and see that I, the Lord, am good (Ps 33.9). You tasted the fruit of disobedience, and you knew that bitter is the food of the bitter counselor. Taste now the fruit of obedience which wards off peril, and know that it is better and more profitable to obey God. You tasted out of due time, and you died. Eat in due time, and you shall live. You chose to learn by trial the outcome of disobedience. Learn also by trial the benefits of obedience. Taste and see that I, the Lord, am good. Exchange experience for experience. Through the perception of evil, you acquired the knowledge of disobedience. Through the perception of good, learn the discernment of obedience. Evilly did Adam stretch forth his hand, not holding in reverence my salvific command, unwilling to discern the Lord's ordinance and the servant's obedience, unwilling by faith to avoid the condemnation for infidelity. He stretched forth his hand, he made a dire exchange, he sold the blessed life which he had, and bought instead, by his choice, lamentable death. He fashioned for himself the death which had been foretold, but nowhere yet existed. He furnished reality for something which had no reality. He changed the clothing of the immortality that is according to grace for the corruption that is from the will. Willingly he became liable to judgement, and in his condemnation he knew the difference between the ordinance of me, the Lord, and the deceit of the Tempter, and disdaining the trustworthy decree, he invited slaughter upon himself from his infidelity, and was likened to vanity" (Ps 143.4).

"Because of all this, again I proffer the entire fruit of obedience to me to those who have died through disobedience. Taste and see that I, the Lord, am most truthful in all things. The offspring of falsehood cannot be found coming from the Truth, nor the flower of death from Life, for opposites cannot coexist. Eat me, Life, and you will live, for this is my desire. Eat the Life that does not fail, for this have I come, that you may have life, and have it more abundantly (Jn 10.10). Eat my bread, for I am the life-giving grain of the wheat (Jn 12.24), and I am the bread of life (Jn 6.35). Drink the wine which I have mixed for you, for I am the drink of immortality. Abandon the folly of impiety, and you shall live. Learn again by experience the things that are good and opportune. Regain through obedience what the disobedience of your Forefather forfeited. He was thrust out of Paradise because of his disobedience. You enter through obedience. Abandon his impiety, and replace it with piety towards me, the Creator. Seek prudence, that you may live, and correct your mind in knowledge of me. If any is quite foolish, let him turn to me, and he will know the light of truth. I am God, first and thereafter, and apart from me there is no God (Is 44.6) begotten of God the Father. I am in the Father and the Father is in me (Jn 14.11), and the Father and I are one (Jn 10.30), and he who has seen me has seen my Father also (Jn 14.9). I am the life and the resurrection (Jn 11.25). I am the bread of life (Jn 6.35, 48) who have come down from heaven (Jn 6.51), and grant life to men. Receive me as leaven into your mass (1 Co 5.6), that you may partake of the indestuctible life that is in me. I am the true vine (Jn 15.1), drink my joy, the wine I have mixed for you. For my cup is intoxicating me (Ps 22.5), intoxicating like the most powerful antidote, joy, against the grief which sprouted in Adam.

Behold, I have prepared a table for you over against those who afflict you (Ps 22.5). Opposite Eden I settled Adam who had violated that celebrated place, that by his seeing the delight no longer permitted he might suffer a ceaselessly smoldering distress. Again, over against those who afflict you have I given you a table, life-giving and joy-creating, which offers in exchange for distress unspeakable joy before those who have envied you. Eat the bread which renews your nature. Drink the wine, the exultation of immortality. Eat the bread which purges away the old bitterness, and drink the wine which eases the pain of the wound. This is the healing of your nature, this is the punishment of the one who did the injury. I became like you, for you, without being changed from my nature, that you might through me become partakers of the divine nature (2 P 1.4). Be changed accordingly, a good change, so that in timely beauty you may be turned from the world to God, from the flesh to the Spirit. I became the true vine in your race, that in me you might bear sweet-smelling fruit. Suck the richness of my ambrosia and grow fat. I am the Lord who gives food to all flesh (Ps 135.25), but especially to those who fear me, just as David foretold, saying: 'Merciful and compassionate is the Lord, He has given food to those who fear Him (Ps 110.4-5).' I once rained manna also on Israel, and I sent from heaven bread prepared without their labor (Ws 16.20). But the beloved people ignored and rejected the wonder, and Israel did not know me, and the people did not understand me (Is 1.3). But as those who ate the manna in the wilderness are dead, not thus do I present my body to you, for he who eats this bread will live forever" (Jn 6.59).

Have you understood these things, beloved? Have the Lord's words clearly shown you the ineffable mysteries of this most holy day? Or do you wish to consider its glories in greater elaboration? For we will disclose them quite gladly, and reveal to the students of the truth things upon which angels will long to gaze (1 P 1.12), not as questioning or contradicting the things which have been divinely foretold, but as making clear, from their first beginnings, the things to which these are akin. But, O considerate children, pray, I beg you, for me, wearied by life, too bent and stooped for walking, that the Lord might grant to me to speak correctly and reason worthily of what is to be said. And carrying me, O dear ones, as of old those from Israel carried the One who was born among us, let us go together to most renowned Sion, and let us gaze with the mind towards the citadel, and see how He who rules the ends of the earth made ready for the Mystical Supper, how the One who sits upon the cherubim (Ps 79.2) reclined at the supper, how He who was eaten in Egypt by way of a type takes the type to Himself, how He who was mystically sacrificed in Egypt here willingly sacrifices Himself, and, having eaten the type, as the fulfiller of types He revealed the truth, at the same time offering Himself as the food of life, so that having joined to the end of the things prophesied of Him the beginning, in turn, of the things so wisely ordained by Him, He might grant the gifts of His love for mankind which would last forever for the race of men by a common dispensation.

Receive from me the account of the divine gospels concerning these gifts. "As they were eating, Jesus took bread, broke it, gave it to His disciples and said: 'Take, eat, this is my body.' And taking the cup and giving thanks, He gave it to them saying: 'Drink of this, all of you; for this is my blood of the new covenant, shed for many for the forgiveness of sins' (Mt 26.26-28)." O the wonder! O that sacred mystery! O that divine initiation! He showed the way by means of the letter, He completed it through the spirit (2 Co 3.6). He taught through types, He gave grace through deeds. In Sion he fulfilled the law of the letter; from Sion He proclaimed the law of grace.

Let us examine the things done in the midst of the supper, what they were and how great. "He rose from the supper and put aside his garments, and taking a towel He girded Himself. Then He put water into a basin, and began to wash the feet of His disciples, and to wipe them with the towel with which He was girt" (Jn 13.4-5). What is more contrary to expectation than this, what more awe-inspiring? He who is clothed with light as with a garment (Ps 103.2) is girt with a towel. He who fettered the waters in the clouds (Jb 26.8) and sealed the abyss with His fearsome name, is bound about by a belt. He who gathers the waters of the sea like a wineskin (Ps 32.7) pours water in a bowl. He who covers His upper chambers with waters (Ps 103.3) with water washed the feet of the disciples. He who measured heaven with His hand's span, and holds the earth in His grasp (Is 40.12), with His undefiled palms wiped off the feet of servants. He for whom "every knee bends, of those in heaven, and on the earth, and under the earth" (Ph 2.10) bowed His neck to attendant servants. The angels saw and recoiled; heaven beheld and shuddered; creation observed and trembled.

"He came then to Simon Peter, and he said to Him: "Lord, are you to wash my feet? (Jn 13.6). Did I not once reveal my unworthiness, saying 'Depart from me, for I am a sinful man, Lord (Lk 5.8)'? And who am I now to presume this? Indeed, if I allow it, will not my pitiable nature, numbed and trembling, perish? Will not all creation accuse my presumption if I should be so overbold? Do not over-burden your servant, O Master. May the sun not behold the rashness of Peter and grow dark against me. Spare you servant Peter, O Lord. I am not worthy to be called your slave. You will not wash my feet forever (Jn 13.8). I tremble as I watch, I recoil as I ponder. God serves man, the King attends the subject, the Master bows to the slave. Refrain, I beg, lest all the earth learn the impiety of Peter."

But what did the wise Dispenser of the Mysteries say in reply? "You do not now know what I am doing, O Peter; you will know afterwards (Jn 13.7). Allow me, then, to complete, even for you, this sacred service. But if not, you do not have a portion with me" (Jn 13.8). When he heard these words, the Leader was altered by hearing them, and was at a loss as to his answer, saying: "Alas, O Lord, I am thwarted in every direction. Presumption is a burden, but refusal is harmful. To say no deserves punishment, but assent is most difficult for me. Nonetheless, let the command of God and not the opposition of the servant prevail, the Wisdom of God, and not the excuse of the servant. I sought to avoid overboldness, but you are commanding submission and acceptance of the sacred work. Do what you wish, O Master, do what you intend, O Lord, and, for the sake of my inheritance with you, wash not only my feet, but my hands and head as well (Jn 13.9). Now I beseech, now I importune: may I obtain the divine washing lest I be deprived of the divine grace; may I comply with your worshipful will lest I incur the loss of your exultation. I shall put forth my feet, I shall stretch out my hands, I shall bow my head, only may I not be separated from the portion of my Lord. Lest I lose the ineffable blessedness, I shall not contrive against myself by resisting God. Let all creation know that I purchase the kingdom of heaven today with a basin."

Upon the conclusion of the divine washing, the Lord sat down and said to them: "Do you know what I have done for you? You call me Lord and Teacher, and you do well to do so, for I am. If, then, I, the Lord and Teacher, have washed your feet, you too should wash one another's feet. I have given you an example, that you should do for one another as I have done for you (Jn 13.12-15). Therefore, imitate me, your Lord, that through this sacred work of mine you may become sharers of the divine nature (2 P 1.4). This best path of exaltation I portray in advance for you. I bent down once to the earth when I bestowed upon your kind existence and felicity, and taking the clay of the earth, I fashioned man, and established a living being upon the earth (Gn 2.7). And now I have seen fit to bend down that I may strengthen the foundations and pedestal of my collapsing creation. I have placed enmity and cursing between the deceiver and the deceived, a wariness of head and heel (Gn 3.15). And now I arm the wounded heel against the serpent, that it may no more limp away from the straight path. I have strengthened your feet to walk upon serpents and scorpions, and every power of the enemy, and they will not harm you at all (Lk

10.19). Through arrogance the one whispering of exaltation tore down the loftiness of the earth-born, first-created one. Smash his insolence by cheerful humility towards one another; pursue this with all your strength. I am the Lord who gives grace to the meek and loathes arrogance. Everyone who exalts himself will be humbled, and he who humbles himself will be exalted (Lk 18.14). Therefore I command you to love one another; by this shall all know that you are my disciples, if you have love for one another" (Jn 13.34-35).

Again I say, beloved, behold how great is the honor of this glorious day. The things celebrated, the presence of God, the offering of the awesome sacrifice, the gift of immortality, and the pledges of endless life summon you to this its splendor. Therefore, my dearest sons and sharers of the heavenly calling (Heb 3.1), let us imitate, to the degree we may, Him who commenced and completed our salvation, Jesus (Heb 12.2). Let us crave the lowliness which is sublime, the love which joins us to God, and a sincere faith in the divine mysteries.

But flee divisions, avoid discords, reject all profane and foolish utterances (1 Tm 6.20), but especially those which the vain-speaking and deceiving deacons of Satan have contrived. I mean those who are clad in the sleeveless garment of a new wisdom, the garment of the desert, but not of the true monk. The Lord commanded us to beware of them very much, off-guard as we are, because of the skin of their garb (Mt 7.15). They have disturbed our spiritual, peace-loving brotherhood, and have caused considerable disorder in your God-protected city. He who with a word silenced the sea (Mk 4.39) will shatter their godless barking, because they have thought ill of Christ, our true God, and have undertaken with mouths profane to destroy utterly the hope of our salvation which we have in Christ—I mean the Resurrection. Where are they now, these God-deniers and monastic wolves who have clad themselves with piety and deny its power, these pseudo-christians who reject the consubstantiality of Christ with the almighty Father because of the Incarnation? Let them tell us, then, these praters, most unreasonable of all: Whose body do the nurslings of the church consume, or at what streams do Truth's children refresh themselves? For if it is the body of God which is distributed, then true God is Christ the Lord, and not mere man or an angel, as they say, a servant and one of the bodiless ones. And if the blood of God is the drink, then again no naked God is that One of the adorable Trinity, the Son of God, but God the Word made man. But if the body of Christ is the food and the blood of Christ the drink, and, as they say, He is mere man, then how is He proclaimed to those who approach the sacred table to be productive of eternal life? And how is it that He is divided here, and everywhere, and yet is not diminished? For mere body is no source of life for those who receive it. Or do they denounce us as false witnesses to God who loves the truth because we proclaim the truth openly and teach the mysteries given by God? But may God's grace excuse me for mentioning these adversaries in this most holy feast.

Let us, then, receive the body of Life Himself who for our sake dwelt in our body as the divinely inspired John says: "Life was made visible" (1 Jn 1.2), and again, "And the Word became flesh, and dwelt among us" (Jn 1.14). This Word is Christ, the Son of the Living God (Mt 16.16), who is One of the Holy Trinity. And let us drink His holy blood for the atonement of our transgressions, and for participation in the immortality that is in Him, all the while believing that He remains Priest and Victim, He the One offering and the One offered, the One receiving and the One distributed, not dividing into two persons the divine and inseparable and, indeed, unconfused unity of One of the all-honorable Trinity. To Him be glory and adoration, along with the Father and the Holy Spirit unto the ages of ages. Amen.

D Encyclopedias

IID1 Isidore of Seville (*c* 560-636), *On Church Services* 1.13-18.

ed PL 83.750-757; *lit* translation of anaphora of Mozarabic liturgy in PEER 109-111.

Born into a prominent Hispano-Roman family, Isidore was educated under the direction of his brother Leander, archbishop of Seville *c* 584-600. Isidore succeeded to his brother's see upon Leander's death.

Isidore's *On Church Services*, one of his earlier works, is dedicated to another of his brothers, Fulgentius, bishop of Ecija. It could more aptly be entitled *On the Origins of Church Services*, for in it Isidore operates on an assumption, inherited from classical antiquity, that knowledge of something's origin or invention is a crucial step towards understanding its meaning.

This selection amply demonstrates Isidore's working out of his thesis, which he borrowed from St. Augustine's First Letter to Januarius (IVB3), that "The things which are done in the services of the church are found to have been established in part by the authority of Sacred Scripture, in part by apostolic tradition and by the custom of the universal church." Book One of *On Church Services* deals with the church and churches (1-2), with liturgical activities (3-23), feasts (24-36), and fasts (37-45); Book Two is concerned with ecclesiastical ministries and per-

sons (1-20), and Christian initiation (21-27). Our excerpt
includes those portions of Book One which deal with the
eucharistic liturgy.

13. Concerning the Praises.

1. The *Praises*, that is, to sing *Alleluia*, is a song of the
Hebrews; its exposition consists of the translation of two
words, that is, *Praise of God.* John makes report about its
mystery in the Apocalypse (19.6), that by the revelation of
the Spirit he saw, and heard the voice of the heavenly army
of angels, like the voice of many waters, and like the voice of
mighty thunders, saying *Alleluia.*

2. Therefore no one should have any doubt that this
mystery of praise, if it be celebrated with worthy faith and
devotion, is joined to the angels. But *Alleluia*, just as also
Amen, is not at all translated from the Hebrew into the
Latin language; not because they cannot be translated, but,
as the learned say, their ancient integrity is maintained
because of their more venerable orgin.

3. In the African lands *Alleluia* is sung not at all times, but
only on the Lord's Days and in the fifty-day period after the
Resurrection of the Lord, to signify the future resurrection
and joy. But among us, according to the ancient tradition of
the Spaniards, except on fastdays and during Lent, *Alleluia*
is sung at all times, for it is written: "His praise is always in
my mouth" (Ps 33.2).

4. That the *Alleluia* is sung at the conclusion, after the
completion of the psalmody or the proclaiming of the readings, the Church does this in hope of the future, indicating
that after the announcement of the Kingdom of Heaven,
which is proclaimed in this life through the two Testaments,
we will have no activity in the future save the praise of God,
as it is written: "Blessed are they who dwell in your
house...they will praise you unto ages of ages" (Ps 83.5).
For that reason the Book of Psalms is also concluded with
praise [*sc* with *Alleluia*, see beginning of Pss 145-150], that it
may be shown that this same praise will be eternal after the
end of the world.

14. Concerning Offertoria.

The Book of Ecclesiasticus indicates that the ancients were accustomed to sing the *offertoria* which are sung in honor of the oblations, when victims were being sacrificed, for it says as follows: The priest, it says, "stretched forth his hand for the libation and poured a libation of the blood of the grape, and he poured it upon the foundation of the altar as a divine odor to the Highest Prince. Then the sons of Aaron cried out, and with wrought trumpets they sounded forth, and caused a mighty sound to be heard for a memorial with God" (Sr 50.16). No differently now too in the sound of the trumpet, that is, in the proclaiming of the voice we are enkindled with song; at once with heart and mouth we shout forth jubilant praises to the Lord in that true Sacrifice by whose blood the world has been saved.

15. Concerning the Mass and its Prayers

The order of Mass and of the prayers by which the sacrifices offered to God are consecrated was first established by Saint Peter. The entire world accomplishes the celebration of the Mass in one and the same way.

The first of these is the prayer of admonition to the people, to stir them up for prayer to God.

The second prayer is one of invocation to God, that He might mercifully receive the prayers of the faithful and their offerings.

The third is made on behalf of those making offerings, or on behalf of the faithful departed that they might obtain forgiveness through this sacrifice.

2. After these, the fourth prayer is made before the Kiss of Peace, that we might all be reconciled to one another in charity, and thus worthily be joined together by the sacrament of the Body and Blood of Christ, for the indivisible Body of Christ does not admit of anyone's dissension.

Next, as the fifth prayer, the *illatio* is said at the blessing of the offering. In it also the entirety of earthly creatures and heavenly powers is summoned to the praise of God, and "Hosanna in the highest" is sung, because when the Saviour was born, from the line of David, salvation came to the world, even to the heights.

3. There follows, as the sixth prayer, the consecration of the Sacrament, that the offering made to God, sanctified by the Holy Spirit, may be changed into the Body and Blood of Christ.

The final prayer is the one with which our Lord taught His disciples to pray, saying: "Our Father, who art in heaven." In this prayer, as the holy fathers have written, seven petitions are contained: in the first three, things eternal are sought; in the following four, things temporal, but their acquisition is sought on account of things eternal.

4. For when we say: "Hallowed be thy name, thy kingdom come, thy will be done, on earth as it is in heaven," these three are, to be sure, begun here, but they are hoped for in that life when the blessing of God, His will, and kingdom among the saints will endure immortally. But for the present, our daily bread which is given both to soul and body is asked for here; here too, after the sustenance of bread, we ask for forgiveness on the basis of fraternal forgiveness; here we ask that we may not enter into the temptation of sin; here, after all the rest, we beg for God's help that we may be delivered from evils. There, on the contrary, there are none of these things.

5. And so, it was this prayer which our Saviour taught; in it are contained both the hope of the faithful and the confession of sins. In foretelling this prayer, the Prophet said: "And it will come about that everyone who will call upon the name of the Lord will be saved" (J1.2.32).

Now these are the seven prayers of the Sacrifice. They have been handed on by evangelical and apostolic teaching, and their numerical scheme seems to have been established both because of the sevenfold universality of Holy Church (Rv 1.4?), and on account of the septiform Spirit of Grace by whose gift the things which are offered are made holy.

16. Concerning the Nicene Creed.

The creed which is proclaimed by the people at the time of the sacrifice was produced by the discussion of the three hundred eighteen holy fathers at the Council of Nicea. Its rule of the true faith excels in so many mysteries of the teaching of the faith that it addresses every aspect of the faith, and there is almost no heresy with which it does not deal in its individual words or sentences. For it tramples upon all the errors of impiety and all blasphemies of Faithlessness, and for that reason it is proclaimed in a common confession by the people in all churches.

17. Concerning Blessings.

The ancient blessing by Moses reveals and sanctions the giving of a blessing by the priests to the people. The blessing was ordered to be given to the people under the sacrament of a threefold invocation. For the Lord said to Moses: "Thus will you bless my people, and I will bless them: May the Lord bless you and keep you. May the Lord make His face to shine upon you and have mercy on you. May the Lord turn His countenance to you and give you peace" (Nb 6.23-26).

18. Concerning Sacrifice.

Now the sacrifice which is offered to God by Christians was first instituted by Christ, Our Lord and Teacher, when He revealed His Body and Blood to the apostles before He was handed over, as we read in the Gospel: "Jesus took bread and the cup, and blessed and gave to them" (Mt 26.26). Melchisedech, The King of Salem, was the first to offer this sacrament figuratively as a type of the Body and Blood of Christ, and was the first to present, by way of an image, the mystery of such a great sacrifice. For he showed the likeness of our Lord and Saviour, Jesus Christ, the

Eternal Priest, to whom is said: "You are a priest forever according to the order of Melchisedech" (Ps 109.4; Heb 7.21).

2. Christians have been commanded to offer this sacrifice upon the abandonment and termination of the Jewish victims whose offering was commanded in the slavery of the old people.

He offered the sacrifice not in the morning, but after dinner in the evening. For thus did it suit Christ to accomplish this around the evening of the day, so that the very hour of sacrifice might indicate the evening of the world. Accordingly, the apostles did not communicate fasting, because it was necessary that the figurative pascha first be fulfilled, and that thus anew they might pass on to the true sacrament of Pascha.

3. It was a part of this mystery that the disciples first did not receive the Body and Blood of the Lord fasting. But now it is received through the entire church by those who are fasting. For thus was it pleasing to the Holy Spirit, through the apostles, that in honor of so great a sacrament the Lord's Body should enter into the mouth of a Christian before other foods, and on that account this practice is observed through the whole world. For the bread which we break is the Body of Christ (1 Co 10.16) who said: "I am the living bread who have come down from heaven" (Jn 6.51). Moreover, the wine is His Blood, the wine of which it was written: "I am the true vine" (Jn 15.1, 5). But bread, because it strengthens the body, is for that reason called the Body of Christ, and wine, because it forms blood in the flesh, is on that account referred to the Blood of Christ.

4. These are visible things, but consecrated by the Holy Spirit, they change into the Sacrament of the Divine Body. Accordingly, as Saint Cyprian says, the cup of the Lord is offered mixed with wine and water because "...we see that in the water the people is understood... [there follows an extended quotation from Cyprian's Letter 63.13; see IVA4].

7. Some say that unless sin stands in the way, the Eucharist should be received daily, for we ask that this Bread be

given to us daily, as the Lord commands, when we say "Give us this day our daily bread." They are right about this, if they receive with religion and devotion and humility, and do not do it relying on their own righteousness with the presumption of pride. Otherwise, if one's sins are such that they remove him from the altar as a dead man, penance should first be done, and then this salvific medicine should be received. For he who eats unworthily, eats and drinks judgement for himself (1 Co 11.29). To receive unworthily is this, to receive at a time when one ought to be doing penance.

8. Otherwise, if the sins are not so great that one is judged in need of excommunication, he should not separate himself from the medicine of the Lord's Body, lest, perchance, he be separated from the Body of Christ by being kept away from it by too long an abstinence. For it is clear that those are alive who are in contact with His Body. Wherefore it is to be feared that, while someone is long separated from the Body of Christ, he will remain a stranger to salvation, as He says: "Unless you eat the flesh of the Son of Man, and drink His blood, you will not have life in you" (Jn 6.54). He who already has desisted from sin should not cease to communicate.

9. Married people, however, should abstain from intercourse and give time to prayer for a number of days, and thus then approach the Body of Christ. Let us read again the books of Kings, and we will find that the priest Abimelech would not give David and his men any of the showbread unless he first asked whether they were pure from women, not indeed from others' women, but from their own wives. And unless he heard that they had been free from intercourse from yesterday and the day before yesterday, he would by no means have given them the loaves which he had first refused (1 S 21).

10. There is as great a difference between the showbread and the Body of Christ as there is between a shadow and the body, between an image and the truth, between the types of things to come and the very things which were prefigured by

the types. Therefore, some days should be selected wherein one may live in continence beforehand, so that he may worthily approach so great a sacrament.

11. We believe that the practice of offering the Sacrifice for the repose of the faithful departed and of praying for them has been handed down from the apostles themselves, because the practice is observed through all the world. For the Catholic Church holds to this, and unless it believed that sins could be forgiven to the faithful departed, it would not give alms or offer the Sacrifice to God on behalf of their souls. The Lord also, when He says: "He who sins against the Holy Spirit, the sin will not be forgiven him, neither in this world nor in the world to come" (Mt 12.32), declares that sins are to be forgiven certain ones then, and are to be cleansed away in a purgatorial fire. Therefore, in a certain passage it was said by Saint Augustine that: "The souls of the departed are" without a doubt "eased by the piety of their living friends, when the Sacrifice . . . is offered on their behalf or alms are given. . .," if any "has prepared for himself some merit while he yet lived in the body whereby whatever is done on his behalf may be of benefit. For such things are not of benefit to all. And why are they not of benefit to all except because of the difference between the lives which each led in the body? . . . In the case of the very good, such works are a thanksgiving; in the case of the not very bad, they are a propitiation; in the case of the very bad, even if these works are of no help to the dead, they are some sort of consolation to the living. In the case of those aided by these works, the aid consists either of their forgiveness being more complete, or, at least, of their condemnation being more endurable (*Enchiridion* Ch. 110)."

IID2 John of Damascus (*c* 675-*c* 749), *An Accurate Exposition of the Orthodox Faith* 86 (= 4.13).

ed B. Kotter, *Die Schriften des Johannes von Damaskos* 2 (Berlin, 1973) 191-198; *tr* FC 37.354-361, revised; *lit* E. P. Benoit, *The Eucharistic Teaching of St. John Damascene* (diss., Washington, D.C., 1946) dated, anachronistic, but very useful.

Yuhannāh ibn Sargīs ibn Mansūr, better known as John of Damascus, the glory of the Arab Christians, was born in Damascus *c* 675 to a prominent Christian family. His grandfather (Mansur) and his father (Sergius) were employed in the civil service of the muslim caliphs. John seems initially to have followed them in such a career, but he retired around or before 715 into the monastery of St. Saba near Jerusalem. Sometime before 726 he was ordained to the priesthood by the Patriarch of Jerusalem, John V. John of Damascus spent the rest of his life at St. Saba, writing to expound and defend the faith.

The work from which our selection is taken is part of a vast compilation entitled *The Fount of Knowledge*, which John wrote at the request of his friend and fellow-monk of St. Saba, Kosmas Melodos (see VIC2), sometime after Kosmas became bishop of Maiuma in 743. *The Fount of Knowledge* is divided into three sections: an introduction to philosophy, called *Philosophical Chapters* or, later, *Dialectica*; a summary catalogue of heresies, called *Heresies in Epitome, How They Began and Whence They Took Their Origin*; and the section from which this excerpt is drawn, *An Accurate Exposition of the Orthodox Faith*.

John promised in his introductory letter to Kosmas that he would add nothing of his own, but, rather, would simply gather and arrange the teachings of his predecessors. In fact, he added his genius for order, his insight, his sense of balance, and his extraordinary piety. This chapter on the eucharist is a brilliant summary and a clear and definitive statement. Not for his hymns and sermons alone does John of Damascus deserve the nickname *Chrysorrhoas*, "Flowing-with-gold."

God who is good, and altogether good, and more than good, who is goodness throughout, by reason of the surpassing wealth of His goodness did not suffer Himself, that is, His nature alone to be good, shared in by no one else. For that reason He made first the spiritual and heavenly powers, next the visible and sensible universe, next man, of the spiritual and sensible. All things, therefore, which He made, share in His goodness according to their existence. For He Himself is existence to all, since in Him are the things that exist, not only because it was He who brought them out of non-existence into existence, but because His energy preserves and maintains all that He made, and especially the living creatures. For they partake of His goodness both in that they exist and in that they share in life. But in truth those of them which have reason have a still greater share, both because of what has already been said, and also because of the very faculty of reason which they possess. For they are somehow more akin to Him, even though He is incomparably higher than all of them.

Man, however, being created with reason and free will, received the power of continual union with God, through his own choice, if, indeed, he abides in goodness, that is, in obedience to His Creator. Since, however, he transgressed the command of His Maker and became liable to death and corruption, the Maker and Fashioner of our kind, through the depth of His mercy (Lk 1.78), was made like unto us (Heb 2.17), becoming man in all things except sin (Heb 4.15), and was united to our nature. For since He imparted to us His own image and His own Spirit, and we did not keep them safe, He Himself took a share in our poor, weak nature, in order that He might cleanse us and make us incorruptible, and establish us once more as partakers of His divinity.

But it was necessary that not only the firstfruits of our nature should partake in the higher good, but also every man who desired it, and that a second birth should take place, and that it should feed on a new nourishment, one suitable to the birth, and thus the measure of perfection be attained. Through His birth, that is, His Incarnation, and

Baptism, and Passion, and Resurrection He delivered our nature from the sin of our first-parent, from the death of corruption, and became the firstfruits of the Resurrection (1 Co 15.20), and made Himself the way and model and pattern (1 P 2.21), in order that we, too, following in His footsteps, may become by adoption what He is Himself by nature, sons and heirs of God and co-heirs with Him (Rm 8.17). He gave us, therefore, as I said, a second birth, in order that, just as we who are born of Adam are made like him and are the heirs of the curse and corruption, so also being born of Him we may be made like to Him and inherit His incorruption and blessing and glory.

But since Adam is spiritual, it was necessary that both the birth and likewise the food should be spiritual too, but since we are of a double and compound nature, it is necessary that both the birth should be double and, likewise, the food compound. We were, therefore, given a birth by water and Spirit, I mean by holy baptism; and the food is the very Bread of Life, Our Lord Jesus Christ, who came down from heaven (Jn 6.51). For when He was about to take on Himself a voluntary death for our sakes, on the night on which He gave Himself up, He established a New Covenant for His holy disciples and apostles, and through them for all who believe in Him. In the upper room, then, of holy and glorious Sion, after He had eaten the old passover with His disciples and had fulfilled the Old Covenant, He washed His disciples' feet, providing a symbol of holy baptism. Then, having broken bread, He gave it to them, saying: "Take, eat; this is my body, broken for you, for the forgiveness of sins." Likewise also He took the cup of wine and water and shared it with them saying: "Drink of this, all of you; for this is my blood of the New Covenant, which is shed for you, for the forgiveness of sins. Do this in remembrance of me. For as often as you eat this bread and drink this cup, you proclaim the death of the Son of Man and confess His Resurrection until He comes."

If, then, the Word of God is living and energizing (Heb 4.12), and the Lord has done all that He willed (Ps 134.6); if

He said "Let there be light" and there was light, "Let there be a firmament" and there was a firmament (Gn 1.3, 6); if the heavens were established by the word of the Lord and all the host of them by the breath of His mouth (Ps 32.6); if the heaven and earth, water and fire and air and the whole universe of these were perfected by the word of the Lord, and also this celebrated living creature, man; if God the Word of His own free will became man, and fashioned flesh for Himself from the pure and undefiled blood of the Holy Virgin without the aid of seed, can He not then make the bread His body and the wine and water His blood? He said in the beginning "Let the earth bring forth the green herb" (Gn 1.11), and even until now, when the rain comes, it brings forth its proper offspring, urged on and enabled by the divine command. God said "This is my body," and "This is my blood," and "Do this," and it is done at His omnipotent command until He comes. For its was in this sense that He said "...until He comes." And the overshadowing power of the Holy Spirit becomes, through the *epiklesis*, the rain to this new cultivation. For just as God made all that He made by the energy of the Holy Spirit, so also now the energy of the Spirit performs those things which are above nature, which it is not possible to comprehend except by faith alone. "How shall this be," said the Holy Virgin, "since I know not man?" And the Archangel Gabriel answered her: "The Holy Spirit shall come upon you, and the power of the Most High shall overshadow you" (Lk 1.34, 35). And now you ask how the bread becomes Christ's body and the wine and water Christ's blood, and I say to you: The Holy Spirit comes and does those things which surpass description and understanding.

Further, bread and wine are employed, for God knows human frailty. For in general, man turns away discontentedly from what is not well-worn by custom; and so, with His usual condescension He does things which are beyond nature through the accustomed things of nature. And, just as in the case of baptism, since it is man's custom to wash himself with water and anoint himself with oil, He joined the grace of the Spirit to the oil and water and made it the bath of regeneration; in like manner, since it is man's custom to eat bread and drink water and wine, he joined his Divinity to these and has made them His body and blood, in order that we may rise to what is supernatural through what is familiar and natural.

The body from the Holy Virgin is in truth body united to divinity, not because the very body which was taken up (Mk 16.19) descends from heaven, but because the bread itself and the wine are changed into God's body and blood. But if you ask how this happens, it is enough for you to hear that it is through the Holy Spirit, just as also from the Holy Theotokos through the Holy Spirit the Lord made flesh to subsist for Himself and in Himself. And we know nothing more, save that the word of God is true and energizes and is omnipotent; but the manner of this cannot be searched out. But one can put it well thus: just as in nature the bread by the eating, and the wine and the water by the drinking are changed into the body and blood of the one who eats and drinks, and do not become a different body from his former one, so the bread of the *prothesis* and the wine and water are supernaturally changed by the *epiklesis* and coming down of the Holy Spirit into the body and blood of Christ, and are not two but one and the same.

Wherefore, to those who partake worthily with faith, it is for the forgiveness of sins and for life eternal and for the safe-guarding of soul and body; but to those who partake unworthily without faith, it is for chastisement and punishment, just as also the death of the Lord became life and incorruption for the enjoyment of eternal blessedness to those who believe, while to those who do not believe and to the murderers of the Lord (1 Co 11.27) it is for everlasting chastisement and punishment.

The bread and the wine are not merely types of the body and blood of Christ, not at all, but the deified body of the Lord itself. For the Lord has said "This is my body," not "This is a type of my body," and "my blood," not "a type of my blood." And on a previous occasion He said to the Jews: "Unless you eat the flesh of the Son of Man, you do not have life in you. For my flesh is true food and my blood is true drink," and again, "He who eats me shall live" (Jn 6.54-58).

Wherefore, with all fear and a pure conscience and certain faith let us approach, and it will be to us altogether as we believe, doubting nothing. Let us honor it in all purity of soul and body, for it is twofold. Let us approach it with burning desire, and with our hands forming the shape of the Cross, let us receive the body of the Crucified. And touching our eyes and lips and brows to it, let us partake of the Divine Coal, in order that the fire of the longing in us, with the additional heat received from the Coal, may completely burn up our sins and illumine our hearts, and that we may be inflamed and divinized by association with the divine fire. Isaiah saw a coal (Is 6.6), but a coal is not plain wood, but wood united to fire. In like manner, the bread of communion is not plain bread, but bread united to divinity. But a body which is united to divinity is not one nature, but has one nature belonging to the body and another belonging to the divinity which is united to it, so that both together are not one nature but two.

With bread and wine Melchisedech, the priest of the Most High God, received Abraham on his return from the slaughter of the alien tribes (Gn 14.18; Hb 7.1). That table prefigured this Mystical Table, just as that priest was a type and an image of Christ, the true Highpriest, for "You are a priest forever according to the order of Melchisedech" (Ps 109.4; Heb 7.17). The loaves of proposition were an image of this bread (Ex 25.30 etc.). This surely is that pure and bloodless sacrifice which the Lord through the Prophet said would be offered to Him from the rising to the setting of the sun (Ml 1.11).

The body and blood of Christ make for the support of our soul and body, without being consumed or suffering corruption, not heading for the privy (Mt 15.17), by no means, but for our being and preservation, a protection against all kinds of harm, a cleansing from all uncleanness, as if He were to take adulterated gold, and purify it by the refining fire, lest in the future we be condemned with this world, for they cleanse diseases and all kinds of calamities. Accordingly the divine Apostle says: "For if we would judge ourselves, we would not be judged. But when we are judged, we are corrected by the Lord, so that we may not be condemned with the world" (1 Co 11.29). This too is what he says: "So that he who partakes of the body and blood of Christ unworthily, eats and drinks condemnation to himself" (1 Co 11.29). Being purified by this, we are united to the body of Christ and to His Spirit, and we become the body of Christ.

This bread is the firstfruits of the bread to come, which is superessential. For the word "superessential" signifies either what is to come, that is, of the age to come, or else that which we take for the preservation of our essence. Whether then it is in this sense or that, it is fitting to speak so of the Lord's body. For the Lord's flesh is life-giving spirit because it was conceived of the Life-giving Spirit. For "What is born of the Spirit is spirit" (Jn 3.6). But I do not say this to take away the nature of the body, but I wish to make clear its life-giving and divine character.

But if some persons called the bread and wine antitypes of the body and blood of the Lord, as did the divinely-inspired Basil [sec VA3], they said so not after the consecration but before the consecration, so naming the offering itself.

It is called a participation, for through it we partake of the divinity of Jesus. It is called communion, and it truly is, because through it we have communion with Christ and share in His flesh and His divinity; also, through it we have communion and are also united with one another. For we partake of one bread, we all become one body of Christ and one blood, and members one of another (Ep 4.25), considered to be of one body with Christ.

With all our strength, therefore, let us beware lest we receive communion from or grant it to heretics. "Give not that which is holy to dogs," says the Lord, "nor cast your pearls before swine" (Mt 7.6), lest we become partakers in their dishonor and condemnation. For if there really is union with one another, then we are truly united by choice with all those who partake with us. For this union is effected by choice and not against our will.

They are called antitypes of future things, not as though they were not truly Christ's body and blood, but because now through them we partake of Christ's divinity, while then we shall partake spiritually through vision alone.

III "At His command": Scriptural Exegesis and the Eucharist

Introduction

This section contains exegetical texts which include teachings on the eucharist. That does not imply that all such texts in this volume are gathered in this section (see materials from John Chrysostom in Section IV), nor that all exegetical material bearing on the eucharist is contained only in professedly exegetical homilies and in commentaries (see below and Appendix).

IIIA. The first part is devoted to passages of Old Testament exegesis. The limited number of selections here is potentially quite misleading, and a few words of explanation are in order. An entire volume could be devoted to selections of Old Testament exegesis touching upon the eucharist, for the prophecies and foreshadowings of the eucharist perceived by the fathers in the Old Testament are superabundant. So many of the standard types and prophecies are dealt with—or, at least, brought up—in other sections of this volume that it seemed best, in the interests of economy, not to include formal exegesis concerning them here, but to list the selections in which they occur in an Appendix to this Introduction, leaving it to the reader's zeal and diligence to pursue them in patristic exegetical texts. Therefore, Section IIIA includes comments on Old Testament texts in which we would not necessarily expect to find a eucharistic reference. The purpose of this approach is twofold: to point up the very fact of references to the eucharist in the exegesis of unlikely texts; and to provide a more balanced view of Origen's thinking on the eucharist than might be obtained from IIIB1 alone.

IIIB. The second part of Section III contains exegesis of specifically eucharistic texts from the New Testament: the Institution Narratives from Matthew (IIIB1, IIIB3, IIIB8), Luke (IIIB10), and First Corinthians (IIIB2, IIIB6), and Christ's eucharistic discourse from John 6 (IIIB4, IIIB7, IIIB9). Additional comments on the Institution Narrative are scattered through the volume—see especially IIA3, IIA4, IIC1, IIC2, IID2, IVA2, IVA3, IVA4, and the conflated institution narratives (themselves a kind of comment) in the eucharistic prayers in VA2-4. For additonal comments on John 6 see especially IIA4, IIIA5, IVA7, and IVA8. The collection in IIIB of multiple specimens of exegesis of the same texts requires no apology, given the variety of exegesis and the dramatically different exegetical styles found here. Selection IIIB5, John Chrysostom's remarks on I Co 10.16-18 ("The cup of blessing..."), fits into neither of the categories of text just described, but is given as a supplement to Chrysostom's very pastoral treatment of the Institution Narrative of 1 Co 11.13-28.

Two other New Testament texts associated with the eucharist which figure prominently elsewhere in this volume are 1 Co 10.17 ("We, though many, are one bread, one body"), crucial to St. Augustine's teaching (see IB6, IIA6.1-3, IIIB7), and Mt 5.23-25 ("Therefore, if you are offering your gift at the altar..."; see Introduction to IVB).

Suggestions for further reading:

C. P. M. Jones, "The New Testament" (with bibl.) in SL 148-169; Bouley 69-87.

Appendix Introduction: The Eucharist and the Old Testament.

1) Christ as Fulfiller of Types (especially of the Passover Observance) in the Institution of the Eucharist:

IIC1, IIC2, IIC3, IIIB3, IVA3

2) The Eucharist as the Fulfillment (and Abolition) of the Sacrifices of the Old Law:

IB6, IIA5, IIA7.1, IIIA2, IIIB1, IIIB2, IIIB3, IIIB6, IVA2

3) Individual Types of the Eucharist:

Noah (Gn 9.20-27): IVA4

Melchisedech (Gn 14.18-19; Ps 109.4): IB5, IB6, IIA4, IIA7.1, IIA8, IID1, IID2, IVA4, VA4, VB1

Passover and Paschal Lamb: IIA5, IIB1, IIC3, IID1, IIIB3, IIIB4, IVA3, IVA4, VB4

Manna (Ex 16.13f; Nb11.7f; Ws 16.20-21): IIA8, IIC1, IIC3, IIIB4, IIIB7, IVC3

Fine Flour (Lv 14.10): IB3

Showbread (Lv 24.5-9): IIA3, IID1, IID2

4) Individual Prophecies of the Eucharist:

Sacrifice of Abel: IB6, IVA2, VA4

Blessing of Judah (Gn 49.11): IIA1, IIA8, (with Is 63.2)   IVA3, IVA4

Ps 22: IIA3, IIA4, IIC3, IIIB1, IVA4, VB2, VB3

Ps 33.9: IB5, IIA3, IIC3, VB1, VB2

Pr 9.1-5: IB3, IB6, IIA8, IIC3, IIIA4, IVA4, VC2

Isaiah's Coal (Is 6.6-7): IIB1, IIC1, IID2

Malachy 1.10-12: IB3, IIA7.1, IID2, IVA2, IVB1

A. Old Testament Exegesis

IIIA1 Origen (c 185-c 254), *Homily on Exodus* No. 13.3. *ed* GCS *Origines* 6.273-274; *lit* P. Jacquemont in EEC 183-193.

In Origen we meet the worthy successor of Clement as head of the Catechetical School of Alexandria. Origen was born c 185 in a devout Christian family, and headed the Catechetical School from 203-231. He was driven from Alexandria by the malice of local bishops, and settled at Caesarea in Palestine, where he directed a school of theology for some twenty years. He suffered torture and prolonged imprisonment in the Decian Persecution, and died c 254.

Origen was the greatest theological writer of his time, and a sign-of-contradiction for ages to come. He was an apologist, a most original speculative theologian, a mystic, and, above all, a student and expositor of scripture. Origen's influence on the church of the fathers is inestimable, if often unacknowledged. The unfortunate Origenist controversy of the fourth and fifth centuries led to the suppression of much of his writing. Those exegetical works from which excerpts have been taken for this volume hang on a sometimes thin, Latin thread. A comment of Origen on Mt 26.23 ("He who dips his hand into the dish with me, he will betray me.") is a fitting epigram on his sufferings at the hands of the ignorant and envious, during his life and after his death: "Such are all in the church who plot against their brothers in whose company they have been frequently at the same table of the body of Christ and at the same cup of His blood."

Origen's teaching about the eucharist is, as with much else in his thought, complex to the point of obscurity. A recent (1978), careful study by Lothar Lies has explored the "spiritualizing tendency" of Origen's concepts of the eucharist. Again, Hans Urs von Balthasar has written lately, in his Preface to the Origen volume of the Paulists' *The Classics of Western Spirituality*: "It has been erroneously held that Origen spiritualized the Eucharist; on the contrary, he sacramentalized Scripture, stating that God's Spirit dwells in it with the same real presence as it does in the church." Origen's eucharistic teaching seems to be two-tiered, at one level quite traditional and orthodox, at another idiosyncratic and esoteric, in which the Sacrament of the Body and Blood of Christ is viewed as a plenary symbol, at once, to use later categories, historical, allegorical, moral, and anagogic.

Origen delivered his homilies on the historical books of the Old Testament (Genesis through 1 Samuel) in Caesarea sometime in the period 238-244, perhaps in 239-242. The thirteen homilies on Exodus survive in the rather free Latin translation by Rufinus of Aquileia, made in the period 403-405 (on Rufinus as translator, see R. E. Heine in FC 71.30-39).

In Homily 13, Origen comments on the description of the building of the Mosaic Tabernacle in Exodus 35*ff.* He offered an allegorical-moral interpretation of the materials required for the building of the Tabernacle and the making of its contents. He enclosed within his running commentary this personal prayer, and a warning, based upon the reception of the eucharist, about the need for the careful reception of the word of God as well.

O Lord Jesus, grant me to have some memorial in your tabernacle. I would prefer, if it were possible, that there be something of mine in the gold from which the throne of mercy is fashioned (Ex 37.6), or with which the ark is covered (Ex 37.1), or from which the candelabrum of light and its lamps are made (Ex 37.17*ff*). Or, if I have not gold, may I be found offering something of silver which could be of use for the columns, or, rather, for their bases (Ex 36.36,38). Or, at least, may I be counted worthy to have some bronze in the tabernacle, whence the clasps could be made (Ex 36.18), and the rest of the things which the word of God describes. Would that it were even possible for me to be one of the princes, and to offer gems for the adornment of the ephod and the pectoral of the priest (Ex 35.27). But because these things are beyond me, may I at least be found worthy to have goats' hair (Ex 36.14) in the tabernacle of God, only so that I may not be found to be barren and unproductive in all things. EACH ONE, therefore, AS HE HAS CONCEIVED IN HIS HEART (Ex 35.6). See that you conceive, see that you hold fast, so that the things which have been said may not, perhaps, slip away and perish. I wish to admonish you by examples from religious observance. You who are accustomed to attend the divine mysteries know how, when you receive the body of the Lord, you keep it with all caution and reverence, lest any part of it fall, lest anything of the consecrated gift slip away. For you believe, and rightly so, that you are guilty, if anything of it fall away through your negligence. But if you employ such caution, quite properly, in keeping the body of Christ, how can you think that it is less of a sin to have treated the word of God with negligence than to treat His body with negligence?

IIIA2 Origen (*c* 185-*c* 254), *Homily on Leviticus* No. 9.10.

ed SC 287.120-122.

Origen delivered his homilies on Leviticus in the same cycle as those on Exodus. Sixteen are extant, again in the translation prepared by Rufinus in 403-405. This is Ori-

gen's brief comment on a part of the rite of Atonement
(Lv 16.13-14). Origen shifts quickly to the New Covenant, the atonement offered once and for all, and the
experience of it in the eucharist.

And so the divine word says: AND HE [Aaron] SHALL
PLACE INCENSE UPON THE FIRE IN THE SIGHT
OF THE LORD, AND THE SMOKE OF THE INCENSE
SHALL COVER THE THRONE OF MERCY WHICH
IS ABOVE THE TESTIMONIES, AND HE SHALL NOT
DIE. AND HE SHALL TAKE SOME OF THE BLOOD
OF THE BULL, AND SPRINKLE IT WITH HIS FIN-
GERS OVER THE THRONE OF MERCY TOWARDS
THE EAST. Now it has taught how the rite of propitiation
on behalf of men should be performed before God among
the people of old. But as for you, who have come to Christ,
the True Priest, who has rendered God propitious towards
you by His own blood, and has reconciled you to the Father
(*cf* Rm 3.25; 5.11), suffer no difficulty concerning blood
from flesh (Dt 12.16 *etc*; Ac 15.29), but learn, rather, of the
blood of the Word, and hear Him as He says to you: "This is
my blood, which will be shed for you for the forgiveness of
sins (Mt 26.28)." He who has been initiated into the mysteries knows both the flesh and the blood of the Word of God.
Let us not, therefore, tarry in these matters which are familiar to those who know them, and cannot be revealed to those
who do not.

IIIA3 Origen (*c* 185-*c* 254), *Homily on Numbers* No. 16.9.
ed GCS *Origenes* 7, 2.151-153.

Origen's homilies on Numbers fit into the same cycle as
those on Exodus and Leviticus. Twenty-eight of them
survive in the translation made by Rufinus in his refuge in
Sicily in 410, the last year of his life. In this extract,
Origen is commenting upon the second vision of Balaam
(Nb 23.18-24), the final verse of which reads, in the

Septuagint version: "Behold, the people will rise up like a
lion cub, and prance like a lion. It will not sleep until it
eats its prey, and drinks the blood of the wounded."
Origen sees this prophecy, spoken of Israel of old, fulfilled in the Christian people, both in the eucharist and in
the words of Christ.

IT [THE PEOPLE] WILL NOT SLEEP, UNTIL IT EATS ITS PREY, AND DRINKS THE BLOOD OF THE WOUNDED

In these words, who will be so obstinate an advocate of
literal interpretation, or, rather, who will be found so insen-
sitive, that he will not be revolted by the sound of the letter,
and of necessity flee to the sweetness of allegory? For how
will this people, so praiseworthy, so splendid, whom his
words praise at such length, come to this, that it will
DRINK THE BLOOD OF THE WOUNDED, since the
food of blood is forbidden by God with such strong commandments that even we, who have been called from
the gentiles, are ordered, as a matter of necessity, to abstain from blood, just as from things sacrificed to idols
(Ac 15.29)? Let them tell us, then, which people is this who
have the practice of drinking blood.

These were the words which caused scandal among those
from the Jews who followed the Lord, when they heard
them in the gospel; and they said: "Who can eat flesh and
blood" (Jn 6.52, 53)?. It is the Christian people, the faithful
people, who hear these things and embrace them, and follow
Him who says: "Unless you eat my flesh, and drink my
blood, you will not have life in you. For my flesh is truly
food, and my blood is truly drink" (Jn 6.54, 56). And,
indeed, He who said these words was wounded for the sake
of men, for "He was wounded because of our sins," as Isaiah
says (Is 53.5). But we are said to DRINK THE BLOOD of
Christ, not only in the rite of the mysteries, but also when we
receive His words in which life consists, just as He says: "The
words which I have spoken are spirit and life" (Jn 6.63). And

so, He was wounded, that One whose blood we drink, that is, we receive the words of his teaching. But those too were no less wounded who preached His word to us, and when we read the words of those men, that is, of the apostles, and attain to life from their words, we are drinking THE BLOOD OF THE WOUNDED.

And so he says IT WILL NOT SLEEP, UNTIL IT EATS ITS PREY. For this people, which is likened to a lion cub or a lion (Nb 23.24), will not rest or sleep until it snatches its prey, that is, until it snatches the Kingdom of Heaven, for "From the days of John the Kingdom of Heaven suffers violence, and the violent seize it" (Mt 11.12). But that you may know even more clearly that these words are written about our people which has been leagued together by the sacraments of Christ, hear how Moses made similar declarations also in other passages, saying: "[They will eat] the butter of cows and the milk of sheep, with the fat of lambs and rams, of the calves of bulls and of goats, with the fat of the pith of the wheat, and they will drink the blood of the grape, wine" (Dt 32.14). And this blood, then, which is called "of the grape," is of that grape which is born of the vine of which the Saviour says: "I am the true vine," but the disciples are "the branches" (Jn 15.1, 5). But "the Father is the farmer," who purges them, "that they may bear very much fruit" (Jn 15.12). So that you are the true people of Israel who know how to drink blood, and you know how to eat the flesh of the Word of God and to drink the blood of the Word of God, and to drink up the blood of that grape which is from the True Vine and from those branches. The fruit of these branches will properly be called THE BLOOD OF THE WOUNDED, which we drink from their words and teaching, so long as we are RISING UP LIKE LION CUBS and PRANCING LIKE A LION.

Let these words about the second vision of Balaam suffice for the time being, but let us pray to the Lord that He may deign to reveal to us interpretations more clear and close to the truth for the understanding of what remains, to the end that, pondering in the Spirit things written through the Spirit, and "comparing spiritual things to spiritual" (1 Co

2.13), we may expound the things which have been written in a manner worthy of God the Holy Spirit who inspired them, in Christ Jesus our Lord, to whom be glory and power unto the ages of ages. Amen.

IIIA4 Origen (*c* 185-*c* 254), *Commentary on the Song of Songs* 3.11.
ed GCS *Origenes* 8.180-181.

> Origen composed the first five books of his Commentary on the Song of Songs *c* 245, during a visit to Athens, and the remaining five books sometime later. Only Books 1-4 survive, again, in a translation prepared by Rufinus in 410. In this brief comment on Sg 2.3, Origen takes us, through Pr 9.2 and Jn 6, into a traditionally eucharistic ambience, but treats it with characteristic ambiguity.

And so, JUST AS THE APPLE TREE AMONG THE other TREES OF THE WOOD, so is the Bridegroom AMONG THE SONS, having fruit which surpasses all, not only in taste, but also in odor, and has its effect on the two senses of the soul alike, that is, both on taste and smell. For Wisdom has prepared His table for us with various abundances (Pr 9.2). On it He not only places the bread of life (Jn 6.41, 48), but also sacrifices the flesh of the Word, and not only mixes his Wine in a bowl, but also provides apples, quite fragrant and sweet, which supply a pleasant taste not only in the mouth and upon the lips, but maintain their sweetness in the throat.

IIIA5 Augustine of Hippo (354-430), *Enarratio on Ps 98* (on Ps 98.9).
ed CCSL 39.1385-1386.

> Augustine's largest work, the *enarrationes*, or sermons on the Psalms, were composed through the period 392-416 or later. Some of these sermons were dictated, but

most were preached, as is the case with the sermon on Ps 98, delivered at Carthage, in the period 411-412. We have excerpted his comment on Ps 98.9. It contains one of his more controversial remarks on the eucharist as *sacrament*, in his sense of the word; for some clarification see IVC5, below.

AND ADORE THE FOOTSTOOL OF HIS FEET, FOR HE IS HOLY.

What should we adore? THE FOOTSTOOL OF HIS FEET. A footstool [*suppedaneum*] is called *scabellum* [footstool]. What the Greeks call *hypopodion*, the Latins have called *scabellum*, and others *suppedaneum*. But notice, brothers, what it is ordering us to adore. In another passage of scripture it says: "Heaven is my throne, but earth is the footstool [*scabellum*] of my feet" (Is 66.1). Does it, then, tell us to worship the earth, because it said in another passage that the earth is the footstool of the feet of God? But how shall we adore the earth, since scripture says clearly: "You will adore the Lord, your God, alone" (Dt 6.13).? It says here ADORE THE FOOTSTOOL OF HIS FEET, but explaining to me what the footstool of His feet is, it says "but the earth is the footstool of my feet." I am in a dilemma: I am afraid to worship earth, lest He who made heaven and earth (Ps 133.3) condemn me; but I am afraid not to adore the footstool of the feet of my Lord, because the Psalm says to me ADORE THE FOOTSTOOL OF HIS FEET. I ask what is the footstool of His feet, and scripture says to me "the earth is the footstool of my feet." In my doubt I turn to Christ, for it is He whom I seek here, and I discover how earth may be worshipped without impiety. For He took earth from earth, because flesh is from earth, and from the flesh of Mary He took flesh. And because He walked here in that flesh, He also gave us that flesh to eat for our salvation. But no one eats that flesh, unless he has first adored it.

We have found out how such a footstool of the feet of God may be worshipped, and how we not only do not sin by worshipping it, but even sin by not worshipping it. But flesh does not give life, does it? The Lord Himself said, when He was speaking about the legacy of this very "earth": "It is the spirit which gives life, the flesh profits nothing" (Jn 6.64). And so, when you bow down and prostrate yourself before any "earth," do not revere it as earth, but as that Holy One whose footstool is that which you adore. For it is on His account that you adore, and so it added here ADORE THE FOOTSTOOL OF HIS FEET, FOR HE IS HOLY. Who is holy? The one in whose honor you adore the footstool of His feet. And lest, when you adore Him, you remain in imagination in the flesh, and not be given life by the spirit, He said: "For it is the spirit which gives life, the flesh profits nothing."

Now, at the time when the Lord bequeathed this, when He spoke of His flesh, and said: "Unless a man eat of my flesh, he will not have eternal life in him" (*cf* Jn 6.54), certain of His disciples, almost seventy, were scandalized, and said: "This is a hard saying, who can understand it?" (Jn 6.61). And they left Him, and walked with Him no longer (Jn 6.67). What seemed difficult to them was His saying: "Unless a man eat my flesh, he will not have eternal life." They understood it foolishly, they thought in a carnal way, and supposed that the Lord was going to cut off some pieces from His body and give the pieces to them, and they said: "This is a hard saying." They were the ones who were hard, not the saying. Indeed, if they were not hard, if they were gentle, they would say to themselves: "He is not saying this without a good reason; there must be some sacrament hidden here." They would have remained with Him, gentle, not hard, and they would have learned from Him what those who remained learned after they had left. For the twelve disciples remained with Him, and when the others left, they pointed out to Him, as if in grief over their death, that those had been scandalized by what He had said, and left. But He instructed them, and said to them: "It is the spirit which gives life, the flesh profits nothing. The words which I have spoken to you are spirit and life (Jn 6.64). Understand what I have said spiritually. You are not going to eat this body which you see, nor are you going to drink the blood which those who will crucify me are going to shed. I have given you a sacrament. Understood spiritually, it will give you life.

Although it must be celebrated visibly, yet it should be understood invisibly." EXALT THE LORD OUR GOD, AND ADORE THE FOOTSTOOL OF HIS FEET, FOR HE IS HOLY.

IIIA6 Theodoret of Cyrus (393-*c* 466), *Commentary on the Canticle of Canticles*, comment on Sg 3.11. *ed* PG 81.125-128

> An Antiochian by birth, Theodoret entered the monastic life as a young man, only to be called to the bishopric of Cyrus, near Antioch, in 423. He was an outstanding pastor, and a prolific writer: apologist, controversialist, theologian, historian, and exegete. He appears first in this volume as an exegete in this short extract. Theodoret proceeds from the marriage-day of Solomon in Sg 3.11 to the Wedding Feast of the Lamb (Rv 19.9), placing us wonderfully into a eucharistic context.

COME OUT AND SEE SOLOMON, O DAUGHTERS OF SION, IN THE CROWN WITH WHICH HIS MOTHER CROWNED HIM, ON THE DAY OF HIS MARRIAGE AND ON THE DAY OF THE JOY OF HIS HEART.

To press on with our interpretation briefly and clearly, avoiding prolixity, the meaning of these words: O DAUGHTERS OF Jerusalem and SION:

That this Sion, again, is the heavenly one the blessed Paul teaches us, saying: "But you have drawn near to Mount Sion, and the City of the Living God, the Heavenly Jerusalem... and the church of the firstborn who have been enrolled in heaven" (Heb 12.22-23). "You, then," they say, "O DAUGHTERS OF SION and Jerusalem, COME OUT AND SEE (for it is impossible for us to see unless we are outside worldly matters), behold the King crowned with love." For He so loved the world (Jn 3.16) that "although He was by nature God, He did not consider it thievery to be equal to god, but He emptied Himself, taking on the form of a slave" (Ph 2.6-7). He so loved the world that "He was led as a sheep to the slaughter, and as a lamb, silent before the shearer" (Is 53.7), and "He redeemed us from the curse of the law, becoming cursed for us" (Ga 3.13). Wherefore it says: "Greater love than this no one can show, than that he lay down his life for his friends" (Jn 15.15). Thus it was that His mother crowned Him.

But it calls Judaea His mother according to His humanity, as being the one who involuntarily crowned Him. For she crowned Him with thorns, intending to dishonor Him; but He, through the thorns, received the crown of love. For willingly He bore the dishonor, and willingly proceeded to His Passion, and therefore it calls this His wedding-day, and the day of the joy of His heart. For on that day came into existence the fellowship of the marriage (cf Rv 19.9). For after the meal, He took bread, gave thanks, broke it and gave it to His disciples, saying: "Take and eat of this all of you, for this is my body, broken for you for the forgiveness of sins. Do this as a memorial of me." Those, then, who eat the Body of the Bridegroom and drink His Blood attain to a sharing in His marriage. For this reason the servants (*diakonoi*) of the Bridegroom invite the daughters of Sion and Jerusalem to come out and see the crown of His love, the crown with which Judaea who bore Him adorned Him unknowingly, and crowned Him on His wedding-day.

B New Testament Exegesis

IIIB1 Origen (*c* 185-*c* 254), *Commentary on the Gospel of Matthew* (on Mt 26.26-28).
ed GCS *Origenes* 11.196-200.

> Origen produced his commentary on Matthew in 249. Of the original twenty-five books, only Books 10-17, on Mt 13.36-22.33, survive in Greek; for Mt 22.34-27.63, we are dependent on the work of an anonymous Latin translator of the fifth century, who translated quite freely, and, occasionally, suppressed difficulties and added explanatory material.

85. BUT WHILE THEY WERE EATING, JESUS TOOK BREAD, GAVE THANKS, BROKE IT, AND GAVE IT TO HIS DISCIPLES, SAYING: "TAKE AND EAT, FOR THIS IS MY BODY." AND TAKING A CUP, AND GIVING THANKS, HE GAVE IT TO THEM SAYING: "DRINK OF THIS, ALL OF YOU, FOR THIS IS MY BLOOD OF THE NEW COVENANT, WHICH IS SHED FOR MANY FOR THE FORGIVENESS OF SINS."

This bread which God the Word declares is His body is the word which feeds souls, word proceeding from God the Word, and bread from Heavenly Bread. It has been placed upon the table about which was written: "You have prepared a table in my sight against those who afflict me" (Ps 22.5). And this drink which God the Word declares is His

blood is the word which gives drink and wonderfully intoxicates the hearts of those who drink. This is the cup concerning which was written: "... and your intoxicating cup, how
glorious it is" (Ps 22.5)! Also, this drink is the fruit of the
True Vine, who said, "I am the true vine" (Jn 15.1), and it is
the blood of that Grape which produced this drink when it
was cast into the winepress of the Passion, just as the bread
too is the word of Christ, made from that Wheat which
"falling   into   the   earth...produces   much   fruit"   (Jn
12.24,25).'

For God the Word was not saying that the visible bread
which He was holding in His hands was His body, but rather
the word, in whose mystery the bread was to be broken. He
was not saying that the visible drink was His blood, but the
word, in whose mystery the drink was to be poured out. For
what else could the body and the blood of God the Word be
except the word which nourishes and the word which
"makes glad the heart" (Ps 103.15)? But why did He not say
"This is the bread of the new covenant," just as He did say
THIS IS THE BLOOD OF THE NEW COVENANT?
Because the bread is the word of righteousness whereby
those who eat it are nourished, but the drink is the word of
the knowledge of Christ, according to the mystery of His
Nativity and Passion. But since the covenant of God with us
was placed in the blood of Christ's Passion, that believing
that the Son of God was born and suffered in the flesh we
should be saved—and not by righteousness, for by that
alone, without belief in the Passion of Christ, there could be
no salvation—on that account, only of the cup was it said
"This is the cup of the covenant" (cf Lk 22.20).

AMEN, I SAY TO YOU THAT I SHALL NOT DRINK
OF THE FRUIT OF THIS VINE SAVE WHEN I SHALL
DRINK IT NEW WITH YOU IN THE KINGDOM OF
MY FATHER.

But something similar was said also about the bread in
Luke: "With longing have I longed to eat this passover with
you...I tell you that from now on I will not eat of it until it
be fulfilled in the Kingdom of God" (Lk 22.15-16). There-

fore, the Saviour will eat and drink that bread and the paschal wine renewed in the Kingdom of God, and He will eat and drink with His disciples. For just as "He did not consider it robbery that He was equal to God. . . . but humbled Himself, even unto death" (Ph 2.6,8). so will He eat bread and drink of the fruit of the vine, and drink it new, and, because of His great goodness and love for men, He will eat and drink with His disciples "when He will have delivered up the Kingdom to God and the Father" (1 Co 15.24). For observe what He says, WHEN I SHALL HAVE DRUNK IT NEW WITH YOU, at no other time than IN THE KINGDOM OF MY FATHER.

But, in another passage, "The Kingdom of God is not food and drink" (Rm 14.17). In a bodily way, and according to the likeness of visible food and drink, "the Kingdom of God is not food and drink," but in a spiritual way, it is, to those who have shown themselves worthy of the heavenly bread and bread of angels, and of that food concerning which the Saviour says: "My food is to do the will of Him who sent me and to complete His work" (Jn 4.34). Moreover, it is possible to demonstrate that we will eat and drink in the Kingdom of God from many passages of the scriptures, especially from the one which reads: "Blessed is he who will eat bread in the Kingdom of God" (Lk 14.15). In the Kingdom of God, then, this passover will be completed, and Jesus will eat it and drink with His disciples. The Apostle's words, "Let no one judge you in respect of food and drink" and the rest "which are the shadow of things to come" (Col 2.16,17), contain a revelation of mysteries to come concerning the spiritual food and drink of which the things which were written about food and drink in the Law are the adumbration. But it is plain that we shall eat true food and drink true drink in the Kingdom of God, using them to build up and strengthen that most true life.

Now he who is a child of Christ, and yet carnal in Christ, may understand in an ordinary way the text: JESUS, TAK-ING BREAD, and, similarly, TAKING THE CUP. But the more prudent may ask from whom Jesus was taking them. For as God gives it, He takes and gives to those who are

worthy to receive the bread and cup from God. Jacob also
indicates how God gives bread when he says: "If the Lord
my God will be with me, and will give me bread to eat and
clothing to put on...of all the things whatsoever you will
give me, O Lord, I will offer tithes to you"(Gn 28.20,22). It
is also written in the Gospel according to John: "Moses did
not give you bread, but my Father gives you the true bread
from heaven" (Jn 6.32). And Jesus always taking bread
from the Father for those who keep the festival along with
Him, gives thanks, breaks it, and gives it to His disciples
according as each of them is capable of receiving, and He
gives it to them saying TAKE AND EAT, and He shows,
when He feeds them with this bread, that it is His body, since
He Himself is the word which is needful for us, both now,
and when it will have been completed in the Kingdom of
God. But now, indeed, it is not yet completed, but it will be
completed then, when we too will have been readied to
receive the full passover which He came to complete, who
came not to destroy the Law, but to fulfill (Mt 5.17); to
complete it now "through a glass, in a riddle" of completion;
to complete it "then, however, face to face, when that which
is complete has come" (1 Co 13.12,10).

If, then, we also wish to receive the bread of blessing from
Jesus who is wont to give it, let us go "into the city" (Mk
14.13 *ff*), into the house of a certain one, where Jesus keeps
"the passover with His disciples" who prepare it for Him by
His instructions, and let us go up to the house's upper room,
large, furnished, and prepared, where, TAKING THE CUP
from the Father, and GIVING THANKS, He gives it to
those who have gone up with Him, saying DRINK ... FOR
THIS IS MY BLOOD OF THE NEW COVENANT. What
is drunk is what is poured forth. It is drunk by the disciples,
but it is SHED FOR THE FORGIVENESS OF SINS
committed by those by whom it is drunk and shed. But if
you ask how it is shed, consider along with that phrase the
passage where it is written "For the love of God has been
poured abroad in our hearts" (Rm 5.5). For if the blood of
the covenant has been poured into our hearts for the forgiveness of sins, then once that potable blood has been

poured out into our hearts, all the sins we have committed
beforehand are forgiven and done away with. For He who
took the cup and said DRINK OF THIS, ALL OF YOU,
does not depart from us as we drink, but drinks it with us
—since He is in each of us—because alone, and without
Him, we are able neither to eat of that bread nor to drink of
the fruit of that True Vine. Do not wonder that He is the
bread, and He eats the bread with us; that He is the drink of
the fruit of the vine, and He drinks with us. For the
Almighty Word of God is called by a variety of names, and
He is beyond numbering in the multitude of His powers,
since all power is one, and it is He.

Then he taught the disciples who had celebrated the feast
with the Master and had received the bread of blessing and
had eaten the body of the Word and had drunk the cup of
thanksgiving. He taught them to sing a hymn to the Father
in return for all these things, and to pass from height to
height, for the faithful can never do anything in a valley .
For that reason, they went up into the Mount of Olives, on
which each olive, like a tree producing fruit, can say "But I,
like a fruitful olive in the house of God" (Ps 51.10). And
those who had not yet become "like new olive plants about
the table" (Ps 127.3), the spiritual table of their Father, they
too could be on the Mount of Olives, of which Zachariah
also prophesies (Zc 14.4). And how aptly was that "Mount
of Mercy" chosen, where He would foretell the scandal of
the frailty of His disciples! He did not wish that it take place,
but foretold that it would, already prepared not to drive the
disciples away as they left Him, but to receive them back as
they returned.

IIIB2 Ambrosiaster (*fl* 366-384), *Commentary on the First Epistle to the Corinthians* (on 1 Co. 11.23-30).

ed CSEL 81, 2.126-129.

"Ambrosiaster" is the name given by Erasmus to the
unknown author of a set of commentaries on the thirteen

Pauline epistles, commentaries attributed to Ambrose in the Middle Ages. All we really know of the author is that he was active in Rome for a period roughly coincident with the pontificate of Damasus (366-384), and, if we follow J.N.D. Kelly, that Jerome did not approve of him, a burden he shared with 99.9% of his contemporaries. Ambrosiaster composed the first Latin commentary on all the Pauline epistles and a curious mélange of exegesis and gossip called *Questions on the Old and New Testaments.* As an exegete he is sober, literal and historical, and possessed of a remarkable knowledge of Jewish tradition.

FOR I RECEIVED FROM THE LORD WHAT I ALSO HAVE HANDED ON TO YOU, THAT THE LORD JESUS, ON THE NIGHT ON WHICH HE WAS BETRAYED, TOOK BREAD, AND GIVING THANKS, BROKE IT AND SAID: "THIS IS MY BODY, WHICH IS BROKEN FOR YOU. DO THIS IN REMEMBRANCE OF ME." SIMILARLY ALSO THE CUP, AFTER THEY HAD EATEN, SAYING: "THIS CUP IS THE NEW COVENANT IN MY BLOOD. DO THIS, AS OFTEN AS YOU DRINK IT, IN REMEMBRANCE OF ME."

He shows them that the mystery of the eucharist, celebrated in the midst of a meal, is not a meal. For it is spiritual medicine, which, eaten with reverence, purifies the one devoted to it. For it is the memorial of our redemption, that mindful of our Redeemer, we may merit to obtain yet more from Him.

PROCLAIMING THE DEATH OF THE LORD, UNTIL HE COMES.
Because we have been set free by the death of the Lord, mindful of this fact, by eating and drinking His flesh and blood which were offered for us, we manifest the New Covenant which we have obtained through them. It is the New Law, which translates the one who is obedient to it to heavenly realms. For Moses also sprinkled the children of

Israel with a calf's blood caught in a bowl, saying: "This is the covenant which God has made in respect to you" (Ex 24.8). This was the figure of the Covenant which the Lord, through the Prophet (Jer 31.31) called New, so that that which Moses handed down would be Old. The Covenant, then, was established by blood, for blood is a witness to divine favor. After its type, we take the mystical cup for the protection of our body and soul, for the Lord's blood redeemed our blood, that is, it made the whole man saved. For the flesh of the Saviour was for the salvation of the body, but His blood was shed on behalf of our soul, just as had been prefigured beforehand by Moses. For thus he said: "The flesh is offered for your body, but the blood for your soul," and on that account blood is not to be eaten (Lv 17.11 ff). If, then, with the ancients there was the image of the truth which has now appeared and been revealed in the coming of the Saviour, how can the Old Testament seem to the heretics to be opposed to the New, since they are witnesses one to the other?

AND SO, WHOEVER EATS THIS BREAD OR DRINKS THE CUP OF THE LORD UNWORTHILY WILL BE GUILTY OF THE BODY AND BLOOD OF THE LORD.
He calls him unworthy of the Lord who celebrates the mystery differently from the way it was handed on by Him. For he who receives it otherwise than it was given by its Author cannot be devout. For that reason, he gives a warning that the mind of one approaching the eucharist of the Lord should be devout according to the order handed down; that there will be a judgement, so that each may explain how he approaches, on the day of the Lord Jesus Christ; that those who approach without the discipline of tradition and behaviour are guilty of the body and blood of the Lord. But what is it to be guilty except to pay the penalty for the death of the Lord? For He was killed because of those who regard His kindness as nothing.

BUT LET A MAN PROVE HIMSELF AND THUS EAT OF THE BREAD AND DRINK OF THE CUP. FOR HE

WHO EATS AND DRINKS UNWORTHILY, EATS
AND DRINKS CONDEMNATION FOR HIMSELF,
NOT DISCERNING THE BODY OF THE LORD.
He teaches that one should approach communion with a
devout soul and with fear, that the mind may know that it
owes reverence to Him whose body it approaches to receive.
He ought to ponder this, that it is the Lord whose blood he
drinks in the mystery, blood which is the witness of God's
favor. If we receive it with discipline, we will not be
unworthy of the body and blood of the Lord, for we shall be
seen to give thanks to the Redeemer.

FOR THAT REASON MANY AMONG YOU ARE SICK
AND AILING, AND MANY SLEEP.
To show that it is true that there will be an examination of
those who receive the body of the Lord, he now shows here
an image of the judgement against those who had thoughtlessly received the body of the Lord, as they were seized by
fevers and illnesses, and many died, that the rest might learn
from them, and, frightened by the example of a few, the rest
might be corrected, knowing that he who received the
Lord's body carelessly is not unpunished, and that he who
has escaped punishment here will be yet more severely
treated, because he scorned the warning.

IIIB3 John Chrysostom (*c* 349-407), *Homily on the
Gospel of Matthew* No. 82, excerpt (on Mt 26.26-8).
ed PG 58.737-740; *tr* LNPF 10.491-493, revised.

John Chrysostom delivered his ninety homilies on Matthew in Antioch, probably in the year 390. Note Chrysostom's concerns with the psychological implications of the
institution of the eucharist, and with the role of the eucharist
in establishing the faith. This selection anticipates Section
IVA of this volume.

AND AS THEY WERE EATING, JESUS TOOK
BREAD, AND GAVE THANKS, AND BROKE IT, AND

GAVE IT TO THE DISCIPLES, AND SAID: TAKE,
EAT; THIS IS MY BODY. AND HE TOOK A CUP, AND
GAVE THANKS, AND GAVE IT TO THEM SAYING:
DRINK OF THIS, ALL OF YOU. THIS IS MY BLOOD
OF THE NEW COVENANT, WHICH IS SHED FOR
MANY FOR THE FORGIVENESS OF SINS.

1. Ah, how great is the blindness of the Betrayer! Even
partaking of the mysteries, he remained the same, though he
had the benefit of the most awesome table, he did not
change. And Luke shows this by saying that after this Satan
entered into him (Lk 22.3; Jn 13.27), not as despising the
Lord's body, but ever after mocking the Betrayer's shamelessness. For indeed his sin became greater for both reasons,
both because he approached the mysteries with such a disposition, and because, having approached them, he did not
become better, neither from fear, nor from the benefit nor
from the honor. But Christ did not prevent him, although
He knew all things, so that you might learn that He omits
nothing which pertains to correction. Wherefore, both
before this, and after this, He continually admonished him
and checked him, both by deeds and words, by fear and by
healing, by threats and by honor. But none of these with-
drew him from that terrible disease.

And so thereafter He lets him go, and by the mysteries
again reminds the disciples of His being slain, and in the
midst of the meal He speaks about the Cross, making His
Passion easy to accept by the continual repetition of the
prediction. For if they were troubled when so many things
had been done and foretold, what would they not have
suffered if they had heard none of these things?

AND AS THEY WERE EATING, HE TOOK BREAD
AND BROKE IT. Why is it that He instituted this sacrament at the time of passover? That you might learn in every
way that He is also the Lawgiver of the Old Covenant, and
that the things in it were foreshadowings of these. Therefore, where the type is, there He puts the truth. But the
evening was a sure sign of the fullness of times (*cf* Ga 4.4),
and that the former things were now come to this, as to their
end.

And He gives thanks, to teach us how we should celebrate this mystery, and to show that He does not come to the Passion unwillingly, and to teach us to bear whatever we suffer with gratitude, thence also offering good hopes. For if the type was a deliverance from such great bondage, even more will the truth set the world free (Jn 8.32), and be handed on for the benefit of our nature. For this reason, He did not bestow the mystery before this, but at the time when the rites of the Law were ever after to cease. And thus He brings to an end the very chief of feasts, and removes the disciples to the other, most awesome table, and says "TAKE, EAT: THIS IS MY BODY, which is broken for many."

And how is it that they were not disturbed at hearing this? Because beforehand He had told them many and great things concerning it. Therefore He discusses it no more, for they had heard enough of it, but He speaks of the cause of His Passion, the taking away of sins. And He calls it BLOOD OF THE NEW COVENANT, that is, of the promise of the gospel of the New Law. For he promised this also of old, and this comprises the Covenant that is in the New Law. And as the Old Covenant had sheep and calves, so this one has the Lord's blood. Hence also He shows that He is about to die, and for that reason He mentions a covenant, and He also reminds them of the former covenant, for that also was established by blood. And again He tells the cause of His death, WHICH IS SHED FOR MANY FOR THE FORGIVENESS OF SINS, and He says "Do this in remembrance of me" (Lk 22.19; 1 Co 11.24). Do you see how He removes and takes them away from Jewish customs? "For as you did that," He says, "in remembrance of the miracles in Egypt, so do this also in remembrance of me." That was shed for the preservation of the firstborn, this for the forgiveness of the sins of the whole world. For THIS, He says, IS MY BLOOD, WHICH IS SHED FOR THE FORGIVENESS OF SINS.

But He said this indicating that His Passion and Cross are a mystery, and thus again comforted His disciples. And as Moses said: "This shall be to you for an everlasting memorial" (Ex 12.14), so He also says "IN REMEMBRANCE OF ME, until I am with you again" (*cf* 1 Co 11.25). Therefore He also says: "With longing have I longed to eat this Passover (Lk 22.15), to deliver to you the new rites, and to give a passover by which I am going to make you spiritual."

And he Himself drank of it. For lest on hearing this they should say: "What then, do we drink blood and eat flesh?" and then be perplexed—for when He began to speak of these things, even at the very words many were scandalized (Jn 6.60ff)—on that account, lest they should be similarly troubled then, He did this first Himself, leading them to a calm participation in the mysteries. For that reason He Himself drank His own blood. "Must we observe that ancient passover also?" someone may ask. By no means. He said DO THIS for this reason, to withdraw us from it. For if this brings about forgiveness of sins, as it surely does, the old passover is now superfluous.

As, then, in the case of the Jews, so here too he has bound up the memorial of the benefit with the mystery, by this means also stopping the mouths of heretics. For when they say "Whence is it manifest that Christ was sacrificed?" we silence them from the mysteries, along with other arguments. For if Jesus did not die, of what are these rites the symbols.

2. Do you see how much diligence has been employed so that it should always be remembered that He died for us? For since the Marcionites and Valentinians and Manichaeans were going to rise up and deny this economy, He constantly reminds us of the Passion also by the mysteries, so that no one may be misled. At the same time He both saves and teaches by means of the sacred table. For this is the chief of blessings, as Paul also urges in every way.

Then, when He had bestowed it, He says I WILL NOT DRINK OF THE FRUIT OF THIS VINE UNTIL THE DAY WHEN I DRINK IT NEW WITH YOU IN MY FATHER'S KINGDOM. For because He had spoken with them about Passion and Cross, He again introduces mention of His Resurrection, speaking of the Kingdom, and thus naming His Resurrection.

And why did He drink after He was risen? Lest the duller sort might suppose that the Resurrection was an illusion. For the common sort make this a proof of the Resurrection. And so even the apostles, persuading them of the Resurrection, say this: "We who ate and drank with Him"(Ac 10.41).

Therefore, to show that they would see Him again, gloriously risen, and that He would be with them once more, and that they themselves would bear witness to the events both by sight and by deed, He says "UNTIL I DRINK IT NEW WITH YOU, you who will bear witness, for you shall see me risen." But what is NEW? In a new, that is, in a novel manner, not having a passible body, but one ever after immortal and incorruptible, and in no need of food.

It was not, then, from need that he ate and drank after the Resurrection, for His body required these things no longer, but for the full assurance of the Resurrection.

And why did He drink not water, but wine, after He was risen? To root out another evil heresy. For since there are certain ones who use water in the mysteries, to show that both when He established the mysteries He had appointed wine, and that when He had risen and was putting an ordinary meal before them, without the mysteries, He used wine, He says OF THE FRUIT OF THE VINE. A vine produces wine, not water.

AND WHEN THEY HAD SUNG A HYMN, THEY WENT OUT TO THE MOUNT OF OLIVES.

Let all those hear this who, like browsing swine, rudely abuse the ordinary table, and rise up drunk. For it is proper to give thanks, and to end with a hymn. Hear this, all you who do not wait for the final prayer of the mysteries, for this is a symbol of it. He gave thanks before giving the eucharist to His disciples, that we also may give thanks. He gave thanks, and sang a hymn after giving the eucharist, that we too may do this very thing.

IIIB4 John Chrysostom (*c* 349-407), *Homily on the Gospel of John* No. 46 (on Jn 6.41-69).
ed PG 59.257-262; *tr* FC, revised.

> The homilies on John, eighty-eight in all, were delivered in Antioch, probably around 391. Chrysostom's psychological and dogmatic treatment of the eucharistic discourse from John 6 gives way, towards the end of the homily, to a splendid encomium on the eucharist.

THE JEWS, THEREFORE, MURMURED ABOUT HIM BECAUSE HE SAID: "I AM THE BREAD THAT HAS COME DOWN FROM HEAVEN." AND THEY KEPT SAYING: "IS THIS NOT THE SON OF JOSEPH, WHOSE FATHER AND MOTHER WE KNOW? HOW, THEN, DOES HE SAY THAT HE HAS COME DOWN FROM HEAVEN?"

"Their God is the belly, and their glory is their shame" (Ph 3.19), said Paul, writing to the Philippians about certain men. Now, it is clear from what had gone before that the Jews were of this sort, and this is likewise clear from the words they addressed to Christ when they approached Him. When He gave them bread and filled their bellies, they kept calling Him a prophet, and sought to make Him king (Jn 6.14-15). But when he taught them about the spiritual food, about eternal life, when He led them away from things of the senses, when He spoke of resurrection, and elevated their minds, when they ought most of all to have marveled at Him, then they murmured, and went away.

Now, if He was in truth the Prophet, as they had just said, "This is indeed the one about whom Moses said: 'The Lord will raise up for you a prophet like me from your brothers; hear him (Dt 18.15, 18)', " they ought to have listened to Him when He said I HAVE COME DOWN FROM HEAVEN. On the contrary, they did not listen to Him, but murmured. Of course, they still held Him in awe because of the recent miracle of the loaves. That is why they did not contradict Him openly. But by murmuring they showed that they resented the fact that He did not give them the table which they desired. And as they murmured, they kept saying: IS THIS NOT THE SON OF JOSEPH?

From this it is clear that they did not yet know His marvelous and strange birth. That is why they still called Him the son of Joseph. Yet, He did not reprove them or say to them: "I am not the son of Joseph." This was not because He was, in fact, the son of Joseph, but because they were not yet able to hear of His miraculous birth. And if they were not ready for a clear revelation of His birth according to the flesh, much more was that the case with that ineffable birth above. If He did not reveal what was lowly, much less would He have treated of those matters. And though it scandalized them very much to think that He was of a lowly and common father, he nevertheless made no revelation, in order that, in removing one scandal, He might not cause another.

What, then, did He reply when they murmured? NO ONE CAN COME TO ME, UNLESS THE FATHER, WHO SENT ME, HAS DRAWN HIM. The Manichaeans pounce on this and say that we can do nothing of ourselves, though the statement actually proves conclusively that we are possessed of a free will. They say: "If a man comes to Him, what need has he of being drawn?" In reality, this does not take away free will from us, but shows our need for help, because He was pointing out here that it is not anyone who happens to do so who comes, but that it is a person enjoying the benefit of such help.

Next He also pointed out the manner in which He draws. That they might not suspect of God some purely material operation, He added: NOT THAT ANYONE HAS SEEN THE FATHER, EXCEPT HIM WHO IS FROM THE FATHER, HE HAS SEEN THE FATHER. "How, then, does He draw?" you will ask. The Prophet foretold this of old, prophesying and saying: THEY SHALL ALL BE TAUGHT BY GOD (Is 54.13; Jn 6.45). Do you see the high dignity of faith, how he predicted that they were going to learn, not from men, nor through a man, but through God Himself? Indeed, that is why He sent them to the prophets, namely, to corroborate His words..

"But," you say, "if He says THEY SHALL ALL BE TAUGHT BY GOD, how is it that some do not believe?" Because His statement was about the majority of men. Besides, even apart from this, the prophecy refers not to all men in general, but to all who are willing. For as a teacher, He is at the disposal of all men, ready to give them His teachings, pouring out His instruction in abundance to all.

AND I WILL RAISE HIM UP ON THE LAST DAY.

In this text the Son has no inconsiderable dignity. For if, to be sure, the Father brings men, it is the Son who raises them up, not, of course, separating His works from those of the Father—for how could that be?—, but showing the equal dignity of their power. Therefore, just as in the passage where He said: "And the Father, who has sent me, bears witness to me (Jn 5.37),"lest any fret about His words, He sent them to the scriptures; so also here, lest they be similarly suspicious, He sends them to the prophets to whom He kept turning, backwards and forwards, to prove that He was not in opposition to the Father.

"But," you will say, "what of those before this time? Were they not taught by God? Then, what is better here?" The fact is that then people learned the things of God through men, but now they learn them through the Onlybegotten Son of God and through the Holy Spirit. Next he added: NOT THAT ANYONE HAS SEEN THE FATHER EXCEPT HIM WHO IS FROM GOD, not saying this here in the sense of causality, but of the mode of His essence. Because, if He had said it in the sense of causality, we are all from God. Where, then, would be the superiority and distinction of the Son? "But why," you will say, "did He not make it clearer?" Because of their weakness. If they were scandalized to such a degree when He said I HAVE COME DOWN FROM HEAVEN, what scandal would they not have taken if He added this?

He calls Himself THE BREAD OF LIFE because He welds together for us this life and the life to come. Therefore, He added: IF ANYONE EATS OF THIS BREAD, HE SHALL LIVE FOREVER. Surely, "bread" here means the teachings of salvation, and faith in Him; or else His body, for both are the sinews of the soul. Moreover, when He said elsewhere: "If anyone hears my word, he will not taste death (Jn 8.52)," they were scandalized, whereas here they did not have a similar reaction, perhaps because they were still in awe of Him on account of the loaves He had brought into being.

2. But notice on what basis He makes a distinction from the manna, by telling them the kind of effect that each of these foods produces. For to show that the manna had no extraordinary effect, He added: YOUR FATHERS ATE THE MANNA IN THE DESERT AND HAVE DIED. Next, He placed before them very convincing evidence that they themselves were deemed worthy of much greater blessings than their fathers, by referring indirectly to those wonderful men who lived at the time of Moses. Therefore, when He had said that they who had eaten the manna had died, He added: HE WHO EATS OF THIS BREAD WILL LIVE FOREVER. And He did not use the words IN THE DESERT without design, but to imply that the manna was not provided for a long period of time, and did not accompany them into the Promised Land. This bread, however, is not such. AND THE BREAD WHICH I WILL GIVE IS MY FLESH WHICH I WILL GIVE FOR THE LIFE OF THE WORLD. With good reason might someone inquire in perplexity at this point whether this was a good time for Him to say these words which were neither constructive nor profitable then, but, instead, were even injurious to those who had already been edified. FROM THIS TIME MANY OF HIS DISCIPLES TURNED BACK, SAYING: "THIS IS A HARD SAYING. WHO CAN HEAR IT?" It seems that these teachings ought to have been given to the disciples alone, as Matthew said, "He spoke to them privately (Mk 4.34; Mt 13.36)."

What answer, then, shall we make to this objection? Even at that time these words were both very profitable and very necessary. Since they were urgently asking for food, but bodily food—and in recalling to Him the nourishment provided for their forefathers, they were stressing the greatness of the manna—in order to prove that all this was type and shadow, while the reality thus foreshadowed was actually present, He spoke of spiritual nourishment.

"But," you will say, "He ought to have said: Your fathers ate the manna in the desert, and I have provided bread for you." But there was a great difference between the two. The latter, indeed, seemed inferior to the former, because the manna was brought down from above, while the latter, the miracle of the loaves, took place below. Therefore, since they were seeking for food brought down from heaven, for this reason He said repeatedly I HAVE COME DOWN FROM HEAVEN.

Now, if someone should inquire, "Why did He also bring up the matter of the mysteries?", we should say this in reply to him: It was just the right time for such words, for the obscurity of what is said always compels the attention of the listener, and makes him listen more carefully.

They ought not, therefore, to have been scandalized, but they should have asked questions and made inquiries. Instead, they went away. If, indeed, they thought He was a prophet, they ought to have believed His words. The scandal, then, consisted in their stupidity, not in the difficulty of His words. And notice, too, how He had gradually bound His disciples to Himself, for it was they who said YOU HAVE THE WORDS OF LIFE. WHERE ELSE SHALL WE GO? Moreover, He here presents Himself, not His Father, as the giver, by saying: THE BREAD WHICH I WILL GIVE IS MY FLESH. However, the crowd did not react as His disciples did, but quite the contrary; THIS IS A HARD SAYING, and they therefore went away.

Yet, the teaching was not strange and novel. For John had implied it earlier, when he hailed Him as "Lamb" (Jn 1.29,36). "Even so, they did not understand it in this way," you will say. I am fully aware they did not, for even the disciples did not completely understand. If they did not know anything clearly about the Resurrection, and for that reason were ignorant of the meaning of the words "Destroy this temple, and in three days I will raise it up" (Jn 2.19), it was much more the case with the words said here, for the former were less obscure than these. For they knew that prophets had raised people from the dead, even if the scriptures do not say this so very clearly; but no scripture had ever said that someone ate flesh. Nevertheless, they believed and followed Him and confessed that He had the words of eternal life. It is the part of a disciple not to fret over the teachings of his master, but to listen and believe and await the proper time for explanation.

"Why is it, then," you will say, "that the contrary also happened, and they TURNED BACK?" This was because of their stupidity. When the question "How?" comes in, unbelief comes in with it. Nicodemus likewise was disturbed in this way when he said: "How can a man enter into his mother's womb" (Jn 3.4)? And these men were similarly perturbed when they said: HOW CAN THIS MAN GIVE US HIS FLESH TO EAT? Now, if you are really looking for the "how?", why did you not say this in the case of the loaves, "How has He multiplied the five into so many?" Because then they were concerned only with being filled, not with observing the miracle. "But on that occasion," you will say, "experience taught them." Well, then, as a result of that, these words also should have been readily accepted. It was for this reason that He worked that miracle ahead of time, so that, instructed by it, they might no more be incredulous about what was said afterwards.

And so, they actually derived no profit from His words at that time, but we have enjoyed the benefit of the very realities. Therefore, we must learn the wonder of the mysteries, what they are, and why they were given, and what is their benefit. "We are one body," scripture says, "and members made from His flesh and from His bones (Ep 5.30)"—let the initiated attend to these words carefully .

3. In order, then, that we may become of His flesh, not by charity only, but also in very fact, let us become commingled with that flesh. This, in truth, takes place by means of the food which He has given us as a gift, because He desired to prove the love which He has for us. It is for this reason that He joined Himself to us, and has brought His body down to

our level, namely, that we might be one, just as a body is joined with the head. For this, indeed, is characteristic of those who love greatly. Job, you see, was implying this when he said of his servants—by whom he was loved with such an excess of love—that they desired to cleave to his flesh. In giving expression to the great love which they possessed, they said: "Who will give to us that we may be filled with his flesh (Jb 31.31)?" Wherefore, Christ has done this very thing to urge us on to greater love; and to show the love He has for us, He has made it possible for those who desire, not merely to look upon Him, but even to touch Him and to eat Him and to fix their teeth in His flesh, and to be commingled with Him, and to satisfy all their longing. Let us, then, come back from that table like lions breathing fire, thus becoming terrifying to the devil, and remaining mindful of our Head and of the love which He has shown for us.

"Parents, it is true, often entrust their children to others to feed, but I do not do so," He says; "I nourish mine on my own flesh. I give myself to you, since I desire all of you to be noble, and I hold out to you splendid hopes for the future. He who furnishes His very self to you here will do so much more for you in the life to come. I wished to become your brother. I shared in flesh and blood (Heb 2.14) for your sake. I have given back again to you the very flesh and blood through which I had become your kinsman."

This blood makes the image of our King bloom in us; it produces an inconceivable beauty; it does not permit the nobility of the soul to fade, since it waters and nourishes it without ceasing. The blood which we form from food is not blood immediately, but it goes through some other stage first. It is not so with this blood, for it at once waters the soul and creates a certain power in it. This blood, when worthily received, drives away demons and puts them far from us, and summons to us the angels and the Lord of the Angels. Where they see the blood of the Lord, demons flee, but angels gather. This blood, poured out, has cleansed the whole world.

The blessed Paul has uttered many truths about this blood in the Epistle to the Hebrews (Heb 9). This blood has

purified the sanctuary and the Holy of Holies. Now, if its
type had so much power, both in the Temple of the Hebrews
and in the midst of the Egyptians, when sprinkled on the
doorposts (Ex 12.7,13), its truth has much more power. This
blood sanctified the golden altar; without it, the highpriest
did not dare to enter the sanctuary; this blood has ordained
priests, this blood has washed away sins, in its types. And if
it had such great power in its types, if death shuddered so
much at the shadow, how would it not be in terror of the
very reality? This blood is the salvation of our souls; by it the
soul is cleansed; by it, beautified; by it, inflamed. It makes
our mind brighter than fire, it renders our soul more brilliant than gold. This blood has been poured forth, and has
made heaven accessible.

4. Awe-inspiring, indeed, are the mysteries of the church;
awesome, indeed, her altar. A fountain sprang up out of
Paradise, sending forth perceptible rivers; a fountain arises
from this table, sending forth spiritual rivers (Gn 2.10; Rv
22.1-2). Beside this fountain there have grown, not willows
without fruit, but trees reaching to heaven itself, with fruit
ever in season and incorrupt. If someone is burning hot, let
him come to this fountain and cool down the feverish heat.
It dispels parching heat and gently cools down things that
are very hot; not things inflamed by the sun's heat, but
things set on fire by burning arrows (Ep 6.16). It does so
because it takes its beginning from above, and has its source
there, and from there is it supplied. Many are the streams of
this fountain, streams which the Paraclete sends forth; and
the Son becomes its custodian, not keeping its channel open
with a hoe, but making our hearts receptive.

This fountain is a fountain of light, shedding abundant
rays of truth. And beside it the powers from on high have
taken their stand, gazing on the beauty of its streams, since
they perceive more clearly than we the power of the oblation
and its unapproachable flashing rays. Just as, if one were to
put one's hand or tongue into molten gold, if that were
possible, he would at once make it golden, so too the oblation affects the soul, but much more so. The stream gushes

up more vigorously than fire; it does not burn, however, but only cleanses what it touches.

This blood was formerly foreshadowed continually in the altars, in the sacrifices of the Law. This is the price of the world; by it Christ purchased the church; by it He adorned her entirely. Just as a man in buying slaves gives gold, and, if he desires to beautify them, does this with gold, so also Christ has both purchased us with His blood, and adorned us with His blood. Those who share in this blood have taken their stand with angels and archangels, and the powers from on high, clad in the royal livery of Christ, and holding spiritual weapons. But I have not mentioned anything great, for they are wearing the King Himself (*cf* Gal 3.27).

However, since it is a great and wonderful thing, if you approach with purity, you come unto salvation; but if you approach with a guilty conscience, you come unto punishment and retribution. "For He who eats and drinks unworthily of the Lord," scripture says, "eats and drinks condemnation to himself (1 Co 11.27, 29)." If, then, those who defile the royal purple are punished in the same way as those who rend it, why is it unfitting that those who receive the body with unclean dispositions have in store for them the same punishment as those who rent it with nails? Indeed, see how Paul has described the fearful punishment in the words: "A man making void the law of Moses dies without any mercy on the word of two or three witnesses; how much worse punishment do you think he deserves who has trodden under foot the Son of God, and has regarded as common the blood of the covenant through which he has been sanctified (Heb 10.28-29)."

Let us who enjoy such blessings, beloved, take heed to ourselves, and when we are tempted to say something shameful, or when we find ourselves being carried away by anger or some other such passion, let us reflect on what privileges we have been granted, what Spirit it is whose presence we enjoy, and this thought will check for us the unruly passions. How long, indeed, shall we be attached to present things? How long shall we remain asleep? How long shall we not take thought for our own salvation? Let us remember what privileges God has bestowed on us, let us give thanks, let us glorify Him, not only by faith, but also by our very works, in order that we may obtain "the good things which are to come (Hb 9.11)," by the grace and love for mankind of our Lord Jesus Christ, with whom glory be to the Father, together with the Holy Spirit, now, and always, and unto ages of ages. Amen.

IIIB5 John Chrysostom (c 349-407), *Homily on 1 Corinthians* No. 24, excerpt (on 1 Co 10.16-18).
ed PG 61.199-201; *tr* LNPF, revised.

> John Chrysostom's homilies on First and Second Corinthians were delivered in Antioch, perhaps after the set of homilies on John, thus in the period 392-397. This excerpt from Homily No. 24 is a commentary on 1 Co 10.16-18, and, curiously, it contains more eucharistic theology, strictly speaking, than III B6 which is concerned with the Institution Narrative of 1 Co 11.23-28. In each, Chrysostom's eucharistic teaching is inseparable from his pastoral concerns for the place of the eucharist in the life of the Christian community and in the lives of individual Christians.

THE CUP OF BLESSING WHICH WE BLESS, IS IT NOT A SHARING OF THE BLOOD OF CHRIST?

What are you saying, O blessed Paul? When you wish to shame the hearer, and are making mention of the awesome mysteries, do you give the title of CUP OF BLESSING to that fearsome and most awesome cup? "Yes," he says, "for that is no mean epithet. For when I say BLESSING, I disclose the entire treasure of God's goodness, and call to mind those mighty gifts." For we also, recounting over the cup the ineffable mercies of God and all that we have been made sharers of, so draw near to Him and communicate, giving Him thanks that He has delivered mankind from error, that He made those far off near to Him (Ep 2.13), that, when they had no hope and were without God in the world, He made them His own brothers and co-heirs (Rm 8.17). For these and all such things we give thanks, and thus approach. "How, then, is your behavior not inconsistent," he says, "O Corinthians, blessing God for delivering you from idols, but running again to their tables?"

THE CUP OF BLESSING WHICH WE BLESS, IS IT NOT A SHARING OF THE BLOOD OF CHRIST?

He spoke very convincingly and very frighteningly. For what he says is this: "This which is in the cup is that which flowed from His side, and of it we partake." But he called it a cup of blessing, because when we hold it in our hands, we thus praise Him, wondering and astonished at His ineffable gift, blessing Him for pouring out this very drink, that we might not abide in error, and not only for pouring it out, but also for imparting it to us all. "Wherefore, if you desire blood," He says, "do not redden the altars of idols with the slaughter of brute beasts, but my altar, with my blood." Tell me, what could be more awe-inspiring than this, what more tenderly kind?

This is what lovers also do. When they see those whom they love desiring what belongs to strangers, and despising their own possessions, lovers give what is theirs, and so persuade their loved ones to withdraw themselves from the gifts of those others. Lovers, however, display this munificence in money and clothing and goods, but no one ever did it in blood. But Christ showed His care and fervent love for us in this too. In the Old Covenant, because they were in an imperfect state, He Himself endured to receive the blood which they used to offer to idols in order to separate them from those idols. This, again, was a proof of His indescribable affection. But now He has transferred the priestly activity to something which is far more awesome and glorious, changing the sacrifice itself, and commanding that He Himself be offered instead of the slaughter of dumb animals.

THE BREAD WHICH WE BREAK, IS IT NOT A SHARING IN THE BODY OF CHRIST?

Why did he not say "partaking?" Because he wished to express something greater and to indicate a great union. For when we receive communion, we do not only participate and receive, but we are also united. For just as that body was united to Christ, so also are we united to Him through this bread.

But why does he add WHICH WE BREAK? One may, indeed, see this done in the eucharist, but not on the Cross, but the very opposite, for "Not a bone of Him shall be broken (Jn 19.36)." But what He did not suffer on the Cross, that He does suffer in the oblation for your sake, and submits to be broken, that He may fill all.

Moreover, because he said A SHARING IN THE BODY, and that which shares is different from what it shares in, he removed even this small difference. For after he said A SHARING IN THE BODY, he sought again to express it more precisely, and so he added FOR WE, THOUGH MANY, ARE ONE BREAD, ONE BODY. "For why am I speaking of sharing?" he says, "We are that very body." For what is the bread? The body of Christ. And what do they become who partake of it? The body of Christ; not many bodies, but one body. For just as the bread, consisting of many grains, was made one, so that the grains are nowhere seen—they exist, indeed, but their difference is not seen because of their being joined together—so also are we conjoined both with each other and with Christ. You are not fed from one body, and the next person from another, but all from the very same one. And so, he adds FOR WE ALL PARTAKE OF THE ONE BREAD. Now if from the same bread, and we all become the same, why do we not also exhibit the same love, and become one in this respect also? For this was indeed the case of old, in the time of our forefathers, "For the multitude of those who believed were of one heart and soul (Ac 4.32)." It is not that way now, however, but the complete opposite. Many and various are the contentions between all, and we are disposed worse than wild animals towards the members of one another. And

Christ joined you to Himself, though you were far removed, but you do not condescend to be united to your brother with the required care, but you cut yourself off, though you have enjoyed the blessing of such great love and life from the Lord. For He has not given His body idly. Rather, because the earlier nature of flesh, that which had been formed from the earth, had become dead through sin and was devoid of life, He brought in as another sort of dough and leaven, so to speak, his own flesh, by nature the same, but free from sin and full of life, and He gave it to all to be shared in, that, nourished by it, and having set aside the former, dead flesh, we might be suited through that very table for immortal life.

BEHOLD ISRAEL ACCORDING TO THE FLESH. ARE NOT THOSE WHO EAT THE VICTIMS SHARERS OF THE ALTAR?

Again, from the Old Covenant, he brings them to this same point. Because they were far beneath the greatness of the things of which he had spoken, he persuades them both from the things of old, and from things to which they were accustomed. And he said well, ACCORDING TO THE FLESH, as if they themselves were according to the spirit. And what he says is like this: "Even from people who are more dense you may be taught that those who eat the sacrifices have a sharing with the altar." Do you see how he suggests that those who seemed to be perfect do not have perfect knowledge if they do not even know that the result of these sacrifices for many is often a kind of sharing and friendship with devils, as habit takes them in bit by bit? For if among men the sharing of salt and of the table becomes an occasion and symbol of friendship, it is possible that this may also happen with devils.

But please consider how, with regard to the Jews, he did not say "they are sharers with God," but THEY ARE SHARERS OF THE ALTAR, for what was placed on the altar was burned. But in the case of the body of Christ it is not so. How? It is a SHARING OF THE LORD'S BODY. For we have a sharing, not with the altar, but with Christ Himself.

IIIB6 John Chrysostom (*c* 349-407), Homily on 1 Corinthians No. 27.3-end (on 1 Co 11.23-28).

ed PG 61.228-232; *tr* LNPF, revised.

> This selection could well be presented in section IV, for Chrysostom takes the Institution Narrative of 1 Co 11.23 *ff* as his point of departure to follow Paul in his concern for the function and significance of the eucharist in the life of the church, with how Christians treat one another, and themselves. It is this abiding concern, evident in all the selections from Chrysostom in this volume, which is, it seems to me, his chief contribution.

Next, wishing also from another point of view to shame them even more, he weaves his words from matters more important still:
FOR I RECEIVED FROM THE LORD, he says, WHAT I ALSO HANDED ON TO YOU: THAT THE LORD JESUS, ON THE NIGHT ON WHICH HE WAS BETRAYED, TOOK BREAD, AND WHEN HE HAD GIVEN THANKS, HE BROKE IT, AND SAID: TAKE, EAT; THIS IS MY BODY, WHICH IS BROKEN FOR YOU. DO THIS IN REMEMBRANCE OF ME.
Why does he make mention of the mysteries here? Because that subject is necessary to him for the matter at hand. "For your Master," he is saying, "considered everyone worthy of the same table, though it is altogether awesome, and far surpasses the dignity of all. But you consider these persons to be unworthy even of your own table, small and mean as it is. And while they have no more than you in spiritual matters, you plunder them in physical things, though even those are not your own." However, he does not speak thus, to prevent his words from becoming harsh. He puts it in a gentler way, saying THAT THE LORD JESUS, ON THE NIGHT ON WHICH HE WAS BETRAYED, TOOK BREAD.
And why does he remind us of that time, of that evening, of the betrayal? Not idly, not without a reason, but to fill

them with remorse by the recollection of that time. For even if one is a stone, when he considers that night, how He was so sad with His disciples, how He was betrayed, how He was bound, how He was led away, how He was judged, how He suffered all the rest, even such a one becomes softer than wax, and is withdrawn from earth and from all its illusions. And so he brings us to the recollection of all those things, putting us to shame by the time and the table and the betrayal, and saying: "Your Master gave up His very self for your sake, and you do not even share a little food with your brother for your own sake."

4. But how does he say that he received it from the Lord, since surely he was not present then, but was one of the persecutors? So that you may learn that that table has nothing greater than the one which comes afterwards. For even today, it is He who accomplishes all and bestows it, just as then.

And not for this reason alone does he remind us of that night, but to bring us to remorse in yet another way. For just as we remember most especially the words which we hear last from those who are dying, and, when we wish to shame their heirs, if they dare to transgress their commands, we say: "Bear in mind that this was the last word your father spoke to you, and that until the evening when he was about to breathe his last he kept repeating these things," so also does Paul, intending thus to make his argument forceful. "Remember," he says, "that this was the final mystical instruction He gave to you, and on the night on which He was about to be slain for us, He gave these commands, and after giving us that supper, added nothing afterwards."

Next he goes on to narrate the very things which were done, saying: HE TOOK BREAD, AND, WHEN HE HAD GIVEN THANKS, BROKE IT, AND SAID: TAKE, EAT; THIS IS MY BODY, WHICH IS BROKEN FOR YOU. If, therefore, you come to the eucharist, do not do anything unworthy of the eucharist. Do not shame your brother, or neglect him in his hunger. Do not be intoxicated, do not insult the church. You come giving thanks for what you have enjoyed, so give back something in exchange and do not cut yourself off from your neighbor. For Christ gave equally to all, when He said TAKE, EAT. He gave His body equally, but you do not even share ordinary bread equally. For the sake of all alike was He broken, and became the body equally for the sake of all.

IN LIKE MANNER, ALSO THE CUP, AFTER SUPPER, SAYING: THIS CUP IS THE NEW COVENANT IN MY BLOOD. DO THIS, AS OFTEN AS YOU DRINK OF IT, IN REMEMBRANCE OF ME.

What do you say? You are making a remembrance of Christ, you despise the poor, and yet you do not tremble? If a son or brother had died, and you were making a remembrance of him, you would have been struck by your conscience if you had not followed the custom and invited the poor. And when you are making a remembrance of your Master, you do not even share the table?

But what is this which He says, THIS CUP IS THE NEW COVENANT? For there was also a cup of the Old Covenant, the libations, and the blood of brute animals. And after sacrificing, they used to catch the blood in a cup or bowl, and thus pour it out. Since He has substituted His own blood for the blood of beasts, He reminds them of that ancient sacrifice, lest anyone should be disturbed by hearing this.

Next, after speaking of that Supper, he connects the present with that time, so that men might be disposed now as if on that very evening, reclining on that very couch, and receiving this sacrifice from Christ Himself, and so he says: FOR AS OFTEN AS YOU EAT THIS BREAD, AND DRINK THIS CUP, YOU PROCLAIM THE LORD'S DEATH, UNTIL HE COMES.

For as Christ said of the bread and the cup, DO THIS IN REMEMBRANCE OF ME, to show us the reason for His giving the mystery, and, in addition, to declare that this is an adequate basis for reverence—for when you consider what your Master has suffered for you, you will be more temperate—so also Paul says here, AS OFTEN AS YOU EAT, YOU PROCLAIM HIS DEATH. And this is that supper. Next, to show that it will endure until the end, he says: UNTIL HE COMES.

THEREFORE WHOEVER EATS THIS BREAD AND DRINKS THE CUP OF THE LORD UNWORTHILY WILL BE GUILTY OF THE BODY AND THE BLOOD OF THE LORD.

And why so? Because He poured it out, and showed the act to be a slaughter, and no longer a sacrifice. And so, just as those who pierced Him then did not pierce Him in order to drink, but to shed His blood, so also does the one who comes for it unworthily gain no benefit from it. Do you see how frightening he makes his words and inveighs against them, showing that if they drink in this way, they partake unworthily of the offerings? How other than unworthily, when one neglects the hungry, when, more than overlooking them, one puts them to shame? For if not giving to the poor expels one from the Kingdom, even though that one be a virgin—or, rather, not giving liberally , for even those virgins had oil, but they did not have it in abundance (Mt 25.1-13)—consider then what sort of wickedness it is to perform such base deeds?

5. "What base deeds?" you say. How do you say "What base deeds?" You have partken of a table so wonderful, and when you should be more gentle than anyone, and like the angels, you become more cruel than any. You have tasted the blood of the Lord, and not even thus do you acknowledge your brother. What pardon can you deserve? Indeed, if you did not know him before this, you should have come to know him from the table. But now you dishonor the very table, for he was counted worthy to partake of it, but you do not count him worthy of your food. Have you not heard how much the one who demanded the one hundred *denarii* suffered, how he made void the gift bestowed on him (Mt 18.28ff)? Do you not consider what you were and what you have become? Do you not, then, remember that if this man is poor in possessions, you were poorer still in good works, full of countless sins? Nonetheless, God delivered you from all of them, and counted you worthy of so wonderful a table. But even so you

have not become more kindly to your fellow man. Therefore, nothing remains but that you should be "handed over
to the torturers (Mt 18.34)."

Let us all hear these words too, all who here approach this
holy table with the poor, but, when we go out, appear not
even to have noticed them, and are drunk, and hurry past
the hungry—the very things of which the Corinthians were
accused! "And when does this happen?" you say. All the
time, to be sure, but especially on the feastdays, when
especially this ought not to take place. At these times,
immediately after communion, there follows drunkenness
and contempt for the poor. And after you have partaken of
the blood, when it is time for you to fast and keep vigil, you
give yourself over to wine and carousing. Now if you happen
to have breakfasted well, you take care that no unpleasant
food spoil the taste of the earlier meal. But after you have
feasted on the Spirit, you bring in satanic luxury. Consider
what the apostles did after they partook of that holy supper.
Did they not turn to prayers and the singing of hymns, to
holy vigils, to the long work of teaching, full of great self-
denial? For at that supper He told and announced to them
great and astounding things, after Judas had gone out to
summon those who would crucify Him. Have you not heard
also how the three thousand who partook of communion
persevered in prayer and teaching (Ac 2.41—42), and not in
drunken feasts and revels (Rm 13.13)? But you fast before
you partake, so that you may somehow appear worthy of
communion; but when you have partaken, and should be
increasing your temperance, you undo everything. And yet
it is not the same to fast before this and after it. For although
it is our duty to be temperate at both times, it is especially so
after we have received the Bridegroom—beforehand, that
you may become worthy to receive; afterwards, that you
may not be found unworthy of what you have received.

"What! Do we have to fast *after* communion?" I am not
saying this, nor do I require it; it would be good, but I am
not forcing you; but I urge you not to feast to excess. For if
one should never live luxuriously, and Paul showed this

when he said "She who gives herself to pleasure is dead while she lives (1 Tm 5.6)," she will be dead all the more at that particular time. And if luxury is death to a woman, it is much more so to a man; and if it is fatal at another time, it is much more so after the communion of the mysteries. And do you, after receiving the bread of life, do a deed of death, and not tremble? Do you not know what great evils are caused by luxury? Unseasonable laughter, disorderly expressions, buffoonery full of destruction, mindless trifling, and other things which it is not proper to mention. And you do these things when you have enjoyed the table of Christ, on the very day on which you have been counted worthy to touch His flesh with your tongue! To prevent this, each one of you should make pure your right hand, your tongue, and your lips which have become a threshold for Christ to walk upon. And when you set a material table, turn your mind to that table, to the supper of the Lord, to the vigil of the disciples, on that night, that holy night. Indeed, if one would consider carefully, the present time is a night. Let us keep watch, then, with the Master; let us be pricked in our hearts with the disciples. It is time for prayers, not for drunkenness, always, indeed, but especially on a feastday. For a feastday occurs for this purpose, not for us to misbehave, not for us to pile up sins, but, rather, that we may eliminate those which exist.

I know that I am saying these things in vain, but I will not stop saying them. For if all of you do not obey, all will not disobey. Or rather, even if you should all be disobedient, my recompense will be greater, but your condemnation will be greater. But that it may not be greater, that is why I will not cease to speak. For perhaps, perhaps, by my perseverance I will be able to reach you.

And so, I urge, let us not behave in this way unto our condemnation. Let us feed Christ, let us give Him drink, let us clothe Him (Mt 25.35ff). These things are worthy of that table. Have you heard holy hymns? Have you witnessed a spiritual marriage? Have you enjoyed a royal table? Have you been filled with the Holy Spirit? Have you joined in the choir of the seraphim? Have you become a comrade of the powers above? Do not throw away so great a joy, do not waste the treasure, do not bring in drunkenness as well, that mother of depression, joy of the devil, parent of countless evils. For from it comes a sleep like death, heaviness of head, and illness, and forgetfulness, and the likeness of death. Furthermore, if you would not care to meet a friend when you have been drinking, do you dare, when you have Christ within, to thrust in upon Him such great drunkenness?

But you are fond of pleasure. So leave off drunkenness. For I, too, would have you enjoy yourself, but with the real pleasure, the one which never fades. What then is the real pleasure, ever flourishing? Invite Christ to dine. Share with Him what is yours, or, rather, what is His. The thingt the former exposes himself to a kind of torrent, a besieging army of maladies, and cannot endure the storm.

That this may not happen, let us follow moderation. For thus we will be in good health, and we will have placed our souls in safety, and will be delivered from evils present and to come. May we be delivered from them and attain to the Kingdom, through the grace and love for mankind of our Lord Jesus Christ, with whom, to the Father, together with the Holy Spirit, be glory, power, and honor, now, and always, and unto the ages of ages. Amen.

IIIB7 Augustine of Hippo (354-430), *Tractate on the Gospel of John* No. 26.12-20 (on Jn 6.50-58). *ed* CCSL 36.265-269; *tr* LNPF, revised.

Augustine's commentary on John is in the form of 124 sermons, or *tractatus*, as they are called. As in the case of the *Enarrationes* on the Psalms, some were preached and some were dictated; various dates have been proposed for their composition, extending from the period 405-410 to sometime after 419/20. Recent work suggests that Tractate 26 was preached, at Hippo, in 414. We have excerpted paragraphs 12-20. In commenting on Jn 6.50-58, Augustine recapitulates most of his eucharistic teaching.

12. THIS IS THE BREAD WHICH COMES DOWN
FROM HEAVEN. The manna signified this bread; God's
altar signified this bread. They were sacraments, differing in
their signs, but alike in the reality which was signified. Hear
the Apostle: "I do not want you to be ignorant, brothers," he
says, "that all our fathers were under the cloud, and all
passed through the sea, and all were baptized unto Moses in
the cloud and in the sea, and all ate the same spiritual food (1
Co 10.1-3)," food of the same spiritual character, to be sure,
but of a different physical character, because they ate
manna, but we eat something else, but theirs was spiritual,
as is ours. But "our fathers," not "their fathers," the ones
whom we are like, not the ones whom they were like. And he
adds: "And they all drank the same spiritual drink."— They
had one kind of drink, we a different one, but only in its
visible aspect, because, for all that, it signified the same
thing in its spiritual power. How was it the same drink?
"They drank," he says, "from the spiritual rock which followed them, and the rock was Christ (1 Co 10.4)." The
source of the bread, the source of the drink. The rock was
Christ in sign; the real Christ is in the word and in flesh. And
how did they drink? The rock was struck twice with a
rod—the double striking signifies the two wooden beams of
the Cross. THIS, then, IS THE BREAD WHICH CAME
DOWN FROM HEAVEN, THAT ANYONE WHO EATS
OF IT MAY NOT DIE. But this is what belongs to the
power of the sacrament, not to the visible sacrament itself,
and to him who eats inwardly, not outwardly, him who eats
in his heart, not him who presses with his teeth.

13. I AM THE LIVING BREAD WHICH COMES
DOWN FROM HEAVEN, living, because I come down
from heaven." The manna also came down from heaven, but
the manna was a shadow, this is the truth. IF ANYONE
EAT OF THIS BREAD, HE WILL LIVE FOREVER.
AND THE BREAD WHICH I WILL GIVE IS MY
FLESH FOR THE LIFE OF THE WORLD. When could
flesh understand that what He called bread is flesh? What
flesh does not understand is called flesh, and therefore all

the more flesh does not understand, because it is called flesh. For they shuddered at this, they said it was too much for them, they thought that this could not be done. IT IS MY FLESH, He says, FOR THE LIFE OF THE WORLD. The faithful know the body of Christ, if they do not neglect to be the body of Christ. Let them become the body of Christ if they wish to live from the Spirit of Christ. Nothing lives from the Spirit of Christ except the body of Christ. Understand, O my brothers, what I have said. You are a human being, and you have a spirit, and you have a body. I term spirit that which is called the soul, the soul upon which your existence as a human being is based, for you consist of soul and body. And so, you have an invisible spirit and a visible body. Tell me what lives from what. Does your spirit live from your body, or your body from your spirit? Every living person will reply—and whoever cannot answer this, I do not know if he is living—What will every living person reply? "Of course, my body lives from my spirit!" Do you too, then, wish to live from the Spirit of Christ? Be in the body of Christ. Does my body live from your spirit? My body lives from my spirit, and your body lives from your spirit. The body of Christ cannot live except from the Spirit of Christ. That is why the Apostle Paul, explaining this bread to us, says: "We, though many, are one bread, one body (1 Co 10.17)." O Sacrament of Piety! O Sign of Unity! O Bond of Charity! He who wishes to live has where he may live, has the means of life. Let him approach, let him believe, let him be incorporated, that he may be made to live. Let him not recoil from the joining of the limbs, let him not be a rotten member which deserves to be amputated, let him not be a deformed member to be ashamed of. Let him be a member lovely, proportionate, and healthy. Let him cleave to the body, living for God, from God. Let him struggle now on earth, to reign afterwards in heaven.

14. THE JEWS THEREFORE ARGUED AMONG THEMSELVES, SAYING: "HOW CAN HE GIVE US HIS FLESH TO EAT?" Of course they argued among themselves, for they did not understand the bread of con-

cord, nor did they wish to receive it. For those who eat such bread do not argue among themselves, since "Though many, we are one bread, one body," and it is through this bread that "God makes people of one mind to dwell in a household" (Ps 67.7).

15. Now what they are asking about, as they argue among themselves, that is, how the Lord could give His flesh to eat, that they do not hear at once, but so far He only says to them: AMEN, AMEN I SAY TO YOU, UNLESS YOU EAT THE FLESH OF THE SON OF MAN, AND DRINK HIS BLOOD, YOU WILL NOT HAVE LIFE IN YOU. "You do not know how it is to be eaten, nor what is the manner of eating this bread; nonetheless, UNLESS YOU EAT THE FLESH OF THE SON OF MAN, AND DRINK HIS BLOOD YOU WILL NOT HAVE LIFE IN YOU." He said these words not, indeed, to corpses, but to living men. Wherefore, so that they would not take Him to mean this life, and argue about that, He went on, adding: HE WHO EATS MY FLESH, AND DRINKS MY BLOOD, HAS LIFE ETERNAL. No one has eternal life who does not eat this bread and does not drink this blood. Men may have temporal life without it, but they cannot have eternal life. So the one who does not eat His flesh and does not drink His blood does not have life in him; and the one who does eat His flesh and does drink His blood has life. His use of the term "eternal" applies to each case. This is not so with that food which we take to sustain this temporal life, for the one who does not eat it will not live, nor yet will the one who does eat it live. For it happens that most, even of those who eat it, die, due to old age, disease, or some mishap. But with this food and drink, that is, with the body and blood of the Lord, this is not the case. For the one who does not receive it does not have life; he who does receive it does have life, and this life is eternal.

Thus He wants this food and drink to be understood to be the society of His body and its members, which is holy church in its saints and faithful ones, predestined, called, justified, and glorified (Rm 8.30). The first of these has already taken place, that is, the predestination; the second and third have taken place, are taking place, and will take place, that is, the calling and the justification; the fourth exists in hope for the present, but will be a fact in the future, that is, the glorification. The sacrament of this reality, that is, of the unity of the body and blood of Christ, is in some places daily, in some places at fixed intervals of days prepared upon the Lord's table and received from the Lord's table, by some unto life, by some unto destruction. And yet the reality of which it is the sacrament is for the life of every man who receives it, and for the destruction of no one.

16. But lest they suppose that in this food and drink eternal life was being promised in such a way that those who receive it would not even now die in the body, He kindly anticipated this supposition, and after He had said HE WHO EATS MY FLESH AND DRINKS MY BLOOD HAS ETERNAL LIFE, He added at once AND I WILL RAISE HIM UP ON THE LAST DAY, so that, for the time being, he may have, according to the spirit, an eternal life in that repose which receives the spirits of the saints, but will not be cheated of the eternal life of the body, but may have it at the res irrection of the dead on the last day.

17. FOR MY FLESH, He says, IS TRULY BREAD, AND MY BLOOD IS TRULY DRINK. For though men seek by means of food and drink to avoid hunger and thirst, nothing truly provides this except that food and drink which makes those who receive it immortal and incorruptible, makes them that very society of the saints in which there will be peace and full and perfect unity. It is for this reason, you see, as men of God before our time have realized, that our Lord Jesus Christ gave His body and blood in things which from plurality are reduced to a unity. For one unity is made from many grains, another unity flows together from many grapes.

18. Finally He explains how what He is speaking of is to come about, and what it is to eat His body and drink His blood. HE WHO EATS MY FLESH AND DRINKS MY BLOOD ABIDES IN ME AND I IN HIM. Therefore, to eat that flesh and to drink that drink is to abide in Christ and

to have Him abiding in oneself. And so he who does not abide in Christ and in whom Christ does not abide is, beyond doubt, one who neither eats his flesh nor drinks His blood, but instead eats and drinks the sacrament of so great a reality unto condemnation for himself (1 Co 11.29), because, though unclean, he has presumed to approach the sacraments of Christ which no one receives worthily except him who is clean, concerning whom is said: "Blessed are the clean of heart, for they shall see God (Mt 5.8)."

19. He says JUST AS THE LIVING FATHER SENT ME, AND I LIVE BECAUSE OF THE FATHER, ALSO HE WHO EATS ME WILL LIVE BECAUSE OF ME. He did not say "Just as I eat the Father, and I live because of the Father, also he who eats me will live because of me." For the Son, who was born equal, does not become better by partaking of the Father in the way that we are made better by partaking of the Son through the unity of His body and blood, signified by that eating and drinking. We, therefore, eating Him, live because of Him, that is, we receive Him as the eternal life which we did not have of ourselves. He, however, lives because of the Father, sent by Him, because He emptied Himself, become obedient even unto the death of the cross (Ph 2.7,8). For if we understand I LIVE BECAUSE OF THE FATHER in the light of what He says elsewhere, "The Father is greater than I (Jn 14.28)," in the same way as we live because of Him, because He is greater than we, this comes about because He was sent. His being sent, you see, was the emptying of Himself and His taking on the form of a servant, (Ph 2.7) and this is a correct understanding as long as one maintains the equality in nature of the Son with the Father. For the Father is greater than the Son as man, but He has the Son as God as His equal, inasmuch as the Son is the same both God and man, the Son of God and the Son of Man, the one Christ Jesus. It was with this meaning, if we understand these words correctly, that He said JUST AS THE LIVING FATHER SENT ME, AND I LIVE BECAUSE OF THE FATHER, ALSO HE WHO EATS ME WILL LIVE BECAUSE OF

ME, as if He were to say: "My emptying, whereby He sent me, brought it about that I live because of the Father, that is, that I refer my life to Him as if to one greater; but that anyone lives because of me is brought about by that participation whereby he eats me. And so, I, being humbled, live because of the Father; man, raised up, lives because of me." But if the statement I LIVE BECAUSE OF THE FATHER was made because He is from the Father and not the Father from Him, it was said without any loss of equality. On the other hand, in saying ALSO HE WHO EATS ME WILL LIVE BECAUSE OF ME, He did not indicate that His equality and ours is the same, but He showed forth the grace of the Mediator.

20. THIS IS THE BREAD WHICH COMES DOWN FROM HEAVEN that by eating it we may live, because we cannot have eternal life ourselves. NOT, he says, AS YOUR FATHERS ATE MANNA, AND ARE DEAD; HE WHO EATS THIS BREAD WILL LIVE ETERNALLY. He wants us to take their having died to mean that they do not live eternally. For, to be sure, even those who eat Christ will die in a temporal way. But they live eternally, because Christ is eternal life.

IIIB8 Cyril of Alexandria (*d* 444), *Commentary on Matthew*, fragments 298, 290.

ed TU 61.255-256; *lit* E. Gebremedhin, *Life-giving Blessing: An Inquiry into the Eucharistic Doctrine of St. Cyril of Alexandria* (Uppsala, 1977).

Cyril was the protegé of his uncle Theophilus, archbishop of Alexandria (see IIC3). He accompanied Theophilus to the infamous Synod of the Oak in 403, and succeeded him in the see of Alexandria in 412. Cyril exhibited many of his uncle's disagreeable characteristics. He is best known as a dogmatic theologian and polemicist, particularly for his attacks on the heterodox Nestorius (see IVA8). In this section, however, we meet Cyril as a commentator, remarkable not so much for the brilliance of his exegesis as for the sublimity of his teaching about the eucharist.

Cyril's commentary on Matthew, written sometime after 428, survives only in the fragments preserved in the *catenae* (chains), continuous commentaries on scripture composed of selections from the earlier works of the fathers.

Fragment 289.

After the Lord took the cup, He gives thanks, that is, in the form of a prayer He speaks with God the Father, manifesting that He is, as it were, the partner and co-signer of the life-giving blessing to be given to us, and at the same time giving us the model of first giving thanks, and then breaking the bread and distributing it. Therefore, we also, when we place the aforementioned objects before the eyes of God, have need of being earnestly reformed unto a spiritual blessing, that partaking of these things, we may be sanctified in body and soul. But He said quite plainly THIS IS MY BODY, and THIS IS MY BLOOD, so that you may not suppose that the things you see are a type; rather, in some ineffable way they are changed by God, who is able to do all things, into the body and blood of Christ truly offered. Partaking of them, we take into us the life-giving and sanctifying power of Christ. For it was needful that He, through the Holy Spirit in us, in a manner proper to God, be mixed, as it were, with our bodies by means of His holy flesh and precious blood. These are ours for a life-giving blessing in the bread and wine, so that we may not be appalled seeing flesh and blood offered on the holy tables of the churches. For God puts the power of life into the offerings, bringing Himself down to our weakness, and He changes them into the energy of His own life. And so that you may have no doubt that this is true, He said clearly THIS IS MY BODY, and THIS IS MY BLOOD. Receive the word of the Saviour with faith, for being the Truth, He does not lie.

Fragment 290.

After Judas went out, the Saviour bestowed on the Eleven the salvific mystery. For since Christ was soon afterwards going to rise with His own flesh to return to the Father, in order that we might have the presence of His body—for without the presence of Christ man cannot be saved, nor freed from death and sin, unless Life is with us—He gave us His own body and blood, that through them even the power of corruption might be undone, and that He might dwell in our souls through the Holy Spirit, and we might become partakers of sanctity, and be called heavenly and spiritual men.

IIIB9 Cyril of Alexandria (*d* 444), *Commentary on the Gospel of John* 4.2, selections (on Jn 6.51 and 53).

ed P. E. Pusey (Oxford, 1872) 1.518-520, 529-531.

> Cyril's commentary on John, written in the period 425-429, is a vast work of continuous commentary, full of dogmatic excursus and polemic argument. Considerations of space limit us to two short extracts from his commentary on the eucharistic discourse in John 6, on Jn 6.51 and Jn 6.53, wherein he elaborates a favorite theme, the life-giving character of the body of Christ.

AND THE BREAD WHICH I WILL GIVE IS MY FLESH FOR THE LIFE OF THE WORLD.

"I die," He says, "for all, that I may give life to all through myself, and I made my flesh a ransom for the flesh of all. For death shall die by my death, and human nature which has fallen will rise again with me. For to this end I became like you, a man, that is, and from the seed of Abraham, that I might become in all respects like my brothers" (Heb 2.17). The blessed Paul understood well what Christ has just now said to us, and he said: "Since, then, the children partook of flesh and blood, He Himself also partook equally of them, that by means of death He might destroy the one who had the power of death, that is, the Devil" (Heb 2.14). For the one who had the power of death, and death itself, could not otherwise have been destroyed, unless Christ gave Himself for us, One as a ransom for all, for He was over all. Therefore, also in the psalms somewhere, offering Himself on our behalf as an unblemished victim to God the Father, He says: "You did not want sacrifice and offering, but you have furnished a body for me. In holocausts and sin-offerings you took no pleasure. Then I said: Behold, I am here. In the title of the book it is written of me: To do your will, O God, has been my desire" (Ps 39.7-9; Heb 10.5-7). For since "the blood of bulls and goats, and the ashes of a heifer" (Heb 9.13) were not adequate for the cleansing of sin, nor yet could the slaughter of brute beasts ever have destroyed the power of death, Christ Himself enters in, in a sense, to undergo punishment for all. "For by His bruises we were healed," as the Prophet says (Is 53.5), and "He Himself bore our sins in His body on the wood" (1 P 2.24). He was crucified for the sake of all and on account of all, that by One dying for the sake of all we might all live in Him. For it was not possible that He be overcome by death (Ac 2.24), nor did corruption exert mastery over Him who is by nature life.

But we will know from His own words that Christ offered His FLESH FOR THE LIFE OF THE WORLD, for He says: "Holy Father, preserve them," and "For their sakes I make myself holy" (Jn 17.11, 19). He says that He makes Himself holy here, not as providing Himself with the benefit of sanctification through purification of soul or spirit, as is thought of in our case, nor yet with the participation of the Holy Spirit, for the Spirit was in Him by nature. He was, and is holy always, and shall be so forever. Rather, He says "I make myself holy" here instead of "I consecrate and offer myself as an unblemished victim for an odor of sweetness," for, according to the Law, that which was brought to the divine altar was made, or, rather, called holy.

Therefore, Christ gave His own body for the life of all, and through His body He makes life to dwell in us again. And how this is, I will say, according to my ability. Inasmuch as the life-giving Word dwelt in flesh, He refashioned that flesh into the good which is peculiar to Him, that is, life; and joined to it, according to the ineffable manner of the union, He rendered it life-giving, as He Himself is by nature. For this reason the body of Christ gives life to those who partake of it. For it expels death whenever it comes into mortals, and it displaces corruption, for it contains the Word, who destroys corruption, perfectly in itself.

Then let those who, because of their folly have never accepted faith in Christ, listen to this: UNLESS YOU EAT THE FLESH OF THE SON OF MAN, AND DRINK HIS BLOOD, YOU DO NOT HAVE ETERNAL LIFE IN YOU. For completely without a share, indeed, without a taste in the life in holiness and blessedness do they remain who have not received Jesus through the mystic blessing. For He is Life by nature, according as He was begotten by the Living Father (Jn 6.57). Moreover, His holy body is no less life-giving, for it was, in a way, gathered to, and, in an indescribable manner, united to the Word who engenders life in all things. Therefore, the body is considered to be His, and is thought of as one with Him. For after the Incarnation it is inseparable, except to the degree that one may know that the Word who has come from the Father, and the temple from the Virgin are not the same by nature, for not of the same essence as the Word from God is the body, and yet they are one by the coming together and the unimaginable concurrence. And since the flesh of the Saviour has become life-giving, as being united to that which is by nature Life, that is, the Word from the Father, whenever we taste of it, then we have life in us, and we are united to His flesh, as it is to the indwelling Word. And therefore, when He raised the dead, the Saviour is found to be acting not by word or by divine commands alone, but He placed a special emphasis on the fact that He was taking His holy flesh as a kind of collaborator in this, to show that it has the power to give life, and that it was already one with Him, for it was really His own body, and not another's. And, indeed, when He raised the daughter of the ruler of the synagogue, saying "Child, get up," He took her hand, as it is written"(Lk 8.54). Giving life, as God, by His all-accomplishing command, but also giving life by the touch of His holy flesh as well, He manifested a single, associated power through both. But also when He approached a city called Nain, and "a corpse was being carried out, his mother's only son," again, "He touched the bier, saying, 'Young man, I say to you, Arise'" (Lk 7.12, 14). And not only to His word does He give power to bring the dead back to life, but, to show that His body is life-giving, as I have already said, He touches the dead, through His body also putting life in those who were already decayed. And if by the touch alone of His holy flesh He gives life to what has become corrupted, how shall we not benefit even more abundantly from the life-giving blessing, whenever we taste it? For it assuredly transforms those who partake of it into its own proper good, that is, immortality.

IIIB10 Cyril of Alexandria (*d* 444), *Homily on the Gospel of Luke* No. 142.

ed R. Payne Smith, Oxford, 1858; *tr* R. Payne Smith, *A Commentary upon the Gospel According to Luke by St. Cyril...* (Oxford, 1859) 664-669, modernized.

Cyril's commentary on Luke is extant, for the most part, only in Syriac translation. Unlike Cyril's other biblical commentaries, it is in the form of homilies, and is more practical and less argumentative, though not without some anti-Nestorian polemic. These homilies are dated to a period from 430 onward.

Here, instead of commenting continuously on the institution narrative from Luke, Cyril makes the scriptural text a point of departure and a frame, and provides, in effect, a sermon on the eucharist and its necessary and beneficial place in the divine economy.

Luke 22.17-22: And He took a cup, and gave thanks, and said: "Take this, and divide it with one another, for I say to you that I will not drink from now on from the fruit of the vine until the kingdom of God has come." And He took bread, and gave thanks, and broke it, and gave it to them, saying: "This is my body which is given for you. Do this in remembrance of me." In like manner also the cup, after He had eaten, saying: "This cup is the New Covenant in my blood which is shed for you. But, behold, the hand of him who betrays me is with me at the table. And the Son of Man indeed goes, according to what has been determined, but woe to that man by whom He is betrayed!"

To be made partakers of Christ, both spiritually and by our senses, fills us with every blessing. For He dwells in us, first, by the Holy Spirit, and we are His abode, according to that which was said of old by one of the holy prophets: "For I will dwell in them," He says, "and lead them, and I will be to them a God, and they shall be to me a people" (Ez 37.27).

But He is also within us in another way by means of our partaking in the oblation of unbloody offerings which we celebrate in the churches, having received from Him the saving pattern of the rite, as the blessed Evangelist plainly shows us in the passage which has just been read. For he tells us that HE TOOK A CUP, AND GAVE THANKS, AND SAID: TAKE THIS, AND DIVIDE IT WITH ONE ANOTHER. Now by His giving thanks, by which is meant His speaking to God the Father in the manner of a prayer, He signified to us that He, so to speak, shares and takes part in His good pleasure in granting to us the life-giving blessing which was then bestowed upon us, for every grace, and every perfect gift (cf Ja 1.17) comes to us from the Father by the Son in the Holy Spirit. And this act, then, was a pattern for our use of the prayer which ought to be offered, whenever the grace of the mystical and life-giving oblation is about to be spread before Him by us. And this, accordingly, is what we do, for first offering up our thanksgivings, and joining in our praises to God the Father both the Son and the Holy Spirit, we so draw near to the holy tables, believing that we receive life and blessing both spiritually and corporeally, for we receive in us the Word of the Father, who for our sakes became man, and who is Life, and life-giving.

Let us, then, inquire, to the best of our ability, what is the view held among us of this mystery, for it is our duty to be "ready to give an answer concerning the hope that is in us," as the wise Peter says (1 P 3.15). The God of all, therefore, created all things in incorruption, and the beginnings of the world were life, "but by the envy of the devil death entered the world" (Ws 2.23-24), for it was that rebel serpent who brought the first man to transgression of the commandment and disobedience by means of which he fell under the divine curse and into the net of death. For it was said to him, "Earth you are, and unto the earth you shall return" (Gn 3.19). Was it, then, right that one who was created for life and immortality should be made mortal, and condemned to death without power of escape? Must the envy of the devil be more unassailable and enduring than the will of God? Not so, for it has been brought to nothing, and the mercy of the Creator has transcended the evil effects of his malice. He has given aid to those upon earth. And what, then, was the manner in which He aided them? One truly great, and admirable, and worthy of God, yes, worthy in the very highest degree of the Supreme Mind. For God the Father is by His own nature Life, and as alone being so, He caused the Son to shine forth, who is also Himself Life, for it could not be otherwise with Him who is the Word who proceeded substantially from Life, from Him who begot Him.

God the Father, therefore, gives life to all things by the Son in the Holy Spirit, and every thing which exists and breathes in heaven and on earth, its existence and life is from God the Father by the Son in the Holy Spirit. Neither, therefore, the nature of angels, nor anything else whatsoever that was made, nor anything that from non-existence was brought into being, possesses life as the fruit of its own nature. But on the contrary, life proceeds, as I said, from the Substance which transcends all, and to it only does life belong, and it alone is able to give life, because it is by nature Life.

How, therefore, can man upon earth, clothed as he is with mortality, return to incorruption? I answer that this dying flesh must be made partaker of the life-giving power which comes from God. But the life-giving power of God the Father is the Onlybegotten Word, and Him He sent to us as a Saviour and Deliverer. And the blessed John the Evangelist clearly tells us how He sent Him, saying: "And the Word became flesh, and dwelt among us" (Jn 1.14). But He became flesh, not by having undergone any change or alteration into what He had not been, nor again by having ceased to be the Word—for He does not know what it is to suffer the shadow of a change (*cf* Ja 1.17)—but rather by having been born in the flesh of a woman, and taken unto Himself that body which He received from her, in order that, having implanted Himself in us by an inseparable union, He might raise us above the power of both death and corruption. And Paul is our witness, where he says of Him and of us, "For inasmuch as the children are partakers of blood and flesh, so He in like manner was partaker of the same, that by death He might bring to nothing him who has dominion over death, that is, the devil, and deliver all those who through fear of death were all their lifetime subject to servitude. For He does not take hold of angels, but He took hold of the seed of Abraham. For which reason it behooved Him in all things to be made like to His brothers," that is, to us (Heb 2.14-17). For He was made in our likeness, and clothed Himself in our flesh, that by raising it from the dead He might prepare a way henceforth by which the flesh which had been humbled unto death might return anew to incorruption. For we are united to Him just as we were united to Adam, when he brought upon himself the penalty of death. And Paul testifies to this, writing thus on one occasion: "For because by man is death, by man is also the resurrection of the dead" (1 Co 15.21), and again on another occasion: "For as in Adam all die, even so in Christ shall all live" (1 Co 15.22). The Word, therefore, by having united to Himself that flesh which was subject to death, as being God and Life, drove corruption away from it, and made it also to be the source of life, for such must the body of Life be.

And do not disbelieve what I have said, but rather accept the word in faith, having gathered proofs of it from a few examples. When you put a piece of bread into wine or oil, or any other liquid, you find that it becomes charged with the quality of that particular thing. When iron is brought into contact with fire, it becomes full of its activity, and, though it is by nature iron, it exerts the power of fire. And so the life-giving Word of God, having united Himself to His own flesh in a way known to Himself, endowed it with the power of giving life. And he Himself assures us of this, saying: "Truly, I say to you, he who believes in me has everlasting life. I am the bread of life" (Jn 6.47-48), and again: "I am the living bread which came down from heaven. If a man eats of this bread, he shall live forever. And the bread which I shall give is my flesh for the life of the world. Truly, I say to you, that if you do not eat the flesh of the Son of Man, and drink His blood, you have no life in you. Whoever eats my flesh, and drinks my blood, has eternal life, and I will raise him up on the last day. For my flesh is true food, and my blood is true drink. He who eats my flesh, and drinks my blood, abides in me, and I in him. As the living Father sent me, and I live because of the Father, so He who eats me shall also live because of me" (Jn 6.51, 53-57). When, therefore, we eat the holy flesh of Christ, the Saviour of us all, and drink His precious blood, we have life in us, being made, as it were, one with Him, and abiding in Him, and possessing Him also in us.

And let none of those whose habit it is to disbelieve say: "Since, therefore, the Word of God, being by nature Life, dwells in us also, is the body of each one of us too endowed with the power of giving life?" Rather, let him know that it is a perfectly different thing for the Son to be in us by a relative participation, and for Himself to become flesh, that is, to make that body which was taken from the blessed Virgin His own. For He is not said to become incarnate and to be made flesh by being in us; but rather this happened once for all when He became man without ceasing to be God. The body, therefore, of the Word was that assumed by Him from the holy Virgin, and made one with Him; but how, or in what manner this was done, we cannot tell, for it is incapable of explanation, and altogether beyond the powers of the mind, and to Himself alone is the manner of the union known.

It was fitting, therefore, for Him to be in us divinely by the Holy Spirit, and also, so to speak, to be mingled with our bodies by His holy flesh and precious blood, which things also we possess as a life-giving blessing, in the form of bread and wine. For lest we should be terrified by seeing flesh and blood placed upon the holy tables of our churches, God, humbling Himself to our infirmities, infuses into the things set before us the power of life, and transforms them into the efficacy of His flesh, that we may have them for a life-giving participation, and that the body of Life may be found in us as a life-producing seed. And do not doubt that this is true, since He Himself plainly says THIS IS MY BODY, THIS IS MY BLOOD, but, rather, receive in faith the Saviour's word, for He, being Truth, cannot lie. And thus you will honor Him, for, as the very wise John says, "He who receives His witness has set his seal that God is true, for He whom God sent speaks the words of God" (Jn 3.33-34). For the words of God are of course true, and in no way whatsoever can they be false, for even though we do not understand how God works acts such as these, yet He Himself knows the way of His works. For when Nicodemus could not understand His words concerning holy baptism and foolishly said, "How can these things be?" he heard Christ say in answer, "Truly, I say to you that we speak that which we know, and testify that which we see, and you do not receive our testimony. If I have spoken to you earthly things, and you do not believe, how will you believe if I tell you heavenly things?" (Jn 3.9, 11-12) For how can a man learn those things which transcend the powers of our mind and reason? Therefore, let this our divine mystery be honored by faith.

But Judas the Traitor, who was eating with Him, was reproved in those words which Christ spoke: BUT

BEHOLD THE HAND OF HIM WHO BETRAYS ME IS WITH ME AT THE TABLE. For he imagined, perchance in his great senselessness, or, rather, as being filled with the arrogance of the devil, that he could deceive Christ, though He is God. But, as I said, he was convicted of being altogether wicked, and hateful to God, and treacherous, and, even so, admission to the table was granted to him, and he was counted worthy of the divine gentleness even to the end, but thereby is his punishment made the more severe. For Christ has somewhere said of him by the Psalmist's voice: "If an enemy had reproached me, I would have borne it; and if he who hated me had spoken against me proud things, I would have hid myself from him. But it was you, my like-in-soul, my neighbor and my acquaintance, who in my company have sweetened food for me, and we went to the house of the Lord in concord (Ps 54.13-15)." Woe, therefore, to him, according to the Saviour's word! For He indeed, according to the good will of God the Father, gave Himself in our place, that He might deliver us from all evil, but the man who betrayed the Saviour and Deliverer of all into the hands of murderers will have for his inheritance the condemnation which is the Devil's fitting punishment. For his guilt was not against one such as we are, but against the Lord of All, by whom, and with whom to God the Father be praise and dominion, with the Holy Spirit, for ever and ever. Amen.

IV "Unity! Verity! Piety! Charity!": The Eucharist in the Christian Community.

Introduction

In Section IV we abandon, in part, the arrangement of selections according to genre for a more topical arrangement, under the general heading "The Eucharist in the Christian Community," under which we include a number of disciplinary and pastoral concerns.

IVA. The first part of this section is concerned with the interplay of the eucharist and orthodox Christian faith and practice. This interplay allows the sort of appeal to shared faith in—and experience of—the eucharist which Leo the Great lodged against Eutyches and his party (see IVA9-10) in a letter to the church of Constantinople in 450:

> In what darkness of ignorance, in what torpor of sloth must they hitherto have lain, not to have learned from hearing, nor come to know from reading, something which in God's church is so unanimously in men's mouths that even the tongues of children do not keep silent about the truth of Christ's body and blood in the sacrament of communion! For in that mystic distribution of spiritual nourishment, what is given and received is of such a nature that, receiving the virtue of the heavenly food, we pass into the flesh of Him who became our flesh.
>
> (Ep 59.2)

Here we are not concerned with separation from the eucharist on account of heterodox belief or behavior (see K. Hein, *Eucharist and Excommunication...*, Bern, 1976). Rather, these passages have been selected to portray the role of the eucharist as a rule of faith in the refutation of heretical teaching (IVA2, IVA3, IVA4, IVA8, IVA9; see also IIC3, IIIB3) and as a test of unity and sincerity (IVA1, IVA10; see also IIA7.2). Some passages, those from Optatus (IVA5) and Augustine (IVA6, IVA7), simply provide examples of important teaching about the eucharist presented in a milieu of anti-schismatic and anti-heretical writing.

The age of the fathers produced no eucharistic heresy as such. Mistaken understanding of the language of type and symbol used in connection with the eucharist gave rise to suspicions (see General Introduction), but there was no real divergence from the general unity of belief however nuanced. The only dispute about the eucharist arose from, to use a scholastic category, the "matter" of the sacrament. Little difficulty was encountered over the use of bread, which was often viewed as symbolizing unity because of its composite nature (see IIA6.1, 2, 3; IIA7.2, IVA8, VA1). Problems arose, however, in various quarters, and for various reasons, over the use of wine. Thus, Filaster of Brescia (Gaudentius' predecessor), in his *Book of Diverse Heresies* of *c*385 reports on an heretical group whom he calls the *Aquarii*: "Another group is the Aquarii, so called because in the heavenly sacraments they offer water, and not that which the catholic and apostolic church is wont to do" (CCSL 9.249). Filaster offers no reason for this use of an unmixed chalice of water, nor, for that matter, do Cyprian (IVA4) and Chrysostom (IIIB3) who speak against the practice; but aquarianism seems to have been a manifestation in practice of a vareity of heretical viewponts.

The simplest situation was the rejection of wine altogether, even in the eucharist, by radical ascetic groups. Less simple is the rejection of wine by millenarians who, because they rejected the mainstream view of the Resurrection as the advent of the Kingdom, put off the use of wine until the millennium, on the basis of Mt 26.29 ("From now on I shall not drink of the fruit of the vine until that day when I shall drink it new with you in the Kingdom of my Father."). The least obvious objection was that of gnostic and other groups who rejected the mixture of wine, symbolizing the divine or heavenly, with water, symbolizing the human or earthly, the sort of symbolism put forward, maybe, by Clement of Alexandria (IIA1).

An oblique refutation of the millenarian objection by John Chrysostom may be found in IIIB3. In IVA we find Irenaeus refuting The Gnostics and Ebionites (IVA2), and Cyprian (IVA4), without going into the causes for aquarian practice, asserting the tradition of the church and explaining the symbolism of the mixed chalice of wine and water (for alternative explanations see IIA3, IIA4, IIB2). The argument against aquarianism probably led to the interpolation of Christ's mixing the chalice in the paraphrases of the institution narrative by Ephraem (IIC1) and in the Liturgy of St. Basil (VA3). The aquarian controversy offers an interesting parallel to later controvesies, like that over the Armenian use of an unmixed chalice of wine, and the Azyme Controversy, in which the "matter" of the eucharist became the center of storms arising from causes extraneous to the eucharist.

IVB. The second part of Section IV contains texts dealing with the dispositions of conversion of self, love of neighbor, and gratitude towards God required for participation in the eucharist. These passages recall Augustine's plea: "...you hear 'The Body of Christ,' and you reply 'Amen.' Be a member of the body of Christ so that your 'Amen' may be true" (IIA6.1). Instructions on the attitude and behavior necessary for worthy participation in the eucharist are provided in the catecheses in IIA, and *passim* in this volume in a variety of settings, especially in connection with Mt 5.23-25 ("Therefore, if you are offering your gift at the altar..."; see IIA3, IIC2, IVA2, IVA5, IVB1, IVD4), and particularly in connection with Paul's warning in 1 Co 11.27-29 ("Therefore, whoever eats this bread or drinks the cup of the Lord unworthily..."), ubiquitous in preaching about the eucharist.

IVC. These selections treat the question of the frequency of communion. Salutary warnings against casual and unconsidered reception of the eucharist had their effect, no doubt, on tender and callous consciences alike, in both cases leading to a less frequent reception of the sacrament. Separating oneself from the eucharist (condemned by Augustine in IVC3, by Isidore in IID1) was a case of doing the apparently right thing for the wrong reason as we see in this remark of Cyril of Alexandria in his comment on John 6.35:

> Since this is the case, let those who have been baptized and have tasted of the divine favor know henceforth that people who go reluctantly to church, who cease for long periods of time to attend the blessing (*eulogia*, i.e. eucharist) that is from Christ, and, because they do not want to partake of Him mystically, allege a damnable reverence, are dismissing themselves from eternal life, are asking to be held excused from being brought to life. Know that their making their excuses, though it seem to be the product of reverence, is, in fact, a snare and a stumbling-block. (PG 73.521)

An emphasis on the august and awesome character of the eucharistic liturgy, of the sort found in the texts in IVD and *passim* in Chrysostom, probably promoted improved behavior on the part of the Christian masses in attendance and increased their appreciation of what had grown routine; but this too was a psychological impediment to frequent access to the sacrament. Awareness of divergence of practice in the frequency of eucharistic liturgies also raised questions about the appropriate frequency of reception. Thus, the texts in IVC address the question of the appropriate response to the two-edged invitation of the eastern liturgies "Holy things for the holy" (IIA3, IVD4, VA3). Two of the selections from Augustine go beyond the question of frequency. The two excerpts in in IVC4 deal with the necessity of the eucharist in this life, over against the life to come. The eucharist is our "Daily Bread" (see IIA6.2 for Augustine's urging of daily communion), but it will not always be so. Another selection from Augustine (IVC5) is included here because it attests to the daily eucharist in the church of Hippo, but more particularly because it gives a valuable insight into Augustine's view of the eucharist as sacrament.

IVD. The selections in this subdivision are self-explanatory. They offer a glimpse of practical preaching about how we should conduct ourselves at the eucharistic assembly, and towards its ministers. IVD complements IVB and IVC in giving us a glimpse of popular piety, or the lack thereof, in the church of the fathers. These texts prevent us from idealizing the congregations of the ancient church, should we be tempted to do so, and they offer, I believe, some solace to contemporary pastors who face the same, perennial problems.

A. "But Our Opinion Agrees with the Eucharist": The Eucharist and Orthodoxy.

IVA1 Ignatius of Antioch (*d* c110), Selections from the Letters to the Churches of Ephesus, Rome, Philadelphia, and Smyrna.
ed SC 10; *tr* ACW, revised.

> St. Ignatius, the Godbearer, the second successor of St. Peter in the see of Antioch, was condemned to death in Antioch and taken for execution to Rome, where he died in the Flavian Amphitheatre *c* 110. The first three of these letters were written during a sojourn in Smyrna on the journey to Rome; he wrote later to the church in Smyrna from Troas.
>
> Ignatius' chief concerns, orthodoxy, unity, fraternal love, against the thought and behavior of the docetists and judaizers of his time, find their pivot in the eucharist, the source and test of all of these ideals.

From the *Letter to the Ephesians*:
5. For a fact, if I in a short time became so closely attached to your bishop—an attachment based not on human, but on spiritual grounds—how much more do I count you happy who are joined to him as the church is to Jesus Christ, and as

Jesus Christ is to the Father! As a result, all things are harmonious in unity. Let no one deceive himself: unless a man is within the sanctuary, he is deprived of the bread of God. Assuredly, if the prayer of one or two has such efficacy, how much more has that of the bishop and the entire church! He, then, who absents himself from the common meeting, by that very fact shows pride and has condemned himself; for the scripture says: "God resists the proud" (Pr 3.34). Let us be zealous, therefore, not to oppose the bishop, that we may be submissive to God.

13. Make an effort, then, to meet more frequently for thanksgiving [*eucharistia*] and praise to God. For, when you meet frequently, the forces of Satan are overthrown, and his baneful influence is destroyed by the unanimity of your faith. Nothing is better than peace. It puts an end to every war waged by heavenly or earthly enemies.

20. If Jesus Christ, because of your prayer, grants me the favor and it is His will, I shall, in the subsequent letter which I intend to write to you, still further explain to you the economy which I have here only touched upon, regarding the New Man Jesus Christ, which is based on faith in Him and love for Him, on His Passion, on His Resurrection. I will do so especially if the Lord should reveal to me that you—the entire community of you!—are in the habit, through grace derived from the Name, of meeting in common in one faith and in Jesus Christ—"who in the flesh was of the line of David" (Rm 1.3), the Son of Man and the Son of God—of meeting, I say, to show obedience with undivided mind to the bishop and the presbytery, and to break the same bread, which is the medicine of immortality and an antidote, that we may not die, but live forever in Jesus Christ.

From the *Letter to the Romans*:

7.2-3. I am writing while still alive, but my yearning is for death. My love has been crucified, and there is in me no fire of love for earthly things. But there is in me a living water (Jn 4.10), which is eloquent and says within me: "Come to the Father." I have no taste for corruptible food or for the delights of this life. Bread of God is what I desire; that is, the flesh of Jesus Christ, who was of the seed of David (Jn 7.42); and for my drink I desire His blood, that is, love incorruptible.

From the *Letter to the Philadelphians*:

4. Take care, then, to celebrate one eucharist. For one is the flesh of our Lord Jesus Christ, and one the cup to unite us with His blood, and one altar, just as there is one bishop with the presbytery and the deacons, my fellow servants. Thus will you conform in all your actions to the will of God.

From the *Letter to the Smyrnaeans*:

6. Let no one be deceived! Even the heavenly powers and the angels in their splendor and the principalities, both visible and invisible, if they do not believe in the blood of Christ, even they will be condemned. "Let him grasp it who can" (Mt 19.12). Let no rank puff up anyone, for faith and love are everything, and to them nothing can be preferred. Observe those who hold erroneous opinions concerning the grace of Jesus which has come to us, how they are opposed to the mind of God! They concern themselves with neither works of charity, nor widows, nor orphans, nor the distressed, nor those in prison or out of it, nor the hungry or thirsty. 7. From eucharist and prayer they hold aloof, because they do not confess that the eucharist is the flesh of our Saviour Jesus Christ, which suffered for our sins, and which the Father in His loving-kindness raised up. And so, those who contradict "the gift of God" (Jn 4.10) perish in their contentiousness. It would be better for them to have love, so as to share in the Resurrection. It is proper, therefore, to avoid associating with such people and not to speak about them either in private or in public, but to attend to the prophets and, especially, the gospel in which the Passion is revealed to us and the Resurrection shown in its fulfillment. Shun divisions as the beginning of evil. 8. You must all follow the lead of the bishop, as Jesus Christ followed that of the Father; follow the presbytery as you would the apostles; reverence the deacons as you would God's commandment. Let no one do anything touching the church apart

from the bishop. Let that celebration of the eucharist be considered valid which is held under the bishop or anyone to whom he has committed it. Where the bishop appears, there is the entire community, just as where Christ is, there is the catholic church. It is not permitted without the bishop either to baptize or to hold an *agape*; but whatever he approves is also pleasing to God. Thus everything you do will be safe and valid (Heb 6.19).

IVA2 Irenaeus of Lyons (*c* 140-*c* 200), *Against Heresies* 4.17.4-18.6; 5.1.3-2.3.

ed SC 100.590-614; 153.24-36; *tr* ANF, revised; *lit* D. Unger,"The Holy Eucharist According to Irenaeus," *Laurentianum* 20 (1979) 103-164.

Irenaeus was probably a native of Smyrna, and as a boy he heard that city's great martyr-bishop Polycarp, a link, according to Irenaeus, to the Apostolic Age. Irenaeus moved westward, to Rome, and then to Lyons, where he became a priest. He was absent from Lyons, on a mission to Rome, during the persecution of 177 (see IA1) in which Bishop Pothinus died. Upon his return, Irenaeus was made bishop.

Irenaeus' principal work, *The Detection and Refutation of the Falsely-named Gnosis* (commonly known as *Against Heresies*), is directed against a variety of gnostic sects and other heretical groups. The entire work survives only in a Latin translation of early but uncertain date.

In Book 4, Irenaeus argues against the contention of the gnostics and Marcionites (see also IVA4) that Creation and the Old Testament were the work of an evil creator-god, or Demiurge, as opposed to the God of the New Testament. In these chapters, Irenaeus shows the true nature of sacrifice: that creation, from which offerings are made, is good as being God's work; that sacrifice is continual from Old Law to New, but made complete in the New Covenant.

In our selection from Book 5, Irenaeus argues against the Ebionites, a radical Jewish-Christian sect who denied the divinity and Virgin birth of Christ (for the Ebionites' aquarianism, see the Introduction to section IV), and against gnostic dualism. Note especially 4.18.4-5 for Irenaeus' appeal to the eucharist as the rule of faith.

4. From all these it is evident that God did not seek from them sacrifices and holocausts, but faith, and obedience, and righteousness, for the sake of their salvation; as God said, when teaching them His will in Hosea the Prophet: "I desire mercy rather than sacrifice, and the knowledge of God more than whole-burnt-offerings" (Hos 6.6). Moreover, our Lord also urged the same thing on them, saying: "But if you had known what this means, 'I desire mercy, and not sacrifice,' you would not have condemned the innocent" (Mt 12.7), bearing witness to the prophets, that they preached the truth, but accusing those men of being foolish through their own fault. 5. Again, giving directions to His disciples to offer to God the firstfruits of His own created things—not as if He stood in need of them, but that they might be themselves neither unfruitful nor ungrateful—He took bread, a part of creation, and gave thanks, saying: "This is my body." And the cup, likewise a part of that creation to which we belong, He declared it to be His blood, and taught the new oblation of the New Covenant. The church, receiving this from the apostles, offers it to God throughout the entire world, to Him who gives us as the means of subsistence the firstfruits of His own gifts in the New Covenant.

Malachy, among the twelve prophets, foretold this as follows: "I have no pleasure in you, says the Lord Almighty, and I will not accept sacrifice from your hands. For from the rising of the sun even to its setting my name is glorified among the gentiles, and in every place incense is offered to my name, and a pure sacrifice; for my name is great among the gentiles, says the Lord Almighty" (Ml 1.10-11). He shows in the plainest manner, by these words, that the former People shall cease to make offerings to God, but that in every place sacrifice shall be offered to Him, a pure sacrifice, and that His name is glorified among the gentiles. 6. But what is the name which is glorified among the gentiles other than that of our Lord, through whom the Father is glorified and man as well? And because it is the name of His own Son, and it was made by Him (*cf* Mt 1.21; Lk 1.31), He calls it His own. Just as a king, if he himself paints a likeness of his son, is right in calling this likeness his own, for both these reasons, because it is of his son, and because it is his own production, so also the Father acknowledges that the name of Jesus Christ, which is glorified in the church throughout the world, is His own, both because it is that of His Son, and because He who inscribed it gave it for the salvation of men (Ac 4.12). Since, therefore, the name of the Son belongs to the Father, and since the church makes offering to Almighty God through Jesus Christ, He says well on both these grounds "and in every place incense is offered to my name, and a pure sacrifice." Now John, in the Apocalypse, declares that the incense is "the prayers of the saints" (Rv 5.8).

18.1. The oblation of the church, therefore, which the Lord commanded to be offered throughout the world, has been accounted by God a pure sacrifice, and is acceptable to Him—not that He stands in need of sacrifice from us, but because the one who offers is himself glorified in what he offers, if his gift be accepted, for, by a gift, both honor and affection towards a king are manifested. And the Lord, wishing us to offer it in all simplicity and innocence, declared: "Therefore, when you are offering your gift at the altar, and you remember that your brother has anything against you, leave your gift at the altar, and go first to be reconciled to your brother, and then return and offer your gift" (Mt 5.23-24). We are bound, therefore, to offer to God the firstfruits of His creation, as Moses also says: "You shall not appear in the presence of the Lord your God empty-handed" (Dt 16.16), so that man, being accounted pleasing to Him in those things in which he has been displeasing, may receive the honor which comes from God.

2. And the class of oblations in general has not been done away with, for there were oblations then, and there are oblations now; there were sacrifices among the People, there are sacrifices also in the church. Rather, the kind alone has been changed, inasmuch as the offering is now made not by slaves, but by freemen. For the Lord is one and the same; but the character of a servile oblation is peculiar to itself, as is also that of the oblation of freemen, in order that, even through the oblations, an indication of freedom might be shown. For with Him there is nothing purposeless, or without significance or meaning. And for this reason the Jews, to be sure, had the tenth part of their goods consecrated to Him. But those who have received liberty set apart all that they have for the Lord's purposes, giving joyfully and freely what is to them less valuable, since they have the hope of greater things, as that poor widow who put all her substance into the treasury of God (Lk 21.1-4).

3. For from the beginning God looked with favor on the gifts of Abel, because he offered with singlemindedness and righteousness, but He had no regard for the offering of Cain, because his heart was divided with the envy and malice which he cherished against his brother, as God said, when reproving his hidden thoughts, "Though you make offering correctly, yet, if you do not divide rightly, have you not sinned? Be at rest" (Gn 4.7), since God is not appeased by sacrifice. For if anyone attempts to offer sacrifice, purely, correctly, legally, merely to outward appearances, while in his soul he does not share with his neighbor that fellowship with him which is right, and has no fear of God—he who thus inwardly cherishes sin does not deceive God by that sacrifice which is outwardly correct. Such an offering will not do him any good, but only the giving up of that which has been conceived within him, so that sin may not, by means of the hypocritical action, make him the murderer of himself. Because of this, the Lord also said: "Woe to you, scribes and pharisees, hypocrites, for you are like whitened sepulchres. For the sepulchre appears beautiful outside, but

inside it is full of dead men's bones and all uncleanness. Even so, you also appear outwardly righteous to men, but inside you are full of wickedness and hypocrisy" (Mt 23.27-28). For while they were thought to make offering correctly so far as outward appearance went, they had in themselves an envy like Cain's. Therefore they too killed the Just One (Ja 5.6), ignoring the counsel of the Word, just as Cain had done. For God said to him, "Be at rest," but he did not consent. Now what else is it to be at rest but to abandon intended violence? And saying similar things to these men, He said: "You blind pharisee, clean the inside of the cup, that the outside may be clean also" (Mt 23.26). But they did not listen to Him. For Jeremiah says: "Behold, neither your eyes nor your heart are good, but in covetousness turned to innocent blood, to shed it, and to injustice and murder, to do them" (Jr 22.17). And, again, Isaiah says: "You have taken counsel, but not of me, and made covenants, but not by my Spirit" (Is 30.1). In order, therefore, that their inner desire and thought, brought to light, might show that God is without blame and works no evil, that God reveals what is hidden, but does no wrong, when Cain was not at all at rest, He said to him: "To you shall he turn, and you shall rule over him" (Gn 4.7). He also spoke to Pilate in a similar way: "You would have no power at all over me unless it were given to you from above"(Jn 19.11). God always hands over the righteous one that, tested by what he has suffered and endured, he may be approved and accepted; and that the evildoer, on the contrary, judged by the actions he has performed, may be rejected. Sacrifices, therefore, do not sanctify a man, for God has no need of sacrifice; rather, it is the pure intention of the offerer that sanctifies the sacrifice, and thus moves God to acceptance, as from a friend. "But the sinner," He says, "who slays a calf for me is as if he had slain a dog" (Is 66.3).

4. Since, then, the church makes offering guilelessly, her gift is rightly reckoned a pure sacrifice by God; as Paul also says to the Philippians: "I am replete, having received from Epaphroditus the things sent from you, an odor of sweet-

ness, an acceptable sacrifice, one pleasing to God"(Ph 4.18). For it is necessary for us to make an offering to God, and in all things to be found pleasing to God the Creator, offering the firstfruits of His own creation, with a pure mind, and in faith without hypocrisy, in well-grounded hope, in fervent love.

Moreover, the church alone offers this pure oblation to the Creator, making offering to Him with thanksgiving, from His creation. But the Jews make offering no more, for their hands are full of blood (Is 1.15), for they did not accept the Word through whom offering is made to God. Nor, again, do all the assemblies of the heretics. For some, by maintaining that the Father is different from the Creator, when they offer to Him what belongs to our created world, they portray Him as covetous of another's property and desirous of what is not His own. Those, again, who maintain that the things around us originated from downfall, ignorance, and passion, while offering to Him the fruits of ignorance, passion, and downfall, sin against their Father, subjecting Him to insult rather than giving Him thanks. But how can they be sure that the bread over which thanks have been given is the body of their Lord, and the cup His blood, if they do not call Him the Son of the Creator of the world, that is, His Word, through whom the wood fructifies, and the fountains gush forth, and the earth gives "first the blade, then the ear, then the full wheat in the ear" (Mk 4.28)?

5. Then, again, how can they say that the flesh which is nourished by the Lord's body and blood goes to corruption, and does not partake of life? Let them, therefore, either change their opinion, or refrain from offering the things just mentioned. But our opinion agrees with the eucharist, and the eucharist, in turn, establishes our opinion, for we offer to Him what is his own, proclaiming fittingly the fellowship and union of the flesh and the spirit. For as the bread, which is produced from the earth, when it receives the invocation of God, is no longer common bread, but the eucharist, consisting of two realities, the earthly and the heavenly, so also our bodies, when they receive the eucharist, are no longer corruptible, but have the hope of resurrection.

6. Now we make offering to Him, not as though He stands in need of it, but giving Him thanks for His gift, and to bless what has been created. For even as God has no need of what is ours, so we do have a need to offer something to God, as Solomon says: "He who has pity on the poor lends to God (Pr 19.17)." For God, who stands in need of nothing, accepts our good works for this purpose, that He may grant us a recompense of His own good things, as our Lord says: "Come, blessed of my Father, receive the kingdom prepared for you. For I was hungry, and you gave me to eat; I was thirsty, and you gave me drink; I was a stranger, and you took me in; naked, and you clothed me; sick, and you visited me; in prison, and you came to me" (Mt 25.34-36). As, therefore, He does not stand in need of these things, even so He desires that we should do them, for our own benefit, lest we be unfruitful. Thus the Word gave to the People that very precept, to make offerings, though He stood in no need of them, that they might learn to serve God, as it is also His will that we, too, should offer a gift at the altar, frequently, and without interruption.

There is, then, an altar in heaven, for towards that place are our prayers and offerings directed; and a temple, as John says in the Apocalypse, "And the temple of God was opened (Rv 11.19);" and a tabernacle, "For, behold," he says, "the tabernacle of God, in which He will dwell with men" (Rv 21.3).

5.1.3 But foolish also are the Ebionites, who do not acknowledge through faith the union of God and human nature, but continue in the old leaven (1 Co 5.7) of their generation. Nor are they willing to understand that the Holy Spirit came upon Mary, and the power of the Most High overshadowed her, wherefore also the One born of her is holy, and the Son of God Most High (Lk 1.35), the Father of all, who accomplished His Incarnation, and revealed the new generation, so that just as through the earlier generation we inherited death, so, through this generation, we should inherit life.

Thus these people reject the commixture of the heavenly wine, and want there to be only the water of this world. They do not accept God into their mixture, but they persevere in that Adam who was conquered and cast out of Paradise. They do not consider that, just as from the beginning of our creation in Adam, God's breathing-in of life, united to the creation, gave life to man, and revealed the reason-endowed animate creature (Gn 2.7), so also, in the end, the Word of the Father and the Spirit of God, united to the substance of the former creation of Adam, wrought a living and perfect man who could receive the perfect Father, so that, as in the animate [Adam] we all died, so in the spiritual [Adam] we should all be brought to life (1 Co 15.22). For Adam did not ever escape from God's hands, the hands to which the Father spoke and said: "Let us create man to our own image and likeness" (Gn 1.26). And for this reason, in the end, not from the will of the flesh, nor from the will of man, but from the good-pleasure of the Father (Jn 1.13), His hands made complete the living man, that Adam should really be according to the image and likeness of God.

2.1. Foolish, moreover, are those also who say that God came into another's property (*cf* Jn 1.11), as if He craved what belonged to someone else, so that He could present human nature, which had been made by another, to that God who had neither made nor created it, and who had been lacking, from the beginning, His own creation of human nature. Therefore the coming of Him, who, according to them, came into another's property, was unjust; nor yet did He truly redeem us by His blood, if He did not truly become man, restoring to His artifact what had been stated at the beginning, that man was made according to the image and likeness of God. He did not defraud another of his property, but took up what was His own with justice and kindness: with justice in respect to our apostasy, redeeming us from it by His blood; with kindness in respect to us who have been thus redeemed. For we gave nothing at all to Him beforehand, nor does He want anything, as if He were in need. It is we, rather, who are in need of communion with Him, and, on that account, with kindness He poured Himself out, in order to gather us into the bosom of the Father.

2. So wholly foolish are they who disdain the entire Economy of God, and deny the salvation of the flesh, and reject its regeneration, saying that it lacks the capacity for incorruptibility. Rather, if this flesh is not saved, then the Lord has not redeemed us by His blood, and the cup of the eucharist is not a communion in His blood, and the bread which we break is not a sharing in His body (1 Co 10.16). For there is no blood except from veins, and from flesh, and from the rest of the substance of human nature which the Word of God came to be, and redeemed by His blood, as His Apostle also says: "In whom we have redemption through His blood, and the forgiveness of sins"(Col 1.14). And since we are His members, and are nourished through creation— the creation He furnishes for us, causing the sun to rise and rain to fall as He pleases (Mt 5.45)—He declared that the cup, which comes from His creation, is His own blood, from which he strengthens our blood; and He affirmed that the bread, which is from creation, is His very own body, from which He strengthens our bodies.

3. Since, therefore, both the mixed cup and the prepared bread receive the word of God, and become the eucharist of Christ's body and blood, from which the substance of our flesh is strengthened and established, how, then, can they say that the flesh, which is fed on the body and blood of the Lord, and is one of His members, is incapable of receiving the gift of God which is everlasting life? As the blessed Paul also says in the Letter to the Ephesians: "We are members of His body, from His flesh and from His bones" (Ep 5.30), saying this not about some kind of spiritual and invisible human nature, for a spirit has neither flesh nor bones (Lk 24.39), but about that arrangement which is authentic human nature, which consists of flesh and sinews and bones, and is fed from the cup, which is His blood, and is strengthened by the bread, which is His body.

IVA3 Tertullian (*c* 160-*c* 225), *Against Marcion* 4.40.

ed CCSL 1.655-657; *lit* V. Saxer, in EEC 132-155.

Tertullian produced a number of antiheretical works, the longest of which is the five books *Against Marcion*. Books 1-3 went through several versions, coming into their present from in 207-208. Books 4-5 were written in the period 208-211, when Tertullian was under Montanist influence, but before he left the church, *c* 212.

Marcion (*d c* 160) posited an opposition between the Law and Love, and maintained that the Creator-God of the Old Testament, the God of Law, was not the God and Father of that Jesus Christ who appeared first in the Synagogue at Capharnaum to proclaim the Gospel of Love. Accordingly, Marcion rejected the Old Testment, and taught that Christ only appeared to be a man and to suffer (docetism). He created His own New Testament, consisting of a doctored version of the Gospel of Luke, and an *apostolicon* of expurgated versions of ten Pauline epistles. He also produced a document called the *Antitheses* wherein he opposed passages from the Law to passages from the Gospel of Love.

In Book 4 of *Against Marcion*, Tertullian undertakes to refute the *Antitheses* on the basis of Marcion's own gospel. In this passage, Tertullian presents Christ, as Giver of the Law, fulfilling in Himself, real God and real Man, the types and prophecies of the Law in the institution of the eucharist, before He really suffered.

Accordingly, He knew also when He should suffer, He whose Passion the Law had prefigured. For out of all the many feasts of the Jews, He chose the day of Passover, for Moses had spoken of this mystery beforehand: "It is the Passover of the Lord" (Lv 23.5). Therefore He also revealed His preference: "With longing have I longed to eat the Passover with you, before I suffer" (Lk 22.15). O Destroyer of the Law, whose longing it was to observe even the Passover. Of course, He was partial to the roast lamb of the Jews! Was it not, rather, the case that it was He who was to be led like a sheep to sacrifice, and, as He was not going to open His mouth, like a sheep before the one shearing Him (Is 53.7), He longed to fulfill the figure of His salvific blood?

2. Moreover, He could have been betrayed by some stranger. Then I could not say that in this detail too the psalm had been fulfilled: "He who ate bread with me has raised his heel against me" (Ps 40.10). Also, He could have been betrayed without a price. In addition, how great a need was there for a betrayer in the case of one who met with the people openly, and could have been attacked instead of betrayed? But that would have been fitting for a different Christ, not for Him who was fulfilling the prophecies. For it was written: "Because they sold the Just One" (Am 2.6), and Jeremiah foretold both the amount and the eventual disposition of the price, when afterwards, upon Judas' repentance, it was collected and given for the purchase of a potter's field, as it is told in the Gospel of Matthew: "And they took the thirty pieces of silver, the price of Him who was appraised"—or "honored"—and paid them for a potter's field" (Mt 27.3-10).

3. And so, having professed that He longed with longing to eat the Passover, as being His own,—for it would have been unsuitable that God desire something which belonged to another—He made the bread, which He had taken and distributed to the disciples, His own body, saying: "This is my body," that is, the figure of my body. But it could not have been the figure, unless it were the body of something real. Something void, like a phantasm, cannot have a figure. Or, if He shaped bread into a body for Himself, because He did not have a real body, then He ought to have delivered up bread for our sakes. That would work in support of the foolishness of Marcion, that bread should be crucified. But why did He call bread His body, and not, rather, the pumpkin which Marcion had instead of a brain? For he does not understand that bread was an ancient figure of the body of Christ who said through Jeremiah: "They plotted against me, saying: 'Come, let us put wood in His bread'" (Jr 11.19), that is, the Cross into His body. And thus He who sheds

light upon the past clearly showed what "bread" meant by calling his body "bread." Similarly, when He established the Covenant sealed with His blood by speaking of the cup, He also proved the reality of His body, for blood can belong to no other body than one of flesh. For even if some type of body other than one of flesh should be brought forward in argument against us, unless it be of flesh, it surely will not have blood.

5. Thus, the proof of the body will stand on the testimony of the flesh, and the proof of the flesh will stand on the testimony of the blood. But that you may also recognize the ancient figure of blood in the wine, Isaiah will help: "Who," he says, "is this who comes from Edom, the redness of His garments from Bosor? Thus handsome in His robe, in vehemence, with strength? Why are your garments red, and your clothing as if from the floor of the winepress well-trodden?" (Is 63.1-3). 6. For the prophetic Spirit, as already viewing the Lord going to His Passion, clothed with the flesh He suffered in, indicates by the redness of His clothing his bloodied garment of flesh, trodden and crushed by the violence of His Passion as if on the floor of a winepress, because men come up from there too as if bloodied from the redness of wine. Genesis delineated Christ even more clearly already in Juda, in the blessing of Juda, from whose tribe Christ's descent in the flesh was to come. "He will wash," it says, "His robe in wine and His garment in the blood of the grape" (Gn 49.11), showing that the robe and garment are the flesh, and the wine the blood. So He who then employed wine as a figure of His blood, also now has consecrated His blood in wine.

IVA4 Cyprian of Carthage (200X210-258), Letter 63.

ed CSEL 3, 2.701-717; *tr* FC, revised.

> Cyprian was a pagan by birth and education, but was converted to Christianity, became a priest, and was chosen to be bishop of his native city of Carthage in

248/49. He presided vigorously over the church of Carthage through years disturbed by persecution and dissension, until his martyrdom on 14 September 258.

Cyprian has left us a variety of treatises, autobiographical, apologetical, and ascetico-pastoral, and some sixty-five letters. Letter 63, written in the autumn of 253 to Caecilius, bishop of Biltha, is the earliest work of Christian antiquity devoted exclusively to the eucharist.

The purpose of Letter 63 is to condemn the heterodox aquarian practice of celebrating the eucharist with bread and water alone (see Introduction to Section IVA). Cyprian simply condemns the practice, leaving its origins and purposes vague, perhaps, as has been suggested, to avoid calling into question the orthodoxy of some of his predecessors in the African hierarchy. In any event, in denouncing the aquarian eucharist, Cyprian elaborated a view of the eucharist which was to have profound influence in western thinking about this sacrament (see, e.g., IIA8, IID1).

Note: Apropos of Cyprian's discussion of Pr 9.1-5 in para 5, compare the heading which introduces Pr. 9.1-6 in Cyprian's collection of biblical *testimonia*, *Ad Quirinum* 2.2 (CCSL 3.30): "That the Wisdom of God is Christ, and concerning the Sacrament of His Incarnation, and Passion, and Cup, and Altar, and the Apostles who were sent forth and preached."

CYPRIAN TO HIS BROTHER CAECILIUS, GREETINGS.

1. Although I know, dearly beloved brother, that very many bishops placed by the divine condescension in charge of the churches of the Lord in the whole world keep the order of evangelical truth and of the tradition of the Lord, and do not depart by human and novel institution from that which Christ, the Teacher, both taught and did; yet, since certain ones, whether through ignorance or through simplicity, in consecrating the cup of the Lord and in minister-

ing to the people, do not do that which Jesus Christ, our Lord and God, the Author and Teacher of this sacrifice, did and taught, I consider it a matter both of obligation and of necessity to write to you a letter concerning this, so that, if anyone is still held captive in this error, upon seeing the light of truth, he may return to the root and origin of the Lord's tradition.

Do not think, dearly beloved brother, that we are writing things merely human and our own, or that we are taking this boldly upon ourselves of our own will, since we admit always with humble and modest moderation our own limitations. But when something is clearly enjoined by God's inspiration and command, it is necessary for the faithful servant to obey the Lord, excused by all, because he who is compelled to fear an offense against the Lord unless he does what is commanded is taking nothing upon himself arrogantly.

2. But we know that we have been warned that, in offering the cup, the tradition of the Lord must be observed and that nothing should be done otherwise by us than what the Lord first did for us, that the cup which is offered in His remembrance should be offered mixed with wine. For since Christ says "I am the true vine" (Jn 15.1), the blood of Christ is, indeed, not water but wine. Nor can His blood, by which we are redeemed and vivified, be seen to be in the cup when wine, wherein the blood of Christ is shown, is wanting to the cup, as is proclaimed by the sacrament and testimony of all the sacred scriptures.

3. For we find even in Genesis, concerning the sacrament, that Noah anticipated this same thing and projected the figure of the Passion of the Lord there because he drank wine, because he was intoxicated, because he was made naked in his home, because he was reclining with his thighs naked and exposed, because the nakedness of his father was noticed by his second son and reported outside, but covered by the other two, the oldest and the youngest, and other matters (Gn 9.20-27) which it is not necessary to pursue, since it is enough to accept this only, that Noah, showing forth a type of future truth, drank not water, but wine, and

so portrayed the figure of the Passion of the Lord.

4. Likewise, in the priest Melchisedech we see the sacrament of the sacrifice of the Lord prefigured according to what the divine scripture testifies and says. "And Melchisedech, the King of Salem, brought out bread and wine, for he was a priest of the Most High God, and he blessed Abraham" (Gn 14.18-19). But that Melchisedech bore the type of Christ, the Holy Spirit declares in the Psalms, saying in the person of the Father to the Son: "Before the morningstar have I begotten you. . . . You are a priest forever according to the order of Melchisedech" (Ps 109.3,4). This order, indeed, is the one coming from that sacrifice and descending thence, because Melchisedech was a priest of the Most High God, because he blessed Abraham. For who is more a priest of the Most High God than our Lord Jesus Christ who offered sacrifice to God the Father and offered the very same thing which Melchisedech had offered, that is bread and wine, His body and blood.

And that antecedent blessing of Abraham extended to our people. For if Abraham believed God and it was imputed to him for righteousness, assuredly whoever believes in God and lives by faith is found a righteous man and is shown to be blessed and justified already in the faithful Abraham, as the blessed Apostle Paul proves, saying: "'Abraham believed God and it was imputed to him as righteousness' (Gn 15.6). You know, therefore, that they who are of faith, these are the sons of Abraham. But the scriptures, foreseeing that God would justify the gentiles by faith, announced to Abraham beforehand that all the nations would be blessed in him. Therefore, those who are of faith are blessed with the faithful Abraham" (Gal 3.6-8). Whence in the gospel we find that sons are raised up to Abraham from stones, that is, collected from the gentiles (Mt 3.9). And when the Lord praised Zacchaeus, He answered and said: "Today salvation has come to this house, for he, too, is a son of Abraham" (Lk 19.9).

Therefore, so that in Genesis, through the priest Melchisedech, the blessing of Abraham should be properly celebrated, the image of the sacrifice went before, established in the bread and wine. Accomplishing and fulfilling this action, the Lord offered bread and a cup mixed with wine, and He who is the plenitude fulfilled the truth of the prefigured image.

5. But also through Solomon the Holy Spirit shows forth beforehand the type of the sacrifice of the Lord, making mention of an immolated victim, and of bread and wine, and also of the altar and of the apostles. "Wisdom," he says, "has built a house and she has set up seven columns. She has slain her victims, mixed her wine in a bowl, and has prepared her table. And she has sent her servants, inviting to the bowl with lofty proclamation, saying: 'Let whoever is simple turn to me,' and to those who lack understanding she said: 'Come and eat of my bread, and drink the wine which I have mixed for you'" (Pr 9.1-5). He declares the wine is mixed, that is, he foretells in a prophetic voice that the cup of the Lord is mixed with water and wine, that it may be manifest that what had been foretold beforehand was accomplished in the Passion of the Lord.

6. This same thing is signified in the blessing of Judah, wherein also the figure of Christ is expressed, that He should have to be praised and adored by His brothers, that he should press down the backs of His departing, fleeing enemies with the hands with which He bore the Cross and conquered death, and that He Himself is the Lion from the tribe of Judah, and reclines sleeping in His Passion, and arises, and is Himself the Hope of the Gentiles (Gn 49.8-10). The divine scripture makes an addition to these things and says: "He shall wash his garment in wine, and his robe in the blood of the grape" (Gn 49.11). But when the blood of the grape is mentioned, what else is shown forth but the wine of the cup, the blood of the Lord?

7. And does not the Holy Spirit, speaking also in Isaiah, testify this same thing concerning the Passion of the Lord, saying: "Why are your clothes red, and your garments as from treading the winepress full and well-trodden" (Is 63.2)? For can water make clothes red, or is it water which is trodden by the feet in the winepress, or squeezed out by the press? The mention of wine is placed there, indeed, that in

the wine the blood of the Lord may be understood and that what was afterwards manifested in the cup of the Lord might be foretold by the prophets who announced it. The treading and pressing of the winepress are also spoken of, since as wine cannot be prepared for drinking unless the cluster of grapes is first trodden and pressed, so we could not drink the blood of Christ unless Christ had first been trodden upon and pressed, and unless He had first drunk the cup (Mt 26.39,42) by which He would give drink to the faithful.

8. But, as often as water is named in the holy scriptures, baptism is preached, as we see signified in Isaiah. "Remember not the events of the past," he says, "the things of long ago consider not. Behold, I am doing new things which now will spring forth, and you will know them. In the wilderness I make a road, in the desert, rivers... to give water to my chosen people, my people whom I have won that they might declare my power" (Is 43.18-21). God foretold there through the Prophet that among the gentiles, in places which before had been without water, rivers should afterwards abound, and should provide water for the chosen people of God, that is, those made sons of God through the birth of baptism.

Likewise, again, it is foretold and predicted beforehand that the Jews, if they should thirst and seek Christ, would drink with us, that is, they would obtain the grace of baptism. "If they have thirsted," he said, "in the deserts, He will bring water to them; He will bring forth water out of the rock for them; the rock will be split and the water will gush out, and my people will drink" (Is 48.21). This is fulfilled in the gospel when Christ, who is the rock (1 Co 10.4), is split by the blow of the lance in His Passion. And He, indeed, reminding us again of what was predicted beforehand by the Prophet, cries out and says: "If anyone thirst, let him come and drink. He who believes in me, as the Scripture says, from within him there shall flow rivers of living water"(Jn 7.37-38).

And that it might be the more apparent that the Lord is speaking there not of the cup, but of baptism, scripture adds, saying: "He said this, however, of the Spirit whom they who believed in Him were to receive" (Jn 7.39). But through baptism the Holy Spirit is received, and thus do those who have been baptized and have received the Holy Spirit come to drink the cup of the Lord. But let it disturb no one that, when the divine scripture is speaking of baptism, it says that we are thirsty and we drink, since the Lord also in the gospel says "Blessed are they who thirst and hunger for righteousness" (Mt 5.6), because what is received with an avid and thirsty desire is drunk more fully and abundantly. Likewise, in another place, the Lord speaks to the Samaritan woman, saying: "Everyone who drinks of this water will thirst again. He, however, who drinks of the water which I will give shall never thirst"(Jn 4.13-14). And by this, indeed, is signified the baptism of the saving water, which, once it is received, assuredly is not repeated again. As for the rest, the cup of the Lord is always both thirsted for and drunk in the church.

9. There is no need for very many arguments, dearly beloved brother, to prove that baptism is signified always by the appellation of water, and that we ought to know that the Lord, when He came, manifested the truth of baptism and of the cup, for He taught that the faithful water, the water of everlasting life, is given in baptism to the believers; but He taught by the example of His teaching that the cup is mixed by the union of wine and water. For taking the cup on the day of His Passion, He blessed it and gave it to His disciples, saying: "All of you drink of this; for this is the blood of the covenant, which will be shed for many for the forgiveness of sins. I say to you, I will not drink henceforth of this fruit of the vine until that day when I shall drink it new with you in the Kingdom of my Father" (Mt 26.27-29). In this passage, we find that the cup which the lord offered was mixed, and that what He called blood had been wine.

Whence it is clear that the blood of Christ is not offered if wine is lacking in the cup and that the sacrifice of the Lord is not celebrated with lawful consecration unless our oblation and sacrifice correspond to the Passion. But how shall we drink the new wine of the fruit of the vine with Christ in the

Kingdom of the Father if we do not offer the wine of Christ also in the sacrifice to God the Father, and do not mix the cup of the Lord according to the teaching of the Lord?

10. The blessed Apostle Paul, moreover, chosen by God and sent and appointed as a preacher of evangelical truth, writes these same things in his Epistle, saying: "The Lord Jesus, on the night on which He was betrayed, took bread and gave thanks and broke it and said: This is my body which is for you. Do this in remembrance of me. In like manner He also took the cup, after they had eaten, saying: This cup is the new covenant in my blood. Do this, as often as you drink it, in remembrance of me. For as often as you shall eat this bread and drink the cup, you proclaim the death of the Lord, until He comes" (1 Co 11.23-26).

But if this is taught by the Lord and the same is confirmed and handed down by His Apostle, that as often as we drink in remembrance of the Lord we should do that which the Lord did, we find that what was commanded is not observed by us unless we also do the same things which the Lord did, and, mixing the cup in like manner, we do not depart from the divine teaching. But that we must not depart at all from the evangelical precepts, and that the disciples ought also to observe and do those same things which the Teacher taught and did, the blessed Apostle teaches more resolutely and forcefully in another passage, saying: "I marvel that you are so quickly deserting him who called you to grace for another gospel, which is not another, except that there are some who trouble you, and wish to alter the gospel of Christ. But even if we or an angel from heaven should preach a gospel to you other than that which we have preached, let him be anathema! As we have said before, so now again I say: If anyone preach a gospel to you other than that which you have received, let him be anathema" (Gal 1.6-9)!

11. Since, therefore, neither the Apostle himself nor an angel from heaven can proclaim otherwise or teach anything else except that which Christ once taught and His apostles preached, I marvel indeed, whence this practice has come, contrary alike to both evangelical and apostolic disci-

pline, that water, which alone cannot represent the blood of Christ, is offered in some places in the cup of the Lord. The Holy Spirit is not silent about the matter of this sacrament in the Psalms, when He makes mention of the cup of the Lord and says: "Your cup which inebriates, how excellent it is" (Ps 22.5)! But the cup which inebriates is assuredly mixed with wine, for water cannot inebriate anyone.

But the cup of the Lord inebriates as also Noah drinking wine in Genesis was inebriated. But the inebriation of the cup and of the blood of the Lord is not like the inebriation coming from worldly wine, since the Holy Spirit says in the Psalm, "Your cup which inebriates," and adds, "how excellent it is," because the cup of the Lord inebriates in such a way that it makes men sober, that it brings minds to spiritual wisdom, that from the taste for this world each one returns to the knowledge of God. And, as the mind is relaxed by that ordinary wine and the soul is eased and all sadness is set aside, so, when the blood of the Lord and the lifegiving cup have been drunk, the memory of the old man (Eph 4.22) is set aside, and there is induced forgetfulness of former, worldly behavior, and the sorrowful and sad heart, which was formerly pressed down with distressing sins, is now eased by the joy of the divine mercy. This can delight the one who drinks in the church of the Lord, but only if what is drunk keeps to the truth of the Lord.

12. But how perverse it is and how contrary that, although the Lord made wine from water at the Marriage, we should make water from wine, since this sacrament also ought to warn and instruct us that in the sacrifices of the Lord we should rather offer wine. For, since among the Jews spiritual grace was lacking, the wine was lacking also, "For the vineyard of the Lord of Hosts is the House of Israel" (Is 5.7).

But Christ, who teaches and shows that the people of the gentiles were their successors, and that we were arriving afterwards, through the merit of faith, into that place which the Jews had lost, made wine from water, that is, He showed that the people of the gentiles instead would gather together and come to the wedding of Christ and His church as the

Jews were departing. For the divine scripture declares in the Apocalypse that the waters signify the peoples, saying: "The waters which you saw, on which that harlot sits, are peoples and throngs and nations of the gentiles and tongues" (Rv 17.15). We perceive that this also is contained in the sacrament of the cup.

13. For, because Christ, who also bore our sins, bore us all, we see that the people are signified in the water, but in the wine the blood of Christ is shown. But when water is mixed with wine in the cup, the people are united to Christ, and the multitude of believers is linked and joined to Him in whom they have believed. This association and mingling of water and wine are so mixed in the cup of the Lord that the mixed elements cannot be separated from one another. Wherefore nothing can separate the church, that is, the multitude established faithfully and firmly in the church, persevering in Him in whom it has believed, from Christ; nothing can keep it from clinging and abiding in undivided love.

But thus, in consecrating the cup of the Lord, water alone cannot be offered, just as wine alone cannot. For, if anyone offers wine alone, the blood of Christ is without us; but if the water is alone, the people are without Christ. But when both are mixed and are joined to each other in the indiscriminate union, then the spiritual and heavenly sacrament is completed. Thus the cup of the Lord is not water alone, or wine alone, but both are mixed together, just as flour alone or water alone cannot be the body of the Lord, unless both have been united and joined and made solid in the structure of a single bread. By this very sacrament our people is shown to be united. Just as many grains, collected and milled and mixed, make one bread, so let us know that in Christ, who is the heavenly bread, there is one body, to which our number has been joined and united.

14. There is no reason, dearly beloved brother, for anyone to think that the custom of certain ones should be followed, if any in the past have thought that water alone should be offered in the cup of the Lord, for we must ask whom they themselves have followed. For if in the sacrifice which

Christ offered, no one but Christ is to be followed, certainly we ought to obey and do what Christ did and what He commanded to be done, since He Himself says in the gospel: "If you do what I command you, no longer do I call you servants, but friends" (Jn 15.14, 15). And that Christ alone ought to be obeyed His Father also attests from heaven, saying: "This is my dearly beloved Son, in whom I am well pleased. Hear Him" (Mt 17.5).

Wherefore, if Christ alone is to be heard, we ought not to attend to what anyone else before us thought should be done, but what Christ, who is before all, did first. Neither ought we to follow the custom of men, but the truth of God, since, through Isaiah the Prophet, God speaks and says: "But in vain do they worship me, teaching the precepts and doctrines of men" (Is 29.13). And again, in the gospel, the Lord repeats this same thing, saying: "You make void the commandment of God to strengthen your own tradition" (Mk 7.13). But also in another place He states: "Whoever does away with one of these least commandments, and so teaches men, he shall be called least in the Kingdom of Heaven" (Mt 5.19).

But if it is not allowed to do away with the least of the commandments of the Lord, how much more forbidden it is to infringe upon matters which are so great, so momentous, so closely connected to the very sacrament of the Lord's Passion and our Redemption, or in any way to change, follow human tradition, to something different from what has been divinely instituted? For, if Christ Jesus, our Lord and God, is Himself the Highpriest of God the Father, and first offered Himself as a sacrifice to the Father, and commanded this to be done in remembrance of Himself, certainly the priest who imitates that which Christ did offers the true and full sacrifice in the church to God the Father; if he offers according to what he sees Christ Himself to have offered, he truly acts in the place of Christ.

15. Otherwise, all of the discipline of religion and truth is subverted, unless that which is prescribed spiritually is kept faithfully, unless in the morning sacrifice what each one

fears is that he should be redolent of the blood of Christ through the savor of wine. "But thus, then, the brotherhood begins to be kept back also from the Passion of Christ in persecutions while it learns in the oblations to be ashamed about His blood and bloodshed." But, in turn, the Lord in the gospel says: "Whoever is ashamed of me, of him will the Son of Man be ashamed" (Mk 8.38). And the Apostle also speaks, saying: "If I were trying to please men, I should not be a servant of Christ" (Gal 1.10). For how can we who blush to drink the blood of Christ shed our blood for Christ?

16. Or does anyone delude himself with this consideration, that, although water alone may be offered in the morning, yet, when we come to the evening meal, we offer a mixed cup? But when we have the evening meal, we cannot call the people to our meal so that we may celebrate the truth of the sacrament with all of the brotherhood present. "But, in fact, the Lord offered the mixed cup, not in the morning, but after dinner." Should we then celebrate the eucharist after dinner so that by increasing the number of the eucharists we could offer the mixed cup? It was fitting for Christ to make offering in the evening of the day, so that the very hour of sacrifice might show the setting, the evening of the world, as it is written in Exodus: "And the entire multitude of the children of Israel shall slaughter it in the evening"(Ex 12.6), and again, in the Psalms: "The lifting up of my hands as an evening sacrifice" (Ps 140.2). We, however, celebrate the Lord's Resurrection in the morning.

17. And since we make mention of His Passion in all sacrifices—for the Passion of the Lord is, indeed, the sacrifice which we offer—we ought to do nothing other than what He did. For scripture says that, as often as we offer the cup in remembrance of the Lord and of His Passion, we should do that which the Lord certainly did. And, dearly beloved brother, let him look to it, if anyone of our predecessors either through ignorance, or through simplicity did not observe this, and did not keep that which the Lord taught us to do by His example and teaching. Pardon from the Lord's mercy may be given to this simplicity, but we cannot be forgiven, we who are now admonished and

instructed by the Lord to offer the cup of the Lord mixed with wine, according to what the Lord offered, and to direct letters to our colleagues concerning this matter, that everywhere the evangelical law and the tradition of the Lord should be kept, and that there should be no departure from that which Christ both taught and did.

18. For what else is it to continue to disdain those things and to persevere in former error than to incur the the the rebuke of the Lord, who reproaches in the Psalm and says: "Why do you declare my justices, and profess my covenant with your mouth, for you have hated discipline and cast my words behind you? If you saw a thief, you kept pace with him, and with adulterers you threw in your lot" (Ps 49.16-18). For to declare the justices and the covenant of the lord and not to do the same thing which the Lord did, what else is that but to cast side His words and to despise the discipline of the Lord, and to commit not earthly, but spiritual robberies and adulteries? For he who steals from evangelical truth the words and deeds of our Lord both corrupts and adulterates the divine teaching, as it is written in Jeremiah: "What has straw to do with the wheat?", he says, "Therefore, behold, I am against the prophets, says the Lord, who steal my words everyone from his neighbor, and lead my people astray by their lies and by their errors" (Jr 23.28, 30, 32)." Similarly, in another passage in the same author: "She has committed adultery with wood and stone. And with all this, she did not return to me" (Jr 3.9,10)."

We ought to observe religiously and beware fearfully and solicitously that this robbery and adultery should not, even now, fall upon us. For if we are bishops of God and Christ, I do not find anyone we ought to follow more than God and Christ, since He Himself, in His gospel, emphatically states "I am the light of the world. He who follows me will not walk in darkness, but will have the light of life" (Jn 8.12). So that we may not walk, then, in darkness, we must follow Christ and observe His precepts, since He Himself, in another place, sending forth His apostles, said: "all power in heaven and on earth has been given to me. Go, therefore, and teach all men, baptizing them in the name of the Father, and of the Son, and of the Holy Spirit, teaching them to observe all that I have commanded you" (Mt 28.18-20).

Wherefore, if we wish to walk in the light of Christ, let us not depart from His precepts and admonitions, giving thanks, that, while He instructs us for the future as to what we should do, He forgives us for the past because we have erred through simplicity. And since already His Second Coming is drawing near to us, more and more His kind and great condescension enlightens our hearts with the light of truth.

19. It is, therefore, fitting to our religion and to our fear, to the position and office of our bishopric, dearly beloved brother, to keep the truth of the tradition of the Lord in mixing and offering the cup of the Lord, and to correct what seems to have been an earlier error among certain people, according to the admonition of the Lord, that, when He comes in His glory and heavenly majesty, He may find us holding firmly to what He told us, observing what He taught, doing what He did. I pray that you, dearly beloved brother, always enjoy good health.

IVA5 Optatus of Milevis (*c* 320-before 392), *Against the Donatists* 6.1-2.

ed CSEL 26.142-146; *tr* O.R. Vassall-Philips, *The Work of St. Optatus...against the Donatists* (London, 1917), revised.

> Optatus, bishop of Milevis in Numidia, is our earliest extant polemicist against the schismatic Donatists. His treatise, vaguely titled in the manuscripts, is generally known as *On the Donatist Schism* or *Against the Donatists*.
>
> The Donatist Schism, which began *c* 311, became a rigorist, exclusionist sect. Purity, variously understood, was to be maintained in the church at any cost. Of such people, some of whom are with us still, St. Augustine said, while commenting upon Ps 95.11: "The clouds of

heaven thunder throughout the whole world that the house of God be built; yet frogs complain from their bog: 'We alone are Christians!'" They denied the validity of non-Donatist ordinations and of the sacraments administered by non-Donatists (see VA8). Optatus' Book VI, from which our extract is taken, is a catalogue of the sacrilegious atrocities of the Donatists. Their zeal led them to the mutilation or removal of altars and the destruction of chalices employed by the catholic clergy. In complaining of their treatment of the altars, "the throne of the body and of the blood of the Lord," and of "chalices which carry the blood of Christ," Optatus gives us a glimpse of his view of the eucharist.

Your wicked behavior with regard to the divine sacraments has, it seems to me, been clearly shown. I now have to describe things done by you, as you yourselves will not be able to deny, with cruelty and stupidity. For what is so sacrilegious as to break up, to scrape, to remove the altars of God, altars upon which you once offered sacrifice, upon which were laid both the prayers of the people and the members of Christ, where Almighty God was called upon, where the Holy Spirit descended in answer to prayer, from which many have received the pledge of eternal salvation, the safeguard of faith, and the hope of the resurrection? Altars, I say, upon which the Saviour forbade the offerings of brotherhood to be placed, unless they were seasoned with peace. He said: "Leave your gift before the altar, and first go back, agree with your brother, so that the priest may be able to make offering for you" (*cf* Mt 5.24). For what is an altar but the throne of the body and of the blood of the Lord?

All these altars you, in your madness, have either scraped or smashed or removed. This inexpiable outrage, if there were any reason for it, might have been carried out by one method only; but, as I think, in one place a good supply of lumber dictated that the altars be smashed, but in other places the scarcity of lumber dictated that the altars be scraped; their removal, by others still, was urged, in part, by reverence. But in each case a disgraceful wickedness was committed when you laid sacrilegious and impious hands upon an object so great.

Why should I report the hired mob of desperados and the wine given them in payment for the crime? This very wine was heated with fragments of the altars, so that it could be drunk with foul mouths in sacrilegious draugths. If, by your envious judgement, we seemed to you to be compromised, what harm had God done you, God, who at those altars was once habitually invoked? In what way had Christ offended you, whose body and blood used to dwell there at appointed times? How had you offended even yourselves, that you should smash those altars on which, long before us, you made offering in a manner you judge to be holy? In impiously attacking our hands there, where the body of Christ used to dwell, you have smitten your own hands as well.

In this way you have imitated the Jews. They laid hands upon Christ on the Cross, you have smitten Him on the altar. If you wished to attack catholics at these altars, you might have spared at least your own former sacrifices there.

Your pride has been revealed in that place where formerly you offered sacrifice with humility. You sin freely where once you were accustomed to pray for the sins of many. By doing this you have willingly joined the company of sacrilegious priests, associated as you are in the crimes of the profane about whom the Prophet Elias made complaint before the Lord. For he spoke in the very words with which you too, among others, have deserved to be accused by him. He said: "O Lord, they have smashed your altars" (1 Kg 19.10). When he says "your," he shows that the altar, where any offering has been made to God, by anyone at all, belongs to God. It might have been enough for your madness that you have rent the members of Christ, that you have divided the peoples of God, long established in unity, by your seductions. You might, in the midst of all this, at least have spared the altars. Why have you smashed the prayers and longings of men along with the altars? For from them the prayer of the people used to ascend to the ear of God. Why did you cut the road of prayer? Why have you labored with impious hands to remove, as it were, the ladder, so that supplication would not have its ascent to God in the customary way?

And though all of you shared in one conspiracy, still, in this matter, while your wrongdoing was the same, you carried it out by different methods. If it was enough to remove, then it was not lawful to smash; if it was necessary to smash, then it is a sin to have scraped. For if, as was agreed among you, it was not lawful merely to scrape the altars, then the man who broke them up seems to have acted rightly, and he is guilty, who by scraping preserved the greater part of them. What is this new and foolish wisdom of yours to seek for what is new in the heart of what is old, as if, having removed the skin, to seek a second skin in the body which the former covered? A gift which is proper to itself and is entire in itself, because it is a unity, can be diminished when something is taken away from it, but it cannot be changed. You scraped, to be sure, as seemed best to you, but what you hate still remains there. What if your conspiracy has determined that the things which we have touched in God's name in the ritual are unclean? Who of the faithful does not know that in the celebration of the mysteries the wood itself is covered by a linen cloth? In the course of these rites the covering can be touched, but not the wood. On the other hand, if the coverings can be penetrated by touch, then so can the wood; and if the wood can be penetrated, then so can the earth. If you scrape the wood, you should also dig up the earth which is beneath. Make a deep hole, while you are searching after what you judge to be purity. But be careful that you do not come all the way to hell, and find there Core, Dathan, and Abiram (Nb 16), the schismatics, your teachers.

It is, then, established that you have both smashed and scraped altars. How is it that in this matter your madness seems to have cooled down somewhat? For we see that later you changed your plan, and that the altars were now no longer either broken or scraped by you, but only removed. If to do this was enough, then you yourselves prove that what you did at first should not ever have been done.

2. But you doubled this monstrous crime when you also smashed the chalices which carry the blood of Christ. You melted them down, thus making money for yourselves in impious trafficking. Nor in this business did you even trouble to select the buyers, but were guilty of sacrilege in selling indiscriminately, and of avarice, in selling at all. You also suffered your own hands to be burnt, hands with which you were accustomed, before us, to handle these same chalices. Still you ordered the sale to take place everywhere. Perhaps wanton women bought them for their own purposes. Pagans bought them, so that from them they might fashion vessels in which to burn incense to their idols. O heinous sin! O unheard-of crime! To take something away from God, to give it to idols, to steal something from Christ, that it might serve for sacrilege.

IVA6 Augustine of Hippo (354-430), *Concerning Baptism* 5.8.9.
ed CSEL 51.269-270

> Augustine's seven books *Concerning Baptism* were written in 400/01, primarily against the schismatic Donatists (see IVA5), who, in common with various present-day schismatics, were much given to the practice of rebaptizing. In our excerpt, while arguing that baptism remains valid, if not in every respect effective, independently of the heretical or vicious dispositions of its minister, Augustine provides, by way of illustration, a profound comment on the relationship of the body and blood of Christ to the dispositions of the individual communicant.

Wherefore, just as the Apostle said of the Law, "The Law is good, so long as one uses it lawfully" (1 Tm 1.8), so also are we able rightly to say about baptism: "Baptism is good, so long as one uses it lawfully." And just as those who did not use the Law lawfully then did not bring it about that the

Law was not good, or of no validity, so also, whoever does not use baptism lawfully, because he lives in heresy or moral corruption, in no way brings it about that baptism is not good, or of no validity. And so, when one is converted either to catholic unity or to a way of life worthy of such a sacrament, he does not begin to have another, lawful baptism, but he begins to have that very same baptism in a lawful manner. Nor does the forgiveness of past sins follow upon baptism, unless the baptism be lawful, and lawfully held. Nor yet, if it is not held lawfully, and sins either are not forgiven, or forgiven ones are repeated, not on that account will the sacrament of baptism become either evil or invalid in the one baptized. For just as Judas, to whom the Lord gave the morsel, not by receiving an evil thing, but by receiving it evilly, provided an opportunity in himself for the Devil (Jn 13.26-27), so also whoever receives the Lord's sacrament unworthily (1 Co 11.27) does not bring it about, because he himself is evil, that it is evil, or, because he did not receive it unto salvation, that he has received nothing. For it will be the body of the Lord and the blood of the Lord nonetheless, even to those to whom the Apostle said "He who eats and drinks unworthily, eats and drinks condemnation for himself" (1 Co 11.29). Therefore, let heretics seek in the catholic church not what they have, but what they do not have, that is, the end of the commandment, without which many holy things may be held, but they cannot be of profit. "But the end of the commandment is charity, from a pure heart and a good conscience and a faith unfeigned" (1 Tm 1.5). Let them hasten to the unity and truth of the catholic church, not that they might have the sacrament of washing, if they have already been baptized, though in heresy, but that they may have it in a manner which leads to salvation.

IVA7 Augustine of Hippo (354-430), *On the Merits and Remission of Sins* 1.34.
ed CSEL 60.33-34.

> Augustine wrote his first work against the Pelagians, the three books *On the Merits and Remission of Sins*, in 412. A number of the views which were, ultimately, to become part of the system of thought called Pelagianism were aired in Africa by the Roman Caelestius, who was condemned in Carthage in 411. Among these views was the denial of the transmission of original sin and, therefore, of the necessity of infant baptism for the remission of sins. Baptism, it was maintained, conferred on children not remission of sins, but sanctification. In this excerpt, just as he urges the necessity of baptism for children, Augustine maintains the necessity of their participation in the body and blood of Christ as well.

Quite rightly do the Punic Christians call baptism nothing other than "Salvation," and the sacrament of the body of Christ nothing other than "Life." Why do they do so except, as I think, because of an ancient and apostolic tradition, on the basis of which they hold it to be an inherent principle of the church of Christ that without baptism and the sharing of the Lord's Table, a man is able to arrive neither to the Kingdom of God nor to salvation and eternal life? Scripture also bears witness to this, according to what we have already said. For what else are those who call baptism "Salvation" maintaining, except what is written: "He has saved us through the bath of regeneration" (Tt 3.5), and what Peter says: "Thus has baptism saved you also, by a like pattern" (1 P 3.21)? In addition, what are they maintaining who call the sacrament of the Lord's Table "Life," except the statements: "I am the living bread who have come down from heaven" (Jn 6.51), and "The bread which I shall give is my flesh for the life of the world" (Jn 6.51), and "Unless you eat the flesh of the Son of Man, and drink His blood, you will not have life in you" (Jn 6.53)? If, then, as so many and such weighty divine testimonies agree, one can hope neither for salvation nor for eternal life without baptism and the body and blood of the Lord, in vain are these promised to children without them. Furthermore, if it is sin alone which separates man from salvation and eternal life, then it is the guilt of sin which is forgiven children through these sacraments. It is written that no one is free of this guilt, "not even if his life be of one day's duration" (Jb 14.5). On this account, there is also the passage in the Psalms: "For in sin was I conceived, and in sin did my mother nurture me in the womb" (Ps 50.7), for either this is said by human nature in general, or, if David said it as applying to his own person, he is not speaking of fornication, for he was born of lawful wedlock. And so, let us have no doubt that also for the baptizing of infants that blood was shed which, before it was shed, was given and handed on in a sacrament, in such a way that it could be said: "This is my blood, which shall be shed for many for the forgiveness of sins" (Mt 26.28).

IVA8 Cyril of Alexandria (*d* 444), Excerpts from Anti-Nestorian Writings.

Cyril's struggle against Nestorius, the Antiochene monk who became archbishop of Constantinople in 428, is one of which the details are many and the issues confused. Cyril chose to assume that in rejecting the Marian title *Theotokos* (Mother of God) in favor of *Christotokos* (Mother of Christ) Nestorius was positing two Christs, one human and one divine, and/or lapsing into Adoptionism and/or Philanthropism. Cyril's temperament and treatment of his adversaries, the rivalry for ecclesiastical hegemony between Alexandria and Constantinople, and the competition between the theological views of the Alexandrian and Antiochene schools of theology have given rise to a "political" interpretation of Cyril's virtual persecution of Nestorius and his allies. Isidore of Pelusium, urging a more temperate approach, wrote to Cyril that "Many of those who were coerced at Ephesus are denouncing you, that you are pursuing your own enmities and exacting vengeance, and not seeking the things that are Christ's in an orthodox way. 'He is,' they say, 'the nephew of Theophilus, and takes after his disposition.'" (Letter 1.310, PG 78.361C).

A more balanced view of the controversy, while acknowledging Cyril's less-than-commendable methods and motives, sees Cyril's violent reaction to the Antiochenes and the most convenient target among them, Nestorius, as an effort to protect a cardinal point of traditional Alexandrian teaching about the eucharist (See II C3, III B9). "the flesh of the Lord is life-giving," against the consequences of a radical dyophysite view which would so sever the divine from the human in Christ as to reduce communion in the body and blood of Christ to participation in mere human flesh and blood (see H. Chadwick, "Eucharist and Christology in the Nestorian Controversy," *Journal of Theological Studies* NS 2 [1951] 145-164).

1. From Cyril's third letter to Nestorius (Cyril, Letter 17.3).
ed ACO 1.1.1.37-38.

Following his condemnation by a synod in Rome in August 430, Nestorius was condemned by a synod held by Cyril in Alexandria in November of that year. Cyril communicated this decision to Nestorius in Letter 17, and undertook, in the same communication, to expound to him the Alexandrian tradition concerning the Incarnation. Our excerpt, which bears on the eucharist, is taken from that exposition.

We will necessarily add this also: Proclaiming the death according to the flesh of the Onlybegotten Son of God, that

is, Jesus Christ, confessing His Resurrection from the dead,
and His Ascension into heaven, we celebrate the unbloody
sacrifice in the churches, and so proceed to the mystical
consecrated gifts, and are sanctified, having become partakers of the holy flesh and precious blood of Christ, the
Saviour of us all. And not as common flesh do we receive it,
not at all, nor as a man sanctified and associated with the
Word according to the unity of dignity, or as having had a
divine indwelling, but as truly the life-giving and very flesh
of the Word Himself. For He is life according to His nature
as God, and when He became united to His flesh, He made it
life-giving. Thus, even if He said to us "Amen, I say to you,
unless you eat the flesh of the Son of Man and drink His
blood" (Jn 6.54), we must not think that it is flesh of a man
like us—for how can the flesh of man be life-giving by its
own nature?—, but as having become truly the very own of
Him who for us both became and was called the Son of
Man.

2. Cyril's Eleventh Anathema and its Explanation:
ed ACO 1.1.5.24-25.

> Cyril appended to Letter 17 a set of twelve anathemas
> (also called "anathematisms" or "chapters") as a test of
> orthodoxy. These came under attack by Antiochene
> theologians, and Cyril composed several works in their
> defense. Here we give Anathema 11 along with the expla-
> nation of it from the set of explanations which Cyril
> wrote during his brief period of house-arrest during the
> Council of Ephesus in 431.

Anathema 11

If anyone shall not confess that the flesh of the Lord is
life-giving, and that it is the very own flesh of the Word of
God from God the Father, but shall pretend that it belongs
to some other, who is connected to Him according to dignity, that is, as having only the divine indwelling, and is not,
rather, as we say, life-giving because it is that of the Word

who is able to give life to all, let him be anathema.

Explanation

We celebrate in the churches the holy, life-giving, and unbloody sacrifice. The body, and also the precious blood, which is offered we believe not to be that of a common man and of anyone like us, but we receive it, rather, as having become the very body and blood of the Word who gives life to all. For common flesh cannot give life, and our Saviour bore witness to this when He said: "The flesh is of no benefit, it is the Spirit that gives life (Jn 6.63)." For since the flesh became the very own of the Word, therefore it is understood to be and is life-giving, as the Saviour Himself said: "As the living Father has sent me, and I live because of the Father, so he who eats me shall live because of me (Jn 6.57)." Since, therefore, Nestorius and those who think as he does ignorantly dissolve the power of this mystery, therefore, and quite appropriately, this anathema came to be.

IVA9 Theodoret of Cyrus (393-*c* 466), *Eranistes*, Dialogue 2, excerpt.
ed G. H. Ettlinger (Oxford, 1975) 151-153.

> Theodoret wrote his *Eranistes, or Polymorph* in 447 or 448. The work is a collection of three dialogues (*Immutable*, *Unconfused*, and *Impassible*) which present and defend the Antiochene tradition concerning the divine and human natures of Christ. The interlocutors are Orthodoxos, the spokesman for orthodoxy (Theodoret), and Eranistes, a collector of a variety of heterodox opinions (hence Polymorph too). It is generally held that Eranistes represents Eutyches, a Constantinopolitan monastic leader possessed, at that time, of powerful political connections and an implacable foe of Antiochene theology (to the extent that he could comprehend it). By a stubborn adherence to a naive understanding of one of Cyril of Alexandria's christological formulae, Eutyches

had lapsed, whether he was aware of it or not, into what came to be called Monophysitism, and was eventually condemned at the Council of Chalcedon.

Both Orthodoxos and Eranistes appeal to the eucharist for illustration and confirmation of their opinions. Note the observance of the contemporary discipline of reticence about the details of the eucharistic liturgy.

Orthodoxos. Tell me then, the mystical symbols offered to the Lord God by the priests, of what things are they the symbols?

Eranistes. Of the Lord's body and of His blood.

Orth. Of the real body, or of one that is not real?

Eran. Of the real one.

Orth. Good. For it is necessary that an image have an archetype; for the painters imitate nature, and paint the images of things that are seen.

Eran. True.

Orth. If, then, the divine mysteries are the antitypes of the real body, then the Lord's body is even now a body, a divine body, to be sure, and the Lord's, not changed into the nature of divinity, but filled with divine glory.

Eran. Your mention of the divine mysteries is quite opportune, for from them I shall prove to you the change of the Lord's body into another nature. So answer my questions.

Orth. I shall answer.

Eran. What do you call the gift that is offered, before the priest's invocation.

Orth. I must not speak openly, for some of the uninitiated may be present.

Eran. Let your answer be enigmatic.

Orth. Food from such-and-such seeds.

Eran. And the other symbol, how do we call it?

Orth. This name is also a commonplace one which indicates a type of beverage.

Eran. But after the consecration, then, what do you call these things?

Orth. The body and blood of Christ.

Eran. And you believe that you partake of the body and

blood of Christ?

Orth. That is my belief.

Eran. Therefore, just as the symbols of the Lord's body and of His blood are one thing before the priest's invocation, but after the invocation are changed, and become something else, so too was the Lord's body changed, after the Ascension, into the divine essence.

Orth. You have been caught in the nets which you have woven, for not even after the consecration do the mystical symbols depart from their own nature! They continue in their former essence, both in shape and appearance, and are visible, and palpable, as they were beforehand. But they are considered to be what they have become, and are believed to be that, and are adored as truly being those things which they are believed to be. Juxtapose, then, the image to the archetype, and you will see the likeness, for the type must bear a likeness to the truth. For too the body possesses, the earlier one, appearance, and shape, and outline, and, generally, the essence of a body. But after the Resurrection it has become immortal, and stronger than corruption, and was counted worthy of enthronement at the right-hand, and is adored by all creation, in that it is the body of the Lord of nature.

Eran. And yet the mystical symbol changes its former name, for it no longer has the name which it was called before, but is called "body." Accordingly, it is necessary that the Truth also be called "God," but not "body."

Orth. Your ignorance is evident. For it is not only named "body," but also "bread of life." Thus even the Lord Himself called it (Jn 6.48), and that divine body we call "body," and "life-giving," and "the Master's," and "the Lord's," teaching thus that it is not the body of some ordinary man, but of our Lord Jesus Christ, who is God and man, eternal and new, "Jesus Christ, the same yesterday and today and unto the ages" (Heb 13.8).

IVA10 Leo the Great (*d* 461), *Sermon* 78.2-3.

ed SC 200.124-126; *tr* LNPF, revised.

Leo I presided over the See of St. Peter from 440-461. He entered into the christological controversy following the Council of Ephesus with his dogmatic letter (sometimes called "The Tome of Leo") sent to Flavian, archbishop of Constantinople, in 449, in which he asserted the faith of the church against Eutyches. Leo's *Tome* was accepted as an authentic statement of the faith by the Council of Chalcedon in 451.

In this sermon, delivered in September 453, Leo urges the authentic mean of faith, between the opposed errors of Nestorius and Eutyches, as a necessary precondition for participation in the eucharist.

But the catholic faith, which withstands all errors, refutes these blasphemies, at the same time condemning Nestorius who divides the divine from the human, and denouncing Eutyches who nullifies the human in the divine, since the Son of the true God, Himself true God, possessing unity and equality with the Father and the Holy Spirit, condescended to be true man, and by the Virgin Mother's conception was not separated from flesh and birth, so uniting humanity to Himself as to remain immutably God, so imparting Godhead to man as not to destroy, but enhance him by glorification. For He who became "the form of a slave" did not cease to be "the form of God" (Ph 2.7, 6), and He is not one joined to the other, but a unity in both, so that ever since "the Word became flesh" (Jn 1.14) our faith is disturbed by no vicissitudes of circumstance, but whether in the miracles of power, or in the degradation of suffering, we believe Him to be both God who is man, and man who is God.

3. Dearly beloved, declaring this confession with all your hearts, reject the wicked lies of heretics, that your fasting and almsgiving may not be polluted by any contagion of error. For our offering of sacrifice is clean, and our gift of mercy is holy, when those who perform them understand

what they are doing. For since the Lord says "Unless you eat the flesh of the Son of Man, and drink His blood, you will not have life in you" (Jn 6.54), you ought so to be partakers of the holy table as to have no doubt whatever concerning the truth of Christ's body and blood. For that is received in the mouth which is believed by faith, and it is in vain for them to answer "Amen" who dispute that which is received.

B "Approach With the Fear of God, With Faith and With Love": Dispositions for Participation in the Eucharist.

IVB1 Anonymous (*c* 100), *The Didache (Teaching) of the Apostles* 14.
ed SC 248.192.

The *Didache* has been a center of on-going controversy since its first publication in 1883. A wide range of dates for its composition has been suggested (from 70 to 200, or later). Unless one accepts the hypothesis of deliberate archaizing, or the incorporation of considerably earlier materials on the part of its compiler, an earlier date of *c* 100 seems the prudent choice. Different locations (Syria, Palestine, Egypt) have been suggested as the *Didache's* place of origin. In any case, it seems to have been compiled in a Jewish-Christian community, or one under significant Jewish-Christian influence, in a place remote from the mainstream of early Christian developments. The *Didache* is a composite document, consisting of a moral tractate (Ch 1-6), a church order (a directory of liturgical observance and ecclesiastical discipline, Ch 7-15), and a concluding prophecy (Ch 16).

Chapter 14 contains the prescriptions for Sunday worship; Chapters 9-10, which contain eucharistic prayers, are given later (VIA1).

On every Lord's Day, after you have assembled, break the bread and give thanks, first confessing your sins, that your sacrifice may be pure. Let no one who has a quarrel with his neighbor gather with you before they are reconciled, lest your sacrifice be profaned (*cf* Mt 5.23ff). For this is what the Lord said: "In every place and time a pure sacrifice is offered to me, for I am a great king, says the Lord, and my name is wonderful among the gentiles" (*cf* Ml 1.11,14).

IVB2 Clement of Alexandria (*c* 150-*c* 215), *What Rich Man is Saved?* 23.
ed GCS *Clemens* 3.174-175.

> This lengthy discourse of Clement deals with the prob-
> lem of wealth in the Christian life. In our excerpt, Cle-
> ment is developing his treatment of Mk 10.29 and Lk
> 14.26; the issue goes beyond wealth to the potential con-
> flict between family ties and the Christian calling.
> Through the rhetorical device of *prosopopoeia* Clement
> presents us with a courtroom drama in which Christ
> portrays Himself in one of the roles of the Logos de-
> scribed in our earlier selection from Clement (IIA1)—that
> of Foster-father who nourishes us with Himself in the
> eucharist.

If, then, one has a godless father or son or brother, and he becomes a hindrance to the faith and an impediment to the life above, one must not be in harmony with him and agree with him, but one must dissolve fleshly kinship on account of spiritual enmity.

Consider the matter as a lawsuit. Imagine that your father stands before you and says: "I gave you birth and reared you. Follow me, be my partner in wrong-doing, and do not obey the law of Christ," and whatever else a blasphemous man, one dead by nature, might say.

But from the opposing side, hear the Saviour: "I gave rebirth to you who were misbegotten by the world for death. I set you free. I healed you. I ransomed you. I shall grant you life unending, eternal, beyond the world. I shall show you the face of God, the Good Father (*cf* Jn 14.8ff). Do not call anyone your father upon earth (Mt 23.9). Let the dead bury their dead, but you follow me (Mt 8.22), for I shall raise you up to the repose and enjoyment of ineffable and indescribable good things which eye has not seen, nor ear heard, nor has it entered into the heart of man (1 Co 2.9), upon which the angels long to gaze (1 P 1.12) and to see the good things which God has prepared for His saints and for His children who love Him (1 Co 2.9). I am your foster-father, I gave myself as bread. No one who has tasted of it ever undergoes the trial of death. And I give daily the drink of immortality. I am the teacher of supercelestial instruction. For your sake I struggled against death, and I paid in full your debt of death which you deserved because of earlier sins and infidelity towards God."

After you have heard the arguments from both sides, judge for yourself, and find in favor of your salvation. And though your brother should say such things, or your child, or your wife, or anyone at all, before all let Christ be victorious in you, for He struggles on your behalf.

IVB3 Basil the Great (*c* 330-379), *The Shorter Rules* No. 172.

ed PG 31.1196; *tr* W.K.L. Clarke, *The Ascetic Works of St. Basil* (London, 1925), revised.

In the course of his eventful life, Basil the Great filled the roles of monastic founder and legislator, of theologian and defender of orthodoxy, and of perfect bishop. Basil was born into a prominent and remarkably devout Christian family (the work of Basil's younger brother, Gregory of Nyssa, also appears in this volume, IIA2). His education took place in his native Caesarea in Cappadocia, in Constantinople, and in Athens. After returning to Caesarea and teaching rhetoric there for a while, Basil experienced a religious quickening, sought baptism, and retired to a life of asceticism, involving himself in the growing coenobitic movement. He maintained close connections with the greater ecclesiastical community, became a priest in 362, and, finally, in 370, was made archbishop of Caesarea, a post he filled with learning, piety, and efficiency until his death.

In this volume, we meet Basil as spiritual director (IV C1), liturgical reformer (VA3), and, here, as monastic legislator. Basil produced two sets of rules, the fifty-five *Longer Rules*, the foundations of coenobitic life, and the 313 *Shorter Rules*, clarifications and supplements to the *Longer Rules*. Each set is in the question-answer format, reproducing Basil's conferences with the monks under his direction. Here Basil teaches us, from the Scriptures, to "Approach with the fear of God, with faith, and with love."

Question No. 172: With what fear, with what sort of assurance and disposition should we partake of the body and blood of Christ?

Reply: Fear is taught us by the Apostle when he says: "He who eats and drinks unworthily eats and drinks condemnation to himself" (1 Co 11.29). Assurance is created in us by belief in the words of the Lord: "This is my body which is given for you. Do this in remembrance of me" (Lk 22.19), in the testimony of John who described first the glory of the Word, and then added the manner of the Incarnation by saying: "And the Word became flesh and dwelt among us, and we beheld His glory, glory as of the Onlybegotten of the Father, full of grace and truth" (Jn 1.14), and in the testimony of the Apostle, as he writes: "Being in the form of God, He did not reckon it robbery to be equal with God, but He emptied Himself, taking the form of a servant, being made in the likeness of men, and found in fashion as a man; He humbled Himself, becoming obedient unto death, indeed, the death of the Cross" (Ph 2.6-8). When, therefore, the soul believes these words, words so very momentous, it learns the greatness of the glory, and is astonished at the surpassing quality of the humility and obedience, that One so great obeyed the Father unto death for the sake of our life, then I think it is disposed towards love for God the Father who "did not spare His own Son, but delivered Him up for us all" (Rm 8.32), and for His Onlybegotten Son who became obedient unto death for our redemption and salvation. And thus is the soul able to obey the Apostle who establishes a good conscience as a sort of benchmark for those who are sound in these matters by saying: "For the love of Christ presses us on, for we judge that if One died for all, then all died. And He died for all, that living they should no longer live for themselves, but for Him who died and rose for their sakes" (2 Co 5.14-15). He who partakes of the bread and the cup should have such a disposition and such readiness.

IVB4 John Chrysostom (*c* 349-407), *Homily on Matthew* 25.3.
ed PG 57.331; *tr* LNPF, revised.

> After commenting on the cure of the Leper recorded in Mt 8.1-4, Chrysostom moves on to a discussion of thanksgiving in the excerpt given here. He proceeds from a consideration of thanksgiving in general to a short discourse on the church's thanksgiving, the eucharist, in particular, and describes the necessary place of the eucharist in the life of the Christian community.

And so, pondering these matters, let us also fulfill all our duties towards our neighbor, and let us continually give thanks to God. For it is wicked, enjoying as we do His bounty every day in fact, not even in word to acknowledge His favor, and to fail to do so when the very act of acknowledgement yields benefits to us. He does not need anything of ours, but we need all things that are His. And so thanksgiving adds nothing to Him, but causes us to be closer to Him. For if men's kindnesses, when we call them to mind, warm us with a greater love for them, so, when we continually recall the Lord's undertakings for our sake, we will be more diligent in respect of His commandments.

For this reason Paul also said "Be thankful" (Col 3.15), for the best safeguard of any favor is the remembrance of that favor and a continual thanksgiving. For this reason also the mysteries, awesome and full of abundant salvation, which are celebrated at every assembly, are called a thanksgiving [*eucharistia*], because they are a recollection of many benefactions and exhibit the totality of God's care for us and dispose us in every way to be thankful. For if His being born of a Virgin was a great wonder, and the Evangelist said in amazement, "Now all this was done. . ."(Mt 1.22)—tell me, how shall we describe His being slain? I mean, if His birth is called "all this," what can we call His crucifixion, the shedding of His blood, His giving Himself to us for a spiritual feast and banquet? Let us, therefore, give thanks to Him continually, and let this activity precede our words and deeds.

But let us give thanks not only for our own blessings, but also for those of others, for in this way we shall be able to destroy envy and to intensify charity and make it more genuine, since it will be quite impossible for you to go on envying those on whose behalf you give thanks to the Lord.

For this reason, when the sacrifice is offered, the priest also bids us to give thanks for the whole world, for those who have gone before, for those now living, for those now being born, and for those who will come after us.

This frees us from earth, and removes us to heaven, and makes us angels instead of men. For they too form a choir, and give thanks to God for His good things bestowed on us, saying: "Glory to God in the highest, and peace on earth, good will among men" (Lk 2.14). "What is this to us angels who are neither on earth nor men?" "It is very important to us, for we have so been taught to love our fellow servants that we consider their blessings as ours."

IVB 5 John Chrysostom (*c* 349-407), *Homily on Matthew* 82.4-6.

ed PG 58.743-746; *tr* LNPF, revised.

> This selection is the conclusion of the homily excerpted in IIIB3. In this portion, Chrysostom praises the eucharist with most vivid and varied imagery. He urges his congregation to participate in the eucharist, but warns against the Judas-like dispositions of sinfulness, sloth, and lack of generosity. Section 6 is a remarkable exhortation to the ministers of the eucharist to do their duty to the body of Christ.

Let us, then, believe God in everything, and contradict Him in nothing. Even though what is said may seem to be contrary to our thoughts and senses, let His word be of greater authority than reason and sight. Let us do this in the mysteries also, not only gazing on the offerings, but keeping His words in mind. For His word cannot deceive, but our senses are easily deceived. His word never errs, but our senses go wrong in very many things. Since, then, the Word says "This is my body," let us be persuaded and believe, and look at it with the eyes of the mind.

For Christ has given nothing perceptible to the senses, and even if in things perceptible, yet all is spiritual. So too in baptism, the gift is bestowed by a perceptible thing, by water, but what is accomplished is spiritual, the birth, the renewal. For if you were incorporeal, He would have given you the incorporeal gifts unclothed, but because the soul has been mingled with a body, He gives you spiritual things in things sensible.

How many now say: "I would like to see His shape, His appearance, His clothes, His shoes." Look! You see Him! You touch Him! You eat Him! You want to see His clothes, but He gives Himself to you, not only to see, but to touch, and eat, and receive within you. Let no one, then, approach with disgust, no one with negligence, but all burning, all fervent, all excited. For if the Jews ate with haste, standing up, wearing their shoes, with their staffs in their hands, you ought to be even more watchful. They, to be sure, were about to go forth to Palestine, and for that reason wore the garb of travellers; but you are about to depart to heaven.

5. And so it is necessary to be vigilant in every way, for no small punishment has been established for those who partake unworthily. Consider how indignant you are against the Betrayer, against those who crucified Him. Take care, then, that you yourself may not become guilty of the body and blood of Christ (1 Co 11.27). They slaughtered the all-holy body, but you receive it in a filthy soul, after such great favors. For it was not enough for Him to become man, to be struck and slaughtered, but He also commingles Himself with us, and makes us His body, not by faith only, but in very fact. Whom, then, should he not surpass in purity who has the benefit of this sacrifice? Than what sunbeam should not that hand be more pure, the hand which is to cut apart this flesh, the mouth which is filled with spiritual fire, the tongue which is crimsoned by that most awesome blood?

Consider with what an honor you have been honored, of what table you are partaking. The One before whom the angels tremble, when they behold Him, and dare not look up without awe because of the brightness which comes from Him—by Him are we fed, with Him we are commingled, and we are made the one body and one flesh of Christ. "Who shall declare the mighty works of the Lord? Who shall cause all His praises to be heard" (Ps 105.2)? What shepherd feeds his sheep with his own limbs? And why do I speak of a shepherd? There are often mothers who, after the travail of childbirth, send out their children to other women as nurses. He did not stand for this; rather, He Himself feeds us with His own blood, and in every way entwines us with Himself.

Consider. He was born of our essence. "But," you say, "this does not pertain to all men." But it does pertain to all! For if He came to our nature, it is quite clear that it was to all. But if to all, then also to each one. "And how was it," you say, "that all have not taken profit from that?" This was not the fault of Him whose choice it was to do this for all, but the fault of those who did not desire it.

He mingles Himself with each one of the faithful through the mysteries. He feeds with Himself those whom He has begotten, and He does not farm them out to another, and thus He also persuades you again that He has taken your flesh. Let us not, then, be remiss, since we have been counted worthy of so much love, of so much honor. Do you not see the babies, how eagerly they grasp the breast, how impetuously they fix their lips upon the nipple? Let us similarly approach this table, and the nipple of the spiritual cup. Or, rather, with much more eagerness let us, as infants at the breast, draw out the grace of the Spirit. Let it be our one sorrow not to partake of this food. The things offered here are not within man's power. He who did these things then, at that Supper, also accomplishes them now. We function as servants, the one who sanctifies and changes them is He.

Let there be no Judas present, no one avaricious. If anyone is not a disciple, let him go away. The table does not receive such ones, for "I keep the passover," He says, "with my disciples"(Mt 26.18). This table is the same as that, it has nothing less. It is not the case that Christ created that one, and man this one. He Himself creates this one also. This is that upper room where they were then, whence they went out to the Mount of Olives.

Let us also go out to the hands of the poor, for that is the Mount of Olives. The multitude of the poor are olive-trees planted in the house of God, dripping the oil which is needful for us there. The five virgins (Mt 25.1-13) had it, and the rest, who did not, perished for that reason. With it, let us go in, that with bright lamps we may meet the Bridegroom. With it, let us go forth from here. Let no inhuman person be present, no one who is cruel and merciless, no one at all who is unclean.

6. I say these things to you who receive, and also to you who minister. For I must address myself to you also, so that you may distribute the gifts with great care. There is no small punishment for you if, conscious of any wickedness in any man, you allow him to partake of this table. "His blood shall be required at your hands" (Ez 33.8). Even though someone may be a general, or a prefect, or even the one who

is invested with the diadem [*sc* the emperor], if he approaches unworthily, forbid him. Your authority is greater than his. If you were entrusted with the task of keeping a spring of water clean for a flock, and you saw a sheep with much mire on its mouth, you would not allow it to stoop down into the stream and foul it. But now, entrusted with a spring, not of water, but of blood and Spirit, if you see any who have sin on them, something more grievous than mire, approaching it, and you are not indignant, and do not drive them off, what pardon can you have?

God has given you this honor for this purpose, that you should discern these things. This is your dignity, this is your security, this is your entire crown, not your going about clad in white and shining vestments. You may say "And how do I know this person or that person?" I am not speaking of the unknown, but the notorious.

I shall say something more fearful. It is not so grievous a thing for the energumens [*sc* those obsessed by demons] to be inside as for those who, as Paul says, "are trampling Christ under foot, and consider the blood of the covenant as common, and affront the grace of the Spirit" (Heb 10.29). For he who has fallen into sin and approaches is worse than one possessed by a demon. For they, because they are possessed, are not punished, but those, when they approach unworthily, are handed over to undying punishment. Let us not, therefore, drive away only the energumens, but all, without exception, whom we may see approaching unworthily. Let no one communicate who is not of the disciples. Let no Judas receive, lest he suffer the fate of Judas. This multitude, also, is Christ's body. Be careful, you who minister at the mysteries, not to provoke the Lord by not purging this body. Do not give a sword instead of food.

Even if such a one comes to communicate from ignorance, forbid him, do not be afraid. Fear God, not man. If you fear man, you will also be laughed to scorn by him. If you fear God, you will be venerable to man also. But if you are afraid to do it yourself, bring him to me. I will allow no one to be so bold. I would give up my life rather than give the

Lord's blood to the unworthy, and I will shed my blood rather than give such awesome blood contrary to what is right. But if anyone does not know who is wicked after some inquiry, there is no blame; these things have been said about public sinners. For if we correct these, God will quickly show us the unknown as well. But if we admit these, why should He then show us those who are hidden?

But I am saying these things, not that we may repel them only or cut them off, but so that we may correct them, and bring them back, that we may take care of them. For in this way we will have God well-disposed, and will find many worthy to receive. And for our diligence and care for others we will receive the great reward. May God grant that we may all attain to it by the grace and love-for-mankind of our Lord Jesus Christ, to whom be glory unto the ages of ages. Amen.

IVB6 John Chrysostom (*c* 349-407), *Homily on First Corinthians* 24,3-end.
ed PG 61.203-206; *tr* LNPF, revised.

> This is the concluding portion of the homily excerpted in IIIB5. Chrysostom provides here an encomium on the historical and eucharistic body of Christ, and interweaves with his praises an exhortation to the correct dispositions for receiving the eucharist.

With this knowledge, beloved, let us take thought for the good of the brothers, and preserve unity with them. For that fearsome and awe-inspiring sacrifice leads us to this, bidding us especially to approach it with unity and fervent love, and made eagles by it, thus to fly to heaven itself. "For wherever the corpse is," He says, "there also will be the eagles" (Mt 24.28), calling His body a corpse by reason of His death. For if He had not fallen, we would not have risen. But He calls us eagles, showing that he who approaches this body must be on high, and have nothing in common with the earth, nor wind himself downwards, and creep; rather, he must be ever soaring heavenwards, and gaze on the Sun of Righteousness (M 4.2), and have the eye of his mind quick-sighted. For this table belongs to eagles, not to crows. Those who now take part in it worthily will also go to meet Him when He descends from heaven, just as those who partake of it unworthily will suffer the ultimate torments.

4. For if one would not receive a king thoughtlessly—why do I say a king? One would not touch a royal robe thoughtlessly, with dirty hands, even if he were in the wilderness, and alone, with no one there. But a robe is nothing but certain threads spun by worms; and if you admire the dye, it too is just the blood of a dead fish. Even so, one would not dare to lay hold of it with unclean hands. If one would not dare to lay hold of a man's garment thoughtlessly, then what of the body of Him who is God over all, spotless, pure, associated with that divine nature, the body whereby we exist and live, whereby the gates of Hades were broken, and the vaults of heaven opened? Shall we receive this with such great insolence? I urge you, let us not slaughter ourselves by our shamelessness, but approach it with all awe and purity. And when you see it set before you, say to yourself: "Because of this body I am no longer earth and ashes, no longer a prisoner, but free. Because of this I hope for heaven, and to receive good things there, immortal life, the portion of the angels, companionship with Christ. This body, even though nailed and scourged, death could not withstand. The sun saw this body sacrificed and turned aside its beams. For this was the veil of the Temple rent then, and the rocks were broken apart, and all the earth was shaken. This is that very body, blood-stained, pierced by the lance, from which gushed the saving fountains, the one of blood, the other of water, for all the world."

Do you wish to learn its power from another source? Then ask the woman with the issue of blood, who did not touch the body, but the garment upon it, and not the whole of the garment, but only the fringe (Mt 9.20-22). Ask the sea which bore it on its back (Mt 14.25). Ask the Devil himself, and say: "Whence do you have that incurable wound? Whence is it that you are powerful no longer? Whence are you taken prisoner? By whom were you seized as you fled?" And he will give no other answer but this: "The body that was crucified." By this were his goads broken up, by this was his head crushed, by this were the principalities and powers made a show of, "For despoiling the principalities and powers, he made a show of them, confidently triumphing over them in Himself" (Col 2.15).

Ask Death also, and say: "Whence is it that your sting has been taken away, your victory abolished (1 Co 15.55), your sinews cut, and you, who beforehand were a terror even to kings and all righteous men, have become a laughing-stock for girls and children?" And he will say that the body is the cause. For when this body was crucified, then the dead rose, then was that prison broken open, and the gates of brass smashed, and the dead set free, and the gate-keepers of Hades all cowered in fear. Had He been one of the many, Death would, on the contrary, have been stronger still; but it was not so. For He was not one of the many, and therefore Death was destroyed. And so, just as those who take food which they are unable to retain, vomit up, because of it, even what was eaten before, so also did it happen to Death. He received that body which he could not digest, and therefore had to cast forth what he already had within him. Indeed, he was in travail while he held Him, and was afflicted, until he vomited Him up. Thus the Apostle says "Having loosed the pangs of death" (Ac 2.24), for never was woman in labor so much in travail as Death was torn and rent while he held the body of the Lord. And what happened to the Babylonian dragon when it took the food and burst asunder in its middle (Dn 14.26), that also happened to him. For Christ did not come forth again through the mouth of Death, but having burst asunder and cut open the middle of the belly of the dragon, from his secret chambers He came forth with great splendor, and flung His beams abroad, not only to heaven, but to the very throne, for to there did He carry up His body.

He has given us this body both to hold and to eat, a thing

proper to intense love. For we often even bite with our teeth those whom we love vehemently. Thus Job too, describing the love of his servants for him, remarked that often, because of their great affection for him, they said: "Who will give us to be filled with his flesh?" (Jb 31.31). Even so Christ has given to us to be filled with His flesh, drawing us on to greater love.

5. Let us draw near to Him, then, with fervor and burning charity, so that we will not have to endure punishment. For in proportion to the magnitude of the benefits bestowed on us, so much more exceedingly are we punished, if we show ourselves unworthy of the bounty. The Magi reverenced this body, even as it lay in a manger, and men profane and foreign, leaving their country and their home, set out on a long journey, and, when they arrived, they worshipped Him with fear and trembling. Let us then, who are citizens of heaven, at least imitate those foreigners. For when they saw Him, although in a manger in a hovel, and with nothing in view such as you look upon now, they drew near with great awe. But you behold Him not in a manger, but on an altar, not a woman holding Him in her arms, but the priest attending, and the Spirit hovering over the offerings with surpassing bounty. You do not see merely the body itself, as they did, but you also know its power, and the entire Economy, and you are ignorant of none of the holy things accomplished by it, for you have been carefully initiated into everything.

Let us, then, rouse ourselves up and be filled with awe, and let us show reverence far beyond that of those foreigners, that we may not, by approaching thoughtlessly and carelessly heap fire upon our own heads. I say these things not to keep us from approaching, but to keep us from approaching without consideration. For as to approach carelessly is perilous, so also not to share in these mystical suppers is famine and death. For this table is the sinews of our soul, the bond of our mind, the foundation of our confidence, our hope, our salvation, our light, our life.

When, with this sacrifice, we depart into the next life, we will tread the sacred threshold with great confidence, protected on every side as with a kind of golden armor. And why do I speak of the world to come, since here this mystery makes earth become a heaven for you? Only open the gates of heaven and look in, or, rather, not of heaven, but of the heaven of heavens, and you will behold what I have been speaking of. For what is most precious of all there, that I will show you resting upon the earth. For as in royal palaces, what is most glorious of all is not walls, or golden roofs, but the body of the king sitting on the throne, so also in heaven, it is the body of the King. But you are now permitted to see this on earth. For it is not the angels or archangels, not the heavens or the heavens of heavens that I am showing you, but their very Lord. Do you see how that which is more precious than all things is seen by you on earth, and not only seen, but also touched, and not only touched, but also eaten? And after receiving it you go home.

Make your soul clean, then, prepare your mind for the reception of these mysteries. For if you were entrusted with carrying a king's child, with the robes, the purple and the crown, you would cast away all that is on the earth. But now that it is not the child of a man, however royal, but the Onlybegotten Son of God Himself whom you receive, do you not tremble, and cast away all love of worldly things, and pride yourself in that adornment alone? Or do you still look towards earth, and love money and pant after gold? What pardon can you have, what excuse? Don't you know that all this worldly luxury is repellent to your Lord? Was it not for this reason that in His birth He was laid in a manger, and took to Himself a humble Mother? Was it not for this reason that He said to the one who was looking for wealth: "But the Son of Man does not have a place to lay His head" (Mt 8.20)?

And what did the disciples do? Did they not observe the same law, taken to the houses of the poor and lodged there, one with a tanner, another with a tentmaker, and with a seller of dye? For they did not ask about the splendor of the house, but about the virtues of men's souls.

Let us imitate them, hurrying past the beauty of pillars

and marbles, seeking the mansions which are above, and let us tread under foot all the pride here below, with all love for money, and acquire a lofty mind. For if we are sober and wary, this world is not worthy of us (Heb 11.38), much less porticoes and arcades. And so, I beg you, let us adorn our souls, let us decorate the house which we are also to have with us when we depart, that we may attain to eternal goods, by the grace and love for mankind, *and the rest.*

IVB7 John Chrysostom (*c* 349-407), *Homily on Ephesians* 3.3-end.
ed PG 62.27-30; *tr* LNPF, revised.

> Chrysostom delivered his homilies on Ephesians, twenty-four in all, in Antioch. This selection is his response to Ep 1.22-23: "And He established Him as the Head over the entire church, which is His body. . ." Here Chrysostom explores the relationship of the individual Christian to the church through the eucharist, and the question of worthiness for participation in the eucharist, worthiness to receive the eucharist and worthiness even to be present at the eucharistic assembly.

However, since our words are about the Lord's body, come, let us turn our thoughts to it, the body which was crucified, which was nailed, which is offered in sacrifice. If you are the body of Christ, carry the cross, for He carried it; endure spittings, endure blows, endure nails. Such was His body. His body was sinless, for "He did not sin, nor was guile found in His mouth" (1 P 2.22). His hands did everything for the benefit of those in need; His mouth uttered nothing unseemly; He heard them say "You have a demon" (Jn 7.20), and He said nothing in reply.

Since we are speaking of the body, know that we, as many of us as partake of the body, as many as taste of that blood, we partake of something which is in no way different or separate from that which is enthroned on high, which is adored by the angels, which is next to Power Uncorrupt. Of that we taste. Oh, how many are the ways to salvation! He made us His own body, He has given us His own body, and yet neither of these facts turns us away from evil. Oh the darkness, the abyss of apathy! "Set your minds on the things above, where Christ is, enthroned at the right hand of God" (Col 3.2,1). And after all this, some set their affections on money, others are taken prisoner by their passions!

4. Do you not see that even in our own body, when any part is superfluous and useless, it is cut off, is cut away? It is of no advantage that it has belonged to the body when it is mutilated, when it is mortified, when it is decayed, when it corrupts the rest. Let us not, then, be too confident because we have once been made members of the body. If this physical body of ours, when it suffers deprivation, if its vital principle should fail, what dreadful evil will it not suffer? When the body does not eat its food, when the pores are stopped up, then it dies. When the vessels are blocked, then it is crippled. So it is with us too, when we close our ears, our soul becomes crippled. When we do not partake of the spiritual food, when, instead of corrupt bodily humors, evil dispositions corrupt us, all these things engender dangerous disease, wasting disease. And then there will be need of cauterizing, need of surgery. For Christ cannot endure that we should enter into the wedding with such a body as this. If He led away and cast out the man who was clothed in dirty garments (Mt 22.11-13), what will He not do to the man who attaches filth to the body, how will He not dispose of Him?

I observe many partaking of Christ's body lightly and incidentally, from custom and ordinance, rather than from consideration and understanding. "When," one says, "the holy season of Lent is at hand, whatever sort one may be, he partakes of the mysteries, or when the day of the Lord's Theophany comes." But this is not the occasion for communion, for neither Theophany nor Lent make us worthy to come forward, but sincerity and purity. With these, come forward always, without them, never. "For as often as" you do this, "you proclaim the death of the Lord" (1 Co 11.26), that is, "you make a remembrance of your salvation, of my kindness."

Consider those who partook of the sacrifices under the Old Covenant, what great abstinence they practised, what they avoided, what they did not do. They were always purifying themselves. But you, when you draw near to a sacrifice at which the very angels tremble, do you measure the matter by periods of time? And how shall you stand before the judgement-seat of Christ, you who dare to receive His body with polluted hands and lips? You would not presume to kiss a king with a foul-smelling mouth, but you kiss the King of Heaven with a reeking soul? That is an outrage.

Tell me, would you choose to come to the sacrifice with unwashed hands? I should think not. No, you would rather choose not to come at all than with dirty hands. And then, as scrupulous as you are in this little matter, do you come with soiled soul and dare to grasp? And yet the hands hold it only for a time, whereas into the soul it is dissolved entirely. Do you not see how the holy vessels are so thoroughly cleansed, so shining? Our souls ought to be cleaner than they, more holy, more brilliant. And why? Because those vessels are kept that way for our sakes. They do not partake of what is in them, they do not perceive Him. But we do, oh yes! Now then, you would not choose to make use of a soiled vessel, and do you come forward with a soiled soul? Note the inconsistency. At the other times you do not come forward even though you are often clean; but at Pascha, however outrageous an act you may have committed, you come. Oh, the force of custom and of presumption! In vain is the daily offering of the sacrifice, in vain do we stand before the altar. There is not one to partake. I am saying these things not to induce you to partake inconsiderately, but that you may make yourselves worthy.

Are you unworthy of the sacrifice, unworthy of communion? If so, then neither are you worthy of the prayer! You hear the herald, standing and saying: "As many as are under penance, all depart." As many as do not partake are under penance. If you are one of those under penance, you should not partake, for he who does not partake is one of those under penance. Why, then, when he says "Depart, all you who are not able to pray," do you have the effrontery to stand still? But no, you are not of that number, you are of the number of those who are able to partake, and yet are indifferent about it, and consider it unimportant.

5. Look, I pray: a royal table is here, angels minister at the table, the King Himself is here. And do you stand gaping? Are your garments dirty, and you have no excuse? Or are they clean? Then sit down and partake. Every day He comes to see his guests, and converses with them all. Even now He is speaking in your conscience: "Friend, how do you stand there without a wedding garment?" He did not say "Why did you sit down?" No, before he sat down, He declared him to be unworthy, even to come in. He did not say "Why did you sit down?", but "Why did you come in" (Mt 22.12)? These are the words that He is at this very moment addressing to all of us who stand here with such shameless effrontery. For every one who does not partake of the mysteries is standing there in shameless effrontery. It is for this reason that those who are in sins are expelled first of all. For just as when a master is present at his table, it is not right that those servants who have offended should be present, but they are sent away, so also here when the sacrifice is brought forward, and Christ, the Lord's Sheep, is sacrificed. Whenever you hear the words "Let us all pray together," whenever you see the curtains drawn up, then consider that heaven is let down from above, and that the angels are descending.

As it is not right that anyone of the uninitiated be present then, so neither is it that one of those who is initiated, but is defiled. Tell me, suppose anyone were invited to a feast, and were to wash his hands, and sit down, and be all ready at the table, and after all, refuse to eat; is he not insulting the man who invited him? Were it not better for such a one not to have come at all? Now it is just in the same way that you have come here. You have sung the hymn; with the rest you have declared that you are of the number of all those who are worthy by not departing with those who are unworthy. Why stay and not partake of the table? "I am unworthy," you will say. Then you are also unworthy of communion in the prayers. For it is not through the offered gifts alone, but also through those canticles that the Spirit descends all around. Do we not see our own servants, scouring the table with a sponge, and cleaning the house, and then setting out the plates? This is what is done by the prayers, by the cry of the herald. We scour the church, as it were, with a sponge, that all things may be set out in a clean church, that there may be "neither spot nor wrinkle" (Ep 5.27).

Unworthy are our eyes of these sights, unworthy our ears! "And if a beast," it says, "touches the mountain, it shall be stoned" (Ex 19.13). Thus they were not worthy so much as to set foot upon it, and yet, afterwards, they came forward and saw where God had stood (*cf* Ps 131.7). And you may, afterwards, come and see; but when He is present, you must depart. You are even less allowed to be here than a catechumen is. For it is not at all the same thing never to have attained to the mysteries, as after having attained to them, to take offense and despise them, and to make yourself unworthy by so doing. I could say more, things more frightening still. But so as not to burden your minds, these will suffice. They who are not brought to their sense by these words will surely not be helped by more.

That I may not, then, be the means of increasing your condemnation, I entreat you, not to stay away, but to make yourselves worthy, both of being present and of receiving. Tell me, were any king to give command and say "If any man does such and so, let him share my table," would you not do all you could for this? He has invited us to heaven, to the table of the great and wonderful King. And do we hesitate, and put it off, instead of hastening and running to it? Then what is our hope of salvation? We cannot lay the blame on our frailty, we cannot blame our nature. It is indolence alone that renders us unworthy.

Thus far, it is I who have spoken. But may He who pricks the heart, He who gives the spirit of compunction, pierce your hearts, and place the seed in the depths of them, that thus from His fear you may conceive, and bring forth the spirit of salvation, and draw near with confidence. For "Your children are like olive plants around your table" (Ps 127.3). Oh, then, let there be nothing old, nothing wild, nothing ungentle, nothing crude! For not so are the young plants that are fit for fruit, for the wondrous fruit, the fruit, I mean, of the olive. And they are thriving, so as all to be around the table, and to come together here, not idly or by chance, but with fear and reverence. For thus with confidence shall you behold Christ Himself in heaven there, and shall be counted worthy of the heavenly kingdom. May God grant that we all may attain to it, in Jesus Christ our Lord, with whom to the Father, together with the Holy Spirit, be glory, might, and honor, now, and always, and unto the ages of ages. Amen.

C "For you have counted us worthy:" Frequency of Participation in the Eucharist.

IVC1 Basil the Great (c 330-379), *Letter* 93.
ed PG 32.484-485; *tr* FC, revised.

> These directives are probably a fragment of a longer letter; they have found their way into Eastern canon collections. Basil approves of daily communion, although, in the light of what is said later in the letter, this may not necessarily imply a daily liturgy. Basil describes his own practice, communion, no doubt as part of a eucharistic liturgy, on Sunday, Wednesday, Friday, and Saturday, and on feast days. The tone of Basil's acceptance of private communion for solitaries and laity contrasts strongly with that of a later pronouncement of the monastic leader Theodore the Studite (*d* 826) on the same subject (PG 99.1661B).

To the Lady Caesaria, concerning Communion.

To communicate every day, to be a sharer in the holy body and blood of Christ is, indeed, a good and beneficial practice, for He says plainly: "He who eats my flesh and drinks my blood has eternal life" (Jn 6.55). Who doubts but that to share continually in life is nothing other than to live in manifold ways. We, for our part, communicate four times in each week: on the Lord's Day, on the fourth day [Wednesday], on the day of preparation [Friday], and on the sabbath [Saturday], also on other days if there is a commemoration of a saint.

But as to a person's being compelled in times of persecution, in the absence of a priest or minister, to receive communion from his own hand—it is a waste of time to prove that this is no offense at all, since events themselves attest the long-standing, traditional character of this practice.

For all those living the solitary life in the wilderness, where there is no priest, reserve communion at home, and receive it from themselves. In Alexandria, and in Egypt, each one, even of the laity, very commonly keeps communion in his house and receives it from himself when he wishes. For when once the priest has consecrated and imparted the sacrifice, he who has received it as complete, once and for all, ought rightly to believe that he is partaking and receiving it from the hand of him who imparted it, even when he partakes of it everyday. Indeed, even in church the priest distributes a portion, and the one who receives it has it at his disposal, and thus moves it to his mouth with his own hand. And so, it is the same situation whether one receives a single portion or many portions at the same time from the priest.

IVC2 John Chrysostom (*c* 349-407), *Homily on First Timothy* 5.5.

ed PG 62.529-530; *tr* LNPF, revised.

The homilies on the two epistles of St. Paul to Timothy were delivered by John Chrysostom during his years in Constantinople (398-404). In this selection we find

Chrysostom extrapolating from his comment on 1 Tm 1.20 ("among these are Hymenaeus and Alexander, whom I have delivered to Satan, that they may be taught not to blaspheme") to explode popular misconceptions about the relationship of frequency to worthiness in the reception of communion.

Many such instances still occur. For since the priests cannot know who are sinners and unworthy partakers of the mysteries, God often takes care of this and delivers them to Satan (1 Tm 1.20). For whenever diseases and injuries, whenever sorrows and calamities, and the like occur, it is for this reason that they come about. This is shown by Paul, saying "For this reason many are weak and sickly among you, and many have fallen asleep" (1 Co 11.30). "But how," you say, "when we approach the mysteries only once a year?" This is indeed the terrible thing, that you determine the worthiness of your communion not by the purity of your minds, but by the interval of time. You think it reverence not to communicate often, not knowing that you are stained by partaking unworthily, though only once, and that to receive worthily, though often, is salutary. It is not presumptuous to receive often, but it is presumptuous to receive unworthily, even though only once in an entire lifetime.

But we are so miserably foolish that, though we keep committing countless offenses in the course of a year, and have no care to be absolved of them, yet we think it enough that we do not regularly make bold insolently to assault the body of Christ, not remembering that those who crucified Christ crucified Him only once. Is the offense, then, the less because committed only once? Judas betrayed only once. Did that fact free him from punishment? Why is time to be considered in this matter? Let our time for communion be a clear conscience.

The mystery at Pascha has nothing more than that which is now celebrated. It is one and the same. There is the same grace of the Spirit. It is always Pascha! You who are initiated understand what I am saying. On the day of preparation [Friday], on the sabbath [Saturday], on the Lord's Day, and on the days of martyrs the same sacrifice is celebrated, "For as often," he says, "as you eat this bread and drink this cup, you proclaim the death of the Lord to" (1 Co 11.26). He does not circumscribe the sacrifice with a temporal limit. Why is that time called Pascha? Because Christ suffered [*paschein*] for us then.

Let no one, therefore, communicate one way then, and in another way now. There is at all times the same power, the same dignity, the same grace, one and the same body; nor is it more holy at one time, and less holy at another. And even you know this, since at Pascha you see nothing out of the ordinary except the ornamental hangings and a more splendid attendance. The only thing that those days have more is that from them began the day of our salvation, that Christ was sacrificed then. But with respect to these mysteries, those days have no superiority.

When you go to take perceptible food, you wash your hands and your mouth. But when you prepare to draw near to this spiritual food, you do not cleanse your soul, but you approach full of uncleanness. "But," you say, "is not the forty days' fasting enough to cleanse this great heap of sins?" But what good is this, tell me? If wishing to store up some precious unguent, one should clean a place for it, but, a little while after storing it, he would throw dung on it, would not the fine fragrance vanish? This takes place with us too. We make ourselves, to the best of our ability, worthy to receive, and then we defile ourselves again! What is the profit? And this we say even of those who are able to cleanse themselves in those forty days.

Let us not, then, I urge you, neglect our salvation, so that our labor may not be in vain. For a person who turns from his sins, and then goes and commits the same again, is "like a dog that returns to its vomit" (Pr 26.11; 2 P 2.22). But if we act as we should, and pay attention to what we are doing, we shall be able to be found worthy of those high rewards. May we all obtain them through the grace and love for mankind of our Lord Jesus Christ, with whom, to the Father and the Holy Spirit be glory, power, and honor, now, and always, and unto the ages of ages. Amen.

IVC3 Augustine of Hippo (354-430), *First Letter to Januarius* (*Ep* 54) 1-5.
ed CSEL 34.158-164; *tr* FC, 12.252-256, revised.

Januarius was a layperson who, in 400, submitted to Augustine a set of questions on liturgical observances. Augustine replied with Letters 54 and 55, which he calls, in his *Retractationes*, "Two Books of Answers to the Inquiries of Januarius." We have excerpted those portions of Letter 54 which are concerned with the eucharist. Augustine's reply abounds with prudence, in his discernment of what is essential and incidental in the church's observances, in his concern for the avoidance of needless scandal, in his insights into the petty psychopathology which can arise over liturgical incidentals, and in his reconciliation of apparently conflicting points of view on the appropriate frequency of participation in the eucharist. The matters discussed here are perennial problems in the life of the church; Augustine's prudence, and his suggestion that such problems can best be resolved "by urging, first, that they remain in the peace of Christ, and then that each act as he devoutly believes he should," are a perennial solution.

AUGUSTINE TO HIS WELL-BELOVED SON, JANUARIUS, GREETINGS IN THE LORD.

1. I should prefer to know beforehand what answer you, were you asked, would give to the questions you have asked me, for in that way I could answer much more briefly by approving or correcting your answers, and quite easily agree with you, or set you right. This, as I said, is what I should prefer. But, in replying to you now, I have preferred to make my answer longer than my delay.

In the first place, I want you to hold as the basic principle of this discussion that our Lord Jesus Christ, as He Himself said in the gospel, has subjected us to His easy yoke and His light burden (Mt 11.30). Therefore, He has bound together the society of His new people with sacraments, very few in number, very easy of observance, most sublime in their meaning, as, for example, baptism hallowed by the name of the Trinity, the sharing of His body and His blood, and whatever else is commended in the canonical scriptures, with the exception of those burdens found in the five books of Moses, which imposed on the ancient people a servitude in accord with their character and the prophetic times in which they lived. But regarding those observances which we keep and, indeed, all the world keeps, and which do not derive from scripture but from tradition, we are given to understand that they have been recommended and ordained to be kept by the apostles themselves or by plenary councils whose authority is so very sound in the church. Such are the annual commemorations of the Lord's Passion, Ressurrection, and Ascension into heaven, of the Coming of the Holy Spirit from heaven, and other such observances as are kept by the universal church wherever it has spread.

2. As to other customs, however, which differ according to country and locality, as, for instance, the fact that some fast on Saturday, others do not; some receive the body and blood of the Lord daily, others receive it on appointed days; in some places no day is omitted in the offering of the sacrifice, elsewhere it is offered only on Saturday and the

Lord's Day, or even only on the Lord's Day; and other such differences as may be noted—there is freedom of observance in these matters, and there is no better rule for the earnest and prudent Christian than to act as he sees the church act wherever he has come. What is proved to be against neither faith nor morals is to be considered a matter of indifference, and is to be observed with due regard for the community in which one lives.

3. I believe you heard this some time ago, but I am nevertheless repeating it now. My mother, who had followed me to Milan, found that the church there did not fast on Saturday. She began to be anxious and uncertain as to what she should do. I was not then concerned with such things, but for her sake I consulted on this matter that man of most blessed memory, Ambrose. He answered that he could teach me nothing but what he himself did, because, if he knew anything better, he would do it. When I thought that he intended to tell us not to fast on Saturday on the basis of his authority alone, without giving any reason, he followed up and said to me: "When I go to Rome, I fast on Saturday; when I am here, I do not. So you also, observe the practice of whatever church you have come to, if you do not want to give or receive scandal." When I told this to my mother, she willingly accepted it. And, recalling this advice over and over again, I have always esteemed it as something I received from a heavenly oracle. For I have often experienced with grief and sorrow the disturbance of the frail by the contentious obstinacy or superstitious anxiety of certain brethren who stir up such controversial questions, thinking that nothing is correct except their own practice. And these are things of the sort that can be decided neither by the authority of holy scripture, nor by the tradition of the universal church, nor by the good purpose of amending one's life, but they are insisted upon simply because somebody thinks up a reason for them, or because a man was accustomed to do so in his own country, or because he saw things done somewhere while on a pilgrimage, and reckoned them to be more correct to the degree that they differed from his own usage.

4. Someone will say that the eucharist is not to be received every day. You ask why. "Because," he says, "those days are to be selected on which a man lives with greater purity and self-restraint, so that he may approach so great a sacrament worthily, for he who eats and drinks unworthily eats and drinks judgement to himself" (1 Co 11.29). Another, on the contrary, says: "Not at all. If the wound of sin and the onset of disease are so great that such remedies must be postponed, then an individual should be debarred from the altar by the authority of the bishop, in order to do penance and be reconciled by the same authority. For this is to receive unworthily, if one receives at a time when he ought to do penance. But he should not deprive himself of communion or restore himself to it by his own judgement, when it suits him. Otherwise, if a man's sins are not so great that he is judged fit for excommunication, then he ought not to separate himself from the daily medicine of the Lord's body."

Someone can quite rightly end the quarrel between them by urging, first, that they remain in the peace of Christ, and then that each act as he devoutly believes he should, according to his faith. For neither of them is dishonoring the body and blood of the Lord, but they are vying with one another in honoring the most salvific sacrament. For there was not a quarrel between Zacchaeus and the Centurion either, nor did one set himself above the other when one, rejoicing, received the Lord into his house (Lk 19.6), and the other said "I am not worthy that you should enter under my roof" (Mt 8.8). Both honored the Saviour in a different and, in a sense, opposite manner. Both were in distress because of their sins. Both found mercy.

For this similarity, the case of the manna is also useful. As among the first people of God it tasted in the mouth of each according to what he preferred (Ws 16.21), so also is it in the heart of each Christian with that sacrament by which the world has been subdued. One person honors it by not daring to receive daily, another by not daring to let a day go by without receiving; but this food is not to be despised, just as the manna was not to be disliked. Thus, the Apostle says it is received unworthily by those who do not distinguish it from other food by the veneration due to it alone. Therefore, when he says "He eats and drinks judgement to himself," he adds immediately "not discerning the body" (1 Co 11.29). This is quite clear, if due attention is given to that entire passage of the First Epistle to the Corinthians.

5. Suppose someone is traveling in a place where, in the ongoing observance of Lent, people do not bathe or relax their fast on the fifth day of the week, and he says "I will not fast today." He is asked why, and he says "Because it is not done in my country." What is he doing but trying to show that his own practice is superior to another's? He will not quote me this from the Book of God, nor contend with the full voice of the universal church wherever it is extended, nor will he demonstrate that the other person acts contrary to the faith, but he in accordance with it, nor will he prove that the other violates good morals, while he preserves them. To be sure, such people violate their peace and quiet by quarreling about such an unimportant matter. I would prefer in matters of this sort that neither one man in another's country, nor the other man in the first's country indicate a distaste for what the people are doing. If someone travels in a strange country, where the people of God are more numerous, more assiduous, and more devout, and there, for example, he sees that the sacrifice is offered twice on the fifth day of the last week of Lent [*sc.* Holy Thursday], in the morning, and in the evening, and, returning to his own country, where it is customary to offer the sacrifice at the end of the day, if he should claim that this is wrong and unlawful because he saw it done differently elsewhere—that way of thinking is childish. We must avoid it among ourselves, but endure it, and correct it among our people.

IVC4 Augustine of Hippo (354-430), *Sermons* (57, 59) *on the Lord's Prayer*, excerpts.

These excerpts might have been presented in section IIA, for they are catechetical. They were not, however, part of the mystagogical catechesis in Hippo, as they were, apparently, in Jerusalem (IIA3) and Milan (IIA4). The sermons from which these excerpts are taken were delivered by Augustine, in different years before 410, in Lent to the *competentes*, or candidates for baptism. They are sermons for the "Handing Over" of the Lord's Prayer—Augustine would teach the Lord's Prayer to the *competentes* and explain it, as he had the Creed, and the *competentes* would have to be prepared to recite the prayer, just as they had recited the Creed, back to their Bishop.

We focus on the explanation of "Give us this day our daily bread," for Augustine makes plain here the absolute necessity of the eucharist for the sustenance of the Christian in this life—the next life is another matter. Augustine's preaching on the Lord's Prayer was influenced by Cyprian's treatise on the same subject; compare these passages with Cyprian, *On the Lord's Prayer* 18 (CSEL 3,1.280-281). Note too, especially in the light of Origen's comments on Mt 26 (IIIB4), the multiple significance of "bread": bread, eucharist, word, preaching, hymnody.

Sermon 57.7

ed PL 38.389-390.

There remain the petitions for this life of our sojourning, and so it continues: GIVE US THIS DAY OUR DAILY BREAD. Give eternal things; give the things of time. You have promised the Kingdom; do not deny the required assistance. You will give us everlasting honor with you; give temporal nourishment on earth. Therefore DAILY, therefore TODAY, that is, in this time. When this life has passed away, we will not ask for daily bread, will we? For then one will not say "daily," but "today." Now one says "daily," when one day passes, and another succeeds. Will we say "daily," when there will be one eternal day?

Of course, this request for daily bread is to be understood

in two ways: for the necessity of fleshly sustenance, and for the necessity of spiritual nourishment. There is need of fleshly food for our daily sustenance, without which we cannot live. There is sustenance, and shelter too, but we understand all of that from the single aspect. When we ask for bread, we include everything. The faithful [*i.e.* baptized Christians] know also a spiritual nourishment, which you too will come to know and receive from the altar of God. That too will be your daily bread, quite necessary for this present life. For we are not going to receive the eucharist when we have come to Christ and have begun to reign with Him forever, are we? Therefore, the eucharist is our daily bread. Only let us receive it in such a way that we are refreshed not only in body, but in mind as well. For the very power which is understood to be there is unity, that, collected into His body, made members of Him, we may be what we receive. Then will it truly be our daily bread.

My preaching to you is also daily bread, and your hearing the readings every day in church is daily bread, and your hearing and singing hymns is daily bread, for these are necessary for our sojourn. When we have arrived there, are we going to listen to a book? No, we are going to see the Word, hear the Word, eat the Word, drink the Word, as the angels do now. Do the angels require books, or expositors, or readers? Not at all. They read by seeing, for they see Truth Himself, and are filled from that Font whence we now receive dew. Mention is made, then, of daily bread, because in this life this request is needful for us.

Sermon 59.6

ed SC 116.192-193.

The Prayer continues: GIVE US THIS DAY OUR DAILY BREAD. Whether we are asking from the Father the sustenance necessary for our body, signifying in bread whatever is necessary for us, or we understand the daily bread to be that which you are going to receive from the altar, we do well to ask that He give it to us. TODAY, that is, in this present time, for it is necessary in this present time, when we hunger. But when we will be in the other life, and hunger will cease to exist, what need will we have to ask for bread? Or, if it be that bread which I said we receive from the altar, we do well to pray that He give it to us. For what are we praying for, but that we may not commit some sin on account of which we would be separated from such bread?

The word of God which is preached daily is also bread. Its not being bread for the stomach does not mean that it is not bread for the mind. But when this life has passed away, we will not seek the bread which hunger seeks, nor will we have need of receiving the sacrament of the altar, for we will then be with Christ whose body we receive. Nor will there be any need for these words, which I am saying to you, to be said, nor will there be need to read a book, when we shall see Him who is the Word of God, through which all things have been made, on which the angels are fed, by which the angels are illumined, by which the angels become wise, not seeking the words of convoluted speech, but drinking in the Only Word, and filled with it, they belch forth praises, and do not grow weary in their praises, for "Blessed," says the Psalm, "are they who dwell in your house, they will praise you unto the ages of ages" (Ps 83.5).

IVC5 Augustine of Hippo (354-430), *Letter* 98.9. *ed* CSEL 34.531-532.

> Augustine wrote Letter 98 to Bishop Boniface of Cataquas, near Hippo, in 408. Boniface had posed to Augustine a set of questions concerning baptism, the last of which was how persons who cannot guarantee the probity of the future life of the infant they present for baptism, since they cannot know the future, are nonetheless allowed to vouch for the infant's faith and conversion, although they cannot know the infant's mind.
>
> In this excerpt, Augustine gives an answer to Boniface's question, and provides us with a remarkable insight

into his own understanding of sacrament, how broad an applicability the word enjoyed with him, and the at once symbolic and effective connection of sacraments to what they represent. In the light of this passage, the enigmatic explanation of the eucharist, which Augustine, commenting on Ps 98.9 (IIIA3), placed in the mouth of Christ, takes on a clearer meaning: "You are not going to eat this body which you see, nor are you going to drink the blood which those who will crucify me are going to shed. I have given you a sacrament."

To be sure, we often speak in the following way: As Pascha approaches, we say that tomorrow, or the day after, is "The Passion of the Lord," although He suffered so many years before, and His Passion occurred only once. Indeed, on that particular Lord's Day we say "Today the Lord has risen," although many, many years have passed since the time when He arose. Why is it that there is no one so foolish as to accuse us of being liars when we speak in this way? It is because we name these days according to a likeness to the days on which those events took place. Thus a day, which is not the actual day, but like to it in the circle of the year, takes its name from the actual day because of the celebration of the sacrament which occurred, not on the very day of the celebration, but long ago. Was not Christ Himself offered in sacrifice once and for all? And yet, in the sacrament He is offered in sacrifice for the people, not only on all the feasts of Pascha, but every day; and it is surely no lie if someone, upon being asked, answers that He is sacrificed. For if sacraments did not have a certain likeness to the things of which they are the sacraments, they would not be sacraments at all. Moreover, it is on the basis of this likeness that the sacraments commonly receive their names from these very things. Therefore, just as in a certain way the sacrament of the body of Christ is the body of Christ, and the sacrament of the blood of Christ is the blood of Christ, so the sacrament of faith [baptism] is faith. Now to believe is nothing else but to have faith, and for this reason, when the answer is given that an infant, who does not yet have the disposition of faith, believes, what is really being answered is that he has faith because of the sacrament of faith, and that he has turned himself to God because of the sacrament of the turning, for even the answer itself is part of the celebration of the sacrament, just as when the Apostle, speaking about baptism, said: "We have been buried along with Christ unto death" (Rm 6.4), he did not say "We have portrayed burial symbolically," but he said, straight out, "We have been buried." Thus he has given the sacrament of so profound a thing no other name that that of the thing itself.

IVC6 John Cassian (*c* 360-*c* 435), *Conference 23 (the Third of Abba Theonas, On Sinlessness)* 21.

ed CSEL 13.670-671; *lit* O. Chadwick, *John Cassian* (2nd ed, Cambridge, 1968) 69-70.

Had John Cassian been an historian, as well as the most influential ascetical writer of the West, he could have left us some fascinating reading. He was a native Latin speaker, born perhaps in Romania, perhaps in Provence. After receiving a first-rate education, and acquiring fluency in Greek, he journeyed *c* 380 to the Holy Land and entered a monastery in Bethlehem. With his fellow-monk Germanus, he undertook extensive journeys to the monastic centers of Egypt to benefit from the wisdom of the spiritual leaders there. His second sojourn in Egypt was broken off by the Origenist controversy, and he and Germanus sought and received refuge and help from John Chrysostom in Constantinople. Cassian and Germanus appeared in Rome in 404 on an embassy on behalf of the exiled Chrysostom. In 415 or 416 Cassian settled at Marseilles, where he founded two monasteries, one for men, one for women, and spent the rest of his life in teaching and writing.

Cassian's *Conferences*, twenty-four in number for the twenty-four elders of the Apocalypse, are a supplement to the monastic rules and teachings which he provided in his *Institutes*. The *Conferences* are Cassian's memoirs of the teachings of the great spiritual directors whom he had encountered in his travels. *Conference 23* takes us to Scete, to Abba Theonas, and provides us with his discussion of the impossibility of sinlessness in the present life. At the end, he takes up the question of the frequency of the reception of Holy Communion, teaching us to avoid the extremes of pusillanimity and pride.

We should not, however, suspend ourselves from the Lord's communion because we realize that we are sinners. Rather, more and more we should hasten to it with eagerness, for healing of soul and purification of spirit, but with such humility and faith that we judge ourselves unworthy to receive so great a favor, and seek it, rather, as a remedy for our wounds. Otherwise, we must not presume to receive communion worthily even once a year, as do some who live in monasteries. They esteem the dignity and sanctity and value of the heavenly sacrament so highly that they consider that only the holy and pure should receive it, rather than that it makes us holy and pure by partaking of it. Surely they fall into a greater arrogance of presumption than they think they are avoiding, because at least when they do receive it, they think they are worthy to receive it. But it is far better to receive the sacrament as a remedy for our ills on every Lord's Day, with that humility of heart whereby we believe and confess that we can never worthily come to those sacred mysteries, than to be carried away by a vain belief that we are worthy to partake of them at least after a year.

D "Let us stand properly, let us stand in awe, let us be attentive...:" Behavior at the Eucharistic Assembly.

IVD1 John Chrysostom (*c* 349-407), *Homily on Matthew* 32.6-7.
ed PG 57.384-386; *tr* LNPF, revised.

> This selection is an excursus which follows upon Chrysostom's comment on Mt 10.12-13 ("As you enter the household, salute it; and if the household is worthy, let your peace come upon it. But if it is not worthy, let your peace come back to you."). Chrysostom warns his congregation in Antioch of the dispositions they must have, and of the consequent behavior they must exhibit at the eucharistic assembly if they are to benefit from the preaching of the word of God and the reception of the eucharist.

Let us not only hear these things, but imitate them as well. For they are said not of the apostles alone, but also of the saints afterwards. Let us, therefore, become worthy to receive them as guests. For according to the disposition of those who receive them this peace both comes and goes away again. For this effect follows not only from the courageous speaking of those who teach, but also from the worthiness of those who receive.

Let us consider it a great loss not to enjoy such peace. For the Prophet also foretells this peace, saying: "How lovely are the feet of those who bring good news of peace." Then, to explain its value, he added: "who bring news of good things" (Is 52.7; Rm 10.15). Christ also declared the greatness of this peace when He said: "Peace I leave with you, my peace I give to you" (Jn 14.27).

And we should do everything to enjoy this peace, both at home and in church. For in the church too the presiding minister gives "Peace," and this peace is a type of that just mentioned, and you should receive it with all eagerness, with a will, before approaching the table. For if not to partake from the table is offensive, how much more offensive is it to reject the one who addresses you.

For your sake the presbyter sits, for your sake the teacher stands, laboring and toiling. What defense, then, will you have if you do not afford him a hearing? For indeed the church is the common home of all, and after you have entered, we come in, following their model [*sc* that of the apostles]; and so, we also proclaim "Peace to all," as soon as we come in, according to that precept.

Let no one, then, be careless, no one daydreaming, when the priests enter and teach, for the punishment appointed for this is not slight. I, for one, would rather enter into any of your houses ten thousand times and be put to shame, than not to be heard when I speak here. This second is harder for me to bear than the first, because this house is of such greater dignity.

Our great riches are truly laid up here, here all our hopes. For what is here that is not great and awesome? This table is far more precious and delightful than yours, and this lamp than your lamp. All those who have put away disease by anointing themselves with its oil in faith and in due season know this. And this coffer too is far better and more necessary than yours, for it contains not clothes, but alms locked up in it, even though few enjoy the profit that comes from almsgiving. This couch is better than yours, for the repose of the divine scriptures is more delightful than any couch.

And if unanimity flourished among us, we would have no home but this. And that there is nothing bizarre in this statement is attested by the "three thousand" (Ac 2.41) and the "five thousand" (Ac 4.4), they who had but one home, one table, one soul, for "the multitude of those who believed," we read, "were of one heart and one soul" (Ac 4.32). But since we fall far short of their excellence, and dwell scattered in our various households, let us, at least whenever we gather here, do so eagerly. Because although in all other things we are beggars and paupers, in these we are rich.

Wherefore, here at least receive us with love when we come in to you. And when I say "Peace to you," say "And with your spirit," and say it not with the voice alone, but also with the mind, not with the mouth, but with the mind also. But if in here you say "Peace also to your spirit," but outside you are my enemy, abusing and spitting at me, and secretly showering me with countless reproaches, what sort of peace is this?

For I, indeed, even though you speak evil of me countless times, bid you peace with a pure heart, with sincere mind, and I can say nothing evil of you ever, for I have a father's heart. And if ever I rebuke you, I do it out of concern for you. But you, by your backbiting me and not welcoming me in the Lord's house—I fear that you are again increasing my depression, not because you abuse me, not because you have cast me out, but because you have rejected peace, and have drawn down upon yourselves that grievous punishment. For although I do not shake off the dust, although I do not turn away, what is threatened remains unchanged.

I, indeed, often bid peace to you, and I will not ever cease from bidding it. And if you receive me with insult, even then I do not shake off the dust (Mt 10.14), not because I am disobedient to the Lord, but because I am on fire for you. Moreover, I have suffered nothing much for you. I have not made a long journey, nor have I come with that garb and that voluntary poverty—I am the first to accuse myself— not without shoes and a second cloak (Mt 10.9-10), and, perhaps, this is why you have failed to do your part. However, this is not an adequate defense for you, for while my condemnation is greater, it does not impart forgiveness to you.

7. Once the houses were churches, but now the church has become a house. Once one might say nothing worldly in a house, now one may say nothing spiritual in a church. Rather, even here you bring in business from the market-place, and while God is speaking, you give up listening in silence to what He says, and bring in contrary things, introducing worldly affairs. And I wish it were only your own affairs, but now you both talk and hear of things which have nothing to do with you.

For this I grieve, and I will not cease grieving. For I cannot change this house for another, but here I must remain until I depart from this life. "Receive us," therefore, as Paul commanded (2 Co. 7.2), for his words referred not to a dining-table, but to the will and the mind. I also seek this of you, charity and fervent, genuine friendship. But if you cannot provide this, at least be a friend to yourselves, and abandon your present negligence. It is enough for my consolation if I see you doing what is right and becoming better men. Thus I will also show forth greater love, even though "the more abundantly I love you, the less I am loved" (2 Co 12.15).

There are many things indeed which bring us together. One table is set for all, one Father begot us, we are all born of the same birth-pangs, the same drink has been given to all, or, rather, not only the same drink, but even to drink from one cup. For our Father, wishing to bring us to familial affection, has devised this also, that we should drink from one cup, a thing which belongs to intense love.

But we are not worthy of comparison to the apostles. I, too, admit this, and would never deny it. For I say that we are not only unworthy of comparison to the apostles themselves, but even unworthy of comparison to their shadows

(Ac 5.15). But for all that, you must do your part. This will not disgrace you, but will benefit you all the more, for when even to unworthy persons you show so much love and obedience, you will receive a greater reward. For I do not speak my own words, since you have no teacher at all on earth (*cf* Mt 23.8-9). But I give you what I have received, and in giving I seek for nothing in return from you but only to be loved. And if I am unworthy even of this, yet by my loving you I shall quickly become worthy. We are commanded to love not only those who love us, but even our enemies (Mt 5.44-46). Who, then, is so hardhearted, who is so savage that after having received such a precept, he should reject and even hate those who love him, full as he may be of countless evils?

We have shared a spiritual table, let us also share spiritual love. For if robbers, sharing a meal, forget their usual behavior, what excuse will we have, who are continually sharing the Lord's body, and do not even imitate their gentleness? And yet to many, not only one table, but even to be of one city has been a sufficient basis for friendship; but we, when we have the same city, and the same house and table, and Way, and Door, and Root, and Life, and Teacher, and Judge, and Creator, and to whom all things are in common (Ac 2.44)—what forgiveness can we deserve, if we are divided from one another?

IVD2 John Chrysostom (*c* 349-407), *Homily on Second Corinthians* 18.3.

ed PG 61.527-528; *tr* LNPF, revised.

Chrysostom preached his thirty homilies on Second Corinthians at Antioch in the years 391-397. In this selection, Chrysostom has moved from a discussion of the final words of 2 Co 8.24 ("before the face of the churches") to a discussion of the power of the prayer of the Christian assembly, and of the need for attentive participation by the laity in the eucharistic prayer.

The prayer of the church freed Peter from his chains and opened the mouth of Paul. The church's assent equips those who come to spiritual rule, and not incidentally. It is for this reason that one who is about to ordain calls at that time for the people's prayers, and they give their assent, and shout acclamations which the initiated know—it is not allowed to disclose everything before the uninitiated.

Moreover, there are occasions on which there is no difference at all between the priest and the layperson, as, for example, when we are to partake of the awesome mysteries, for we are all alike counted worthy of the same things. Under the Old Covenant the Priest ate some things, and those below him others, but it was not lawful for the people to partake of the things of which the priest partook. It is not that way now, but one body and one cup are set before all.

And in the prayers, also, one may observe the people's considerable contribution, for the prayers are made in common by the priest and by the people on behalf of the energumens and those under penance. All say one prayer, the prayer filled with compassion. Again, when we exclude from the holy precincts those who cannot partake of the holy table, another prayer must be offered, and we all alike fall upon the ground, and all alike rise up. When the Peace is to be received and given in turn, we all kiss alike. Again, in the most awesome mysteries, the priest prays for the people, and the people also pray for the priest, for the words "And with your spirit" are nothing but this. The offering of the thanksgiving [*eucharistia*], again, is in common, for the priest does not give thanks alone, but all the people as well. For, having received their assent, only after they agree that it is fitting and right to do so, does he begin the thanksgiving. And why are you surprised that the people sometimes pray aloud along with the priest, since they send up those sacred hymns along with the very cherubim and the powers above?

Now I have said this in order that each one of the laity may also be vigilant, that we may understand that we are all one body, having such difference among ourselves as members from members (Rm 12.4 ff); that we not load everything upon the priests, but that we ourselves may also care for the whole church as for our common body. This course will provide for greater safety and for your greater growth in virtue.

Note how frequently the apostles admitted the laity to share in their decisions. For when they ordained the seven, they first conferred with the people (Ac 7.2-3), and, when Peter ordained Matthias, with all who were present there, both men and women (Ac 1.15 ff). For here there is no haughtiness of rulers, no servility of the ruled, but a spiritual rule, which usurps—by taking on itself the greater share of the labor and care for you, and not by seeking greater honors. For the church should live as one household, it should be as one body, just as there is one baptism, and one table, and one source, and one creation, and one Father.

IVD3 Caesarius of Arles (470-542), *Sermons* 73, 74, and 78.

ed CCSL 103.306-309, 310-312, 323-325; *tr* FC, revised.

Caesarius was the most important Gallic churchman of his day. He entered the great monastery of Lerins in 490/91, and received his monastic formation there. He was sent to Arles on a number of monastic missions, and became increasingly involved in the ecclesiastical community. He was chosen to be archbishop of Arles in 503. His interest in the monastic life continued, but he devoted himself to his see, reforming its pastoral care, and presiding over a number of important and influential synods.

Caesarius' sermons give us our most vivid portrait of him. He was an energetic and popular preacher. His discourses are simple and to-the-point. Though they are devoted to the practical, immediate needs of his own people, any pastor can see that they have a perennial relevance.

Sermon 73

An Admonition, Encouraging All the People to Remain Faithfully in Church until the Divine Mysteries are Celebrated.

I beg, and with paternal devotion I urge you, dearly beloved, that as often as Mass is celebrated, either on the Lord's Day or other important holydays, no one leave church until the divine mysteries are completed. Although there are many people whose faith and piety give us reason to rejoice, there are still more who think too little about the salvation of their souls. These leave church as soon as the divine lessons have been read. In fact, while the lessons are being read, some of them are so busy with idle and worldly gossip that they neither hear them themselves nor allow others to do so. We might blame such people less if they did not come to church, because they clearly offend God all the more in the very place where they might have won forgiveness of their sins.

2. Therefore I ask you, brothers, to receive the suggestion of our lowliness, not only patiently, but even gladly. If you take careful notice you will realize that Mass is not completed when the divine lessons are read in church, but when the gifts are offered, when the body and blood of the Lord are consecrated. You yourselves can read in your houses the prophetic, apostolic, and gospel readings, or you can listen to others while they read them. But you cannot hear or see the consecration of the body and blood of Christ anywhere but in the house of God. Therefore, anyone who wants to offer the entire Mass with profit to his soul ought to remain in church with reverent body and contrite heart until the Lord's Prayer is said and the blessing imparted to the people.

When the majority of the people—in fact, what is worse, almost all of them—leave the church as soon as the lessons have been read, to whom will the priest say "Lift up your hearts"? Moreover, how can they reply that they have lifted them up when they go down into the streets both in body and in heart? Or how will they cry out with trembling and with joy "Holy, holy, holy ... Blessed is He who comes in the name of the Lord"? Again, when the Lord's Prayer is said, who will be able to exclaim with humility and truth "Forgive us our trespasses, as we forgive those who trespass against us"? Indeed, even those who remain in church utter the Lord's Prayer with their lips unto their own judgment, rather than as a remedy, if they have not forgiven debts to their debtors, for they are proven to have failed to fulfill this in action. And to no purpose they say "Deliver us from evil," when they themselves do not cease to return evil for evil.

If, then, those who are in church are in danger if they refuse to fulfill what they promise, what do those think of themselves whom either insatiable desire or love for this world keeps so involved that it does not allow them to remain in church for the space of one hour? It is not enough for them that throughout the week they are continually occupied with their needs or, perhaps more truly, with their desires. Still, after an hour or two, in which they seem to be present in church more in body than in spirit, turning their backs on the sacrifices and the priests of God, they return with no delay to embrace worldly pleasure. These people do not know what they are looking for, or what they are leaving. They follow darkness and desert the light, they embrace shadows and despise the truth. They lose the sweetness of Christ and seek out the bitterness of the world, they love vanity and look for falsehood (Ps 4.3). Truly, one who is in a hurry to leave church does not know how much good is accomplished in the celebration of Mass.

3. If a king or some influential person had invited such people to a meal, I wonder if they would dare to depart before the entire meal was finished. Even if no person detained them, their gluttony would. Why do we not leave the banquet of a man until it is concluded, except that we want to fill our stomachs more than is probably necessary, and fear to offend the man? Why do we quickly leave a

spiritual and divine banquet? I fear to mention it lest, perhaps, some become angry, yet I will speak out because of the imminent danger both to me and to you. We do this because we do not care for the soul's food, and have neither fear of God nor respect for man (Lk 18.2).

However, through God's mercy not all are blameworthy in this matter. Many can be found who remain in church with great devotion until the blessing over the people is given, and persist in humble prayer, not only for themselves, but also for others. God, who has given them such devotion that they remain in church, will also grant them a reward. On the other hand, those who are careless He will condemn by His just judgement. Therefore, brothers, warn those who are unwilling to say the Lord's Prayer and receive the blessing. Do not cease to rebuke them, telling them, and quite plainly threatening them that it does them no good to hear the divine readings if they depart before the divine mysteries are completed. However, we cannot and should not blame those who are occupied in works of public necessity and those who are prevented from remaining through some infirmity. But let them examine their consciences as to whether necessity or their own will holds them back.

4. Therefore, again and again I beg and entreat you that every Lord's Day, and especially on the major feasts, no one leave church until the divine mysteries are completed—with the exception, of course, of those we mentioned before who might be prevented by serious illness or by public necessity from remaining any longer. I speak truly, brothers: It is obstinate and exceedingly impious for Christians not to have the reverence for the Lord's Day which the Jews are seen to observe on the Sabbath. Since the latter unfortunate people observe the Sabbath in such a way that they do not dare to do any secular work on it, how much more should those who were "redeemed, not with gold or silver, but with the precious blood of Christ" (1 P 1.18-19) pay attention to their price, and make time for God on the day of the Resurrection, and take thought more carefully for the salvation of their souls? Finally, if throughout the Lord's Day we neglect to engage in reading and prayer, we sin against God,

and not lightly, then how great a wrong it is if we do not have the patience to stay in church for the space of an hour or two while the divine mysteries are celebrated. What is worse, love for this world so intoxicates us that its fleeting shadows and the pleasures of worldly desires constantly draw us to vain and false joys which produce true grief.

5. For this reason, again and again I beg you: Let none of you leave church until the divine mysteries have been completed. Remain in church in such a way that no one of you is busy with idle or worldly gossip. I advise you humbly and tell you what I must say, and you should hear: The man who despises the herald will face the judge. However, if a man hears me willingly and strives to fulfill what I have asked, I believe that out of God's mercy glorious rewards will be given to him, both in this life and the next. On the other hand, whoever prefers to despise me will not be able to excuse himself before the tribunal of Christ by saying that he was not restrained from evil or that he was not called by continual warnings to what is holy and pleasing to God. In God's mercy, however, we trust that you will not incur judgement for contempt, but that, instead, you will attain to the kingdom through willing obedience, with the help of our Lord Jesus Christ, who, with the Father and the Holy Spirit, lives and reigns unto ages of ages. Amen.

Sermon 74

An Admonition that the People Should Attend Mass to the End.

If you would learn and observe carefully what grief and bitterness there is in my soul when I see you unwilling to stay for the entire Mass, dearly beloved, you might have pity on both yourselves and me. Surely, he who understands what is taking place in church when the divine mysteries are being celebrated realizes the evil they do who without some great necessity leave church when the Mass is not yet finished.

Therefore, if you want to free me from tribulation of soul, and to absolve yourselves from sin, do not despise my plea. Fear, rather, what the Lord has said about priests: "He who hears you, hears me; and he who rejects you, rejects me" (Lk 10.16).

Whoever is neither afraid nor ashamed to rush out of church, although the Mass is not yet completed, let him not doubt that he sins doubly, as he forsakes the divine mysteries, and insults and saddens the priest who is solicitous for his welfare. If our humbleness invited you to perform some difficult worldly tasks, we are sure that your charity would afford us obedience. However, when we call you, not to earthly, but to heavenly pursuits, not to temporal ones, but to those which will benefit your soul forever, not looking for temporal gain, but summoning you to heavenly treasures, consider in what peril they remain who feign obedience. Indeed, dearly beloved, when you leave church I do not grieve so much because you make me suffer any physical loss; rather, it is because I want you to be perfect that I perceive you offending God with such sorrow.

2. Therefore, again and again, I beg you, when you come to church, because we who are the Lord's least worthy representative invite you to a banquet that is not earthly, where human food is served, but to a heavenly, spiritual banquet, where the bread of angels is set before you, do not reject or despise your Lord's banquet, so that He may not despise you in the blessedness of His Kingdom. Indeed, you ought to fear that judgment in the gospel whereby the Lord said that those who had been invited to the wedding feast, and disdained to come, were unworthy, and commanded others to be invited (Mt 22.2 ff). It should not be considered with indifference, but should be feared, that those who were unwilling to come because of worldly preoccupations were judged unworthy by the very words of the Lord. Therefore, in order that this may not be said of us also, let us, as I have already implored, have patience for the space of one or two hours until the food of souls is placed on that spiritual table and the spiritual sacraments are consecrated. Moreover, since, when the prayers are finished, the Lord's blessing is

bestowed upon you, not by a man, but through a man, receive the heavenly dew of divine blessing with a grateful and loving soul, a reverent body, and a contrite heart, in order that, according to the Lord's promise, it may become in you "a fountain of water, springing up unto life everlasting" (Jn 4.14).

3. Various, different occupations prevent all from remaining in church. Physical infirmity keeps one, the public welfare another, their own whim binds still others, and draws them away like captives. How many even now in the marketplace or in the halls of the basilicas have time for lawsuits or business! How many in the entrances of the basilicas or in the offices are occupied with gossip or idle conversation! No small number of clerics is commonly among them! What kind of benefit can such derive from sacred scripture when they do not even allow the sound of it to reach their ears? Rather, there is fulfilled in them that which was written, "like the deaf asps which stop their ears so that they do not hear the voice" of the scriptures "charming them" (Ps 57.5, 6). Therefore, you upon whom God has deigned to bestow His fear and love, and who come to church with great compunction, should frequently reproach those who are unwilling or, perhaps, unable to come here. Warn them and give them salutary advice to fear what is written: "The burdens of this world have made them wretched." Now we are not saying that they should not be concerned about their food and clothing, but we are asking this, that for the space of one or two hours, while the lessons are read and the divine mysteries celebrated, they should not leave the church, and let them at least labor for their souls as much as they hasten to labor for their bodies. Although they ought to provide for their souls much more than they do for their bodies—because what has been made according to the image of God is better than what was formed from the slime of the earth—this much we urge at present, that they strive to provide for both, at least equally, what they need. Let them prepare for the body what is sufficient for the short time in this world, and for the soul what it needs forever in eternity.

4. And therefore I beg you, dearly beloved, that wherever
you will be, you will zealously carry all that you have heard
in this preaching under the Lord's inspiration to your neighbors and relatives who either cannot come to church with
you or, what is worse, perhaps will not, as well as to those
who, though they do come, leave early. For, just as I will be
guilty if I neglect to speak to you, so you also, if you do not
remember what you have heard in order to teach it to others,
ought to fear that you will have to give an account for them.
Therefore, with the Lord's inspiration, strive to fulfill what
the Apostle says: "If a person is caught doing something
wrong, you who are spiritual should instruct such a one in a
spirit of gentleness" (Gal 6.1). The same Apostle also
preaches not only to the clergy, but to the laity and to
women, saying: "Reprove the restless, comfort the faint-
hearted, support the weak" (1 Th 5.14). Provided that you
are willing to rebuke one another in charity in case of sin, the
Enemy will be able to take you by surprise only with difficulty, or not at all. If he does take you by surprise, the evil
which was done is easily amended and corrected. Then is
fulfilled in you what was written: "A brother who helps his
brother will be exalted" (Pr 18.19), and "He who causes a
sinner to be brought back from the error of his way saves his
soul from death, and covers a multitude of sins" (Ja 5.20).
With the help of our Lord Jesus Christ, to whom is honor
and dominion, together with the Father and the Holy Spirit,
unto ages of ages. Amen.

Sermon 78

An Admonition to Observe Silence in Church.

A few days ago I gave you some advice with paternal
concern and devotion. Because of those whose feet hurt or
who suffer some other physical disability, I even asked, in a
sense, that when drawn-out accounts of the martyrs or,
indeed, any rather long lessons are read, those who cannot

stand should sit down in humility and silence, and listen attentively to what is read. But now some of our daughters think that all of them, or, indeed, very many of them, even of those who are physically well, should do this regularly. Yes, when the word of God has begun to be read, they want to lie down, just as they would do in their beds. If only they would merely lie down, and with thirsting hearts hear the word of God in silence! Then they would not be so busy with idle tales that they themselves do not hear or allow others to hear what is being proclaimed. Therefore, I beg you, venerable daughters, and I exhort you with fatherly care: whenever the lessons are read or the word of God is preached, let no one lie down on the ground, unless, perhaps, a serious illness compels her. Even then, no one should lie down, but should sit up and listen attentively and with eager heart to the words that are proclaimed.

2. I ask you, brothers and sisters, tell me: What seems greater to you, the word of God or the body of Christ? If you want to answer the truth, you surely must say that the word of God is not less than the body of Christ. Therefore, with as great care as we take when Christ's body is given to us, so that none of it may fall out of our hands onto the ground, with just so much care we should see to it that God's word which is dispensed to us may not fall away from our hearts because we are thinking or talking about something else. The person who hears the word of God with inattention is surely no less guilty than the one who allows the body of Christ to fall on the ground through his own carelessness.

3. Still, I would like to know if, at the hour when the word of God is preached, we were to give precious jewels, earrings, or gold rings, our daughters would stand and take them. Doubltess they would take most eagerly what was offered to them. However, because we cannot and should not offer bodily ornament, we are not heard willingly. Yet it is not fair that we who administer spiritual riches should be judged useless. If anyone willingly hears the word of God, he should not doubt that he has received earrings for his soul, sent from the fatherland of Paradise. If a man is encouraged to give something to the poor, then whenever he extends his

hands in almsgiving, he will receive bracelets given by Christ. Truly, as the pleasure-loving flesh is adorned for a short time with earthly ornaments so that it may please carnal eyes to its own ruin or that of others who are filled with lust, so a holy soul is adorned by divine words as with the spiritual and eternal pearls of good works, that thus happily adorned, it may attain to the company of its heavenly spouse and to the wedding banquet, and will not have said to it what is written in the gospel: "Friend, how did you come in here without a wedding garment?" (Mt 22.12), lest naked and despoiled of the ornaments of good works he hear: "Bind his hands and feet, and cast him forth into the darkness outside, where there will be weeping and the gnashing of teeth" (Mt 22.13). Rather, because of its adornment of good works, may that longed-for word be addressed to it: "Well done! Good and faithful servant, enter into the joy of your Lord" (Mt 25.21).

4. I beg you, daughters, listen carefully to my words. If a mother wanted to adorn her daughter, and the girl, scorning the ornaments she receives, kept bending down and moving restlessly from side to side, so that her mother could not dress her as she wished, would she not be justly rebuked and slapped? Consider me the mother of your souls. I want to adorn you in such a way that no spot or wrinkle (Ep 5.27) may appear in you before the tribunal of the eternal Judge. Desiring to provide for your souls not only ornaments but also medicines, I wish to sew up the tears, mend the rips, heal the wounds, wash away the spots, repair the losses, and adorn with spiritual pearls that which is sound. If I do not hesitate to give them, why should anyone receive them with scorn? Since earthly, temporal adornments of the body are purchased at a great price if no one is found to give them, how much more fitting it is, then, that you receive with perfect charity eternal ornaments for your souls which are offered without any cost, although we have acquired them with great labor? When we provide you with pearls from the fatherland of Paradise, we seek no other reward in this life but to see you listen patiently and willingly to the words which are addressed to you and, according to your strength,

with God's help, fulfill them in your actions.

5. Beloved brothers and venerable daughters, we are not saying these things because we believe that you do not receive the word of God willingly. Through the goodness of God our soul exults and rejoices over your obedience more than can be thought or said. Still, because we want you to rise continually to better things, we presume to admonish you with paternal solicitude even with regard to the things which you do perfectly. Moreover, since not all men and women would come to the vigil today, I beg you, sons and daughters, faithfully to report what has been said to you to those who were absent. Thus you may obtain a reward, not only for your own amendment, but for that of others as well.

IVD4 Anastasius II, Patriarch of Antioch (*d* 608/09), *Sermon on the Eucharistic Assembly.*
ed PG 89.825-849; *lit Clavis patrum graecorum* 3.462.

This sermon, along with much else, has long been attributed to the Abbot Anastasius of Sinai (*d* after 700). The efforts of Stergios Sakkos to make sense of the literary conglomerate of *Anastasiana* led to his ascribing this sermon to Anastasius II, sometime monk of Sinai, who succeeded his namesake Anastasius I to the see of Antioch in 599, and died in civil disturbances there in 608 or 609. Sakkos' ascription of the sermon to Anastasius II must be regarded as tentative, but the sermon is definitely not suited, one hopes, to a monastic milieu, and of the various *Anastasii* sorted out by Sakkos, either Anastasius I or Anastasius II would seem to have the best claim to it.

The sermon is of great interest, for its invective against improper behavior in church and against various kinds of insincerity incompatible with participation in the eucharist, for its mystagogical elements, and for its very considerable borrowings from John Chrysostom, an earlier preacher from Antioch who found much to complain of in his congregation's behavior. Note: The reference to the

Jewish writers who left an account of the martyrdom of St. James is probably a confused reference to Hegesippus and Josephus, cited by Eusebius in *Ecclesiastical History* 2.23.

The grace of the Holy Spirit, throughout all the divine Scriptures, always urges us to keep the divine commandments of God, but especially the exhortation given through the Prophet David, which is sung daily in psalmody. For the Book of Psalms teaches the elements of reverence for God, makes prescriptions concerning faith, teaches sobriety, points the way to fear of God, discourses on retribution, on compunction, on discipline, on repentance, on compassion, on God's love and patience, on purity, on long-suffering, on fasting, on alms-giving.

Constant attention to prayer and the divine Scripture is the mother of all the virtues, for through prayer we receive every request and gift from God. "In the assemblies bless God" (Ps 67.27), it says, and "In the midst of the assembly I shall praise you" (Ps 21.23). Wherefore the Prophet, as if speaking in the person of God, places before us the necessity of unremitting, constant attention to God, saying: "Take time and know that I am God" (Ps 45.11). For without attention and constancy in prayer, and in the divine reading of Scripture, it is impossible either to receive what we request or to know God truly.

For if in the worldly schools of the arts, after spending a considerable amount of time, one is scarcely able to attain to a rudimentary level of knowledge, how much more is it necessary, in the case of one who desires to attain to the knowledge of God and to be well-pleasing to Him, to devote time to God, and to keep his soul borne aloft towards Him with fervent ardor to the end of life? Do you not observe those who obtain worldly, temporal power, how whenever they grasp an opportunity, they are pushed and impelled by their own thoughts as if driven by a fire, and each of them says: "What an opportunity I have come upon! What great power is mine! How widely I rule and am obeyed! How promptly the good things of life attend to me! I shall grow rich, I shall build, I shall plant, I shall snatch, I shall expand,

I shall lay hold of the opportunity before it is gone. I shall not delay, I shall not be careless, for I do not know what tomorrow will bring." By these and similar considerations the majority of men are driven on, as if pushed and impelled by demons; they are choked by temptations and worldly cares, and bear no fruit (*cf* Mk 4.19). They give no thought to the soul, to death, to punishment, to judgement.

But it may be that we lack self-knowledge and deceive ourselves. Would that this were all; at least the evil would be less. But we also hate one another, and revile, and plot, and envy, and slander and jeer. None of us attends to his own sins, no one is anxious about his own burden (Ga 6.5); rather, we enquire carefully into the sins of our neighbors. We are filled with filth (Lk 11.39) up to our throats, and we are not at all concerned. Unto old age we busy ourselves with the affairs of others, and not even in old age do we examine our own sins. We perceive even the small imperfections of our brothers, but we do not see the beam in our own eye (Mt 7.3). We are bent down with the weight of our own sins, and yet we research the faults of others. But even that does not shame us! We spare no one, we respect no one; rather, we bite everyone, we devour everyone, the humble, the great, the guilty, the innocent, priests, our teachers, our guides, those who admonish and exhort. For this reason God's wrath comes upon us (Ep 5.6), for this reason we are chastised unto many afflictions and misfortunes, because of the callousness which possesses us.

For great is our blindness, great our apathy, great our heedlessness. We have no compunction, nor fear of God, no amendment, no repentance, but our whole mind is upon evil and luxury and drunkenness. Moreover, often we are occupied throughout the entire day at the theater, in obscene talk, and the other works of the devil. We do not grow weary, and indeed, because of these activities we give no thought to food, home, and other necessities. But in the church of God we do not wish to offer one hour to God, for prayer and the readings, but we hasten to escape from God's church as if from a conflagration. If the reading from the

divine Gospel is somewhat long, we are irritated and we
fidget about. When the priest is offering prayers, if he
prolongs them even a little, we grow dismal and distracted.
And when he is offering the bloodless Sacrifice, if he lingers
even for a short time, we are bored and depressed, we yawn,
and are as anxious to escape quickly from prayer as from a
trial in court. Just so quickly do we wish to ecape from
prayer, and we are urged on by the devil to get away to
foolish and dissolute activities. Great is our wretchedness,
beloved. For though we ought in every prayer and supplication to be ardent and intense, and especially at the offering
of the spotless mysteries, though we ought to stand before
the Master with fear and trembling at the eucharistic assembly, we do not make offering before Him with a pure conscience, with a crushed and contrite spirit (Ps 50.19); rather,
we transact legal business and attend to our many vain
concerns in the midst of these assemblies.

Some think not about with what purity and repentance
they approach the sacred table, but about in what garments
they will be dressed up. Others who have come do not see fit
to remain until the conclusion, but try to find out through
others what is going on in the liturgy and whether the time
for communion has come. Then they jump in at a run, like
dogs, snatch the mystical bread, and leave. Others, though
present in the temple of God, do not keep quiet for even one
hour, but prattle away to one another, giving themselves to
foolish talk rather than prayers. Yet others leave the celebration of the divine liturgy, and give themselves over to the
pleasures of the flesh. Others give neither time nor attention
to their consciences, to cleanse them of the filth of sins
through recollection, but gather up even greater burdens of
sin for themselves as they spy out the beauty and figures of
the women, making a brothel of the church of God through
their senseless lust. Yet others bargain about business and
property, making that most awesome hour into an exchange
and market place. Others occupy themselves during the
liturgy with slandering one another and even the very priests
who are offering the sacrifice. Certain women must be
included among these. In addition, as many of these as are

slaves to the devil do not tarry in the church of God so much for the sake of prayer as for the purpose of leading astray, by displaying themselves, many of the more naive.

Now that my exhortation includes the two classes, that is men and women, I shall return to the original plan of my discourse, speaking with grief such things as our disdain and carelessness have wrought for us who appear to be Christians.

What is more dreadful than the practice whereby, though we have greed and wickedness and a multitude of sins within us, we wash our hands with a little water, and thus take to ourselves that holy body and the divine blood shed for the salvation of the world, unclean and defiled as we are. Do you not see how when Judas received the Master's body unworthily and deceitfully he was immediately condemned, and provided an even greater opportunity for the evil one? For it says: "And when he took the morsel, immediately Satan entered into him" (Jn 13.27), not that the devil had no regard for the bread, but to convict the one who had received it, for he received his own judgment (1 Co 11.29). Tell me: with what sort of conscience do you approach the mysteries, with what sort of soul, what kind of disposition, when you have within a conscience which accuses you? Tell me, if you were carrying dung in your hands, would you dare to touch royal garments? But why speak of that case? You would not touch your own clothes with dirty hands. No, first you would scrub and wipe off your hands, and then you would touch your clothes. Why do you not show God the honor you bestow on cheap clothing and garments? And what kind of pardon will you obtain, tell me? For merely entering God's church and venerating the divine forms of the holy icons and the venerable crosses is not in itself pleasing, nor yet is washing your hands with water in itself a cleansing, but rather to flee from sin and wash away its filth, and with confession and tears and a humble spirit to wipe out the stains of sins, and thus approach the undefiled mysteries.

Someone might say: "Weeping and lamenting over myself is unpleasant for me!" Why? Because you do not engage in spiritual toil, because you lack discernment, because you do not ponder the fearsome day of judgement! Nevertheless, if you cannot weep, at least you might grieve and look sad, and curtail your laughter, and cast away your haughtiness, and stand before the Lord with fear, with eyes lowered towards the earth, and with a cast-down spirit confess to Him. Do you not observe those who attend an earthly king, often enough a godless one, how they attend on him with all reverence, gazing upon him with fear, neither speaking, nor moving about, nor yielding to distraction, but waiting on him in quiet and awe? We, on the contrary, conduct ourselves in the church of God just as we do at the theater or the bath, laughing, joking, blathering, deceiving ourselves, not even realizing that we are in a church.

Do you not know that God's church is a hospital and a harbor? If, then, you remain ill while in the hospital and are not cured, when will you be healed? If you are tempest-tossed in the harbor, where will you be at rest? Stand, I entreat you, with reverence, stand with fear at the fearsome time of the anaphora, for with what disposition and attitude each of you attends at that time, just so is he offered up to the Lord, for the anaphora is so called because it is an offering-up to God. Stand before God, then, with tranquillity and compunction. Confess yours sins to God through the priests. Condemn your actions, and do not be ashamed. For there is shame which leads to sin, and there is shame which is glory and grace (Si 4.21). Accuse yourself before men, that the Judge may acquit you before the angels (*cf* Lk 12.8) and all the world. Seek mercy, seek pardon, seek forgiveness of your past sins and deliverance from future ones, that you may fittingly approach the mysteries, that with a clear conscience you may receive the body and blood, that they may be for your cleansing and not your condemnation. Listen to the divine Paul, as he says: "Let each examine himself, and then eat of the bread and drink of the cup. For he who eats and drinks unworthily eats and drinks condemnation for himself, not discerning the body of the Lord. Wherefore there are many infirm and ill among you, and many sleep" (1 Co. 11.28-30). Do you observe that illness and death are quite frequent consequences of the unworthy reception of the divine mysteries?

But perhaps you will say: "And who is worthy?" I know, I know! But nevertheless, you will become worthy only if you desire to. Acknowledge that you are a sinner; sever yourself from sin; keep away from sin, from wickedness, from anger. Show the works of repentance; take upon yourself temperance, gentleness, forbearance. Manifest a compassion which comes from the fruits of righteousness towards those in need, and you have become worthy. Pray to God in a contrite spirit, and He will grant your requests; since, unless you do this, you are wasting your time in church. This is not my opinion, but the word of the Lord, for He says: "Why do you say 'Lord, Lord,' and fail to do my will" (*cf* Mt 7.21)? Moreover, "Faith without works is dead" (Ja 2.20). "What then," one says, "because my works are evil is it pointless for me to pray, pointless to spend time in God's church?" I do not say that, nor will I allow it. Rather, my urging is that we pray as we should, that when we come to pray we conduct ourselves in a fitting, godly way, lest Christ say also to us, as He did to the Jews: "'My house shall be called a house of prayer,' but you have made it a den of thieves" (Mt 21.13). For if those who were selling and buying in the Temple of the Jews were beaten and driven out by the Lord, of what punishment, of what hell will they be reckoned worthy who abuse one another and hold grudges? What shall we suffer, we who have sworn allegiance to God, but are the subjects of the devil?

For inasmuch as the priest is the mediator of God and men (1 Tm 2.5), and propitiates God for the forgiveness of the sins of the multitude, observe how he forearms everyne and makes affirmation, as if saying to the people something like this: "Since, O people, you have established me as your mediator to God at this mystical table, I urge you to be earnest in your attention along with me. Withdraw from all worldly thoughts, abandon all concern for things temporal, for this is the time for earnest prayer, not for vain activity. Hear what the deacon says to you: 'Let us stand properly, let us stand in awe, let us attend to the holy anaphora.' Let us bend our necks, let us confine our thoughts, let our minds be winged, let us ascend to heaven. 'Let us have our minds and hearts on high,' let us raise the eyes of the soul upwards to God, let us pass by heaven, let us pass by the angels, pass beyond the cherubim, and let us run to the very throne of the Lord, let us grasp the spotless feet of Christ, let us weep and do violence (*cf* Lk 16.16) to His mercy, let us confess at His holy, heavenly, and spiritual altar."

The priest assures us of these things when he says: "Let us lift up our hearts." Then what do we answer? "We have lifted them up to the Lord." What are you saying? What are you doing? Your mind is distracted with things corruptible and temporal, it is occupied with status and property and pleasure and litigation, and you say "I have lifted it up to the Lord"? Pay attention, I urge, lest, perhaps, you do not have your mind up to the Lord, but downwards to the devil. What are you doing, O man? The priest is offering the unbloody sacrifice to the Lord for your sake, and you pay no attention? The priest strives on your behalf, standing in the sanctuary as if in a fearsome tribunal. He is making urgent invocation that the grace of the Holy Spirit may come upon you from above, and you have no care at all for your salvation? Do not do this, I pray. Abandon this evil and vain attitude. Cry out along with the priest who strives for you, work along with him who prays for you. Devote yourself to your salvation. "Great power has a just man's constant entreaty" (Ja 5.16). It is constant if you struggle along with the priest, and show the fruits of repentance (Lk 3.8), since "If one is building and one is tearing down, what do they gain but labor" (Si 34.23). Is it not a great atrocity of tearing down, not only to lie to Christ at that awesome time of the divine liturgy, but also to hold grudges against your brothers, although you say in the Prayer: "And forgive us our trespasses as we forgive those who trespass against us."?

What do you say, O man? Why are you so boldly insolent to God? You harbor resentment against your brother, sharpening a sword against him, contriving plots against him, and, carrying this evil poison in your heart, you cry out to God: "Forgive me my offences, just as I have forgiven him who offended me"? Did you come to God's house to pray or to lie, to receive grace or to embrace anger, to obtain forgiveness of sins or an increase of offenses, to acquire salvation or retribution? Don't you see that we impart the kiss of peace to one another at that awesome time in order that we may approach the Lord with a clean heart, having cast away "all bondage of wickedness" (Is 58.6) and hardness of heart?

What are you doing, O man? When the six-winged angels assist, covering the mystical table, the cherubim stand in attendance, and the seraphim cry out the thrice-holy hymn with a clear voice, when the bishop bows down in reverence, making propitiation for you, and all attend with fear and trembling, when the Lamb of God is slain and the Holy Spirit comes from above, when unseen angels go quickly around the entire people, noting and recording the souls of the faithful, do you not shudder at your inattention, at your greeting your brother with a Judas' kiss, at your concealing long-standing grudges and a serpent's poison against your brother in your heart? How do you not tremble and collapse, when you say to Him who knows the secrets of the heart "Forgive me as I have forgiven my brother"? How is such a prayer as yours different from a curse? Look, by your prayer you are accusing yourself. "If I forgive, forgive; if I pardon, pardon. If I am compassionate, be compassionate. If I maintain a grudge against my fellow servant, hold a grudge; if I am wrathful, be wrathful; with what measure I measure, let it be measured to me; if my forgiveness is feigned, let your mercy be feigned. I condemn myself, O Master, for I have heard your frightening word 'With what measure you measure, it shall be measured in return for you (Mt 7.2),' and 'If you do not forgive men their offenses, your heavenly Father will not forgive you (Mt 6.15).' Persuaded by the sentence of your truthful words, I have forgiven, I have pardoned those who have sinned against me; forgive, then, O Master, as I have forgiven my fellow-servants!"

Let these be our words, this our constant prayer, when we are present at the time of the fearsome and awe-inspiring liturgy. The priest, aware of this, after the consecration of that bloodless sacrifice, lifts up the Bread of Life, and shows it to all. Then the deacon cries out and says: "Let us attend," that is, he says "Attend to yourselves, brothers. Observe, shortly before you gave assent: 'We have lifted our hearts to the Lord.' And again, professing a clear conscience and forgiveness of wrongs, you said to God 'Forgive us our trespasses as we forgive those who trespass against us,' and for that reason you also kissed one another. But since I too am a man, and I do not know your thoughts, I cast judgement away from me, for I do not know who is worthy or unworthy of communion in these mysteries, and therefore I tell you to attend to yourselves and realize in whose presence you are standing."

Then the priest continues and says: "Holy things for the holy." What is he saying? "Take care, beloved, how you approach communion in the divine mysteries lest someone of you, coming forward to receive, hear: 'Do not touch me (Jn 20.17), get away from me, you who practice grudge-holding and lawlessness. Go far away, you who do not pardon your brother. And come then, and offer your gift (Mt 5.24), and you will be found worthy of communion. Cast away from you all filth of evil, and come then, and receive the cleansing Coal'" (Is 6.6-7). Say to Him: "O Lord, I know that I am guilty of many sins and offenses, but because of your commandment, I have pardoned my brothers, that I also may be counted worthy of pardon from you, O Lord." These thoughts, and the like, the priest suggests to you in this brief utterance.

Therefore, let us pardon our brothers, and cast away from ourselves all evil and wickedness, wishing to walk worthily of the calling whereby we have been called (Ep 4.1). Do not say "I have forgiven my brother frequently, and yet again he has sinned against me," for you too will hear the same thing from the Lord. Do not say "He has sinned greatly and terribly against me. He has had designs on my house; he has claimed my land; he has killed my son; he has done me many foul deeds; he has thrown me into prison; he has handed me over unto death, and I cannot forgive." Do not, beloved, do not speak thus, I pray. For as much as you forgive your brother, so much, and more, will the Lord forgive you.

Follow the example of St. Stephen, the proto-martyr. What did he say when he was being stoned? "Lord, do not assign this sin to them" (Ac 7.59). Imitate James the Brother-of-God, of whom even the Jewish writers report that he prayed for those who were doing away with him, and said: "Lord, forgive them, for they do not know what they are doing." Imitate the Lord Himself, who accepted death for our salvation, and if your brother wishes to hang you on a cross, cry out along with the Lord, and say: "Father, forgive them (Lk 23.34) this sin." Consider the man who owed his master 10,000 talents. When you hear "10,000 talents," understand the burdens of sin. When he fell down before his master, when he begged, when he implored, he was forgiven all that debt. But because he held grudges and did not forgive his fellow-servant, he obtained forgiveness no more, but was handed over to everlasting torment (Mt 18.23-35). Thus the harboring of resentment alone was enough to destroy him, more than all those heavy sins of the 10,000 talents. Wherefore, I plead, let us flee this wicked and unforgiveable sin.

And if you want to learn how the darkness of harboring resentment is worse than every other sin, just listen. Every other sin is completed in a short time, is quickly done with, as for example, when one commits fornication, and later realizes the magnitude of his sin, and returns to his spiritual senses. But harboring resentment is an unceasing, burning passion. He who is possessed by this passion, when he rises from sleep, when he retires, when he prays, when he journeys, he bears a ceaseless, unremitting poison in his heart, with the result that one who is thus enslaved neither enjoys God's favor nor obtains forgiveness of sins. For where the harboring of resentment has been implanted, there nothing is of any benefit, not fasting, not prayer, not tears, not confession, not supplication, not virginity, not almsgiving, not any of these things, for the harboring of a grudge against one's brother undoes all.

Moreover, note this well. He did not say "If you are offering your gift at the altar, and remember that *you* have anything against your brother," but "you remember that *your brother* has anything against you. . . go away, be reconciled with your brother, and come then and offer your gift" (Mt 23.24). If, then, we are obliged to heal the evil and wickedness of our brother, what pardon will we have, who not only fail to do this, but also harbor grudges against our brothers, concealing the wicked venom of a serpent within ourselves? I hear many people saying frequently: "Alas! How am I to be saved? I cannot fast; I do not know how to keep vigil; I am unable to live in continence; I cannot bear to withdraw from the world. How then can I be saved?" How? I will tell you: Forgive and you will be forgiven; pardon and you will be pardoned (*cf* Lk 6.37). Behold! a single, short way to salvation! I will show you a second way. Which? "Judge not, and you will not be judged" (Lk 6.37). Behold, yet another way without fasting, without vigils, without weariness.

So do not judge your brother, even if you see him sinning with your own eyes. For there is one Judge and Lord, and He will "repay each one according to his works" (Rm 2.6), and there is one day of judgement at which we shall be present, with our deeds revealed, and receiving God's mercy. "For the Father judges no one, but He has entrusted all judgment to the Son" (Jn 5.22). He, then, who judges before the coming of Christ is Antichrist, because he snatches at the dignity of Christ. Let us not, then, judge our brothers, I pray, that we may be counted worthy of pardon. You may, indeed, observe him sinning, but you do not know with what kind of an end he will finish his life. That thief who was crucified with Jesus was a murderer, a homicide, and Judas was an apostle and disciple of Jesus, one of the original disciples. But in a short space of time they changed places, and the thief proceeded to the Kingdom, and the disciple to perdition. Granting that your brother is a sinner, how do you know his other deeds? For there are many who sin often quite publicly, and do great penance in secret, and we see them sinning, but know nothing of their penance and amendment, and with us they are judged to be sinners, while with God they have found justification.

And so I urge that we harbor no resentment, that we judge

no man, until the just Judge (2 Tm 4.8) comes, "who will also illumine the hidden things of darkness, and reveal the desires of hearts" (1 Co 4.5). But particularly do not pass judgement on a priest of God concerning private and doubtful activities of which you have heard him accused. Do not say: "The celebrant is a sinner; he has been condemned; he is unworthy; and the grace of the All-Holy Spirit will not come down." Think nothing of this sort. It is someone else who knows and judges secret things. "Know thyself," that everyone is higher than you, and resign judgment to the just Judge. Let the priest not err in the teachings which have to do with God, then you are no judge of the rest; unless you've lost your senses, you know your limitations and your true worth. "What then," someone says, "isn't a bishop subject to judgment and the canons of the church?" Certainly! But he will not be judged by you, but by God, or, frequently, by a bishop greater than he. What right have you, a sheep, to judge the shepherd? Why, like the Pharisee, do you snatch at the judgement reserved to God, and at the sacred dignity neither committed nor entrusted to you by God?

Wherefore, I pray, judge no one, especially a priest of God. But with faith, with a lively repentance, and with a clear conscience approach the divine mysteries, and you will obtain the sanctification of all things. Even if it were an angel who offers the unbloody Sacrifice, but you approach unworthily, not even the angel will cleanse you of your sins. That what I say is true, Judas himself gives evidence, for he received the divine bread from the immaculate hands of the Master Himself, but because he received it unworthily, Satan entered him at once.

And if you wish to hear a story showing that to refrain from judging anyone frees a man from sins, but on the other hand, to pass judgement seals sins fast, then listen.

Men are still living in the flesh, Christ the Lord is my witness, who were eyewitnesses of this. There was a certain man of those who are in the monastic life who lived his life in all carelessness and indolence. He fell ill with a mortal illness, but though his last breath was approaching, he did not fear his death at all, but was departing from the body with all thanksgiving and eagerness. One of the God-beloved fathers who had gathered there questioned him saying: "Brother, believe me, on the basis of what we have observed, we thought you spent your life in all indolence and neglect, and we do not know how you can be so carefree at this time." The brother replied: "Really and truly, honored fathers, I have spent my life in all indolence and neglect, and just now, at this very hour, the angels of God brought me the accounting of my sins. They read off the sins which I committed since the time when I renounced the world, and said to me: 'Do you acknowledge these?' And I said: 'Yes, indeed, I know them quite well. And yet from the time when I renounced the world and became a monk, I have not judged any man nor have I held a grudge. And I pray that the word of Christ may hold good for me as well, for He said: "Judge not, and you will not be judged," and "Forgive and you will be forgiven"' (Lk 6.37). And when I said this to the angels, at once the account of my sins was torn up, and behold, I am departing to Christ with all joy and freedom from anxiety." And when the brother had told this to the fathers, he yielded up his spirit to the Lord in peace, to the great benefit and edification of those present. May we too be counted worthy of the benefit, edification, and portion of keeping ourselves unwounded by any passing of judgement and harboring of resentment, by the grace and love for mankind of our All-holy and Merciful God, for to Him belongs all glory, honor, and adoration with His Onlybegotten Son and life-giving Spirit now and ever, and unto the ages of ages. Amen.

V. "Singing, proclaiming, shouting the hymn of victory, and saying...": Eucharistic Prayer and Chants.

Introduction

This final section provides A) a modest selection of eucharistic prayers (anaphoras), B) an anthology of texts of eucharistic chants, and, since we have entered the realm of liturgical texts, C) two early poetic compositions for the liturgical observance of Great and Holy Thursday.

VA. These four eucharistic prayers have been included here, even though they and many more are readily available in PEER, because the eucharistic prayer was a crucial, and, until it was veiled in pseudo-mystical silence in the sixth and seventh centuries, a perennial mode of eucharistic teaching. This is surely not to say that these prayers had a wholly, or even primarily catechetic function, or that they were, in their classic forms, easily and wholly comprehensible by the masses of the people (though they were in the vernacular, the great eucharistic prayers were *never* in the vulgar language). The prayers did not, any more than preaching about the eucharist, exist in a vacuum. They were proclaimed in an interplay of text, music, light, color, space, texture, movement, and fragrance, in a milieu ideally suited to teach the whole person, to the extent of his/her capacity, and to the extent that the mystery could be taught, the nature of the sacrament of the Body and Blood of Christ in *context*. Thus, regular attendance and attention to the eucharistic liturgy could lead to the formation of those dispositions inculcated by the texts in the preceding portions of this volume:

I. An awareness of the true nature of the sacrifice of the Mystical Body, and of the fact that the Sacrifice of Christians differs from any that had gone before;

II. An appropriate understanding of the sacrament, without recourse to jargon or vulgarization;

III. An appreciation of the situation of the eucharist (our eucharist) in the Divine Economy, and of why the eucharist is offered again and again;

IV. A realization of the place of the eucharist in the life of the church, and in the lives of its members.

The text from the *Didache* (VA1) gives an example of a eucharistic prayer (if, in fact, it is one) from the period of experimentation and extemporization. Eucharistic prayer became more formulaic, both in language and in structure, according to Bouley, due to the convergence of a number of trends and requirements: development of a specifically liturgical vocabulary, separation of the eucharist from the communal meal which had been its earlier setting, greater frequency of eucharistic liturgies, the limited ability of some of the clergy to extemporize, and a concern for orthodoxy (and for precision of expression) in the eucharistic prayer. The anaphora of Hippolytus (VA2) is a model eucharistic prayer, not a text for recitation, from the period of extemporization within a set of very strong and traditional formulaic structures. The liturgy of St. Basil (VA3) and the Roman Canon (VA4) are written, fixed anaphoras. The contrasts between these last two are great and multiplex. These prayers offer a mere hint of the rich diversity in the eucharistic prayer of the catholic church, and indicate that, even after the shift from "freedom to formula," true freedom has not been lost.

(Note: The scriptural sources of the insitution narratives have not been identified in the texts, for that would have been too unwieldly; see the work of Lietzmann in "Suggestions for further reading.")

VB. The communion chant texts in this section date from the later chronological limit of the age of the fathers (VB1, VB2, VB5), or even from well beyond it (VB3, VB4). They have been included in this volume because they show the abiding influence of patristic understandings of the eucharist (both in content and in choice of scriptural texts), and because they were one of the ways in which the message of the fathers was passed on to succeeding centuries.

VC. Yet another medium for the handing on of patristic teachings in encapsulated form was hymnody, of which two early specimens are offered here. They correspond in content to the sermons in IIC, and in synthetic quality and ease of transmission to the syntheses in IID.

Suggestions for further reading:

Bouley 151-158, 245-253; SL (Chapter III, The Eucharist) 147-240; on the conflated institution narratives of the eucharistic prayers see H. Lietzmann, *Mass and Lord's Supper,* tr D.H.G. Reeve, Leiden, 1979, 20-40; on the silence imposed on the eucharistic prayers by clerical laziness and a mistaken understanding of mystery see Bouyer 366-379; on some of the consequences of this see R. Taft, "How Liturgies Grow: the Evolution of the Byzantine 'Divine Liturgy,'" *Orientalia Christiana Periodica* 43 (1977) 355-378; for an account of the presentation of the details of the eucharistic liturgy in catechesis see ARI 37-49.

A. Prayers

VA1 Anonymus (*c* 100), *The Didache (Teaching) of the Apostles* 9-10.
ed SC 248.174-182; *lit* Bouley 90-99, Bouyer 115-119.

Just as the date and place of origin of this work have been subjects of controversy (see comment on IVB1), so also has the nature of the prayers and instructions given in chapters 9-10. The weight of recent opinion leans heavily towards accepting these prayers as eucharistic; they follow the prescriptions for baptism (7) and fasting and private prayer (8). The precise structure of the eucharist provided for, and the manner of its possible articulation with an associated meal have yet to be satisfactorily determined, and remain matters of hypothetical reconstruction (see Bouley 95-97). These prayers were set down as models for those who were considered to need them, or felt that they needed them, in presiding over the eucharist. They were derived from structures and formulae already traditional in Jewish Christianity.

9. Regarding the eucharist, give thanks [*eucharistize*] thus: First, concerning the cup:

We give thanks to you, our Father,
for the holy vine of David your servant,
which you have made known to us through Jesus your Servant.
To you be glory unto the ages!
Concerning the broken bread:

We give thanks to you, our Father,
for the life and knowledge
which you have made known to us through Jesus your Servant.
To you be glory unto the ages!
As this broken bread was scattered over the hills,
   and then, when gathered, became one,
so may your church be gathered
   from the ends of the earth into your Kingdom.
For yours is the glory and the power,
   through Jesus Christ, unto the ages!

Let no one eat and drink of your eucharist but those baptized in the name of the Lord; to this, too, the saying of the Lord is applicable: "Do not give what is holy to dogs (Mt 7.6)."

10. After you have been satisfied, give thanks [*eucharistize*] thus:

We give you thanks, O holy Father, for your holy name
which you have enshrined in our hearts,
and for the knowledge and faith and immortality
which you have made known to us through Jesus your
Servant.
To you be glory unto the ages!
You, Master Almighty,
have created all things for the sake of your Name,
and have given food and drink to the sons of men for
enjoyment, that they may give thanks to you.
But to us you have granted spiritual food and drink
for eternal life through Jesus your Servant.
For all this we give thanks to you, for you are mighty.
To you be glory unto the ages! Amen.

Be mindful, O Lord, of your church, to deliver it from all
evil, and to perfect it in your love;
and gather it, the sanctified, from the four winds
into your Kingdom which you have prepared for it.
For yours is the power and the glory unto the ages!

May grace come and this world pass away!
Hosanna to the God of David!

If anyone is holy, let him come!
If anyone is not, let him repent!
Maranatha!
Amen.

But permit the prophets to give thanks [*eucharistize*] as they wish.

VA2 Hippolytus of Rome (*c* 170-*c* 235), *The Apostolic Tradition* 4.

ed PE 80-81; *lit* Bouyer 158-182, Bouley 118-128.

Since the first publication of the text of the Bohairic-Coptic version of this work in 1848, scholarship has reached a labored and nuanced consensus which attributes *The Apostolic Tradition* to Hippolytus, a presbyter of uncertain origin, resident in Rome, and engaged in controversy with the ecclesiastical establishment there until his martyr's death in the persecution of Maximinus.

Hippolytus' *Apostolic Tradition* dates from *c* 215. Its original Greek text has been lost, but it survives in a number of oriental versions and adaptations, and, in part, in a Latin version. The work is a polemically conservative guide to ecclesiastical observances. After describing the procedure for the consecration of a bishop in Ch 2-3, Hippolytus provides in Ch 4, given here, a model text to guide that bishop's improvisation of the eucharistic prayer. The prayers are a model; they do not necessarily represent Roman practice of *c* 215, but they cannot have been radically at variance with the prayer formulas of eastern origin which constituted the Roman tradition at that time. This, our earliest complete anaphora, is an individual's concretization of widely familiar structures and formulas.

Let all offer the kiss of peace to him who has been made a bishop, saluting him because he has been made worthy. Let the deacons present the oblation to him, and, after placing his hands upon it, along with the entire presbytery, let him say, giving thanks:

The Lord be with you.
And let all say: And with your spirit (2 Tm 4.22).
[Let us lift] up our hearts.
We have them [lifted] to the Lord.
Let us give thanks to the Lord.
It is fitting and right (2 Th 1.3).

And then let him continue as follows:

We give thanks to you, O God, through your beloved servant Jesus Christ, whom you have sent to us in the last times (Ga 4.4) as Saviour and Redeemer and Angel of your Will (Is 9.5). He is your inseparable Word, through whom you have created all things (Jn 1.3), and in Him you were well-pleased (Mt 3.17). You sent Him from heaven into the womb of the Virgin, and He, dwelling in the womb, was made flesh, and was manifested as your Son, born of the Holy Spirit and the Virgin.

When He had fulfilled your will, and obtained (Ac 20.28) a holy people (1 P 2.9) for you, He stretched forth His hands when He suffered, that He might free from suffering those who believed in you.

When He was handed over to His voluntary suffering, that He might destroy death, and burst the bonds of the devil, and tread upon the nether world, and illumine the just, and fix the limit, and reveal the Resurrection, taking bread, He gave thanks to you, and said: Take, eat, this is my body, which will be broken for you.

Similarly also the cup, saying: This is my blood which is shed for you. When you do this, you are making a remembrance of me.

Wherefore remembering His death and Resurrection, we offer to you the bread and the cup, giving thanks to you because you have accounted us worthy to stand in your presence and serve you. And we ask that you send your Holy Spirit upon the oblation of holy church, and that gathering it together into one, you grant to all who partake of the holy things a fullness of the Holy Spirit for the strengthening of faith in truth, that we may praise you and glorify you through your Servant Jesus Christ, through whom be glory and honor to you, to the Father and to the Son with the Holy Spirit in your holy church, both now, and unto the ages of ages. Amen.

VA3 The Anaphora of the *Divine Liturgy of St. Basil.*

ed F. E. Brightman, *Liturgies Eastern and Western* (Oxford, 1896) 321-341; *lit* Bouyer 290-304, Bouley 236-237, P. G. Cobb in SL 173-176.

The anaphora of this liturgy or, at least, the greater part of it, barring slight interpolations, is considered to be the work of St. Basil. It is an elaboration of an earlier version (text translated in PEER 34-37) which may have been the traditional anaphora of Cappadocia, of the Antiochene type, or of an earlier formulation by Basil himself, working in this tradition. Bouyer describes Basil's composition as "a biblical patchwork," but goes on to say: "Despite the peculiarly artificial character that such a method of composition risked giving St. Basil's eucharist, his familiarity with Scripture together with the synthetic power of his thought, since he went not merely to the wording, but to the themes themselves, made his text one of the most beautiful eucharistic formularies of tradition." Though the Liturgy of St. Basil was initially the more common byzantine liturgy, it was displaced in popularity by the Liturgy of St. John Chrysostom, and now it is used in the eastern churches only ten times per year.

The text translated here is from Brightman's reconstruction of the byzantine liturgy of the ninth century. He based his text of the Liturgy of St. Basil on the famous Barberini Euchologion of the eighth century, supplemented by a Grottaferrata manuscript of the ninth-tenth century for the central part of the anaphora which is lacking in the Barberini MS. Materials inserted by Brightman from other sources to establish his reconstruction are included here and we have continued beyond the anaphora in this translation to illustrate allusions to the communion rite which occur elsewhere in this volume. The *Historia Ecclesiastica* of Germanus I (IIB1) is an elucidation of the Liturgy of St. Basil.

And after the Creed the deacon says:

Let us stand properly, let us stand with awe, let us be attentive to offer the holy anaphora in peace.

People: Mercy, Peace, a sacrifice of praise (Ps 49.14; Heb 13.15)!

Priest: The grace of our Lord Jesus Christ, and the love of God the Father, and the communion of the Holy Spirit be with you all (2 Co 13.14).

People: And with your spirit (2 Tm 4.22).

Priest: Let us lift up our hearts (Lm 3.41).

People: We have [them lifted up] to the Lord.

Priest: Let us give thanks to the Lord (Jdt 8.25).

People: It is fitting (2 Th 1.3) and right.

The priest begins the holy anaphora:

O Existing One, Master, Lord (Jr 1.6), God the Father, almighty, worshipful, it is truly fitting and right and becoming to the magnificence of your holiness (Ps 144.5) to praise you, to hymn you, to bless you, to worship you, to give thanks to you, to glorify you, the only God (Jn 5.44) essentially existing, and to offer to you with a contrite heart and in a spirit of humility (Dn 3.39) this our spiritual worship (Rm 12.1), for you are the One who has bestowed upon us the knowledge of your truth (Heb 10.26). And who is able to declare your powers, to make heard all your praises (Ps 105.2), or to narrate all your wondrous deeds (Ps 25.7) at all times (Ps 33.1)? O Master, Master of all (Jb 5.8), Lord of heaven and earth (Mt 11.25), and of all creation (Jdt 9.12) visible and invisible, who sit upon a throne of glory and gaze upon the depths (Ws 9.10+Dn 3.55 var), without beginning, unseen, incomprehensible, uncircumscribed, unchanging, the Father of our Lord Jesus Christ (2 Co 11.31), the great

God and Saviour (Tt 2.13), our Hope (1 Tm 1.1), who is the
image of your goodness (Ws 7.26), the identical seal, in
Himself manifesting you the Father (Jn 14.8), the Living
Word (Heb 4.12), true God (1 Jn 5.20), before the ages (Ps
54.20) Wisdom (1 Co 1.24), Life (Jn 14.6), Sanctification (1
Co 1.30), Power (1 Co 1.24), the True Light (Jn 1.9), by
whom the Holy Spirit was revealed, the Spirit of Truth (Jn
14.17), the Grace of adoption (Rm 8.15), the Pledge of the
inheritance to come (Ep 1.14), the Firstfruits of eternal
goods, lifegiving Power, the Font of sanctification, by
whom all the spiritual and intellectual creation is enabled to
worship you and to render to you endless glorification, for
all things serve you: the angels praise you, the archangels,
thrones, dominations, principalities, powers (Col 1.16), and
the many-eyed cherubim; the seraphim attend you, one with
six wings and one with six wings; with two they cover their
faces, and with two their feet, and with two they fly, as they
cry out antiphonally (Is 6.2-3) with unwearying mouths and
never-silent divine praises,
aloud singing, crying aloud, shouting the hymn of victory
and saying:
People: Holy, holy, holy Lord of Hosts, heaven and earth
are filled with your glory (Is 6.3). Hosanna in the highest!
Blessed is he who comes in the name of the Lord. Hosanna
in the highest (Mt 21.9)!

The priest says in a low voice:

Along with these blessed powers, O Master, Lover-of-
Men, we sinners also cry aloud and say: Most truly are you
holy, and all-holy, and there is no measure of the magnificence of your holiness (Ps 144.5), and you are holy in all
your works (Ps 144.14). For in righteousness and true judgement you have brought all things upon us (Dn 3.28,31), for
you formed man, taking dust from the earth (Gn 2.7), and
you ennobled him with your own image, O God, and placed
him in the Paradise of Delight (Gn 3.23), promising him
immortality of life and the enjoyment of eternal goods in the
observance of your commandments. But when he disobeyed
you, the true God who created him, and had been led astray

by the deceit of the serpent, and had been rendered mortal by his own transgressions, by your just judgement, O God, you sent him into exile, from Paradise into this world, and you returned him unto the earth from which he had been taken (Gn 3.19), while establishing for him an economy of salvation by rebirth in your Christ. For you did not dismiss forever (Dn 3.34) the artifact which you had made, O Good One, nor were you unmindful of the works of your hands (Ps 137.8), but you visited him through the depths of your mercy (Lk 1.78) in manifold ways (Heb 1.1). You sent the prophets (1 Ch 36.15). You accomplished deeds of power through your holy ones who were well-pleasing to you (Gn 5.22) in every generation and generation (Est 9.27). You spoke to us through the mouths of the prophets (Lk 1.70), your servants (Rv 10.7), foretelling (Ac 3.18) the salvation that was to come. You gave the Law for our assistance (Is 8.20). You appointed angels for our guardians. But when the fullness of the times came (Ep 1.10), you spoke to us in your own Son, through whom you also made the ages (Heb 1.2). Though He is the effulgence of your glory, and the imprint of your essence, supporting all things by the word of His power (Heb 1.3), He did not consider it robbery to be equal to you, God (Ph 2.6) the Father; but, God before the ages, He was seen on earth and lived among men (Ba 3.38), and incarnate from the Holy Virgin, He emptied Himself, taking the form of a slave (Ph 2.7), conformed to the body of our lowliness (Ph 3.21), that He might make us conformed to the image (Rm 8.29) of His glory (Ph 3.21). For since through man sin entered into the world, and through sin death (Rm 5.12), it was the good-pleasure of your Only be-gotten Son, who is in your bosom, God the Father (Jn 1.18), born of a woman (Ga 4.4), the holy Theotokos and ever-virgin Mary, born under the Law (Ga 4.4), to condemn sin in His own flesh (Rm 8.3), that those who died in Adam should be made alive in Him; your Christ (1 Co 15.22). He lived as one of us in this world, and gave precepts of salva-tion. He turned us away from the error of idols, and brought us to the knowledge (Col 1.10) of you, the true God (Jn 17.3) and Father. After He acquired us as His very own people (Tt

2.14), a royal priesthood, a holy nation (1 P 2.9), and cleansed us in water (Ep 5.26), and sanctified us by the Holy Spirit (Rm 15.16), He gave Himself (Tt 2.14) as an exchange (Mt 16.26) to death by which we were held fast (Rm 7.6), for we had been sold by sin (Rm 7.14), and through the Cross He descended into Hades, that He might fill all things (Ep 4.10) with Himself. He loosed the pangs of death (Ac 2.24), and rose on the third day, and established for all flesh the way of the resurrection from the dead, according as it was not possible that the Guide of Life (Ac 3.15) should be held fast (Ac 2.24) by corruption. He became the Firstfruits of those who sleep (1 Co 15.20), the Firtborn from the dead, that He might be the first of all in all things (Col 1.18). And ascending into heaven, He took His seat at the right hand of the Majesty on high (Heb 1.3), and He will come (Mt 24.50) to repay each according to his works (Rm 2.6).

But He left us, as memorials of His salvific Passion, the things which we have set forth according to His commands. For when He was about to go to His voluntary and celebrated (4 Mc 10.1) and life-giving death, on the night on which He surrendered Himself (1 Co 11.23) for the life of the world (Jn 6.51), He took bread into His holy, immaculate hands, and lifted it up to you, God the Father. He gave thanks, blessed it, hallowed it, broke it, and gave it to His holy disciples and apostles, saying: Take, eat; this is my body, broken for you for the forgiveness of sins. Similarly He also took the cup from the fruit of the vine, mixed it, gave thanks, blessed it, hallowed it, and gave it to His holy disciples and apostles, saying: Drink of this, all of you; this is my blood, shed for you and for many for the forgiveness of sins. Do this as a remembrance of me, for as often as you eat this bread and drink this cup you proclaim my death (1 Co 11.26), you confess my Resurrection.

And so, we also, O master, mindful of His salvific sufferings, of His life-giving Cross, of His three-day burial, of His Resurrection from the dead, of His Ascension into heaven, of His Enthronement at your right hand, God the Father, and of His glorious and dread Second Coming,
aloud offering to you your own, from what is your own, in all, and for all

People: we praise you, we bless you, we give thanks to you, O Lord, and we pray to you, O our God.

Wherefore, O Master All-holy, we too, sinners and your unworthy servants, who have been counted worthy of serving at your holy altar, not on account of our works of righteousness (Dn 9.18; Tt 3.5), for we have not done anything good upon the earth, but on account of your mercies and your compassions which you have poured forth lavishly upon us (Tt 3.5-6), we are emboldened to approach your holy altar, and having set forth the antitypes of the holy body and blood of your Christ, we pray and call upon you, O Holy of Holies, that, by the benevolence of your goodness, your All-holy Spirit may come (Ac 19.6) upon us and upon these proffered gifts, and bless them and sanctify them and make (*and he signs the holy gifts saying*) this bread the precious body of our Lord, God, and Saviour Jesus Christ, Amen! and this cup the precious blood of our Lord, God and Saviour Jesus Christ, Amen! that which was poured out for the life of the world (Jn 6.51), Amen! and that you would join all of us who partake of the one bread (1 Co 10.17) and cup to one another unto a communion of one Holy Spirit (2 Co 13.14), and that you would bring it about that none of us partakes of the holy body and blood of your Christ unto judgement or condemnation (1 Co 11.34), but that we may find mercy and grace (Heb 4.16) along with all the saints from of old (Lk 1.70) who have been well-pleasing (Gn 5.22), forefathers, fathers, patriarchs, prophets, apostles, preachers, evangelists, martyrs, confessors, teachers, and every just spirit of those who have been made perfect (Heb 12.23) in the faith *aloud* especially our all-holy, immaculate, highly-blessed Lady, the Theotokos and ever-virgin Mary, *and as the diptychs are being read by the deacon, the priest prays* St. John the Forerunner and Baptist, saint *N.*, whose memorial we are celebrating, and all your saints, by whose prayers visit us, O God.

And be mindful of all who have fallen asleep in the hope of the resurrection to eternal life, and grant them rest where the light of your countenance (Ps 4.7) visits them.

Again we pray you, be mindful, O Lord, of your holy, catholic, and apostolic church from the ends to the ends of the earth (Ps 71.8), and give it peace, for you have acquired it by the precious blood of your Christ (Ac 20.28; 1 P 1.19); and establish this holy habitation until the consummation of the world (Mt 28.20).

Be mindful, O Lord, of those who have presented these gifts, and of those for whom and through whom and on account of whom they presented them.

Be mindful, O Lord, of those who bear fruit (Col 1.10) and do good works in your holy churches, and of those who attend to the poor, to reward them with your abundant and supercelestial gifts, to grant them heavenly goods in return for earthly (Jn 3.12), eternal goods in return for temporal (2 Co 4.18), incorruptible goods in return for corruptible (1 Co 9.25).

Be mindful, O Lord, of those in the wilderness and mountains and caves and ravines of the earth (Heb 11.38).

Be mindful, O Lord, of those who live in virginity and piety and the religious life.

Be mindful, O Lord, of our most pious and faithful emperor whom you have deemed fit to rule over the earth (2 Ch 22.12). Crown him with the armor of truth, with the shield of your good-pleasure (Ps 5.13); overshadow his head on the day of battle (Ps 139.8); strengthen his arm (Ez 30.25); exalt his right hand (Ps 88.14); strengthen his sovereignty; subdue to him all the barbarian nations (Ps 46.4) who crave war (Ps 67.31); grant him security and inalienable peace; speak to his heart (Is 40.2) good things concerning your church and all your people, that in his tranquillity (Jr 29.7) we may lead a calm and quiet life in all piety and devotion (1 Tm 2.2).

Be mindful, O Lord, of every authority and power (Tt 3.1), and of our brothers in the palace, and of all the army. Preserve the good in goodness, and make the wicked good by your kindness (Ps 118.68).

Be mindful, O Lord, of the people attendant here, and of those who for commendable reasons are absent, and have mercy upon them and upon us according to the abundance of your mercy (Ne 13.22). Fill their storehouses with every good thing (Ps 143.13; Dt 6.11). Preserve their marriages in peace and harmony; bring up the children; educate the youth; support the elderly; console the faint-hearted (1 Th 5.14). Gather the scattered (Ps 105.47); lead back those who are wandering and join them to your holy, catholic, and apostolic church. Set free those who are vexed by unclean spirits (Lk 6.18). Sail along with those who sail; journey along with those who journey. Defend the widows; protect the orphans; free the prisoners; heal the sick.

Be mindful, O God, of those under judgements and in the mines, and in exile, and in bitter servitude, and in every affliction, necessity, and mishap, and of all who entreat your great depths of mercy, and of all those who love us, those who hate us, and those who have bidden us, unworthy as we are, to pray on their behalf.

And be mindful of all your people, O Lord our God, and pour forth upon all the wealth of your mercy, and grant to all what they require for salvation. And those whom we have not remembered, due to ignorance, or forgetfulness, or the abundance of names, you remember, O God, who know the age and name of each, who have known each one from his mother's womb. For you , O Lord, are the Help of those without help, the Hope of those without hope (Jdt 9.11), the Saviour of the storm-tossed, the Harbor of seafarers, the Physician of the diseased; be yourself all things to all, you who know each one and his request, each household and its need. And deliver, O Lord, this flock, and every city and region from famine, pestilence, earthquake, flood, fire, the sword, and foreign invasion and civil war.

Among the first, be mindful, O Lord, of our Father and Bishop *N*. Grant him to your holy churches in peace, safety, honor, health, enjoying length of days, rightly dividing the word of your truth (2 Tm 2.15).

(*The Diptychs of the Living*)

Be mindful, O Lord, of the entire episcopate of the

orthodox who rightly divide the word of your truth (2 Tm 2.15).

Be mindful, O Lord, according to the abundance of your mercies (Ps 50.3), of my unworthiness also. Forgive me every transgression, voluntary and involuntary, and do not on account of my sins keep the grace of your Holy Spirit from the proffered gifts.

Be mindful, O Lord, of the presbyterate, of the diaconate in Christ, and of every clerical order, and do not make ashamed any of those who encompass your holy altar (Ps 25.6).

Visit us in your goodness (Ps 105.4, 5), O Lord, be manifested to us in your abundant mercies. Grant us temperate and favorable weather, give tranquil showers to the earth for bearing fruit, bless the crown of the year of your goodness (Ps 64.12), O Lord. End the divisions of the churches, quell the ragings of the nations (Ps 2.1), destroy quickly the uprisings of heresies by the power of your Holy Spirit. Receive us all into your Kingdom, as sons of light and sons of day (1 Th 5.5). Show us your peace, and grant us your love, O Lord our God, for you have bestowed all things on us (Is 26.12),

aloud and enable us with one mouth (Rm 15.6) and with one heart (Ac 4.32) to glorify and praise your all-honorable and magnificent name of the Father and of the Son and of the Holy Spirit, now, and always, and unto the ages of ages.
People: Amen!
Priest: And may the mercies of our great God and Savior Jesus Christ be with you all (Tt 2.13).
People: And with your spirit (2 Tm 4.22).

And while the deacon says the middle litany...
Deacon: Having made memorial of all the saints, again and again in peace let us pray to the Lord.
People: Lord have mercy!
Deacon: For the precious gifts offered and sanctified, that our God who loves mankind, who has received them to His holy and celestial and spiritual altar for an odor of spiritual

fragrance (Ep 5.2) may send down to us in return divine grace and the gift of the Holy Spirit, let us ask.

People: Lord have mercy!

Deacon: That he would free us from all affliction, wrath, danger, and necessity, let us pray to the Lord.

People: Lord have mercy!

Deacon: Assist, save, have mercy, and protect us, O God, by your grace.

People: Lord have mercy!

Deacon: Having asked for unity of faith and the communion of the Holy Spirit, let us commend ourselves, and one another, and our entire life to Christ God.

People: To you, O Lord!

    ... the priest says the accompanying prayer:

O our God, the God of Salvation (Ps 67.21), teach us to give thanks in a manner worthy of your favors which you have given and give us (Tb 12.6). You are our God, who have accepted these gifts. Cleanse us of every defilement of flesh and spirit (2 Co 7.1), and teach us to attain complete holiness in fear of you (2 Co 7.1), that receiving a portion of your sacraments in the pure witness of our conscience (2 Co 1.12), we may be made one by the holy body and blood of your Christ, and that, having received them worthily, we may have Christ dwelling in our hearts (Ep 3.17), and may become the temple of your Holy Spirit (1 Co 6.19). Yes, O our God (Jdt 9.12), and make none of us guilty (1 Co 11.27) of these your awesome and celestial mysteries, nor made infirm (1 Co 11.30) in soul and body from partaking of them unworthily. Rather, allow us until our last breath worthily to receive the hope of your sacraments as provisions for the journey of eternal life, for an acceptable defense before the fearsome judgement-seat of your Christ (2 Co 5.10), that we too, along with all the saints who have been well-pleasing to you (Gn 5.22) from the ages, may become sharers of your eternal good things which you have prepared for those who love you (1 Co 2.9), O Lord, *aloud* and count us worthy, O Master, with confidence (Heb 4.16) and without condemnation, to make bold to call upon you as Father (1 P 1.19), Heavenly God, and to say:

The people [*say*] *the* Our Father,who are in heaven, hallowed be your name; your Kingdom come; your will be done, as in heaven, so also on earth. Give us today our daily bread, and forgive us our offenses, as we forgive those who offend us, and lead us not into temptation, but deliver us from evil (Mt 6.9-13),

Priest, aloud: for yours is the kingdom, and the power, and the glory (Mt 6.13var), of the Father and of the Son and of the Holy Spirit, now, and always, and unto the ages of ages.

People: Amen.

And after the "Amen" the priest says: Peace to all.
People: And to your spirit.
And while the deacon is saying Let us bow our heads to the Lord, *the priest says the accompanying prayer*:

Master, O Lord, the Father of all mercies and God of all comfort (2 Co 1.3), bless, sanctify, protect, fortify, strenghten those who have bowed their heads to you, separate them from every evil work (2 Tm 4.18), join them to every good work (Col 1.10), and count them worthy to partake, without condemnation, of these immaculate and life-giving mysteries, for the forgiveness of sins (Mt 26.28), for the communion of the Holy Spirit (2 Co 13.14), *aloud* by the grace, and mercies, and love-for-mankind of your Only-begotten Son, with whom you are blessed, together with your all-holy and good and life-giving Spirit, now, and always, and unto the ages of ages.

People: Amen.

Prayer of the elevation of the bread:

Attend, O Lord (Dn 9.18 var) Jesus Christ, our God, from your holy dwelling-place (1 K 8.39), and come to bless us (Ps 79.3), you who are enthroned on high with the Father and present invisibly here with us, and deign by your mighty hand (Dt 9.26) to impart to us, and through us to your entire people...

and, after the deacon says Let us be attentive!
the priest raises the holy bread and says:

Holy things for the holy!

And after the people say:
One is holy, One is Lord, Jesus Christ (1 Co 8.6), to the glory
of God the Father (Ph 2.11)!
*he takes the portions of the holy body and puts them into the
holy cups and says:* Unto the fullness of the Holy Spirit!

The ekphonesis of communion:
Deacon: Approach with the fear of God, with faith, and
with love (1 Tm 1.14)!
The koinonikon [see VB1] is sung.

VA4 The *Canon* of the Roman Mass.

ed PE 426-438 (preface from CCSL 161A.23); *lit* Bouyer
227-243, Bouley 200-215, A. G. Martimort, *The Eucharist*
(*The Church at Prayer* 2, New York, 1973) 131-170.

Hippolytus' anaphora (VA2) provides us with an
example of a eucharistic prayer presumably acceptable, if
not in every respect typical, in the Roman church of the
first decades of the third century. Profound changes
occurred between the composition of Hippolytus' model
anaphora and the all-but-final redaction of the Roman
Canon at the end of the sixth century. The Roman church
shifted from Greek to Latin as its liturgical language, and
produced an anaphora probably in the pontificate of
Damasus (366-384), of sufficient stability that it could be
adopted by the church of Milan (*cf* Ambrose's quotations
from it in *On the Sacraments* [IIA4]). Rome was moving
to a middle ground between the eastern usages, with their
set of alternative, but invariable anaphoras, and other
western usages in which the greater part of the prayers of
the anaphora varied according to season and feast. The
Roman church adopted a single *Canon actionis*—the
norm, or rule, of the action, or offering—with the option
of limited adjustment or supplement to accommodate the
feasts of the liturgical year. This basic structure is apparent in the pontificate of Vigilius (537-555), and was given

its final form by Gregory the Great, the Dialogist, Pope of Rome (590-604).

The festal supplements to the Canon in this translation (between asterisks) are those from Holy Thursday, from what came to be known as the *Missa chrismalis* or Chrism Mass. By the time of the so-called Gelasian Sacramentary (*c* 750; Roman material dating from *c* 650, or earlier), the Roman church had three masses for Holy Thursday: 1) the morning mass in the titular churches, originally for those ending their fast on Holy Thursday (see IVB4), eventually associated with the reconciliation of penitents; 2) the papal Chrism Mass, around noon, for the blessing of the oil of the sick, the chrism, and the oil of the catechumens; and 3) the presbyteral evening mass, particularly commemorative of the Last Supper. Only the prayer for the blessing of the oil of the sick occurs here, because the blessing of the chrism and the oil of the catechumens occurred after the anaphora, between the communion of the pope and that of the clergy and laity.

The Lord be with you.
And with your spirit (2 Tm 4.22).
[Let us lift] up our hearts (Lm 3.41).
We have [lifted them up] to the Lord.
Let us give thanks to the Lord our God.
It is fitting and right (2 Th 1.3).

Truly it is fitting and right, just and salutary, for us always and everywhere to give thanks to you, O Lord, holy Father, almighty, eternal God, *and humbly to beseech your Mercy that for those who are to be made new by the baptism of the spiritual bath you may strengthen the creature of chrism unto a sacrament of perfect salvation and life, that, when the sanctification of unction has been poured forth and the corruption of their first birth removed, the innocent odor (2 Co 2.15) of an acceptable life may perfume the holy temple (1 Co 3.16,17) of each; that, imbued with royal and priestly and prophetic dignity (Lk 10.24; 1 P 2.9) by the sacrament

which you have established, they may put on the garment of
an incorruptible gift,* through Christ our Lord, through
whom the angels praise your Majesty, the dominations
adore you, the powers tremble before you, the heavens and
the hosts of heaven and the blessed seraphim with united
exultation together celebrate you. We pray that you may bid
our voices also to be admitted along with theirs, saying in
humble praise:
Holy, holy, holy Lord God of Hosts; the heavens and the
earth are filled with your glory (Is 6.3). Hosanna in the
highest! Blessed is He who comes in the name of the Lord.
Hosanna in the highest (Mt 21.15)!

Therefore, we humbly pray and ask of you, most merciful
Father, through Jesus Christ, your Son, our Lord, that you
accept and bless these gifts, these offerings, these holy and
unblemished sacrifices, which we offer to you first for your
holy catholic church; may you deign to grant it peace, to
guard it, to bring it together, and govern it throughout the
world; and also for your servant, our pope *N*.

Be mindful, O Lord, of your servants and handmaids,
NN, whose faith you know, and of whose piety you are well
aware, and of all who stand here present, who offer to you
this sacrifice of praise (Ps 49.14). For themselves, and all
their own, for the redemption of their souls (Ps 48.9), for the
hope of their salvation (1 Th 5.8) and security, they offer
their prayers (Ps 49.14) to you, the eternal, living and true
God (1 Th 1.9), in communion together, *and celebrating
the most sacred day on which our Lord Jesus Christ was
handed over (1 Co 11.23) for our sake,* and also revering
the memory, in the first place, of the glorious, ever-virgin
Mary, the Mother of God, our Lord Jesus Christ, and also
of your blessed apostles and martyrs Peter, Paul, Andrew,
James, John, Thomas, James, Philip, Bartholomew, Matthew, Simon and Thaddaeus, Linus, Cletus, Clement, Six-
tus, Cornelius, Cyprian, Laurence, Chrysogonus, John and
Paul, Cosmas and Damian, and all your saints. By their
merits and prayers may you grant that in all things we may
be defended by the aid of your protection. Through Christ
our Lord.

This offering, therefore, of our service, and also of your entire household, *which we offer to you on the day on which our Lord Jesus Christ entrusted to His disciples the celebration of the mysteries of His body and blood,* we ask you, O Lord, that you graciously accept it, that you order our days in your peace, and bid that we be snatched from eternal condemnation, and numbered in the flock of your chosen ones. Through Christ our Lord.

Of this offering, we ask, O Lord, that you may deign to render it in all respects blessed, approved, valid, spiritual (Rm 12.1) and acceptable, that it may become for us the body and blood of your well-beloved Son, our Lord and God, Jesus Christ, who, on the day before He suffered *for the salvation of us all, that is, today,*took bread in His holy and worshipful hands; with His eyes raised to heaven (Mt 14.19 *etc*) to you, God, His almighty Father, He gave thanks to you; He blessed it, broke it, and gave it to His disciples, saying: Take, and eat of this, all of you, for this is my body. Similarly, after supper, also taking this glorious cup (Ps 22.5) in His holy and worshipful hands, again giving thanks to you, He blessed it and gave it to His disciples, saying: Take, and drink of this, all of you, for this is the cup of my blood of the new and eternal Covenant, the mystery of the faith, which shall be shed for you and for many, for the forgiveness of sins. As often as you will do these things, you will do them for a remembrance of me.

For this reason we too, O Lord, we your servants who are also your holy people, are remembering the blessed Passion of Christ your Son, our Lord God, and His Resurrection from the dead, and also His Ascension in glory into heaven. And thus we offer to your glorious Majesty, from the gifts which you have given, a pure victim, a holy victim, an unblemished victim, the holy bread of eternal life (Jn 6.48), and the cup of everlasting salvation (Ps 115.13). May you deign to look upon them with a kindly and glad countenance, and to accept them, just as you deigned to accept the offering of your servant Abel the Righteous (Gn 4.4; Mt 23.35; Heb 11.4), and the sacrifice of our patriarch Abraham (Gn 22.1-14; Heb 11.17), and that which your highpriest Melchisedech offered to you, a holy sacrifice, an unblemished victim (Gn 14.18; Heb 7). We humbly pray you, Almighty God, bid that these may be borne by the hands of your angel to your altar on high in the sight of your divine Majesty, that as many of us as shall receive the most holy body and blood of your Son by partaking of this altar (1 Co 10.18) may be filled with every heavenly blessing and grace. Through Christ our Lord.

[*Note*: On the variable use of the following prayer, and the association with it of the names of the departed, see Martimort 165-166.]

Be mindful as well, O Lord, of those who have gone before us with the seal of the faith and sleep in the repose of peace *NN*. We pray that you grant to these, and to all who rest in Christ a place of restoration, light, and peace. Through Christ our Lord.

To us, also, sinners, your servants, who trust in the multitude of your mercies (Ps 50.3), may you deign to grant some sharing and fellowship with your holy apostles and martyrs, with John, Stephen, Matthias, Barnabas, Ignatius, Alexander, Marcellinus, Peter, Felicity, Perpetua, Agatha, Lucy, Agnes, Caecilia, Anastasia, and with all your saints; admit us into their company, not calculating what we deserve, but, we pray, granting forgiveness. Through Christ our Lord.

Send forth, O Lord, your Holy Spirit, the Paraclete, from heaven into this rich oil of the olive (Rm 11.17), which you have deigned to bring forth from the greenwood for the restoration of the body, that by your holy blessing it may be, for each one who attains to the anointing, a protection for soul and body, to eliminate all pains and infirmities, every illness of the body. May it be your perfect chrism, with which you have anointed priests, kings, prophets, and martyrs, blessed by you, enduring in our flesh, in the name of our Lord Jesus Christ through whom, O Lord, you ever create, sanctify, vivify, bless, and bestow good things on us.

Through Him, and with Him, and in Him, to you God, the Father almighty, in the unity of the Holy Spirit, are all honor and glory, through all ages of ages. AMEN.

B Eucharistic Chants.

Psalmody accompanied the reception of communion in the church of the fathers. An initial refrain, intoned by a cantor, was taken up by the people, and sung by them between the verses of the psalm sung by a cantor. A number of psalms were employed, the most popular being Ps 33, with v. 9a, "Taste and see that the Lord is good," as its refrain (see St. Cyril of Jerusalem, *Mystagogical Catechesis* 5 [IIA3] for a mention of the cantor intoning this verse). St. Augustine mentions the use of v. 6a, "Approach Him and be illumined," as the refrain. St. John Chrysostom describes the use of Ps 144, with v. 15, "The eyes of all hope in you, and you give them their food in due season," as its apt refrain.

When communion psalmody was altered, and subsequently abandoned, in part as a result of the ever growing infrequency of communion by the laity, its vestiges, the refrains, were left as communion antiphons. These are verses from the Psalms and other scriptural texts, and nonscriptural compositions in prose and verse. Their number was increased over the centuries to accommodate the new feasts of the evolving liturgical year. These communion antiphons are known by a variety of names (Greek *koinonikon*, Roman *antiphona ad communionem* or *communio*, Gallican *trecanum*, Ambrosian *transitorium*, Mozarabic *ad accedentes, etc*). The following examples have been selected for presentation here because of their antiquity and/or their express bearing on the eucharist.

VBI The Greek *Koinonikon*: Some *koinonika* for Great (Holy) Week in Jerusalem.

ed A. Papadopoulos-Kerameus, *Analekta Hierosolymitikes Stachyologias* 2 (Petrograd, 1894) 82, 107; *lit* T. H. Schattauer, "The Koinonicon of the Byzantine Liturgy: An Historical Study," *Orientalia Christiana Periodica* 49 (1983) 91-129.

> The communion chant of byzantine Christianity accompanies, in modern practice, the fraction of the consecrated bread, its commixture with the consecrated wine, the admixture of heated water, and the communion of the clergy. In earlier practice, it accompanied the communion of the people.
>
> Our examples here are taken from the so-called *Typikon of the Anastasis* (Jerusalem, Stavrou MS 43), which was copied in 1122, but reflects considerably earlier practice. It describes the services for Great Week and Pascha in Jerusalem.
>
> The first is the *koinonikon* for the Liturgy of the Presanctified Gifts for Wednesday of Great Week:

Melchisedech the priest
with bread and wine
blessed Abraham (Gn 14.18-19);
but you, the Lamb of God (Jn 1.29,36),
have saved us with your body and blood.
Praise God in His holy ones,
praise Him in the firmament of His might (Ps 150.1).

> The rest are a set of alternative *koinonika* for the Divine Liturgy of St. James celebrated on Great and Holy Thursday:

[1.] Of your Mystical Supper,
today, O Son of God,
as a partaker receive me.
For not to your enemies
will I disclose your mystery,
nor a kiss shall I give you,

as did Judas,
but like the Thief I acknowledge you:
"Remember me, O Lord,
in your Kingdom" (Lk 23.42).

[2.] Taste and see [that the Lord is good] (Ps 33.9).

[3.] Fed on the body
of the holy table,
and watered with the blood
of the divine bowl (Pr 9.2),
perceive God's amazing mystery,
for the forgiveness of sins (Mt 26.28)
and for eternal life (Jn 6.27).

> The first of this set, the troparion (short, non-scriptural
> hymn) "Of your Mystical Supper," is, in a sense, the best
> known of byzantine *koinonika*. It is of Constantinopoli-
> tan origin, introduced there into the Great Thursday
> Liturgy in the ninth year of Justin II (573/4). In more
> recent practice, it has been used quite commonly as a
> generic hymn for the communion of the people, with a
> variety of elaborate musical settings (see K. Levy, "A
> Hymn for Thursday in Holy Week," *Journal of the
> American Musicological Society* 16 [1963] 127-175). It is
> found, in Latin translation ("Cenae tuae mirabili..."), as
> the post-gospel antiphon in the Ambrosian mass for Holy
> Thursday.

VB2 Communion Antiphons from the *Antiphonary of Bangor*.

ed F. E. Warren, *The Antiphonary of Bangor* (HBS 10,
London, 1895) 30-31.

> The *Antiphonary of Bangor* (Milan, Bibliotheca
> Ambrosiana MS C.5. inf.) is our most precious relic of

the ancient Irish liturgy. It was copied at the monastery of Bangor during the abbacy of Cronan (680-691), and traveled from there to the Irish foundation of Bobbio in No. Italy. The following antiphons are found in a cluster under the rubric *Ad communionem*.

For Communion:

We have received the body of Christ, and have been given to drink of His blood; we will fear no evil, for the Lord is with us (Ps 22.4).

Another:

Taste and see, alleluia,
how good the Lord is, alleluia (Ps 33.9).

Another:

With my lips I will utter a hymn, alleluia,
when you teach me, I will answer forth your righteousness, alleluia (*cf* Ps 34.28).

Another:

Take to yourselves this sacred body of the Lord and the blood of the Saviour,
unto everlasting life, alleluia.

Another:

How sweet in my mouth are your words,
O Lord, alleluia (Ps 118.103).

Another:

This is the living bread which has come
down from heaven, alleluia,
he who eats of it will live forever, alleluia (Jn 6.51-52).

Another:

Revived by the body and blood of Christ, let us
always say to you, O Lord, alleluia.

VB3 *Transitoria* from the Ambrosian Liturgy.

ed M. Magistretti, *Monumenta veteris liturgiae Ambrosianae* 2.2 (Milan, 1904) 410.

> An eleventh-century choir book of the Ambrosian liturgy (Milan, Biblioteca del Capitulo metropolitano MS 2102) from the collegiate church of San Vittore in Val Travaglia (NW of Milan) provides the following cluster of communion antiphons for the Sundays after Pentecost.

By the grace of God, let us take up the gifts
received from Christ, not unto condemnation,
but to save our souls.

Your body is broken, O Christ, your cup is
blessed (1 Co 10.16). Let your blood be always
a source of life for us, to save our souls,
O our God.

Angels have surrounded the altar, and Christ
administers the bread of the saints and the
cup of life for the forgiveness of sins (Mt 26.28).

He who eats my body and drinks my blood abides
in me and I in him, says the Lord (Jn 6.57).

Our years and days decline towards their end;
since there is time, let us correct ourselves

for the praise of Christ; let our lamps be
lit (Lk 12.35), for the High Judge is coming
to judge the nations, alleluia, alleluia.

Angels stand at the side of the altar, and the
priests consecrate the body and blood of Chirst,
singing and saying: Glory to God in the highest (Lk
2.14).

We have received the body of Christ, and have
been given to drink of His blood; we will fear
no evil, for the Lord is with us (Ps 22.4).

Receive the heavenly sacrament with fear, and
be filled with the sweetness of Christ. The Lord
has given us the bread of heaven; mankind has eaten
the bread of angels (Ps 77.24-25).

Let us love one another, because God is love,
and he who loves his brother is born of God,
and sees God (1 Jn 4.7); and in this is the love
of God made complete (1 Jn 4.17), and he who does
the will of God endures forever (1 Jn 2.17).

Approach the altar of God; cleanse your
hearts, and be filled with the Holy Spirit,
receiving the body and blood of Christ
for the forgiveness of sins (Mt 26.28).

Grant peace, O Lord, Father, to the priests
and deacons who break the body of the Lord,
alleluia, alleluia, alleluia.

The fragrance of Christ has brought us all
together; come, be filled with the sweetness
of Christ.

VB4 Fraction Chants.

These are not, strictly speaking, communion chants, but
the striking character of these chants sung at the fraction
of the consecrated bread warrants our including a few
examples here. The first is an antiphon from the Moza-

rabic liturgy for Holy Thursday from an antiphonary of Léon (Léon, Biblioteca Catedral MS 8), copied there in the abbacy of Abbot Ikila (917-970).

ed L. Brou, J. Vives, *Antifonario visigotico mozarabe de la Catedral de Léon* (Barcelona-Madrid, 1959) 266.

For the fraction of the Bread:

Remember us, O Christ, in your Kingdom (Lk 23.42), and make us worthy of your Resurrection.

The second is from a Bolognese *graduale-troparium* of the first half ot the eleventh century (Rome, Bibliotheca Angelica MS 123); the antiphon is appointed to be sung at the fraction in the Easter Vigil mass.

ed Paléographie musicale 18 (Berne, 1969) f.111v.

At the fraction:

This is the Lamb of God (Jn 1.29, 36) who has come down from heaven (Jn 6.51), whose body is broken on the altar, alleluia. And he who receives of it with a pure heart (Mt 5.8), his soul will live forever.

According to tradition, the fraction chant of the Roman liturgy, the *Agnus Dei*, was introduced by the Syrian Pope Sergius I (687-701). Though some regional variants existed in the earlier Middle Ages, it came into universal use as one of the common chants of the mass in the form which remains current today. Remarkable parallels exist: in some versions of the Divine Liturgy of St. James, the celebrant says the following prayer at the commixture: "Behold the Lamb of God who takes away the sin of the world, slain for the salvation of the world," and in the Georgian version of the Liturgy of St. John Chrysostom, the *Taste* (the generic term in Georgian, and in other usages, for the *koinonikon*, from Ps 33.9), sung, apparently, during the fraction and commixture, is: "O Lamb of God, who have taken away the sins of the world, have mercy on us. Praise the Lord from the heavens" (Ps 148.1)."

The following is the *Agnus Dei* text in a troped form. Scholars have been unable to agree upon a precise, universally applicable definition of a trope. For our present purposes, it is enough to point out the obvious: the base text of the *Agnus Dei* has been embellished with a prooemium and intercalated verses. This example is from a manuscript of the end of the eleventh century from St. Martial of Limoges (Paris, Bibliothèque nationale lat 1139).

ed G. Iversen, *Corpus Troporum* 4 (Stockholm, 1980) 45.

To this high feast
come all you,
to receive the sacred body,
with one voice crying out:
LAMB OF GOD, WHO TAKE AWAY THE SINS OF THE
WORLD (Jn 1.29-36),
whose blood saved the Israelites in Egypt,
HAVE MERCY ON US.

LAMB OF GOD, WHO TAKE AWAY THE SINS OF THE
 WORLD,
who enrich the hearts of the faithful with the
feast of your own flesh,
HAVE MERCY ON US.

LAMB OF GOD, WHO TAKE AWAY THE SINS OF THE
WORLD,
intact, unharmed, living and everlasting Bread,
GRANT US PEACE.

VB5 The Irish Communion Hymn "*Sancti, uenite.*"
ed AH 51, 298-299.

The church of the fathers, as we have seen, made no explicit provision for extensive, non-scriptural communion hymns. One hymn, however, survives from the early Irish church, which is expressly appointed to be sung during the communion of the clergy.

This anonymous hymn, "*Sancti, uenite,*" has come down to us in the *Antiphonary of Bangor*, though the hymn itself is probably of a much earlier date than that manuscript. Legend associates it with the dispute between Sts. Patrick and Sechnall. The arrival of the angry Patrick interrupted Sechnall's celebration of mass just before reception of communion. They met outside the church and were reconciled, "And so they made peace then, Patrick and Sechnall. And whilst they were going round the cemetery, they heard a choir of angels singing around the oblation in the church; and what they sang was the hymn beginning, "*Sancti uenite Christi corpus,*" etc.; hence this hymn is sung in Ireland when one goes to the body of Christ, from that time onward." (J. H. Bernard, R. Atkinson, *The Irish Liber Hymorum* [HBS 14] 5). The composition of this hymn in the Patrician period is quite unlikely, but its very primitive character suggests that it was composed well before the Bangor Antiphonary was copied. The rubric for this hymn in the Antiphonary is *Hymn when priests receive communion*; thus it was, in early usage at least, sung only during the communion of the clergy.

Hymn when priests receive communion:

Holy ones, come, receive the body of Christ,
and drink the holy blood by which you are redeemed.

Saved by the body and blood of Christ,
fed on them, let us sing praise to God.

By this sacrament of body and blood
all are freed from the jaws of Hell.

The Bestower of Salvation, Christ the Son of God,
has saved the world by Cross and blood.

Sacrificed on behalf of all, the Lord
has been Himself both priest and victim.

The Law wherein sacrifice of victims was bidden
is the foreshadowing of the divine mysteries (Heb 8.4-5).

The Giver of Light and Saviour of All
has granted a glorious grace to His holy ones:

all approach with pure mind and faith
to receive an eternal guarantee of salvation.

The Guardian of the saints, their Ruler as well,
is the Lord, the Grantor of everlasting life to the faithful.

He gives the bread of heaven (Ps 77.24) to the hungry,
proffers drink to the thirsty from the Living Spring (Jn 6.35).

Alpha and Omega (Rv 1.8), Christ the Lord Himself,
has come, will come to judge mankind.

C Hymns for Great and Holy Thursday.

We conclude this section with two longer hymns for Thursday of Great (Holy) Week. These may be viewed as hymnodic counterparts to sermons for this feast (see IIC).

VC1 Flavius, Bishop of Châlon-sur-Saône (*d* 591), "*Tellus ac aethra iubilent.*"
ed AH 51.77-78.

This hymn is ascribed in its manuscript tradition to Flavius, and scholarship has tentatively accepted his authorship. In medieval usage, the hymn was appointed to be sung at the *Mandatum*, or *pedilavium*, the ceremonial foot-washing conducted on Holy Thursday. The hymn refers, in its second-to-last stanza, to the reconciliation of penitents and the consecration of chrism (see VIA4), both prominent features of the Holy Thursday observances, incidental to the commemoration of the

383

Last Supper. In its rhythm, stanzaic structure, and
number of stanzas (less the doxology), Flavius' hymn
conforms to the generic ambrosian hymn pattern
modeled on the compositions of St. Ambrose.

Let heaven and earth rejoice
at the great Prince's Supper
which has purged Adam's breast
with the food of life.

On this night the Creator of all
in a most mighty mystery
changes His flesh and His blood
into food for the soul.

Rising from this noble feast
He gives men an example,
for lowliness' sake
approaching Peter's feet.

The slave is appalled at the service,
when he beholds the angels' Master
carry water, and a towel,
and kneel upon the ground.

"O Simon, let yourself be washed!
My acts are mysteries, and disclose
—as I, the Highest, fetch lowly things—
the honor due from dust to dust."

The Foot-washer reclines upon the couch,
and completes His honeyed discourse,
in which He marks the foe
who ponders schemes of death.

O savage wolf, Judas most wicked,
you give a kiss to the gentle Lamb,
giving over to bonds the royal body
which cleanses the squalor of the world (Jn 1.29,36).

Today those imprisoned
in flesh and heart are freed.
The chrism is blessed, the anointing
whence hope leaps up for the pitiful.

To the Victor over death sing glory,
glory bright with praise,
with the Father and Holy Spirit,
for He has ransomed us from death.

VC2 St. Kosmas Melodos (*fl* 743), *Kanon for the Fifth Day of Great Week.*

ed W. Christ, M. Paranikas, *Anthologia graeca carminum christianorum* (Leipzig, 1871) 190-193; *lit* E. Wellesz, *A History of Byzantine Music and Hymnography* (2nd ed, Oxford, 1961) 198-245.

The kanon entered into Orthros (the morning office) in the seventh century. This complex poetic form consists of eight odes, each of which was originally appended to one of the biblical odes (canticles) sung at Orthros:

Ode 1: The Canticle of Moses in Exodus (Ex 15.1-9)
[Ode 2: The Canticle of Moses in Deuteronomy (Dt 32.1-43)]
Ode 3: The Prayer of Hannah, Mother of Samuel the Prophet
(1 S 2.1-10)
Ode 4: The Prayer of Habakkuk the Prophet (Hb 3.2-19)
Ode 5: The Prayer of Isaiah the Prophet (Is 26.9-19)
Ode 6: The Prayer of Jonah the Prophet (Jon 2.2-10)
Ode 7: The Prayer of the Three Young Men (Dn 3.26-45, 52-56)
Ode 8: The Hymn of the Three Young Men (Dn 3.57-88)
Ode 9: The Canticle of the Theotokos (Lk 1.46-55) and
The Prayer of Zachariah, Father of the Forerunner
(Lk 1.68-79).

The long and comminatory second canticle was omitted,
except in Lent; indeed, accoiding to recent opinion, it did
not appear at all in the Orthros service familiar to Kosmas
and John of Damascus, hence the absence of a second ode
from this kanon. The popularity of the kanon and the
musical prominence given to it led to a diminution of the
liturgical prominence of the canticles and, finally, to the
elimination of all save one of them (the Canticle of the
Theotokos), leaving only the kanon and the *Magnificat*,
except in Lent and in the Pascha-Pentecost period, when the
other canticles were recited.

The primary role of the kanon at the time of its development and first flowering was to relate the unvarying canticles to the particular feast or season being celebrated. The
festal content of the ode is linked to its antecedent canticle
most commonly, though not invariably, through quotation
or allusion to the canticle in the text of the ode, and also
through analogical or typological alignment of canticle and
feast.

St. Kosmas Melodos and St. John of Damascus were
considered the premier composers of kanons. According to
tradition, they were foster-brothers. Kosmas was a monk of
St. Saba, and became bishop of Miauma, near Gaza, in 743.

First Ode (Ex 15.1-9)

With division is the Red Sea rent,
the wave-nourishing deep is dried up;
it has become at once a passage to the unprotected,
and a tomb to the fully-armed;
and a God-pleasing song was raised:
"Gloriously glorified (Ex 15.1) is Christ our God!"

The Universal Cause and Creator of Life,
the boundless Wisdom of God
has built a house for His pure self (Pr 9.1)
from a Mother who knew not man (Lk 1.34);
for clothing Himself in a bodily temple,
Gloriously glorified is Christ our God!

Initiating His friends,
He readies the soul-nourishing Table;
the very Wisdom of God mixes
an ambrosial bowl (Pr 9.2) for the faithful.
Let us approach with piety, and cry
"Gloriously glorified is Christ our God!"

Let us, the faithful, all hear
the uncreated and connatural Wisdom of God
inviting with lofty proclamation (Pr 9.3),
for He cries: "Taste,
and knowing that I am good (Ps 33.9), cry out
'Gloriously glorified is Christ our God!'"

Third Ode (1 S 2.1-10)

Though the Lord and Creator of All,
God impassible,
you became poor (2 Co 8.9), uniting creation to yourself,
and you proffered yourself as the passover (1 Co 5.7)
to those for whom you were about to die,
saying: "Eat my body,
and you will be strengthened (1 S 2.1) in faith."

The very Deliverance of all the human race,
O Good One,
you gave drink to your disciples,
filling full the cup of gladness;
for you offer yourself as a sacrifice,
saying: "Drink my blood,
and you will be strengthened in faith."

"The fool who is the betrayer among you,"
you foretold to your disciples,
Long-suffering One,
"he will not know these things,
and, void of understanding, will not comprehend.
But you abide in me,
and you will be strengthened in faith."

Fourth Ode (Hb 3.2-19)

The Prophet, plainly foreseeing (Hb 2.1)
your ineffable mystery (Hb 3.2),
O Christ, declared long ago:
"You have established the mighty love
of your power (Hb 3.4), Merciful Father,
for you sent your Onlybegotten Son, O Good One,
as an atonement into the world."
Proceeding to the suffering
which was the font of freedom from suffering
for all those descended from Adam,
O Christ, you said to your friends:
"I have longed to share this passover with you (Lk 22.15),
since the Father has sent me, the Onlybegotten Son,
as an atonement into the world."

Fifth Ode (Is 26.9-19)

Bound fast by the fetters of love,
the apostles consecrated themselves
to Christ the Lord of All, and
those who proclaim the gospel of peace to all
had their beautiful feet (Is 52.7) washed.

He who controlled the boundless
and superabounding water in the firmament,
He who curbed the abysses
and checked the seas,
the Wisdom of God pours water in a basin,
the Master washes the feet of slaves.

The Master shows the disciples
a model of humility;
He who clothes the sky with clouds (Ps 146.8)
girds Himself with a towel,
and bends His knee

to wash the feet of slaves,
He in whose hand is the life of all who are (Jb 12.10).

Sixth Ode (Jon 2.2-10)

The ultimate abyss, that of sins, has enclosed me (Jon 2.6),
and no longer able to endure its waves,
like Jonah I cry out to you, O Master,
"Lead me back from corruption (Jon 2.7)."

"You call me Lord and Teacher,
O my disciples, and indeed I am (Jn 13.13),"
the Saviour declared, "therefore,
follow the example (Jn 13.15),
the one you behold in me.

He who is clean
has no need for his feet to be cleansed (Jn 13.10).
You are clean, O disciples, you are,
but not all of you, for the evil impulse
of one of you rages out-of-control."

Seventh Ode (Dn 3.26-45, 52-56)

The young men in Babylon
did not fear the flames of the furnace.
Though cast into the midst of the flame,
bedewed (Dn 3.50) they sang:
"Blessed are you, O Lord,
the God of our Fathers" (Dn 3.26).

With nodding head, Judas
set in motion evil plans,
seeking an opportunity to hand over (Mt 26.16)
to condemnation the Judge,
who is Lord of All,
the God of our Fathers.

"One of you," Christ declared
to His friends, "will betray me."
Forgetful of their joy, they were seized
by grief and fear, saying:
"Who is it? Tell us,
O God of our Fathers."

"Whoever overboldly puts his hand
with me into the bowl,
for him it were better never
to have entered the gates of life" (Mt 26.24).
He revealed him, speaking thus,
the God of our Fathers.

Eighth Ode (Dn 3.57-88)

In peril for their fathers' laws,
the blessed young men in Babylon
disdained the king's senseless decree;
and united to the fire by which they were not undone,
they sang out a hymn
worthy of the Mighty One;
"Praise the Lord, O His works,
and exalt Him unto the ages." (Dn 3.57).

The blessed dinner-guests in Sion,
faithful to the Word,
attended the Shepherd like lambs;
and united to Christ from whom they did not depart,
fed by the divine Word,
they cried out in thanksgiving:
"Praise the Lord, O His works,
and exalt Him unto all ages."

The hateful Iscariot, heedless,
by intent, of the law of friendship,
readied for betrayal the feet
which Christ had washed; and though he ate

your bread, the divine Body,
he raised His heel against you (Jn 13.18), O Christ,
and knew not how to cry out:
"Praise the Lord, O His works,
and exalt Him unto all ages."

The man without conscience received
the Body which redeems from sin
and the divine Blood poured out
for the sake of the world;
but he was not ashamed to drink
what he sold for a price;
he took no offense at his wickedness,
and knew not how to cry out:
"Praise the Lord, O His works,
and exalt Him unto all ages."

Ninth Ode (Lk 1.46-55; Lk 1.68-79)

O faithful, come, let us enjoy
the Master's hospitality,
the immortal Table
in the Upper Room,
with minds on high,
having learned the transcendent word
from the Word
whom we magnify (Lk 1.46).

"Go," said the Word
to the disciples, "and prepare
in an upper room, where the mind is firmly set,
the passover for those whom I initiate
with the unleavened word of truth (1 Co 5.8),
and magnify
the power of grace.

The Father begot me, creative Wisdom,
before the ages;

He established me as the beginning of His ways
for the works now mystically accomplished (Pr 8.22);
for though I am the uncreated Word by nature,
I make my own the voice
of the nature I have now assumed.

As I am a man
in reality, not a mirage,
so divinized is the nature which,
by the manner of the exchange,
is united to me.
Wherefore know that I am one Christ
who saves that of which and in which I am."

Index

393